TROUBLING TRICKSTERS

Indigenous Studies Series

The Indigenous Studies Series builds on the successes of the past and is inspired by recent critical conversations about Indigenous epistemological frameworks. Recognizing the need to encourage burgeoning scholarship, the series welcomes manuscripts drawing upon Indigenous intellectual traditions and philosophies, particularly in discussions situated within the Humanities.

Series Editor:
Dr. Deanna Reder (Métis), Assistant Professor, First Nations Studies and English, Simon Fraser University

Advisory Board:
Dr. Jo-ann Archibald (Sto:lo), Associate Dean, Indigenous Education, University of British Columbia

Dr. Kristina Fagan (Labrador-Métis), Associate Professor, English, University of Saskatchewan

Dr. Daniel Heath Justice (Cherokee), Associate Professor, Indigenous Studies and English, University of Toronto

Dr. Eldon Yellowhorn (Piikani), Associate Professor, Archaeology, Director of First Nations Studies, Simon Fraser University

For more information, please contact:
Lisa Quinn
Acquisitions Editor
Wilfrid Laurier University Press
75 University Avenue West
Waterloo, ON   N2L 3C5
Canada
Phone: 519-884-0710 ext. 2843
Fax: 519-725-1399
Email: quinn@press.wlu.ca

TROUBLING TRICKSTERS

REVISIONING CRITICAL CONVERSATIONS

Deanna Reder and Linda M. Morra, editors

INDIGENOUS STUDIES SERIES

Wilfrid Laurier University Press

This book has been published with the help of a grant from the Canadian Federation for the Humanities and Social Sciences, through the Aid to Scholarly Publications Programme, using funds provided by the Social Sciences and Humanities Research Council of Canada. We acknowledge the support of the Canada Council for the Arts for our publishing program. We acknowledge the financial support of the Government of Canada through the Book Publishing Industry Development Program for our publishing activities.

 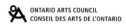

Library and Archives Canada Cataloguing in Publication

Troubling tricksters : revisioning critical conversations / Deanna Reder and Linda M. Morra, editors

(Indigenous studies series)
Includes bibliographical references and index.
Issued also in electronic format.
ISBN 978-1-55458-181-8

1. Tricksters—North America. 2. Tricksters in literature. 3. Folk literature, Indian—North America—History and criticism. 4. Indians of North America—Folklore. 5. Indians of North America—Social life and customs. I. Reder, Deanna [date] II. Morra, Linda M. III. Series: Indigenous studies series (Waterloo, Ont.)

PS8089.5.I6T76 2010   398.2089'97   C2009-904028-X

Library and Archives Canada Cataloguing in Publication

Troubling tricksters [electronic resouce] : revisioning critical conversations / Deanna Reder and Linda M. Morra, editors

(Indigenous studies series)
Includes bibliographical.
Electronic monograph.
Issued also in print format.
ISBN 978-1-55458-205-1

1. Tricksters—North America. 2. Tricksters in literature. 3. Folk literature, Indian—North America—History and criticism. 4. Indians of North America—Folklore. 5. Indians of North America—Social life and customs. I. Reder, Deanna [date] II. Morra, Linda M. III. Series: Indigenous studies series (Waterloo, Ont.)

PS8089.5.I6T76 2010a   398.2089'97

Cover image: *Wesakichak5*, by Steve Keewatin Sanderson. Cover design by Martyn Schmoll. Text design by Catharine Bonas-Taylor.

This book is printed on FSC recycled paper and is certified Ecologo. It is made from 100% post-consumer fibre, processed chlorine free, and manufactured using biogas energy.

Printed in Canada ·

Contents

DEANNA REDER

Preface

While it is commonly quipped that the "Indian is a European invention,"[1] that no Indigenous person in North America called themselves "Indian" before the arrival of Columbus, in much the same way no Indigenous community had "tricksters"—the term is the invention of a nineteenth-century anthropologist.[2] Instead, the Anishinaabeg told stories about Nanabush,[3] the Cree told stories about Wesakecak,[4] the Blackfoot told stories about Naapi,[5] the Stó:lō told stories about Coyote, and all these stories continue to be told and retold to this day. That being said, just as many Indigenous people in North America now refer to themselves as Indians, and many storytellers talk and write about tricksters, drawing not only on traditions in which they may or may not have been raised but also on their imaginations and the work of other Native authors.

It has only been since the late 1980s that an infrastructure has been established to publish, distribute, and teach Indigenous fiction in Canada. Literary critics, virtually all non-Indigenous, looked for strategies to discuss this literature. The products of the Canadian education system themselves, many were, not surprisingly, uninformed about basic legal terms (What is a Status Indian? Who qualifies as Métis?) and historical contexts (the Indian Act, residential schools, the Sixties Scoop), never mind the rich and intricate epistemologies and storytelling genres of individual Indigenous nations. One way in which critics sought to begin critical conversations and surmount this lack of background was to draw upon discussions in postmodernism, post-colonialism, and the work in the U.S. on and by Gerald Vizenor. Trickster criticism emerged as one of the first critical approaches for Indigenous literature in Canada, an approach that at one point became so popular that in recent years it has become somewhat of a cliché.

This volume seeks to reignite interest in trickster criticism, albeit not the discussions of old. Twenty-first-century trickster criticism is influenced by the recent work of nationalist critics who have called for ethical literary studies that are responsible to Indigenous people and communities. More often than not this requires that scholars identify themselves in relation to their material and to the nation they write about. This means that critics must not only have an understanding of the particular context from which a story emerges but also that they imagine their audience to include Indigenous people, whether as scholars, students, or general community members.[6]

It is no exaggeration to state that this volume marks the coming of age for Indigenous literary studies in Canada, an area marked by an awkward absence of Indigenous scholars, reflecting the often poor ability of universities, especially literature departments, to attract and engage Indigenous students. This is not to suggest that the study of Indigenous literatures be limited to Indigenous people, but rather that this absence is somewhat akin to having Women's Studies departments fully staffed by men. For this reason it is an encouraging sign that this volume contains the work of several emerging Indigenous critics, some still completing their doctoral work alongside more senior scholars, including a Canada Research Chair and an Associate Dean for Indigenous Education. As is said in the territory where I live and work, following Coast Salish protocol: "I raise my hands to you." This anthology also includes the work of non-Indigenous critics who have long been part of and helped grow this field, as well as junior scholars trying to find their place in cultural approaches: "I raise my hands to you." This volume also includes discussions with or reflections from visual artists (and one archaeologist), as well as the work of established writers, whose writing continues to encourage us: "I raise my hands to you." And to Lisa Quinn at Wilfrid Laurier University Press, who has been an enthusiastic supporter from the beginning, and to my co-editor, Linda Morra, who first invited me to work with her on this project, who is a crackerjack editor, an absolutely delightful person to collaborate with, and I suspect the hardest working critic in the field: "I raise my hands to you." Hai Hai.

Notes

1   See Louis Owens, *Mixedblood Messages: Literature, Film, Family, Place* (Norman: U of Oklahoma P, 2001), 116.
2   The term "tricksters" is attributed to nineteenth-century anthropologist Daniel Brinton, who first used the word to describe the category of characters found

within Indigenous mythic traditions. As Suzanne J. Crawford and Dennis F. Kelley argue, this term has negative connotations; see *American Indian Religious Traditions: An Encyclopedia* (Oxford: ABC-CLIO, 2005), 1123.

3 Also called Nenabush, Nanabozho, Wenabozho, etc.

4 Also called Wisakechak, Wesakaychak, Wisakedjag, etc.

5 Also called Old Man, Napi, Napiw, etc.

6 This approach is timely, a way to shift the focus of research from the effects of colonization to the contributions and potential of Indigenous worldviews. I suspect that the next generation of literary critics might very well return to pan-Indian approaches in the discussion of literature, because national or tribal specific approaches are unlikely to satisfy or resonate with a growing urban Indigenous readership, many of whom have no connection to home communities, language, or culture, and identify instead with the cities in which they live. Because the term "pan-Indian" is associated with the monolithic homogenous notion of the "Indian," I wonder if the powwow term, "inter-tribal," might better explain future approaches that hold within them possibilities to unify and celebrate our belonging together. Until then, however, I look forward to the particular tack that the field has taken, to rely upon the intellectual contributions of Indigenous nations to provide new ways of reading.

A Preface
Ruminations about *Troubling Tricksters*

I was attending a conference recently when another academic politely asked about the nature of our book—the collection of essays, creative pieces, and interviews that Deanna Reder and I gathered and selected for *Troubling Tricksters*. When I characterized the anthology and gave a general description of its contents, he responded, "I hope someone is working on Sheila Watson and suggesting how 'postmodern' her use of the trickster is." It was an interesting remark, both in its focus on a non-Native writer who had used a trickster figure in her work of fiction and in demonstrating the persistence of identifying a trickster through a decidedly postmodern lens. I refrained from comment, not out of a sense of judgment, but out of a sense that, unfortunately, I might have made precisely that kind of remark not so long ago. Indeed, my own work has not been free of these kinds of assumptions and connections, to which an article I had written on Mordecai Richler's *The Incomparable Atuk* some years ago would bear witness. At the time, I had made use of Allan Ryan's *The Trickster Shift*, which was the most current piece of criticism on the subject—but which in its generality does not satisfactorily address the kinds of questions and issues that the contributors address herein.

In feeling that there was yet more to be done on the subject, Dr. Manuela Costantino (Department of English, UBC) and I made a preliminary attempt on the subject by organizing a panel at the annual Congress of the Humanities and Social Sciences in 2007, at which a shorter version of a paper that appears in this anthology was presented. In formulating the scope and nature of the collection, Deanna Reder then stepped in and gave it the shape it now assumes. To put it in vastly understated terms, I am most deeply grateful to and appreciative of her: she is a most extraordinary woman from whom I learned exponentially in the process of working on the anthology and in putting the selected pieces together. She is the real force and intelligence behind this book.

In reading over the anthology again, I am freshly reminded of some of our original objectives. Since the late 1980s, tricksters have been seen as emblematic of a postmodern consciousness rather than as part of specific Indigenous cultures, histories, storytelling; and since tricksters have often been used in the service of a predominantly white and colonial culture that characterized this figure as exotic, tricksters need to be relocated within specific Indigenous socio-historical contexts, and understood properly within those contexts. The conversation I mentioned at the outset of this preface merely reinforced my sense of rationale for our book and provided further justification about why it was so vital. Greater accountability, responsibility, and more finely developed, ethical criticism—these are the words and phrases that kept flooding over me as I read over the essays, interviews, and creative pieces selected for the anthology.

I am deeply grateful to each of the contributors for making *Troubling Tricksters* what it is—a "troubling," provocative, compassionate, savvy, and timely book that showcases the complexity of, and the need to ground the trickster in, Indigenous socio-historical contexts. I feel thoroughly honoured and privileged to be a part of it. I am also thankful to Lisa Quinn, the editor at Wilfrid Laurier University Press, who was enthusiastic about this project from the outset; to the readers of the manuscript, whose suggestions were extremely useful; to Bishop's University for providing funding towards the publication process and for showing support for our work; to Sylvie Côté, a blessing in the form of the Director of Research Services at Bishop's University; to the members of the Department of English at Bishop's University for their kindness and support; to my students of English 352, especially Serena Trifiro, Tanja Schnell, Verena Jager, Katharina Forster, Taylor Evans, Ben Wylie, Whitney Carlson, and Pat Corney, with whom I shared many of the ideas from the manuscript and with whom discussions about the subject were a source of stimulation and pleasure; and to those friends (especially Mercedes Watson, Brendan Davis, Matsuo Higa, Barbara Richardson, Anna Sedo, Margaret Tucker, and Bruce Gilbert) and family for being so loving and kind as Deanna and I worked through the manuscript.

LOOKING BACK TO THE "TRICKSTER MOMENT"

KRISTINA FAGAN

What's the Trouble with the Trickster?

An Introduction[1]

I must admit that, when first asked to contribute to this collection of essays on the trickster, I was apprehensive. My first encounter with trickster figures had been in the late 1990s when I was writing my dissertation on humour in Indigenous literature in Canada. At that time, the trickster was a particularly trendy topic among critics and it seemed, as Craig Womack recently put it, that "there were tricksters in every teapot" ("Integrity" 19). Focusing on the trickster seemed to appeal to literary critics as an approach that was fittingly "Native." The trouble was that the trickster archetype was assumed to be an inevitable part of Indigenous cultures, and so the criticism paid little attention to the historical and cultural specifics of why and how particular Indigenous writers were drawing on particular mythical figures. As a result, the critics' trickster became an entity so vague it could serve just about any argument. Unsatisfied with much of the critical work on the trickster, I critiqued it in a section of my dissertation entitled, "What's the Trouble with the Trickster?" As I recently re-read that piece, I could see, in retrospect, the ways in which the troubles in the trickster criticism of the 1990s reflected broader problems in the study of Native literature at that time. I also realized that these problems have since then been articulated and begun to be addressed by the movement known as Indigenous (or American Indian) Literary Nationalism. I have therefore revised the original piece to give a sense of how the critical treatment of the trickster has fit into and reflected the developing study of Indigenous literature, from the 1990s to the present.

I want to separate clearly the creative depiction of figures such as Coyote and Nanabush from literary criticism about "the trickster." The work of many

Indigenous writers in Canada—including such influential figures as Thomas King, Tomson Highway, Beth Brant, Daniel David Moses, and Lenore Keeshig-Tobias—has included mythical figures that could be described as tricksters. And some of these writers have used the term "the trickster" when describing their creative work, in some cases making strong claims for the importance of the trickster, and of a connected "comic worldview," to Indigenous peoples. In Canada, the most famous spokesperson for the trickster-worldview theory is Tomson Highway, who has repeatedly asserted that Christ is to Western culture as the trickster is to Native culture (Highway XII, quoted in Hunt 59 and in Hannon 41): "One mythology says that we're here to suffer; the other states that we're here for a good time" (quoted in Hannon 41). Later in this essay, I explore some possible reasons for this popularity of tricksters among contemporary Indigenous writers in Canada.

The object of my critique is not the Indigenous writers' use of tricksters, much of it emerging in the 1990s, that seeks to explain this use: Allan Ryan's *The Trickster Shift* (1999), Kenneth Lincoln's *Indi'n Humor* (1993), and many essays asserted the "trickster spirit" in Indigenous creative work.[2] Any humorous work by an Indigenous author seemed to be considered the result of a trickster influence. We can see this single-minded approach to Indigenous humour when, for instance, Blanca Chester claimed that "Native satire ... is *always* connected to the trickster" (51, italics mine) and Drew Hayden Taylor pronounced, "while the physical manifestation of Nanabush, the trickster, appears in precious few plays, his spirit permeates *almost all* work presented as Native theatre" (51–2, italics mine). The working assumption seemed to be that the trickster was hiding in every work of Indigenous literature and it was the critic's job to find him.[3]

The popularity of the trickster among Canadian critics of Indigenous literature in the 1980s and 1990s can be traced to an increasing public awareness of Indigenous cultural difference from mainstream Canada. Elijah Harper's blocking of the Meech Lake Accord in 1987 and the Oka Crisis in 1990 made mainstream Canadians sit up and take notice as Native people in Canada became increasingly politicized and outspoken. In 1988 came parliamentary approval of the Multiculturalism Act and a resulting public discussion of cultural diversity. At the same time, literary Canada began to become more aware of issues of cultural difference. As Margery Fee points out in her essay in this collection, the much-discussed "Writing Thru Race" conference in 1994 called the literary community's attention to "the notion that different cultural locations are just that—different. They produce different needs and require different forms, both literary and socio-political" (Monika Kim Gagnon and Scott Toguri McFarlane, quoted in "The Trickster Moment"

92). Given this sense of needing to acknowledge the "difference" of Indigenous writing, then, and given the kinds of claims that Highway and others were making for the trickster as a marker of this difference, it is unsurprising that Canadian literary critics seized upon the trickster as a culturally appropriate means of approaching Indigenous literature.

Yet there is always a danger in focusing on cultural symbols of difference. As Helen Hoy ponders in *How Should I Read These?*, even as a critic seeks to be culturally sensitive, he or she can "by deploying fixed and static signs of Indianness participate in present-day neo-colonial 'strategies of containment'" (166). In other words, those cultural symbols can easily become labels, commodities, and stereotypes, ways of explaining and controlling that which is unfamiliar. And the trickster, as he appeared in most criticism of the 1990s, did indeed become a "fixed and static sign of Indianness." Many literary critics treated the figure as timeless, as a manifestation of Indigenous "tradition," understanding "tradition" as "the perfect transmission of beliefs and statements handed down unchanged from one generation to the next" (Mauzé 5). They asserted general characteristics of "the" Native trickster and drew on examples from multiple tribes, regions, and times (i.e., Cox 17, Dickinson 176). Such a comparative mythological approach was rarely used within anthropology or most literary criticism at the time, yet it continued in the criticism of Native literature. Marc Manganaro suggests that comparative mythology is appealing when dealing with unfamiliar cultures, since it is indeed a "strategy of containment" that authoritatively gathers complex histories and cultures, "reducing multiplicity and chaos into uniformity, harmony, and order" (170). From this perspective, we can see that the pan-tribal trickster archetype offered a way of managing the issue of Indigenous "difference" without requiring extensive research into the complexity of particular Indigenous peoples. Of course, this pan-tribalism extended well beyond trickster studies; within the study of Indigenous literature at this time, Indigenous people were generally unquestioningly grouped together as products of "Indigenous culture" and "colonialism."[4]

Stripped of the burden of belonging to any particular time or place, the trickster was then free to represent the critics' ideals. The tendency to idealize the trickster was part of a larger rhetoric of idealization in the study of Indigenous literature. Rey Chow, in her *Ethics after Idealism*, defines "idealism" as the tendency "to relate to alterity through mythification; to imagine the 'other,' no matter how prosaic or impoverished, as essentially different, good, kind, enveloped in a halo, and beyond the contradictions that constitute our own historical place" (xx). And indeed, in much literary criticism, Indigenous people were positioned as the political "good guys" who stood for all that is non-centred, non-oppressive, spiritual, and benevolent. In studies of the trickster, this limited depiction of Indigenous people amalgamated with a similar idealization of humour. The critical response to humour is most often more celebratory than critical, particularly in an approach to humour that has been called the "mythological strain" (Purdie 151). This approach explores humour and comedy in terms of mythological forms, such as the carnival, the trickster, the fool, and the birth-rebirth cycle. Humour is seen as expressing certain universal forces—such as mysticism, fertility, creativity, and nature—and arising out of the unconscious, of lower classes, of past cultures, or of "primitive" cultures. Rather than focusing on the social uses of humour, this approach "comes to locate *all* laughter as *valuably* involved with energies that are distinct from social convention" (Purdie 151). A typical example is Lance Olsen's 1990 study, *Circus of the Mind in Motion: Postmodernism and the Comic Vision*. Olsen centres his analysis on the circus, which he associates with an idealized "comic vision" that is fundamentally subversive and playful (18). Despite this emphasis on subversion, however, Olsen removes his analysis from socio-historical context, claiming that "postmodern humour" is not the product of a period, but a state of mind (18). He regards the "comic vision" as determined not by time, but by culture. Thus, he distinguishes between a "tragic vision," which he claims is distinctively Western, and a non-Western "comic vision" that emphasizes interconnectedness, creative survival, and adaptability (24).

Much like Olsen, many critics in the 1990s associated non-Western culture (in this case, the trickster) with postmodern ideals. Paradoxically, the trickster was often presented as a *stable* symbol of chaos, disorder, and resistance. For instance, in an essay on Thomas King, Blanca Chester writes, "[t]he trickster *always* works from out of chaos rather than within an ordered system" (51, italics mine). Such depictions of the trickster are popular largely because they serve a certain critical fashion, one that emphasizes the constructedness and unknowability of the world. The trickster is read as a metaphor of postmodernism, challenging stable categories and forms. The critic can thus fit their material into current theoretical trends, while simultaneously appealing to the cultural "authenticity" and hence the authority of an "indigenous theory." Robert Nunn is accurate in his suggestion that "the trickster is a metonym of those energies of cross-culturality, hybridity and syncreticity" (97), but it is largely critics who have made it such a metonym. For instance, both Sheila Rabillard and Peter Dickinson, in essays on Tomson Highway, slide almost imperceptibly from discussions of the trickster to discussions of hybridity, gender transgression, and queer sexuality, implicitly equating the subjects. In one such slide, Dickinson writes, "Thus, as a figure through which to reimagine both narrative and political/cultural communities, and, more-over, as a 'chance' operation in language aimed at subverting outmoded mythic structures and destabilizing the ontological fixity of 'authentic' or 'essential' representations of the Indigene (be they in the social sciences or humanities), the Trickster—whether metamorphosized as Coyote, Nanabush, Raven, or Weesageechak—inhabits a site of profound gender ambiguity" (176). Similarly, Carlton Smith writes, "King's Coyote emerges not so much as a representative of anthropomorphic, embodied versions of trickster but rather as a linguistic construct sent forth to disrupt our acceptance of certain 'old stories'" (516). In these typical quotations from trickster studies of the time, we can see the move away from an "embodied" figure with roots in Indigenous lives towards a trickster that is primarily a metaphor for a partic-ular theoretical stance. Ironically, both Rabillard and Dickinson castigate Paul Radin's 1956 study of the trickster for making the same critical move that they do, reading the trickster through the lens of his own culture. By over-emphasizing the ordering and teaching functions of trickster tales, Rabillard says, Radin "demonstrates the desire for purity, boundary, and definition that exercises the dominant culture in relation to the colonized North Ameri-cans" (4). Academic culture had changed since Radin's time; the desire there-after was for impurity, permeability, and ambiguity. But the tendency to see in Native culture what fit the current critical climate remained the same.

Having extracted the use of the trickster from its particular cultural con-text and made it a tool in the critic's own theoretical project, the final criti-cal step was to reapply it to the creations of Native people. "Trickster" became an adjective, a label to put on Native humour, art, theatre, and literature. But such classification can be critically limiting. One popular device was to identify a particular character in a piece of Native literature as a trickster. For example, writing on Thomas King's *Medicine River*, Herb Wyile writes: "Though Harlen is a realistic character, he also reflects the typical ambivalence of the trickster.... Thus King's evoking of the figure of the trickster further distinguishes the novel from the Western tradition (in that the trickster is a central figure of Native cultures)" (112). Wyile's association of Harlen with the trickster is based not on any specific allusions to the figure, but merely on the character's comic ambivalence. This equation of the character and the trickster is rendered inevitable by the quick and sweeping assertion that "the trickster is a central figure of Native cultures" (112). Wyile quickly and sim-ply explains both the novel and the character of Harlen as characteristically Native. Pomo-Coast Miwok writer Gregory Sarris critiques William Gleason's reading of Louise Erdrich's *Love Medicine* for just this kind of critical catego-rization. Gleason writes about Erdrich's character Gerry Nanapush, "Gerry is Trickster, literally" (quoted in Sarris 127). Sarris responds that Gleason is trying to "nail down the Indian so we can nail down the text. The Indian is fixed, readable in certain ways, so that when we find him or her in a written text we have a way to fix and understand the Indian and hence the text" (128). Sarris here identifies the critical sleight of hand inherent in such readings; the trickster, presented as a symbol of instability, became a way of stabilizing Native texts.

Sometimes, the author him- or herself was stamped as a trickster. For example, two articles about Tomson Highway and his writing have implicitly and explicitly equated the playwright with the trickster (Hannon, Wigston), part of a rhetoric that describes Highway as natural, animal-like, magical, and spiritual. Drew Hayden Taylor takes an ironic view of this kind of labelling of Indigenous writers:

> That seems to be the latest fad with academics. Subscribing all actions and at least one character in a written piece to the trickster figure. As playwright/poet Daniel David Moses describes it, "They all like to play 'Spot the Trickster.'" ... So perhaps, just for clarity's sake, I should take the time to make sure these no doubt intelligent people understand that it's just the inherent trickster tendencies that exist on a subconscious level in all literary works penned by Aboriginal writers and are representative of our culture. In other words, I'm not responsible for these views or criticism, the trickster made me do it.
>   Yeah, they'll buy that. ("Academia" 99)

Taylor here points to a serious problem with many readings that look at Indigenous texts in terms of the trickster: they ignore the agency of the Indigenous author or artist.

This tendency to underestimate the active role of the artist can be seen in Allan Ryan's 1996 dissertation and subsequent 1999 book on humour in contemporary Canadian Indigenous art, both entitled *The Trickster Shift*. They provide an excellent survey of humourous art and a valuable collection of the views of Indigenous artists and writers on humour. However, Ryan's analysis of this material is limited by his use of an overgeneralized trickster theory. In his introductions to both his dissertation and his book, Ryan establishes his theoretical approach to Native humour. He clearly allies himself with the "worldview" school of comic theory when he states his conviction that there is "indeed a sensibility—a spirit—at work (or at play) in the practice of many of these artists, grounded in a fundamentally 'comic' (as opposed to 'tragic') worldview and embodied in the traditional Native trickster" (*Trickster* 1999, 3). The structure of this sentence is telling; Ryan makes the comic (or trickster) "spirit," rather than the artists, the active subject of the sentence. The artists and their practice are presented not as using and drawing on tradition, but as guided by a tradition and a "worldview." Thus, for example, Ryan later writes, "[t]he tribal Trickster may in fact revel in the opportunity afforded by the postmodern moment" ("Trickster" 1995, 37). The trickster appears to be the one making artistic choices.

Ryan's study de-historicizes Indigenous artists by grounding his trickster theory in a cross-cultural past. He relies heavily on anthropological readings of the trickster, from numerous places and times, and then unquestioningly applies them to contemporary art. He slides simply and unquestioningly from the past to the present: "It is hardly surprising that the interplay of irony and parody so prevalent in traditional trickster narratives would emerge as a major feature of contemporary Native artistic practice" ("Trickster" 1995, 20). With such a slide, Ryan obscures the contemporary context in which Native artists are using traditions. Also, while he considers the influence of the trickster, he does not substantially consider the influence of Native artists on each other. In ignoring historicity in favour of "traditionality," Ryan obscures the complex political and social functions of these artists' humour. Having stripped the trickster of historical specificity, Ryan then explicitly claims the figure in the name of current theory: "Clearly, the Native Trickster, when conceptualized as 'postmodern,' can be considered 'postcolonial' as well" ("Trickster" 1995, 39). This claim allows him to move further away from the question of how and why the trickster figure is actually used. Indeed, the trickster becomes a label for the artists' artistic process: "the 'Trickster shift' is best understood as process—as creative practice and subversive play whose ultimate goal is a radical shift in viewer perspective" ("Trickster" 1995, 11). With "trickster" referring to everything that Indigenous artists do, it loses its usefulness as a term of analysis.[5]

Much has changed since the peak of trickster criticism in the 1990s. Arguably, the most significant change has been the entry of more Indigenous people into the academy and into the ranks of literary critics. Indigenous scholars have generally been unwilling to accept an idealized rhetoric that would situate our people as the passive recipients of either a traditional and spiritual, or a postmodern and hybrid, worldview. In an effort to describe the cultural, historical, and political grounding of Indigenous peoples as well as the complex interrelations between them, a number of Indigenous scholars have adopted an approach to literature that is sometimes known as Indigenous (or American Indian) literary nationalism.[6] Although it is difficult to generalize about such a diverse group of scholars, they are connected in their call for cultural and historical specificity in the study of Indigenous literature, as opposed to the generalizing and essentializing that have been so common in the field, and particularly in trickster criticism. Womack, for example, explains: "[w]e are trying to avoid the kind of literary work that has been so very popular in our field in which people avoid historical research and base their criticism exclusively on tropes and symbols [such as the trickster]" ("A Single Decade" 7). According to Robert Warrior, a historicized and critical perspective becomes particularly important when faced with claims that, like the claims Highway has made about the trickster, call upon a spiritual and cultural authority. Instead of viewing such claims as "the truth" about Indigenous people, Warrior explains, we need to approach them as statements made by a particular person at a particular time for particular reasons. Quoting Edward Said, Warrior argues that what he calls "secular" criticism allows "a sense of history and of human production, along with a healthy skepticism about the various official idols venerated by culture and by system" (206). In the field of Indigenous literature, one could argue that the "official idols" have included the "trickster" himself, as well as writers whose voices have been taken as those of absolute cultural authority.

A culturally specific approach may sometimes mean that we leave the word "trickster" behind altogether, since, as Womack points out, it is not a word in traditional Indigenous cultures and languages: "there is no such thing as a trickster in indigenous cultures … tricksters were invented by anthropologists" ("A Single Decade" 19). I discovered, when team-teaching with Cree writer and elder Maria Campbell, that there is much more to say about the figure whom the Cree know as "Elder Brother" than there is about vague, pan-tribal tricksters. Close attention to a particular cultural figure also tends to eliminate much of the idealization that I described earlier in this essay. For instance, according to Campbell, despite the lack of gendered pronouns in the Cree language, "Elder Brother" is not genderless; he is a male who sometimes disguises himself as female. I am not an expert on Cree culture and do not want to make any authoritative pronouncements on this matter; I simply want to point out that Campbell's understanding of the Cree trickster challenges some of Highway's claims and the flurry of critical claims about the trickster's subversion of gender. Womack says that he similarly learned to challenge the critical idealization of the trickster while living in Blackfoot country and learning about Naapi: "'Naapi' means 'foolish one.' Somehow, as a literary trope, we seem to have instead mistaken him or her for a role model and ignored some of the more oppressive characteristics of this figure (look at the rapes, for example, that are sometimes part of trickster stories)" ("Integrity" 116). The complexity of particular Indigenous mythical figures would be less of a surprise to historians, anthropologists, and folklorists, who have been working with a more culturally specific approach to Indigenous studies for some time, while literary critics continued in a comparative, cross-cultural mode. For example, folklorist Barre Toelken, in his essay, "Life and Death in Navajo Coyote Tales," explains how, when working on Navajo Coyote stories in the 1960s, he originally took an idealized view of the stories; he viewed them as exclusively positive forces that helped establish the Navajo social order and had healing powers. Finally, after several years, his Navajo friends informed him that he was only partly right. Coyote stories, they told him, also have a much darker side, one that has been little acknowledged outside of Navajo communities: "Since words and narratives have the power to heal, they may also be used to injure and kill" (396). Witches can use the power of Coyote tales to harm and to create disorder that is "contrary to community values" (400). They use the stories "separately, divisively, analytically, in order to attack certain parts of the victim's body, or family, or livestock" (396).

I offer the example of Toelken in part as a corrective to the uncritical idealization of trickster figures and stories. But I also want to emphasize that he discovered that trickster stories could be deliberately used for a variety of purposes, depending on the teller and his or her goals. And this brings me back to an earlier point—that it was not only critics who were obsessed with tricksters in the 1980s and 1990s. As Fee puts it, "for a while, everyone who was anyone wrote at least one trickster story, play, or poem" ("The Trickster Moment" 106). And although, as Womack says, anthropologists may have invented the trickster, Indigenous artists were certainly using the term. So how are we to understand this creative trend, if not as the product of a timeless, cross-cultural trickster tradition? I would argue that, like the Navajo storytellers, contemporary Indigenous writers were using tradition to suit their purposes. "Tradition" is continually reinvented, with contemporary cultural responses being framed in reference to the past and to "traditionality" (Hobsbawm and Ranger). Like all other peoples, Native people have adapted their traditions, dropping some, adapting others, and encouraging still others. Thus, while the focus on the trickster in Indigenous writing was indeed based in part on tribal history, it was just as much a contemporary artistic and political trend. The invocation of this "traditional" figure was strategic, and served to legitimate certain activities or interests. As Marie Annharte Baker asserts, when we see a Native trickster used in a play (or, I would add, any other piece of cultural production), "we must become aware not only of the special circumstances of that creation and its circular totality, we must know something of the playwright, actor, director, or the events of the day which give inspiration to a particular rendition. You are forced to be particular to understand" (227).

Although there is no space in this foreword for the kind of particularity for which Baker calls, a brief look at the history of the "trickster trend" in Indigenous writing in Canada may help to clarify how Indigenous people strategically draw on certain traditions. In Canada, the popularity of tricksters in Indigenous literature in the 1990s can be traced, at least in part, to Toronto in the mid-1980s. There, Highway had been doing some reading on trickster figures: "I studied Greek mythology, Christian mythology in the Bible, native mythology here and in other native tribes down in the States— Navaho and Hopi. I began to uncover this incredibly vital character" (quoted in Hannon 38). He, Makka Kleist, Doris Linklater, and Monique Mojica then held a series of workshops through Native Earth Performing Arts "to learn the tools necessary to approach the traditional Native trickster figures" (Preston 139). Native Earth recruited the help of non-Native performers, Richard Pochinko and Ian Wallace, who were trained in mask-making and European clowning techniques (Nunn 99). Out of these workshops arose the strategic body, "The Committee to Re-establish the Trickster" (Ryan, *Trickster* 1999, 4).[7] These workshops were also the improvisational beginnings of Highway's enormously popular and influential plays, *The Rez Sisters* (1988) and *Dry Lips Oughta Move to Kapuskasing* (1989). With the nationwide popularity of these plays, Highway became a public figure and an influential spokesperson for the trickster, repeatedly asserting the figure's centrality in the Native worldview. His statements have had a profound effect, undoubtedly spurring on some other Native artists and writers in their use of the trickster.

Of course, this very brief narrative of the rise in the popularity of Native tricksters is not at all definitive. There are many other strands to this story. For instance, Thomas King, a Cherokee-Greek writer, has said that his use of the Coyote figure was heavily influenced by his reading of the transcribed stories of Harry Robinson, an Okanagan storyteller. I offer these narratives to suggest that Highway's and other writers' use of the trickster was not simply the inevitable passing on of a tradition that they learned at their mothers' knees. As Fee writes, "[t]he tradition of oral storytelling rarely connects seamlessly with the contemporary written tradition except in anthologies [and, I would add, in much criticism on Native Literature]" ("Anthology" 146). Rather, it seems, the emergence of the trickster in contemporary Native writing took place in a very urban, cross-cultural, organized, and strategic manner. This conscious recreation of a tradition does not mean that the contemporary manifestations of the trickster tradition are in any way "fake." But they are, like all instances of "tradition," recreated because of specific and current needs. Again, it is not within the scope of this essay to explore fully what these needs are; I will simply offer some quick possibilities. For instance, the concept of the trickster seems to have been particularly appealing and useful to urban Native artists. The urban Native community is tribally mixed, and living with a wide array of cultures and possible lifestyles. In this situation, the "trickster," being pan-tribal and endlessly adaptable, but still identifiably Native, may offer a useful symbol of city life. Highway himself explains that this figure has a particular appeal in the city: "Weesakeechak walks down Yonge Street; in fact, he prances down Yonge Street … Weesakeechak is making the city into a home for Native people" (Hodgson, para. 43). Highway and other gay Aboriginal artists may also have found the overt sexuality and gender-bending of some trickster figures useful and appealing. As much as gay Indigenous people across the continent have adopted and adapted the pan-Native figure of the "two-spirited person," so the figure of the trickster has been used to bring a legitimacy and "traditionality" to the challenging of heterosexual norms (Carroci 115). Highway's trickster, in fact, has a distinctly campy sensibility, one that is surely connected to urban gay culture as well as to Cree culture.

Although some Indigenous artists made a strategic choice to focus on the trickster, others have spoken against the trickster monopoly. At a round-table discussion at the Congress of the Humanities and Social Sciences in 2000, Cree writer and actor Anne Marie Sewell was one of several Indigenous participants who raised concerns about the critical focus on the trickster: "The public always wants something from Native people. Sometimes they want me to bleed for them and tell them about the "issues." And lately, I feel like everyone wants me to put on my trickster face, my survivor face. I feel like I'm supposed to be funny. I'm Native, so I must be funny." Ojibway writer and literary critic Armand Ruffo made similar comments about the focus on humour and tricksters: "Not only does all the critical attention to humour in Native literature create the impression that all Native literature has to be funny, but it unwittingly hacks off the roots of Aboriginal literature by concentrating on one narrow aspect of the oral tradition" (quoted in Hulan and Warley 126). Métis poet Marilyn Dumont writes with frustration about the pressure to "infuse everything you write with symbols of the native world view, that is: the circle, mother earth, the number four or the trickster figure" (47). Just as Highway and his contemporaries had used the trickster to carve out space for their work, Sewell, Ruffo, and Dumont were reacting against the trickster to make space for different kinds of Indigenous writing.

The tide seems to have turned against trickster criticism in recent years. The complaints of some Indigenous writers, the critique from Indigenous nationalist critics, and the changing of academic fashion seem to have left few people working on the trickster. Renate Eigenbrod's recent monograph on Aboriginal literature uses the word trickster only in distancing quotation marks (162). And, in as authoritative a source as *The Cambridge Companion to Native American Literature* (2005), the trickster is only very briefly mentioned, with the following skeptical commentary: "Whether such easy celebration [of the hybrid, postmodern, identity-shifting trickster] actually chimes with the lived reality or is more of a literary and utopian gesture has been a matter of some debate, as has the reason for its popularity with non-Indian readers. Does it allow connections to be made across cultures or is it just more easily consumable by white readers because it has lost its specificity and communal identity in a cosmopolitan and postmodern mélange?" (79). And, in 2007, Ojibway scholar Niigonwedom Sinclair actually called for a moratorium on studies of the trickster.

So where does that leave this new collection of essays on the trickster? I would suggest that these essays represent a new approach to trickster studies, one that has clearly been influenced by the nationalists' call for cultural and historical specificity. For example, in the first section of this anthology, Niigonwedom James Sinclair clearly lays out the debates as articulated by eminent Native American literary nationalists, and challenges scholars to produce work committed to the continuance of Indigenous nations. Then, Margery Fee looks at cultural production during what she calls the "Trickster Moment," situating the latter as part of the cultural appropriation debates of the 1980s and 1990s. Modelled on both of these approaches, Linda Morra's paper considers the ethical implications of the use of the trickster in the works of such non-Indigenous Canadian writers as Sheila Watson, Mordecai Richler, and Gail Anderson-Dargatz.

The second section, focused on Raven, opens with Richard Van Camp's story of Raven and the Dogrib people, who hid Raven's beak under the dress of an elderly powerful medicine woman—the comic value of the narrative derives in part from the old woman's subsequent pleasure with the beak's performative abilities. Jennifer Kelly's paper then critiques the story and shows how a Western cultural and historical perspective, even one informed by previous knowledge of Dene trickster narratives, may limit one's understanding of such works. Kelly's essay is followed by an interview with Christopher Kientz, showcasing how his production company, *Raven Tales*, redevelops such trickster tales, beginning with those related to the Raven, for the needs of a modern audience. Sonny Assu's biographical submission explores the challenges of an artist whose cultural legacy was denied him for the vast part of his childhood, and addresses how his art rediscovers that legacy, even as it is negotiated within a pervasive consumer cultural context. The third section brings together essays on three different traditions, each grounded in particular communities: Métis (Warren Cariou's reading of Rigoureau); Blackfoot (Eldon Yellowhorn's retelling of Naapi); and Cree (Deanna Reder's examination of a comic book Wesakecak).

The fourth section, on Coyote and Nanabush, begins with Thomas King's 1990 poems, "Coyote Sees the Prime Minister" and "Coyote Goes to Toronto," reprinted here in order to be reread in a contemporary political context and in terms of contemporary ecological concerns. Jo-ann Archibald's short excerpt, which comes from the preface to her book *Indigenous Storywork: Educating the Heart, Mind, Body, and Spirit*, discusses the role of Coyote in Stó:lō storytelling. In "(Re)Nationalizing Naanabozho," Daniel Morley Johnston reconsiders Gerald Vizenor as a literary nationalist, whose concepts of survivance and trickster hermeneutics still have revolutionary potential. Judith Leggatt examines what she refers to as "the emergence of a cross-cultural trickster poetics" by working through Gerald Vizenor's concepts in relation to works by Anishinaabe writers Lenore Keeshig-Tobias and Marie Annharte Baker and their respective references to Nanabush and Coyote. Leggatt argues that these writers find a way of articulating a comic vision of Anishinaabe trickster discourse that contradicts previous academic interpretations. The last piece, by Niigonwedom James Sinclair, offers a fusion of theory and storytelling in a gripping contemporary incarnation.

In the final section, Anishinaabe scholar Jill Carter reconsiders Vizenor's notion of "Trickster discourse" as she analyzes the work of Spiderwoman Theater and the role of the female body as evidence of survivance. Implicitly, in its focus upon the competing allegiances suggested by Spiderwoman Theater's location in New York and its participants' varying national ties, her paper also calls attention to the issue of borders and nations as currently inscribed in Western maps. In another examination of borders, Christine Kim uses Hiromi Goto's *The Kappa Child* to consider the implications when a Japanese kappa surfaces in Blackfoot territory and lives alongside Blackfoot tricksters; she invites readers to consider how contiguous existences inform and challenge current understandings of culture and history, and how these may also provide us a way of "imagining harmonious coexistences that do not resort to strategies of colonial violence." The final contribution, Thomas King's reprinted essay, "How I Spent My Summer Vacation: History, Story, and the Cant of Authenticity," suggests that, although stories may alter in detail, as he has overtly argued elsewhere, their fundamental importance to identity and nationality cannot be underestimated.

These essays are very different from the trickster studies with which I found myself so frustrated nearly a decade ago. In my view, the solution to the "troubles" that I have described here does not lie in abandoning the study of trickster figures. Some of the nationalist critics (and indeed I myself) have criticized literary critics' focus on a "cultural" approach to Indigenous literature (as opposed to a political or historical one) as a way of avoiding difficult research and challenging political issues. But culture—particularly the oral stories and Indigenous languages in which "tricksters" live—is clearly important to Indigenous communities, as evidenced in their efforts to keep those languages and stories alive and vibrant. The key, perhaps, is not to assume "an explicit analogy between writer and culture" (Sullivan 112), but to remain aware of the agency and individuality of Indigenous writers. There is a balance to be sought between an awareness of the complexity and multiplicity and the need to generalize meaningfully about Indigenous people. Métis scholar Emma LaRocque articulates the complexity of trying to understand what has been called the "Aboriginal worldview":

> [T]here is an Aboriginal ground to Aboriginal literature. The foundational bases to Aboriginal worldview refer to the modes of acquiring and arranging knowledge within the context of original languages, relationships, and cultural strategies. This ground, though, is layered and 'unsedimented' for there is here a complex imbrication of cultural continuity and discontinuity. (220)

Understanding that "Aboriginal ground to Aboriginal literature" is what the critics who wrote about the trickster in the 1980s and 1990s were trying to do. And it is what we in the field are still trying to do—although with the benefit of more knowledge and a much more developed field. Looking back over the past decade, the changes in the study of Indigenous literature have been striking. I wonder what they will be saying about the trickster ten years from now.

Notes

1   I would like to thank my doctoral supervisor, Ted Chamberlin, as well as my dissertation committee members, Russell Brown and Neil ten Kortenaar, for their helpful comments on the original version of this piece. Thanks also to Deanna Reder for encouraging me to unearth this piece of my dissertation and for her inspiring suggestions for revision.

2   In the area of Canadian Aboriginal literature, for instance, see Cox; Dickinson; Leggatt; Matchie and Larson; Rabillard; and Smith.

3   For the sake of simplicity, I will refer to the trickster as "he," recognizing that some claim that trickster figures have no fixed gender.

4   I have written elsewhere on the problems of looking at Aboriginal culture through the lenses of culture and colonialism. See "Tewatatha:wi: Aboriginal Nationalism in Taiaiake Alfred's *Peace, Power, Righteousness: An Indigenous Manifesto.*"

5 Most of this limited theorizing happens in Ryan's introduction. In his analyses of specific artworks, Ryan is much more historically grounded, showing himself to be aware of the ways in which Native artists are influenced by contemporary events and by each other. However, his overall argument and analysis are limited by the inability of his "trickster theory" to accommodate the artists' active and contemporary choices. Also, Ryan can only view the art as "subversive," a view that ignores aspects of humour that do not seem to fit within the transgressive, postmodern, "trickster" type.

6 The most influential work along these lines has come from Native American critics, particularly Jace Weaver (Cherokee), Craig Womack (Creek), Robert Warrior (Osage), Daniel Heath Justice (Cherokee), Devon Mihesuah (Choctaw), Elizabeth Cook-Lynn (Crow Creek Sioux), and Simon Ortiz (Acoma Pueblo), but there are also influential nationalist scholars in the Canadian context, such as Taiaiake Alfred (Mohawk), and Janice Acoose (Métis-Saulteaux).

7 For more on the Committee to Re-establish the Trickster, see Fee in this volume.

Works Cited

Baker, Marie Annharte. "An Old Indian Trick Is to Laugh." *Canadian Theatre Review* 68 (Fall 1991): 48–9.

Campbell, Maria. Personal communication with Kristina Fagan. Saskatoon, 2002.

Carrocci, Massimiliano. "The Berdache as Metahistorical Reference for the Urban Gay American Indian Community." In *Present Is Past: Some Uses of Tradition in Native Societies*. Ed. Marie Mauzé. Lanham, MD: UP of America, 1997. 113–29.

Chester, Blanca. "Green Grass, Running Water: Theorizing the World of the Novel." *Canadian Literature* 161/162 (Summer/Autumn 1999): 44–61.

Chow, Rey. *Ethics After Idealism: Theory-Culture-Ethnicity-Reading*. Theories of Contemporary Culture Series. Bloomington: Indiana UP, 1998.

Cox, Jay. "Dangerous Definitions: Female Tricksters in Contemporary Native American Literature." *Wicazo Sa Review* 5:2 (Autumn 1989): 17–21.

Dickinson, Peter. *Here Is Queer: Nationalisms, Sexualities, and the Literatures of Canada*. Toronto: U of Toronto P, 1999.

Dumont, Marilyn. "Positive Images of Nativeness." In *Looking at the Words of Our People: First Nations Analysis of Literature*. Ed. Jeannette Armstrong. Penticton, BC: Theytus, 1993. 45–50.

Eigenbrod, Renate. *Travelling Knowledges: Positioning the Im/Migrant Reader of Aboriginal Literatures in Canada*. Winnipeg: U of Manitoba P, 2005.

Fagan, Kristina. "Tewatatha:wi: Aboriginal Nationalism in Taiaiake Alfred's *Peace, Power, Righteousness: An Indigenous Manifesto*." *American Indian Quarterly* 28:1–2 (Winter/Spring 2004): 12–29.

Fee, Margery. "Aboriginal Writing in Canada and the Anthology as Commodity." In *Native North America: Critical and Cultural Perspectives*. Ed. Renée Hulan. Toronto: ECW, 1999. 135–55.

———. "The Trickster Moment, Cultural Appropriation, and the Liberal Imagination in Canada." In *Troubling Tricksters: Revisioning Critical Approaches*. Ed. Deanna Reder and Linda M. Morra. Waterloo, ON: Wilfrid Laurier UP, 2009. 59–76.

Hannon, Gerald. "Tomson Highway and the Trickster: Scenes from the Life of Playwright Tomson Highway." *Toronto Life* 25:4 (March 1991): 28–44, 81–5.

Highway, Tomson. *The Rez Sisters*. Saskatoon: Fifth House, 1988.

Hobsbawm, Eric, and Terence Ranger, eds. *The Invention of Tradition*. Cambridge: Cambridge UP, 1992.

Hodgson, Heather. "Survival Cree, or Weesakeechak Dances Down Yonge Street: Heather Hodgson Speaks with Tomson Highway." *Books in Canada* 28:1 (Fall 1999): 2–5. <www.booksincanada.com/article_view.asp?id=632>.

Hoy, Helen. *How Should I Read These?: Native Women Writers in Canada*. Toronto: U of Toronto P, 2001.

Hulan, Renée, and Linda Warley. "Comic Relief : Pedagogical Issues Around Thomas King's *Medicine River*." In *Creating Community: A Roundtable on Canadian Aboriginal Literature*. Ed. Renate Eigenbrod and Jo-Ann Episkenew. Penticton, BC: Theytus; Brandon, MB: Bearpaw, 2002. 125–46.

Hunt, Nigel. "Tracking the Trickster." Review of Tomson Highway's *Dry Lips Oughta Move to Kapuskasing*. *Brick* 37 (Autumn 1989): 58–60.

LaRocque, Emma. "Teaching Aboriginal Literature: the Discourse of Margins and Mainstreams." In *Creating Community: A Roundtable on Canadian Aboriginal Literature*. Ed. Renate Eigenbrod and Jo-Ann Episkenew. Penticton, BC: Theytus; Brandon, MB: Bearpaw, 2002. 209–34.

Lincoln, Kenneth. *Indi'n Humor: Bicultural Play in Native America*. New York: Oxford UP, 1993.

Manganaro, Marc. *Myth, Rhetoric, and the Voice of Authority: A Critique of Frazer, Eliot, Frye, and Campbell*. New Haven, CT: Yale UP, 1992.

Matchie, Thomas, and Brett Larson. "Coyote Fixes the World: The Power of Myth in Thomas King's *Green Grass, Running Water*." *North Dakota Quarterly* 63:2 (Spring 1996): 153–68.

Mauzé, Marie. "On Concepts of Tradition." In *Present Is Past: Some Uses of Tradition in Native Societies*. Ed. Marie Mauzé. Lanham, MD: UP of America, 1997. 1–15.

Murray, David. "Translation and Mediation." In *The Cambridge Companion to Native American Literature*. Ed. Joy Porter and Kenneth Roemer. Cambridge: Cambridge UP, 2005. 69–84.

Nunn, Robert. "Hybridity and Mimicry in the Plays of Drew Hayden Taylor." *Essays on Canadian Writing* 65 (Fall 1998): 95–119.

Olsen, Lance. *Circus of the Mind in Motion: Postmodernism and the Comic Vision*. Detroit: Wayne State UP, 1990.

Preston, Jennifer. "Weesageechak Begins to Dance: Native Earth Performing Arts Inc." *The Drama Review: A Journal of Performance Studies* 36:1 (Spring 1992): 135–59.

Rabillard, Sheila. "Absorption, Elimination, and the Hybrid: Some Impure Questions of Gender and Culture in the Trickster Drama of Tomson Highway." *Essays in Theatre/Etudes Théâtrales* 12:1 (November 1993): 3–27.

Radin, Paul. *The Trickster: A Study in American Indian Mythology.* New York: Philosophical Library, 1956.

Ryan, Allan J. "The Trickster Shift: A New Paradigm in Contemporary Canadian Native Art." Diss., U of British Columbia, 1995. Ann Arbor, MI: UMI, 1996.

———. *The Trickster Shift: Humour and Irony in Contemporary Native Art.* Vancouver: U of British Columbia P, 1999.

Sarris, Gregory. *Keeping Slug Woman Alive: A Holistic Approach to American Indian Texts.* Berkeley: U of California P, 1993.

Sewell, Anne Marie. Roundtable on Aboriginal Literature. Congress of the Humanities and Social Sciences. Edmonton, May 2000.

Sinclair, Niigonwedom J. Comment at Roundtable on Aboriginal Literature. Canadian Association of Commonwealth Literatures and Languages. Congress of the Humanities and Social Sciences. Saskatoon, May 2007.

Smith, Carlton. "Coyote, Contingency, and Community: Thomas King's *Green Grass, Running Water* and Postmodern Trickster." *American Indian Quarterly* 21:3 (Summer 1997): 515–34.

Sullivan, Rosemary. "Northrop Frye: Canadian Mythographer." *Journal of Commonwealth Literature* 18 (1983): 1–13.

Taylor, Drew Hayden. "Academia Mania." In *Funny, You Don't Look Like One: Observations of a Blue-Eyed Ojibway.* Rev. ed. Penticton, BC: Theytus, 1998. 95–9.

———. "The Re-Appearance of the Trickster: Native Theatre in Canada." In *On-Stage and Off-Stage: English Canadian Drama in Discourse.* Ed. Abert-Reiner Glapp with Rolf Althof. St. John's, NL: Breakwater, 1996. 51–9.

Toelken, Barre. "Life and Death in Navajo Coyote Tales." In *Recovering the Word: Essays on Native American Literature.* Eds. Brian Swann and Arnold Krupat. Los Angeles: U of California P, 1987. 388–401.

Warrior, Robert. "Native Critics in the World: Edward Said and Nationalism." In *American Indian Literary Nationalism.* Ed. Jace Weaver, Craig S. Womack, and Robert Warrior. Albuquerque: U of New Mexico P, 2006. 179–223.

Wigston, Nancy. "Nanabush in the City." *Books in Canada* 18:2 (March 1989): 7–9.

Womack, Craig S. "A Single Decade: Book-Length Native Literary Criticism between 1986 and 1997." In *Reasoning Together: The Native Critics' Collective.* Ed. Craig S. Womack, Daniel Heath Justice, and Christopher B. Teuton. Norman: U of Oklahoma P, 2008. 3–104.

———. "The Integrity of American Indian Claims: Or, How I Learned to Stop Worrying and Love My Hybridity." In *American Indian Literary Nationalism.* Ed.

Jace Weaver, Craig S. Womack, and Robert Warrior. Albuquerque: U of New Mexico P, 2006. 91–177.

Wyile, Herb. "'Trust Tonto': Thomas King's Subversive Fictions and the Politics of Cultural Literacy." *Canadian Literature* 161/162 (Summer/Autumn 1999): 105–24.

Trickster Reflections
Part I

To teach Indigenous literature with a belief in the full humanity of Indigenous people is to inevitably engage in an act of political resistance. (52)
   —Daniel Heath Justice, "Renewing the Fire: Notes Toward the Liberation of English Studies"

Native American Indian literatures are tribal discourse, more discourse. (4)
   —Gerald Vizenor, "A Postmodern Introduction," *Narrative Chance: Postmodern Discourse on Native American Indian Literatures*

Boozhoo.[1]
   I have a trickster story. It is my own. It is also now yours.
   It's about my experiences with what we might call "Tricksters."[2]
   My earliest remembrances were at home, when I was around nine, in stories my dad would read and tell before I went to bed. Virtually every night, when we weren't too tired, my sisters and I would gather on the couch and my Dad would bring out a copy of *The Adventures of Nanabush: Ojibway Indian Stories* (collected from a group of Rama Ojibway elders, Toronto: Doubleday, 1979). Sometimes, he would just narrate other ones he knew. Afterwards, as he usually did, my father asked us questions, mostly to reflect on the stories: what we might do if we were Nanabush, why Nanabush did the things he did, what we liked, didn't like, or might change if one of us told the story. Often, we would answer using our knowledge from school, television, and popular culture (for me: whales, hockey, and Optimus Prime). Sometimes, my father would relate these stories to similar Waynaboozhoo or Nanabosho narratives,

even if they carried different details. At other times, he would demonstrate how parts of these stories held responsibilities we carry as Anishinaabeg: to respect ourselves, our bodies, our spirits, and our minds—according to the Seven Sacred Teachings.[3] Mostly we laughed, learned from one another, and grew as a family.

Growing up, I witnessed hundreds of other trickster narratives, mostly in "ceremonial" settings, from namings to sharing circles to Midewiwin lodges. Sometimes I heard them in classrooms, read them in books, and watched them on TV. For the most part, these narratives were used for educational, medicinal, and community-building purposes—in events like initiations, healings, and tribal agreements. Sometimes, these stories were grotesque, sanitized, and silly, but virtually always resembled at least a shadow of the stories my father told (and continues to tell).

Now, I utilize trickster stories in my critical and creative pursuits as an Anishinaabeg scholar, teacher, and writer. I use them to demonstrate that Anishinaabeg literary theories in fields such as signification, semiotics, and the novel—that coincidentally dialogue well with historical ideas found in Plato's allegory of the cave, Coleridge's "symbol," and post-structuralism— are available, complex, and rich on their own terms. Other Anishinaabeg scholars such as Gerald Vizenor, Gordon Henry, Louise Erdrich, Lenore Keeshig-Tobias, and Armand Ruffo use similar stories to make other Anishinaabeg-specific arguments in other philosophical arenas. Other times, I simply read or tell Nanabush stories to my daughter before bed, ask her questions, and laugh with her.

This is a modern-day continuance of a very old Anishinaabeg intellectual tradition—storytelling. Years ago, this exchange took place in the winter, when clan and family relatives resided in large (and/or sometimes several) lodges and communities to share resources, food, and stories.[4] Nowadays, this process continues in ceremonial lodges, over kitchen tables, at universities, and—in my family's case—on living room couches.

Stories continue to be the predominant vessels in which Anishinaabeg knowledge is carried. Go anywhere where Anishinaabeg are and you will find them. Some stories are funny, some more serious, some educational, some less, some more—but all are meant to share some aspect of Anishinaabeg knowledge. Some are "classical" narratives used for ceremonial purposes. Some are in modern contexts of everyday events. Some are short, others long. Some take many visits and several "chapters" to share. Some require more than one storyteller. Some are terrible, mean-spirited, and false, too. Some are all of these and more.

Now, as before, stories reflect the experiences, thoughts, and knowledge important to Anishinaabeg, and collectively map the creative and critical relationships, and philosophies and histories of kin. Among other reasons, stories create, define, and maintain our relations with each other and the world around us, and when shared, cause us to reflect, to learn, to grow, as families, communities, and a People. Stories also indicate where we are in the universe, how we got here/there, and often indicate where we need to go. Although many do this through collective joy and beauty, not all stories build positive relations—some can wear them down and destroy them—and require great courage, negotiation, and thought to understand. Still, all are worth hearing out.

Anishinaabeg storytelling, therefore, is not a simple one-dimensional act but a complex historical, social, and political process embedded in the continuance of our collective presence, knowledge, and peoplehood. In the introduction to her edited anthology, *Stories Migrating Home: A Collection of Anishinaabe Prose*, Anishinaabe literary critic Kimberly Blaeser identifies that "Story remains the heartbeat of Indian community.... The accounts may have morals, suggesting an appropriate action or relationship, or they may simply allude to the general or specific mystery of life, but they always reinforce our connections. By centering us in a network of relationships, stories assure the survival of our spirits. Stories keep us migrating home" ("A Gathering of Stories" 2–3). These "heartbeats" demonstrate the dynamism of Anishinaabeg existence.

Storytelling of this nature, of course, requires a creative, critical, and ultimately active audience. Interviewed by Blaeser for her study of his work, *Gerald Vizenor: Writing in the Oral Tradition*, Anishinaabe author Gerald Vizenor suggests that what constitutes the process of Native storytelling is when "[t]he listener is active, not passive. The listener makes the story, but the story is also set up in a way that it can be personal and recognizable too ... All of this I am suggesting is discourse. It's a discourse between the listener, the implied author, the narrator, and the events that took place (that are called upon), the character ... We imagine it by telling and by listening" (25). By participating in the lives of stories, imagining them, and incorporating them into personal perceptions and expressions (just as my father encouraged), Native and Anishinaabeg audiences become participants in this collective process of knowledge creation and dissemination. In these interests, some stories are deemed valuable to a community's knowledge and therefore saved, maintained, and retold for years and years—others not so much. For years, seasons, and generations, certain stories appear, disappear, and mesh with other influences, experiences, and ideas in an ever-expanding, community-based, canon formation.

For Anishinaabeg, a large part of this ongoing and collective intellectual process is the dissemination of aadizookaanag, "traditional" or "sacred" stories. Many of these educational narratives and histories are shared through interpretation of pictograph texts, such as those found on birchbark scrolls or petroglyphs, and taught through the use of sand and earth. Some are told in biblical scripture. Others are conveyed through metaphors, allegories, and "texts" found throughout the world and the universe. And, though often referred to as parts of an "oral tradition," these stories engage and take up countless philosophies and processes of individual and collective writing— ranging from signifiers that are "fleeting" (as in gesture, dance, or song) to others more "permanent" (like beadwork or tattoos).[5] And, as in the creation of all texts, elements of history, authorship, and subjectivity are definitively present.

The task of interpreting, retelling, and theorizing aadizookaanag requires a cultural fluency that, according to some, takes a lifetime to learn. According to Anishinaabeg storyteller Basil Johnston, stories such as these have three meanings: a "surface meaning" (derived from the basic words), a "fundamental meaning" (derived from contextual analysis), and a "philosophical meaning" (derived from identifying the beliefs inherent to the worldview, or epistemology, being expressed) ("Is That All There Is?" 100). All three must be taken into account to understand a single aadizookaan fully, and none must be left out. Equally considerable are when aadizookaanag are connected to certain ceremonial protocols, "belong" to particular individuals or groups (such as communities/families/clans), and hold deep ties to concepts found in Anishinaabemowin.

A significant part of aadizookaanag are what are sometimes called "trickster stories." In some community versions, the story revolves around a figure named Naanabozhoo; in others it is Wenabozhoo, Nanabush, Manabozhoo, Nanabozoo, and so forth. Some just use "Trickster." For the most part, these stories involve some aspect of the creation of the earth, and relate to the ongoing spiritual, mental, emotional, and physical growth of Anishinaabeg. And, while much debate consists on how these stories relate precisely to reality and humanity, Anishinaabeg trickster narratives are distinctly related to some aspect of what is claimed as an Anishinaabeg "perspective" or "worldview." Take, for example, Johnston's claim that "the [Anishinaubeg] dreamed Nanabush into being. Nanabush represented themselves and what they understood of human nature" ("Is That All There Is?" 101), or Anishinaabe Midewiwin elder Edward Benton-Banai's description that "[t]hese things that Waynaboozhoo learned were later to become very useful to Indian people. He has been looked upon as kind of a hero by the Ojibway. These 'Waynaboozhoo Stories' have been told for many years to children to help them grow in a balanced way" ("The Great Flood" 92). Many of these stories are used to instruct and guide Anishinaabeg adults and elders, too.

Today, most Anishinaabeg storytellers tell trickster narratives in the interests of continuing Anishinaabeg culture and tradition. Some stories are delivered orally, some are published on paper, while others are still read or written on birchbark, sand, rocks, dirt. Some even make up parts of short stories and novels Anishinaabeg storytellers write. Trickster stories are sometimes only one part of a larger body of interrelated narratives these knowledge keepers hold and tell, but they often contain rich and complex elements such as multiplicity, humour, and eroticism—so they often call great attention to themselves.

It would be very difficult to come up with any exhaustive definition of Naanabozhoo, or any of his other Anishinaabeg incarnations. What can be said is that this figure teaches, demonstrates, and engages existence in the universe with a vibrant, active, and dynamic spirit. His presence usually ensures that something interesting, divergent, and/or potentially world-altering will occur. Referring back to *The Adventures of Nanabush*, for example, Nanabush not only recreates the earth after a great flood, but signifies the birch tree with markings, gives woodpeckers a red crest, initiates peace with Waub-Ameek (the Giant Beaver), and imparts medicine to the red willow for Ojibway peoples. Creation is a constant theme, and Nanabush's curiosity, intelligence, playfulness, as well as anger, foolhardiness, and desire lead to provocative moments of growth, complexity, and beauty. Perhaps put best by Vizenor, "Naanabozho ... is an ironic creator and, in the same instance, the contradiction of creation" (*Manifest Manners* 170). While this means that Anishinaabeg trickster narratives (even told by the same teller) may contradict each other, carry different details, and conclude differently, what's central is that Anishinaabeg knowledge, philosophies, and perspectives are available, inherent, and evident in them. Of course, some stories take up other interests as well.

How Anishinaabeg-specific intellectual tenets are derived is through such things as examining Johnston's "three meanings," Vizenor's "active listening," and the formulation of responsible, ethical, and Anishinaabeg-centred literary approaches. This starts in the recognition that most everything in Anishinaabeg trickster stories—the gender, shape, lineage, actions, and very name, for example—depend on the storyteller(s), the context(s), the time(s), and the who/what/where/when/why a story is being told, as well as both to and for. It also continues in the identification that many trickster narratives are "myths," but much in the way Jarold Ramsey defines them, as "stories whose shaping function is to tell the people who knew them who they are; how, through what origins and transformations, they have come to possess their particular world; and how they should live in that world, and with each other" (*Reading the Fire* 4). While admittedly I take issue with Ramsey's use of past tense and the term "possess," the point here is that trickster narratives are part of what define Anishinaabeg claims to spiritualities, laws, and aesthetics. For instance, I would posit that these stories formulate a part of living, ever-changing, and evident Anishinaabeg notions of justice, nationhood,[6] and even a Constitution.

As a part of aadizookaanag (and the larger canon of Anishinaabeg literature), trickster narratives are part of an ongoing legacy Anishinaabeg storytellers take up to honour, maintain, and critically strengthen relationships between themselves, their communities, and the universe. Although few agree precisely on details of Naanabozhoo's adventures—and creation, contradiction, and diversity seem to be the only sure-fire tenets—these stories are committed and embedded in explorations of Anishinaabeg philosophies, experiences, and existence. Sometimes direct references to Anishinaabeg communities, territories, and politics are evident, sometimes less so, but these aspects are always present. Sometimes history is easily recognizable, other times more metaphorical, but this is also a crucial part of these stories. Some tellers share stories that undermine Anishinaabeg peoples, communities, and sovereignties, too. Specific and contextual, these stories are a significant part of how Anishinaabeg intellectuals assert their presences, share their voices, and participate in the growth of Anishinaabeg knowledge as a result.

Even after tens of thousands of years of narrative interests, centuries of colonial invasion, and millennia of ongoing technological, contextual, and political change, Anishinaabeg storytellers are still intertwining themselves, their communities, and the cosmos. Many of these stories reflect and promote positive growth, some are more destructive, but all are in the voices of living, modern, Anishinaabeg, reflecting the experiences and knowledges of a collective worldview. Trickster stories, therefore, are one part of how Anishinaabeg claims to subjectivity, identity, and nationhood are actualized, disseminated, and ongoing. They are also a fulfillment of the responsibility Anishinaabeg hold as active contributors to the diversity of the universe. Although these stories have a home, the universe informs these stories as much as the universe is informed by them. Like the beating of a drum, the shake of a jingle dress, and the late-night reading of Nanabush stories to three children, this is how Anishinaabeg therefore contribute to the ongoing growth, health, and continuance of individual, community, and universal traditions.

• • •

When I was first approached to contribute to an academic anthology about what we might call "Tricksters," my initial feeling was one of unease.[7] Y'see, I've spent much of my scholastic life learning to hate institutional treatments of these kinds of stories, and, to be frank, the last thing I want to do is contribute mud to already murky water. But, having now read, experienced, and endured several literary approaches that perpetuate some very colonial and imperial practices on Indigenous knowledge systems, not to mention the fact that my daughter is almost school-aged, I feel I need to say something. Hopefully, by adding my voice and experience, I can show how harmful these theories can be, participate in the ongoing growth of our field, and suggest some critical tenets to avoid repeating these dangerous discourses.

Before I do this, however, let me share what I feel are the two most fundamental questions I ask myself whenever I am reading a text that theorizes Native literature(s):[8] Is this research responsibly and ethically engaging with, and in some way contributing to, the Indigenous knowledge system it is drawing from? And, who is benefiting from this research?[9] In my next immediate and accompanying thoughts: Who is the intended audience of this text? Is there an identifiable individual, community, or group? Are there Indigenous faces in any of these? Who/Where/When are these faces? Are they living? Are they healthy? Are they real? Are they being listened to? Are they referenced? Are they speaking? What are they saying?

My reasons for such interests are relatively simple. I assert that if theorists keep their work grounded in specific social, political, cultural, and material struggles of Native life by sincerely engaging, listening to, and dialoguing with voices from Indigenous intellectual traditions, critical methodologies invested in Indigenous continuance are emerging. Now I may not agree with the critic's method, politics, or pedagogy, but if real-life Native peoples and communities, in all of their complexities, are considered as active participants in a theory regarding their literatures, the writer is contributing to a historical process and practice of Indigenous intellectualism. Only a culturally ignorant and myopic criticism—that denies Indigenous voices a central place in discussions of Indigenous lives, cultures, and realities—could do otherwise.

In this vein, I want to encourage many of my colleagues in the academic world to reflect upon the ways Indigenous creative and critical outputs are theorized. Also, I wish to propose that all of us (re-)consider the critic's responsibility to the people and communities in which Indigenous literatures come from. So, let me offer what I believe should be(come) an unwavering tenet of our field: ***Indigenous literatures have specific spatial and historical relations, based in individual and collective Indigenous subjectivities, and these*** *should not be separated in any criticism that purports to interpret, explore, and/or describe them.* Although these relationships can be spiritual, interpersonal, intrapersonal, and/or material, they are always political. And while, arguably, some are more successful than others, Indigenous literatures demonstrate attempts by creative and critical Indigenous peoples to actualize webs of connections between themselves, their communities, and creation. Whether it be written or spoken, in novels or ceremonies, with tricksters or not, literary expressions show evidence of a commitment to speak about individual and communal Indigenous perspectives, knowledges, and philosophies of the past, present, and future—most times in the interests of growth, presence, and continuance. And, as with political subjectivities, there are crucial reference points, specifically based in history, place, and context.

I assert that this tenet has been ignored in many past and present scholarly treatments of Native literatures, and some myopic approaches are dominating and undermining our field.[10] This vein of thought is evidenced by the lack of many scholars to engage ethically, be responsible to, and ultimately support Indigenous knowledge systems while using, dissecting, and theorizing Native trickster stories for personal interest and benefit.[11] Even more specifically, critics have used "findings" in trickster stories to support several one-sided and problematic claims about Indigenous psychologies, epistemologies, and intellectual processes. Most often, these assertions take the form of broad, generalized, ahistorical, and atemporal theories that have little relationship to the storyteller(s) who tell them, requiring a complete denial of and divorce from the Indigenous political processes in which they are embedded. Older theories have posited that trickster stories are evidence of archaic, superstitious, and inferior thought patterns—arguments for Native difference and deficiency. Later strands terminate literary difference in the (ultimately assimilative) interests of "equality." More recent approaches— often wielded in studies of works by Louis Owens, Gerald Vizenor, and Thomas King—use a righteous liberal rhetoric to argue a totalizing postmodern cultural relativism and to claim that tricksters are the ultimate globalized trope: a figure that knows no home, has no responsibilities, and transgresses all boundaries. Many of these theories have also historically accompanied colonial policies and practices interested in Indigenous erasure, removal, and genocide—and should be grounded in these specific times, places, and subjectivities.

The central (and perhaps most blatant) example of this sort of criticism is the well-known and extremely influential anthropological and psychoanalytical study on tricksters and trickster stories in North America, Paul Radin's *The Trickster: A Study in American Indian Mythology*, first published in 1956.

While American and European theories regarding trickster characters and stories date back centuries—most notably by Daniel Brinton, Henry School-craft, and Franz Boas—most posited that tricksters "proved" Native American cultural difference and permanently deficient behaviour. Radin's text, how-ever, signals an important turn in criticisms of Native literatures. It is the first sustained book-length attempt by a Western scholar to theorize Native Amer-ican trickster stories in mainstream critical and popular terms. Its legitimacy is signified by the participation of three of the world's leading academics in their fields at the time: the renowned anthropologist, Radin; Greek-myth scholar Karl Kerényi; and respected psychologist Carl G. Jung.[12] It is also arguably the first attempt by a scholar to use evidence of tricksters to argue for a widespread humanistic relevance in Native storytelling traditions. This moment is important to reflect upon, particularly in order to understand its implications today.

Although descriptions of this text lie elsewhere, I will provide a basic overview here. In essence, Radin's text is one of the first attempts in the "modern" period to interpret, categorize, and codify Indigenous trickster stories, recorded orally from Native informants, and structure their form and content into a social scientific discourse for the purposes of trying to understand American Indian "thought." To a small measure, it is an activist text, interested in presenting aspects of Native American cultures, histories, and "authentic" versions of their myths to a broader, academic, mainstream audience and suggest their inclusion in a larger, evolutionary chain of human development. It also, in an even smaller way, seeks to locate and discuss Amer-ican Indian myths in some cultural contexts. Much more directly, though, Radin (with Kerényi and Jung) seeks to reduce Indian cultures and stories into a singular, monolithic version and explain them in such a way as to serve Amer-European needs and perspectives.

Working solely with versions recorded, translated, and recounted from Native informants by himself and other anthropologists, Radin's thesis is sim-ple: that Native American trickster stories show evidence, preserved in "its ear-liest and most archaic form," of one of the most widespread, global "expressions of mankind," a character that is

> at one and the same time creator and destroyer, giver and negator, he who dupes others and who is always duped himself. He wills nothing consciously. At all times he is constrained to behave as he does from impulses over which he has no control. He knows neither good nor evil yet he is responsible for both. He possesses no values, moral or social, is at the mercy of his passions and appetites, yet through his actions all values come into being. (xxiii)

Recounting a forty-nine-part story cycle of the Trickster in Winnebago (Ho-Chunk) tradition (Part I) and comparatively adding "Supplementary Trickster Myths" from other tribes (Part II), Radin concludes:

> The overwhelming majority of all so-called trickster myths in North America give an account of the creation of the earth, or at least the transforming of the world, and have a hero who is always wandering, who is always hungry, who is not guided by normal conceptions of good or evil, who is either playing tricks on people or having them played on him and who is highly sexed. Almost everywhere he has some divine traits. (155)

If one ignores the "secondary addition(s), elaborations and reinterpretations," Radin argues that one can see a "true trickster cycle" existent amongst Native American tribes, and one that shows evidence of "a remodeling of an older form" of human struggle (165–8). Specifically, according to Radin, the Native American trickster figure therefore resembles a character that straddles the liminal boundary between humanity's spiritual and physical realms—evidenced by his physical and spiritual deformities and exaggerations—and is, "primarily, an inchoate being of undetermined proportions, a figure foreshadowing the shape of man" (xxiv). As a culture-hero who teaches, demonstrates, challenges, satirizes, and gives form to man's rightful place in the world, he literally creates a new universe as he destroys the old, for his sole purpose is to instruct and signify man's development. In Radin's opinion, "[w]hat happens to him happens to us" (169).

As Radin posits, and as Kerényi and Jung support in their commentaries, American Indian trickster stories represent a stage of rudimentary human thought. As Jung so casually puts it, "[c]onsidering the crude primitivity of the trickster cycle, it would not be surprising if one saw in this myth simply the reflection of an earlier, rudimentary stage of consciousness, which is what the trickster obviously seems to be" (201). Found in other ancient story-telling traditions and "archaic" societies in ancient Greece, China, Japan, and the Semitic World, trickster tales all share an interest in articulating ambiguous distinctions between human and divine realities, with the final goal being in the development of "civilized" codes of morality, values, and ideology (xxiii). For instance, the "childishness" and "stupidity" of the Trickster force primitive man to abandon his "original state," thereby leading to a higher stage of mental and social development where such "therapeutic" narratives can (and must) be abandoned (202–3, 205–7). Thus, according to Radin, we see in American Indian trickster stories the evocation of "new" spiritual and physical senses of selves and the evolutionary demonstration of an ongoing process towards civilization that all human societies have followed (168–9).

To be fair, the time period and discourse in which this book exists sheds light on its shaping, published as it was in a wave of American liberal reformation movements on the heels of World War II. The 1940s and 1950s were a time of change for Indians in U.S. discourse and political policy. Up to this point, Native Americans had been long constructed in the public imagination as a dying, savagely inferior, and culturally pitiful group in need of help— a point Roy Harvey Pearce argues in his widely popular (and problematic) book of 1953, *Savagism and Civilization: A Study of the Indian and the American Mind*.[13] With the end of World War II and the civil rights movement, widespread public calls for inclusion and "justice" for Natives in America gained traction.

Responding to civil rights activists (championing their own anti-racist, inclusionary, and de-segregationist agenda) and some Native leaders, the U.S. federal government in 1946 instituted the Indian Claims Commission, giving it a mandate of *compensating* and *terminating* the special relationship Indians had with the federal government. This policy, often referred to as "Termination," sought to "as rapidly as possible … make the Indians within the territorial limits of the United States subject to the same laws and entitled to the same privileges and responsibilities as are applicable to other citizens of the United States, [and] to end their status as wards of the United States" (as quoted in Canby 25).[14] "In reality," Chippewa historian Duane Champagne remarks, Termination was a U.S. move to renege on treaty obligations and "resurrect" late nineteenth-century assimilationist tactics (319). Adopted as "official congressional policy on August 1, 1953," Termination facilitated several federal and state practices and programs that sought to exterminate tribal sovereignty and force Natives into American society, including "legal" taxation, seizure of tribal lands, and relocation into cities (Canby 25–8, Rawls 39–50).

By this time in history, Native American communities were accustomed to resisting colonial assaults, displacement, and invasions in a multitude of ways. They had learned throughout the nineteenth and early twentieth centuries—during countless treaty negotiations, the Dawes (General Allotment) Act, and boarding school policies—that Native claims to land, livelihood, and sovereignty were not in the primary interests of America. And, although some Natives continued to advocate for their communities on the U.S. national stage, more turned their attention to localized struggles and interests, such as fighting oppressive laws, resisting arbitrary Indian Agent decisions, and continuing to practise traditions and ceremonies. After John Collier's

Indian Reorganization Act (IRA) of 1934, some tribes began to practise "limited" forms of self-government, which included drafting constitutions, reclaiming land and resources taken during Allotment, and establishing tribal business corporations (Deloria and Lytle 171–82). These actions were of some help in ongoing Native struggles. Other groups vehemently refused the provisions of the IRA, and more intrusions by the Bureau of Indian Affairs. Likely due to a long history of draconian treatment by federal and state governments, overwhelming social and economical needs as a result of colonization, and the demands of everyday life, most Native peoples still focused much of their attention locally in the interest of maintaining their community's sovereignty and continuance. World War II radically altered the landscape in both Native and non-Native worlds. During the conflict, thousands of Native peoples left their communities to fight or work in factories, funding of on-reserve schools and programs was drastically cut, and tribal lands were "leased" to non-Native interests for the war effort. Many Native men and women never returned to reservation life, while others brought their national and international experiences home—and in turn introduced new ideas and interests to their communities. Some kin resisted these "foreign" influences, frequently resulting in conflicts of ideology and competing community interests (often described over-simplistically along such lines as "traditionals" versus "progressives" or "full-bloods" versus "mixed-bloods").

Meanwhile, civil rights discourses dominated the U.S. mainstream and deeply influenced Indian policy, as the "American" was emphasized in "Native American." In *The Nations Within: The Past and Future of American Indian Sovereignty*, Vine Deloria, Jr., and Clifford Lytle write:

> We can mark out the two decades from 1945 to 1965 as the barren years. Self-government virtually disappeared as a policy and as a topic of interest. Indian Affairs became a minor element in the American domestic scene; Indians became subject to new forms of social engineering, which conceived of them as a domestic racial minority, not as distinct political entities with a long history of specific legal claims against the United States. (190)

As Deloria and Lytle identify, long-standing treaty obligations were cut in the name of "encouraging" Native American independence when, for legislators, "[a]ll that mattered was that Indians be made to conform to the norm of American society" (191). "Termination" was intended to be the last move for Native assimilation into America.

As before, many Natives continued to resist erasure. In 1944, a group made up mostly of returning World War II Native veterans interested in advocating for "sovereignty and self-determination" founded the National Congress of American Indians (NCAI). Although it would take years to have much force politically, decades later the NCAI was pivotal in Red Power. Other acts of resistance included struggles over land and resources, legal challenges against federal dam and mineral projects, and, of course, localized practices that had gone on for centuries—including the engagement, maintenance, and continuation of culturally, historically, and socially autonomous lives through community, ceremony, and story. Although all of these tactics were effective to a degree, discourses and power structures of American imperialism, expansionism, and popular sentiments towards "equality"—all leading to similar attacks on sovereignty—undermined many efforts.

Readers, by this point, may wonder why I am referencing political history in an essay on literary criticism. My point is that each cannot be separated from the other. Radin's book was released in 1956, only three years after Pearce's *Savagism and Civilization*. Both books champion arguments for ornamental Native inclusion in America—after, of course, they become "civilized." Not coincidentally, 1956 was also the year Termination became official policy. It would be impossible not to see that these books, and several others of the time, are firmly embedded in certain discourses of cultural "progressivism" with assimilationist ends. In other words, both U.S. Indian policy and academia were deeply invested in "civilizing" Natives into the mainstream.

Radin's *The Trickster*, on one hand, does have some important and timely arguments. Calling for a humanistic relevance in Native cultures and the inclusion of Natives in U.S. society was somewhat radical, particularly considering the xenophobia rampant at the time. Positing that Indians practice "rudimentary" cultures but have an evolutionizing *human* mind could also be somewhat productive, particularly in civil rights debates where mainstream acceptance is the goal. *The Trickster*, with its high-profile scholarship, could even be seen as one important step in the institutional legitimatization of Native studies and literatures. However, the text can also dangerously be used to assert a pernicious discourse that Indians are, and seemingly will forever be, less civilized than anyone else (especially if they continue to maintain such "archaic" traditions as trickster stories). It could be paternalistically construed that Natives must be "encouraged" to cease telling trickster stories so that they don't remain in their uncivilized difference.

There is also, however, something important to identify in *The Trickster*. Radin's text does have evidence of Native peoples resisting colonialism and practicing their cultures, politics, and intellectual traditions. How? Through trickster stories. Most highlighted is one Ho-Chunk individual (and likely community's) history and experience "obtained" from "Sam Blowsnake ... an old Winnebago Indian living near the village of Winnebago, Nebraska," in a "cycle" of Wakdjunkaga stories "in 1912" (3–49, 111). As mentioned, these years were highlighted by some devastating assaults on Native sovereignty, including reservation policies, the Dawes Act, and increasingly intensified boarding school policies that forced Native children through a brutal assimilative process. When considered in this context, some stories take on possible new meanings, including when Wakdjunkaga murders two children "borrow[ed]" from a younger brother (8–11), swims in the ocean and "aimlessly" searches for land while no one answers questions about where it is (11–12), and experiences an erection while lying on a "lovely piece of land" (18–19). Or, more specifically, how would the stories of Wakdjunkaga "wandering," his forging of a community with other displaced creatures "because the world is soon going to be a difficult place to dwell," their discovery of a home "with red oaks growing upon it," the Trickster turning "pieces of his penis" into "potatoes," "turnips," 'artichokes," "ground beans," and "rice" for human beings to eat, and his settlement "where the Missouri enters the Mississippi" (22, 39, 53) be considered in the context of the politics, perspectives, and history of Blowsnake's community (the Winnebago Tribe of Nebraska) and their stories of migrations, wars with other tribes, and removal from Kentucky to Nebraska ("History")?

These enlightening specifics, among many others, are virtually absent in Radin's analysis. Instead, we get a thoroughly selective analysis that privileges structuralist parts of trickster stories (orality, characterization, and humanism) over specific local, political, and historical contexts of the literatures. While this is certainly evidence of the intellectual trend of the time, it is also blatantly obvious that these editorial choices register colonial interests in their discursive and political implications. Although the stories come from intellectual histories, Radin streamlines these literatures into widely understood categorical themes and patterns—reflecting his interest in how they can prove all-encompassing relativistic theories. And, even though the stories do document some parts of his informants' epistemologies, experiences, and politics, Radin engages in the process of Native intellectual dispossession by denying aspects of their specific locations, histories, and subjectivities. Viewed in this way, cultural expressions are authorless artifacts and objects, temporal only in the role they play in human "development," and political only in terms of how they demonstrate a myopic pattern of "civilization." Much like politicians and policy-makers of the time, Radin is ready to place Native peoples into a global (and arguably American-centric) hegemonic narrative, removing their perspectives, knowledges, and claims to their critical and creative territories. Perhaps put best by critic Franchot Ballinger, Radin's book is ultimately "too governed by Euro-American categorization, too reliant on western dualistic perception," and overly occupied with non-Native interests (20–1).

The Trickster, however, while still influential in critical and mainstream circles,[15] is only one part of a larger ideological trajectory. Even though it would be impossible to contextualize all of the following movements completely, most seem to reflect several similar and disturbing trends that echo Radin. Most disconcerting is how selectively distanced and comfortable many of these movements are from historical and real-life Native intellectual struggles. In the late 1960s, for instance, Claude Lévi-Strauss argues in *Structural Anthropology* that trickster characters act as a "mediator" in human cultures between two polar opposite positions, providing evidence that human "mythical thought always progresses from the awareness of oppositions toward their resolution" (221). And Victor Turner follows Lévi-Strauss in saying that trickster characters reflect a universal human interest in, and move towards, liminality (576), proving to other scholars such as Mary Douglas that cultural stories such as these are "fictive, man-made, arbitrary creations" (200).

Comparable trends can be found in ethnographic studies of the 1970s and 1980s, arguably the first forays by modern-day literary critics into Native literatures. Studying this early scholarship on Native literatures (what he terms "mode-one discourse"), Cherokee scholar Chris Teuton remarks that these critics are interested in "criticism as an act of cultural translation ... focusing specifically on questions of definition: 'what is Indian literature' and 'who is an Indian author,'" as well as devising "correct" ways in which to collect orally recorded stories (200–1). Two such examples are *Traditional Literatures of the American Indian: Texts and Interpretations*, edited by Karl Kroeber and published in 1981, and the 1987 anthology *Recovering the Word: Essays on Native American Literature*, edited by Brian Swann and Arnold Krupat.

Traditional Literatures of the American Indian is a collection of ten translations of "Traditional American Indian Orations," with accompanying critical commentary by Kroeber, Ramsey, Dennis Tedlock, Barre Toelken, Tacheeni Scott, and Dell Hymes. Steeped in formalist and structuralist traditions, these critics attempt to represent the texture, text, and context of Native oral literary aesthetics and uncover "authentic" ways in which to translate, record, and reflect "traditional" stories and their accompanying cultural consciousnesses. Most use trickster stories to do this. Constantly lamenting an inability to reflect accurately Native voices, Kroeber claims that all contributors seek "not ways of attaining a single definitive reading of a story or a set of stories, but, instead, ways of entering into the rich complexity of meanings provided by traditional American Indian literary art" (8). Interestingly, this is attained because Native stories "appeal to enough common features in human nature to allow us at least entrance to their pleasures" (9).

Recovering the Word: Essays on Native American Literature, edited by well-known American critics Brian Swann and Arnold Krupat, contains many ethnographic studies of trickster stories as well. Mostly found in the second section of the book, "Interpreting the Material: Oral and Written," interpretive models are placed onto tribal orations, stories are recounted, translated, and categorized, and generalizations are suggested regarding each story's cultural epistemologies, techniques, and literary worthiness. For example, William Bright attempts to formulate an all-encompassing definition of Native tricksters, echoing the conclusion that the character is intended to act as a human mediator (379). Barre Toelken constructs four "levels of meaning" for Navajo Coyote stories (entertainment, moral, medicine, witchcraft), and argues that they reflect particular parts of tribal psyche (disorder, integration, humour, destruction), while then promptly informing scholars that the first two categories (entertainment and moral) are available for critical scrutiny while the third and fourth levels (medicine and witchcraft) would likely result in further degradation to Navajo culture (396–400). Howard Norman studies Swampy Cree Wesucechak stories and determines that the character "teaches by negative example"—an odd claim considering that he later shares stories where "Wesucechak gave the Cree language, and became the thief of it" (402, 404).

What is most interesting is how, for the most part, this criticism is distanced from the interests and activities of the very communities in which these trickster stories were taken. By the mid-1960s, long-standing colonial policies and practices, assimilative trends, and failures to recognize and support Native rights, sovereignty, and economic development had hampered and undermined many parts of Native life. Strikingly, situations were comparable in Canada and the United States.[16] In fact, in 1969, Canada was drafting its own Termination-like policy with Prime Minister Pierre Trudeau's "Statement of the Government of Canada on Indian Policy," the aptly named "White Paper." By the early 1970s, a large-scale resistance movement, primarily begun by Native peoples in urban areas, exploded.

For the most part, this resistance was characterized by a demand for Native recognition, rights, and sovereignty, and was heralded by Native intellectuals. Two books in particular stand out. The first, Cree activist Harold Cardinal's *The Unjust Society: The Tragedy of Canada's Indians* declared that a "Buckskin Curtain," made out of "indifference, ignorance, and, all too often, plain bigotry," separated and ghettoized Natives from their communities and mainstream society, evident in repeated "betrayals of our trust ... a dictatorial bureaucracy [that] has eroded our rights, atrophied our culture and robbed us of simple human dignity" (2). In *Custer Died for Your Sins: An Indian Manifesto,* Vine Deloria, Jr., described how this wall was systematically and historically established, enforced, and reified by U.S. federal governments, agencies, universities, churches, private companies, mainstream citizens, and many Indians themselves. These forces ensured that Native lives remained under the legal and social control, construction, and whim of imperialist institutions, stereotypical claims about Native peoples, and status quo hegemony. This all created an atmosphere, Deloria writes, in which "[t]o be an Indian in modern American society is in a very real sense to be unreal and ahistorical" (2). Cardinal and Deloria could have been describing some scholars and critics studying trickster stories, too.

Fed up with regular attempts to assimilate Indian cultures and communities, "Red Power" dominated Native discourses throughout the 1970s. "Red Power was," according to Alvin M. Josephy, Jr., "a determined and patriotic Indian fight for freedom—freedom from injustice and bondage, freedom from patronization and oppression, freedom from what the white man cannot and will not solve" (2). At the same time, an Indigenous cultural revitalization and resurgent interest in traditional teachings, ceremonies, and traditions occurred. For many Native peoples long displaced and/or isolated from their communities, sacred lands, and cultural spaces, an opportunity was seized to return "home," rejoin tribal nations, and participate in relearning traditional teachings, histories, and stories. Some built cultural lives in urban centres, whereas others connected on reservations and sacred spaces—(re-)claiming older spaces and (re-)establishing new ceremonial institutions such as the Potlatch, the Sun Dance, or the Midéwiwin Lodge. This process is captured in Acoma Pueblo writer Simon Ortiz's 1977 book, *The People Shall Continue.*[17]

As part and parcel of this, Native artistry experienced surging growth and popularity, particularly stories, poetry, and novels written in English. Although Indigenous intellectuals had been disseminating narratives in the "oral tradition," pictography, codices, wampum, drums, rock, earth, and sand for centuries, a "Native American Renaissance" was declared. The commercial and critical success of Native authors such as N. Scott Momaday and Maria Campbell led countless storytellers to publish children's books, novels, books of poetry, and other forms of art. A striking amount of these include, or are about, tricksters—so much so that by 1996, critics Barbara Babcock and Jay Cox called the "Trickster" the "most popular, problematic, and powerful figure in Native American literature" (99).

Oddly, and even though trickster stories must have been influenced by such crucially important and landmark history and politics, these parts are absent in these criticisms. While many of these anthropologists and ethnographers did important work in legitimating Native artistry, introducing tropes to the mainstream and highlighting certain cultural parts of these stories, their findings (and thus their conclusions) are ultimately half-finished. Specific community and individual histories, politics, and subjectivities are as important aesthetics, perhaps at times even more so, than oral, humanistic, and structural ones. For the most part, these approaches study Native literatures according to dominant discourses, standards, and values, and are interested in showing how characters such as the Trickster validate certain political interests, theories, and tastes that facilitate and validate non-Native entryways.

Some of these criticisms also suggest disturbing conclusions on the role of trickster stories in Indigenous intellectual systems. Referring back to Toelken and Norman, these conclusions can lead to some tragic and romantic stereotypes when absent of political and historical contexts. The same could be said of ethnographic lamenters of the "oral tradition." As Muskogee Creek critic Craig Womack remarks of these approaches, "on the stories most popular with ethnographers, the ones that usually get cast in the aforementioned structural categories (creation, hero, trickster, and monster slayers, and so on)" is a sentiment invested in an inherent "diminishment argument," determined to show Native literatures as impossible to "fix" into written text, translations, and interpretations. This uncovers the insipid nature of such a critical approach, asserting that "[r]ather than assuming that outside approaches have been the problem, we assume that the literature itself is the problem" (*Red on Red* 63–4).

Which brings us to the long-standing argument, from Radin into today: that tricksters are expressive "mediators" for Native cultures. As Indigenous intellectualism, activism, and struggles for land, recognition, and rights have continued over the past twenty-five years, post-structuralism and post-colonialism have become arguably the most popular lenses of literary criticism. Interested in fragmentation, multiplicity, cultural relativism, and the deconstruction of power relations, post-structural and post-colonial theorists have been keenly interested in trickster stories for the way in which they prove a "postmodern condition" in Native literatures. In much of this work, theories lauding mediating, liminal, and "mixedblood" interests in Native trickster stories (and, by default, Native cultures) are claimed.[18] As Babcock and Cox, two such proponents, claim, the Trickster "knows no bounds, lives in a world before/beyond classification, and is always in motion," as he is "[t]imeless, universal, and indestructible … Mythical and primordial, [a] champion of possibility and enemy of spatial, temporal, and cultural boundaries" (99).

An adoration of Native American tricksters, and particular manifestations in the works of Louis Owens, Gerald Vizenor, and Thomas King, have been taken up by many post-structuralists. Employing such theorists as Jacques Derrida, Louis Althusser, Michel Foucault, and Judith Butler, critics have claimed that tricksters predominantly engage and up-end all discourses of ideology, power, and "claims of truth" (what Vizenor often calls "terminal creeds"). Although it would be imprecise to paint all with the same brush, most critics posit that what Native American trickster stories show is that there is nothing outside of discourse, everything is mediated by conflicts and power dynamics, and "good" criticism points this out. For instance, there are no "essences," only delusional claims to subject positions—including "Indian," "European," "male," "female," or even "good" and "evil"—primarily as they suggest something "pure." "Trickster discourse," a theory often attributed to Vizenor, shows that nothing is "truth"; everything is recreated and mediated in language by practices of heteroglossia, dialogism, and "play"—including language, politics, and identity.[19] Human identities, in particular, are constantly being remade as hybrid, borderless, and fluid, while "Native identities"—if there are such things—are mediated in precisely the same way. When employing Owens, critics often employ his use of "frontier," or contact zone between cultures, to explain this space where re-creation occurs. In King, it's usually his use of Coyote, humour, and mixed-race characters. That these theorists often refer to "oral traditions" as a basis for their work also "prove" a "slippery" and "transient" mobility and interest. The perfect trickster trope in the work of Owens, Vizenor, and King, therefore, is the "mixed-blood," an idea that critic David Murray claims has been paralleled to "the traditional figure of the shape-shifting trickster who can change identities" and "has been quite widely adopted and circulated as corresponding to postmodern ideas of constantly reinvented identity, and a lack of fixed values or identity" (79).

Much of this vein of "trickster criticism" shows evidence of what Terry Eagleton describes as a trend in post-structuralism to "scatter" all meaning "along the whole chain of signifiers" and obsess over language's instability and infinite play through "a process of division or articulation, of signs being themselves only because they are not some other sign" (therefore a sign "must always be repeatable or reproducible ... part of its identity") (110–2). This vein of thought, as Eagleton points out, has very real consequences:

> nothing is ever fully present in signs: it is an illusion for me to believe that I can ever fully be present to you in what I say or write, because to use signs at all entails means that my meaning is always somehow dispersed, divided and

never quite at one with itself. Not only my meaning, indeed, but me: since language is something I am made of, rather than merely a convenient tool I use, the whole idea that I am a stable, unified entity must also be a fiction. Not only can I never be fully present to you, but I can never be fully present to myself either. (112)

This also means that subjective claims to "truth," "reality," and "history" are impossible, and literary criticism following this path has tended to focus on the absence of unified meaning as conclusions of ambivalence, ambiguity, and undecidability in all literatures (125–6).

Some, by this point, may be wondering why Vizenor, Owens, and King—all of whom reference Native (and tribally specific) history, take up Native (and tribally specific) struggles, and engage Native (and tribally specific) discourses throughout their trickster stories—are viewed predominantly as working in "liminal" spaces and solely interested in undermining Native claims to identity. Or, some may point out that Indigenous identities have never been "pure" as, even long before European contact, intellectual and intertribal intermixing, trade, and mediation have always taken place. Or, some may wonder why there is an overwhelming emphasis on Native identities that "defer meaning," particularly when tribal nations and communities seek control over membership (a crucial part of self-government practice). Or, some even may identify that—on the heels of five hundred years of Indigenous claims of land, nationhood, and knowledge on this continent—it's remarkably convenient for theories to come along that pin Native intellectual production to European arrival, pronounce that Native identities are embedded in "mixed-blooded-ness" (which is ironically an "essence," indicating highly problematic blood quantum premises), and revisit such long-standing stereotypes of Natives "caught" between two cultures.

Other critics of post-structural and post-colonial theorists, such as bell hooks, question the political motivations of post-structuralist critics who celebrate cultural pluralism but fail to recognize the historical and political legacies embedded in American society. A blanket one-case-fits-all critique of essentialism, the negation of cultural claims and identities, and discourses that claim subjectivity is infinitely refractable and groundless does not help the colonized "find new strategies of resistance" (2480–3). Or, as Ella Shohat notes in her 1992 essay "Notes on the 'Post-Colonial,'" many theories of "post-colonialism," while potentially helpful, are often divorced from political and social realities for oppressed peoples and ignore historical and social resistance movements pursued by colonized peoples (100–6). There are also real dangers, she warns, in suggesting that theories of "hybridity" and "syncretism," originating in critiques of European cultural and political hegemony, are easily applicable to other cultures (108–12). Building on this critical trajectory, Cherokee critic Jace Weaver suggests in his essay "From I-Hermeneutics to We-Hermeneutics: Native Americans and the Post-Colonial," that until post-colonial theorists take seriously the political interests and advocacy in Native religious and cultural expressions, notions of land, and community formations, "the post-colonial moment for Native Americans will not yet have arrived" (11–15, 20–2). Weaver also warns that some uses of post-structuralist theories ensure that "[h]ybridity, postmodernism, and postcoloniality are the twenty-first-century 'smelting pot' in which diverse metals become alloyed into one" (*American Indian Literary Nationalism* 28).

One wonders, in the case of certain strands of post-structuralism, if the costs are too high for such a totalizing investment in cultural relativism. Can the Indigenous be taken out of Indigenous literatures? Can community contexts, specificities, and knowledges be removed from tribal, or pan-tribal, literatures? Can we remove politics, histories, and even parts of *reality*, from Indigenous literatures, expressions, aesthetics? What end goals does this serve? Who benefits? Who is at the centre of Indigenous identities? Will Indigenous communities be supported and maintained in this regard? Will these theories relate to today's Indigenous peoples' efforts to provide a future land, cultural, and intellectual base for their children? What are the implications of a criticism that avoids, rather than engages, some of the central issues that Indigenous peoples are struggling for, telling stories about, and speaking about? Will this help build our field of Indigenous literatures and the specific intellectual systems in which many stories emerge? And finally, what happened to diversity in pluralism?

In the interests of "multiplicitous" truths, theories interested in deconstructing power relations, colonial discourses, and subjectivities do have critical importance. Arguably the field of Native literary studies would not be where it is today without a lot of hegemonic languages, ideologies, and "truths" being interrogated, split, and opened up. Strong scholars of Indigenous literatures who use post-structuralist theories—such as Vizenor, King, Owens, Weaver, Blaeser, Chadwick Allen, Cheryl Suzack, James Cox, Alan Velie, A. LaVonne Brown Ruoff, Margery Fee, Annharte, Terry Goldie, and Qwo-Li Driskill—remind us that Indigenous storytellers can be interested in building and supporting Native claims of nationhood, identities, and aesthetics while at the same time tackling important issues surrounding meaning, cultural interplay, and colonization. At the same time, these scholars don't remove subjectivities, contexts, or histories from their work. Mindful of these issues, these critics show evidence of J. Edward Chamberlin's call for post-structural and post-colonial theories to be devised collaboratively with Indigenous peoples and their struggles so that they are "ultimately less about finding ways of saying no and more about finding ways of saying yes" ("From Hand to Mouth" 141).

I don't argue that trickster stories have some dynamic aesthetics, oral or otherwise. I don't argue that trickster stories aren't hard to pin down, hard to translate, hard to record, and told to subvert and mediate conflict in human existence (some are about sex, after all). I don't contend that trickster stories aren't intended to destabilize imposed and static claims, binary thinking, and ossified beliefs about (and certainly by) Native peoples and their cultures. I also don't argue that trickster stories aren't meant to teach us all about being human—the ugly parts, the pretty parts, and all of the parts in between. What I don't believe, not for a second, is some of the primary beliefs underlying this legacy of "trickster criticism": that trickster stories reflect Indigenous "archaic" and disappearing thinking patterns, teach Native peoples that cultural expressions are "fictions" and sole expressions of "liminality," and don't privilege deeply held concerns and interests in defining and locating specific subjectivities, politics, and histories. What seems to be divorced from the directions of most of these theories of trickster stories, and particularly the rush to place them in larger narratives, is a—yes, I'll say it—"truth": Native storytellers of the Americas are not interested in giving up their own, nor their nations,' creative and critical sovereignties. In fact, many seem to privilege their specific Indigenous identities, cultures, and communities. Even if stories are told about acquiescing to colonialism, giving up local identities, and "cultural death," they most often teach about the importance, responsibility, and relevance of family, community, nation-hood—not that they must be cast away. Why would Native elders, parents, and knowledge keepers continue to be so adamant, historically and today, in telling these stories as a part of resisting assimilation, participating in community knowledge, and teaching their children to be one of the People? Shouldn't a responsible and ethical criticism include the fact that Natives are *both* humans and members of living Native nations, especially in the colonial context of five hundred years of denying one or the other?

I say there's room in trickster stories for human and Indigenous knowledge(s), and that's what these stories *really* teach us. In fact, that is what I believe every Indigenous story I have ever read or heard, spoke or wrote, laughed or cried at, has shown me. To claim an Indigenous subjectivity, to learn within an Indigenous community, and be a citizen of an Indigenous nation, is to be uniquely, and beautifully, human, too: full of politics, full of spirit, full of strength—and all the complexities therein. And, hopefully with allies, Indigenous peoples will continue to struggle with, for, and because of our Indigenous cultures, communities, and knowledges.

Getting back to literary criticisms of Indigenous literatures, even though texts are produced, recorded, and collaborated on by Indigenous writers, speakers, and informants, and often sold on a global market, these stories are not without homes. As with all homes and families, the cornerstones of community, there are responsibilities in maintaining and respecting those relationships. To engage in the process of interpreting these stories, therefore, a critic cannot ignore, divorce, or deny these relations, particularly when Indigenous communities, histories, and knowledge systems are deeply invested in their value. If Thomas King is right, and "the truth about stories is that's all we are," as Justice points out, "then the work of the literary scholar has profound ethical implications. Our vocation is the telling, preservation, interpretation, and creation of stories. Stories are what we *do*, as much as what we *are*" (*Our Fire Survives the Storm* 206, original emphasis).

This is why, I assert, scholars theorizing Indigenous literatures must continue to formulate responsible critical tenets for our field, and reflect on ethics. Of course, this is a process that began well before me, but it is my intention to encourage more of it here by suggesting some possible trajectories scholars might want to keep in mind in their works while studying Native stories. While these are crucial in studies of trickster stories, these can also be used as lenses for other Indigenous literatures as well. Importantly, these are meant as starting points, not end points, and I profess to be no expert— only an interested party amongst many. As evident by the multiple voices that follow, this trail has already started. I hope many of us walk it together.

Responsible and ethical criticisms of Indigenous literatures recognize the full humanity of Indigenous peoples. As Justice identifies in the epigraph to this paper, criticism has for too long been invested in dehumanizing Indigenous peoples while furthering a project of colonialism in the Americas. To invest in a criticism that explores the full humanity (which includes tribal-specificity) of Indigenous peoples is to invest in a truly revolutionary act. Most of all, engaging this wide-ranging complexity is part of upending colonial discourses and meaningfully participating in the interests of Indigenous knowledge systems. Speaking of the politics of Indigenous erotica, arguably one of the greatest literary threats to colonialist hegemony and Indigenous erasures, Kateri Akiwenzie-Damm remarks that after five hundred years of mainstream misrepresentation, bastardization, and ignorance, "We need to see images of ourselves as healthy, whole people. People who love each other and who love ourselves. People who fall in love and out of love, who have lovers, who make love, who have sex. We need to create a healthy legacy for our peoples" (148). Human beings (and their stories) come with interests and ties that are political, social, sexual, material, and more. These must be included in studies of Native literatures.

Responsible and ethical criticisms of Indigenous literatures situate stories in specific times, places, and contexts. Native peoples, like all human beings, tell stories that reflect specific experiences, influences, and interests. These are always contextual and often promote a method of continuance somehow related to the interconnected nature of our communities, our families, and the world around us. Criticism should take this up. As Womack writes, "We need to prioritize dates, events—in short, history. Not just distant history but recent events. Instead of making universal, overarching assumptions about Indians, the compassionate critic should delve into historical particulars. We need an improvement over the kind of literary work that has been so very popular in relation to Native literature in which people avoid historical research and base their criticism exclusively on tropes and symbols" (*American Indian Literary Nationalism* 171). In Abenaki critic Lisa Brooks's new study *The Common Pot: The Recovery of Native Space in the Northeast*, she brilliantly shows how Native literatures of this region have deep historical ties to land as well. This attention brings criticism closer to First Nations peoples and their current situations, interests, and struggles. Justice points out that this is also a directive from Native writers and their literatures, too, as,

> one thing is certain from the work of most Indian writers: being Cherokee, Creek, Choctaw-Cherokee, or Anishinaabe, or any of the self-designations of the Indigenous peoples of this hemisphere, includes a fundamental affirmation of the Indian nationhood of a specific community that expresses a tribal-specific identity that's rooted somewhere in a tribal-specific language, sacred history, ceremonial cycle, and geography. Why else would we cite tribal affiliation? Why would we acknowledge kin, ancestors, and spirits if not to acknowledge their specificity? Why would so many use their Indigenous language to name particular spirit beings, or give geographic details of a particularly meaningful place, if not to locate them in a specific linguistic, geographic, and sometimes historical relationship? (*Our Fire Survives the Storm* 214).

Scholars such as Bonita Lawrence (in her important book *"Real" Indians and Others: Mixed-Blood Urban Native Peoples and Indigenous Nationhood*) show that pan-tribal literatures can certainly be considered in specificities as well.

Responsible and ethical criticisms of Indigenous literatures respectfully consider Indigenous-centred literary approaches as fruitful possibilities. Indigenous storytellers are, in countless ways, politically invested in the sustenance and continuance of the relationships and communities in which they reside. As stated, this is usually embodied in some aspect of Indigenous community, but not always. Stories are the lifeblood between storyteller, community, and universe—how they relate, how they interact, how they change as a result. This interconnectivity is a fruitful space that is as full of perspectives, creativity, and growth as it is full of controversy, polemics, and politics. Speaking of this literary tradition, Armand Ruffo points out in his essay, "Why Native Literature?" that "it is said that one cannot be a Native writer and not be political; it comes with the territory" (670). As Ruffo argues, it is these claims for Native aesthetics and perspectives where "the literature itself tells us what it is" and "theories of criticism, ways of approaching the literature" emerge (667). While these might not be the sole interest of a Native storyteller, they are almost always a strong one.

Responsible and ethical criticisms of Indigenous literatures legitimate a long-standing and wide-ranging Indigenous intellectualism and recognize this intellectual history. Tomson Highway remarks that "Native people have a literary tradition that goes back thousands of years before 1492. Mainstream audiences in Canada don't know that we have a mythology that is every bit as potent as mythologies anywhere else—not least of all Christian mythology—and that it is applicable to the specific landscape and the relationship of a specific people to that landscape.... Our literature, our literary tradition, our history, our language, our culture is first rate" (as quoted in Preston 140). It is also in the best interests of theorists, if they are *sincerely* interested in accurately developing meaningful approaches to North American cultures, canons, and critical legacies, to investigate Indigenous intellectual traditions, for they are the most expansive, wide-ranging, and influential knowledge processes in this area of the world. I agree with Womack when he writes: "Tribal literatures are the *tree*, the oldest literatures in the Americas, the most American of American literatures. We *are* the canon. Native peoples have been on this continent at least thirty thousand years, and the stories tell us we have been here even longer than that, that we were set down by the Creator on this continent, that we originated here. For much of this time period, we have had literatures. Without Native American literature, *there is no American canon*" (*Red on Red* 6–7, original emphasis). We need all critics to engage critically with these (hi)stories—embodied in the works and words of Native writers, thinkers, and community members—and simultaneously contribute to the intellectual processes of which they are a part. As critic Sam McKegney writes, this means that "one must engage—listen, learn, dialogue, debate," and allow oneself to be informed by Indigenous thinkers but remain critically and honestly engaged, without apology (44). And, as Osage critic Robert

Warrior points out in his seminal book *Tribal Secrets: Recovering American Indian Intellectual Traditions*, this also includes the crucial recognition that Indigenous peoples have continuing critical and intellectual histories worthy of examination on their terms (xvi–xvii).

This body of work, of course, is underpinned by its own theories, approaches, and knowledge bases, none of which have ended as well. Critics engaging in these literatures must take this into consideration, particularly when investing so heavily in criticisms formulated outside of Indigenous contexts, histories, and experiences. And, without really needing to be said, responsible literary criticisms of Native literatures listen, employ, and make as a central tenet Native intellectual voices.

In terms of post-structuralism and post-colonialism, King reminds scholars in his important essay "Godzilla vs. Post-Colonial" that these lenses are useful, but that

> the term ["post"] itself assumes that the starting point for the discussion is the advent of Europeans in North America. At the same time, the term organizes the literature progressively suggesting that there is both progress and improvement. No less distressing, it also assumes that the struggle between guardian and ward is the catalyst for contemporary Native literature, providing those of us who write with method and topic. And, worst of all, the idea of post-colonial writing effectively cuts us off from our traditions, traditions that were in place before colonialism ever became a question, traditions which have come down to us through our cultures in spite of colonization, and it supposes that contemporary Native writing is largely a construct of oppression. (11–12)

Simply, Native writers write about more than resistances to colonialism. To use Womack's metaphor, European invasion on our territories is a branch on the tree, albeit a heavy one, but ultimately only a branch. Criticism should take up all struggles of our intellectual traditions that embody the entire spectrum of Native existences.

Responsible and ethical criticisms of Indigenous literatures are responsible to an audience that *includes* real-life, modern Indigenous peoples in it. I assert that no research or literary criticism is objective, and should be (at least) interested in methods of Indigenous continuance. Métis critic Jo-Ann Episkenew reminds us, "When analyzing literary works, most scholars are very conscious that ideology is embedded in the text; what they often forget is the ideology that they bring to their reading" (54). In the ideological, imagined, and intended audience of a body of criticism on Native literatures, if there are intentionally mutated, mutilated, and/or fantastically deformed representations of Native peoples (or worse, completely erased), necessary questions should be posed as to the critic's politics, what their purpose is in using this information, and what their work's implications are. As Labrador Métis scholar Kristina Fagan points out in "'What About You?': Approaching the Study of 'Native Literature,'" "critics need to be honest about their fundamental critical assumptions. What is our guiding theory? How are we defining our terms and categories? What do we believe is the purpose of 'Native Literature?'" (247).

Responsible and ethical criticisms of Indigenous literatures do not assume that Native cultural expressions are "ending," nor do they adopt a "deficit" model of change, especially if reality says otherwise. Cultural adaptability, innovation, and growth have always been a tenet of Indigenous cultures. How could they have maintained themselves for millennia otherwise? Tribal and pan-tribal communities, cultures, and nations have always changed with influence, and on some degree by their own terms. Characterizing Native cultures as inherently weak, passive, and lacking in the face of Western advancement, particularly considering the history on this continent regarding that gesture, is to deny countless evident and multivalent resistances and to ultimately participate in an imperialist justification for their erasure. Native nations, one must remember, have not disappeared, and are very much dynamic, complex, and alive today. Speaking of literary approaches invested in describing Native cultures as incapable of reconciling change, deficient, and disappearing as a result of cultural influences from the west, Weaver reminds us that "Native interest in incorporating elements from other cultures long predated European encounter. Vast trading networks carried goods throughout North America, and trade argots were developed to facilitate commerce—all before any had seen a white man. Natives showed themselves adept at adopting and adapting anything that seemed to be useful or to have power. Yet each new item, tool, or technology was used to strengthen, not weaken, their people" (*American Indian Literary Nationalism* 29). Instead of seeing Native cultures, peoples, and literatures as the problem, we need to see that, for the most parts, the issues have been in critical lenses themselves. If past, problematic theories continue to be revisited, this must be considered.

Responsible and ethical criticisms of Indigenous literatures dream of (and point to) important new possibilities for literary criticisms of Indigenous writing, as well as leave space for the reader to dream of (and point to) possibilities too. Indigenous signification has a long and storied history on this continent. No Native community, I would argue, has ever been "illiterate," but has used forms of writing in multitudes of ways. Equally, we have told stories in complex and diverse ways. For instance, the use of Roman orthography should not be the start or end point, nor the be-all and end-all of Indigenous literacy, intellectualism, or stories. Also, although I recognize how important historically constituted studies of orality in Native literatures have been, these have also proven to be reductivist and limiting in scope, particularly in relation to Indigenous signification systems continuing today (such as books, drums, tattoos, sand teachings, wampum, tagging, and footprints).

Grounded political and historical approaches, as I have tried to suggest in this essay, are one way to examine this history. Speaking in his 1981 essay "Towards a National Indian Literature: Cultural Authenticity in Nationalism," Simon Ortiz identifies, quite rightly, that it is "the oral tradition" which has sustained and manifested Indigenous communities, histories, and stories, and "given rise to the surge of literature created by contemporary Indian authors" (10). However,

> it is not the oral tradition as transmitted from ages past alone which is the inspiration and source for contemporary Indian literature. It is also because of the acknowledgement by Indian writers of a responsibility to advocate for their people's self-government, sovereignty, and control of land and natural resources. And it is to look at racism, political and economic oppression, sexism, supremacism, and the needless and wasteful exploitation of land and people, especially in the U.S., that Indian literature is developing a character of nationalism which indeed it should have. It is this character which will prove to be the heart and fibre and story of an America which has heretofore too often feared its deepest and most honest emotions of love and compassion. It is this story, wealthy in being without an illusion of dominant power and capitalistic abundance, that is the most authentic. (12)

Ortiz's approach is only one route. Literary approaches considering Indigenous technological and environmental innovation, semiotics, and theology are some directions scholars may want to invest in and use to uncover Indigenous narrative theories (and some have). It seems to me that this would be an excellent space in which to devise many theories on tricksters, too.

Responsible and ethical criticisms of Indigenous literatures promote dialogic exchanges that include all interested parties, Indigenous or otherwise. Even the staunchest Indigenous sovereigntist agrees: we are all interconnected. Indigenous peoples, allies, and other interested parties must all be at the table, bringing their honest concerns, beliefs, and interpretations of Indigenous literatures for a true dialogue to happen, continue, and grow. These must be initially without judgment, recognizing that all positions, disagreeable or not, have historically situated contexts. Although we will undoubtedly make mistakes and be quick to judge (including, I admit, myself at times), we should invite everyone to the literary feast (even if they might not come). Everyone, though, must bring some food so that everyone will benefit. And, with respect, everyone should try each other's food, even if we don't love it.

Responsible and ethical criticisms of Indigenous literatures provoke, evoke, and invoke change, growth, and beauty that is understandable by many, even if devised by few. Speaking of Indigenous theorizing, Lee Maracle writes in "Oratory: Coming to Theory" that "[t]here is a story in every line of theory. The difference between us and European (predominately white male) scholars is that we admit this, and present theory through story. We differ in the presentation of theory, not in our capacity to theorize" (236). Ultimately, she claims,

> No brilliance exists outside of the ability of human beings to grasp the brilliance and move with it. Thus we say what we think. No thought is understood outside of humanity's interaction. So we present thought through story, human beings doing something, real characters working out the process of thought and being.
>
> For Native people, the ridiculousness of European academic notions of theoretical presentation lies in the inherent hierarchy retained by academics, politicians, law makers, and law keepers. Power resides with the theorists as long as they use a language no one understands. In order to gain the right to theorize, one must attend institutions for many years, learn this other language, and unlearn our feeling for the human condition. Bizarre.
>
> If it cannot be shown, it cannot be understood. Theory is useless outside human application. (238–9)

Simply, we all have a responsibility to listen respectfully to, learn from, and engage with Indigenous peoples and communities with whom we live, from whom we draw, and with whom we share this world. As many have documented, Indigenous storytellers make their worlds through words, sentences, stories. As literary critics of these literatures, we have an exciting opportunity to participate in this process. By maintaining responsible, real-life connections with Indigenous peoples and their stories, we hold the potential to invoke positive change, inspire, and perhaps even contribute, in the process of more creations. We can also add to an everlasting process of Indigenous continuance. By being mindful of our past legacies—some brutal, some beautiful—we can define trajectories including real, living Indigenous peoples as a central part of the world. And maybe, just maybe, we can devise some responsible approaches, have a few conversations, and have a few visions of our own. Then, we can help grow, build, and rebuild the world—just like tricksters.

In the meantime, I have to go read some *Nanabush* stories to my daughter. Miigwech.

Notes

1   This is the traditional greeting of many Anishinaabeg, intended to honour the teachings of Wenaboozhoo.

2   I realize that the use of the category/term "Trickster" is contentious in Indian Country, with some critics and storytellers decrying and/or refusing to use it. This derision is primarily due to its overuse, inappropriate connotations, and problematic descriptions associated with the name, particularly in academic circles. Cree critic Neal McLeod, for example, calls the term, "inaccurate" in that it

> suggests to some that this sacred being is little more than a buffoon. The concepts centred on the word in English include such words as "trickery," "tricky," and "trick," which indicate something less than the truth. One could argue that this is part of the same dynamic that exists when courts and governments have argued that Indigenous lands have been historically empty of laws and governance structures (the notion of terra nullius). The term "trickster" is part of this same trickery, making Indigenous narratives conceptually empty and potentially devoid of truth. (97)

Anishinaabe storyteller Basil Johnston, in his seminal essay "One Generation from Extinction," argues that "scholarly" uses of the term "Trickster" all too often describe sacred characters such as "Nanabush, Raven, Glooscap, Weesaukeechauk" in reductive, simplistic, and stereotypical terms, creating the impression that "Indian stories are nothing more than fairy tales or folklore, fit only for juvenile minds" (95–6). Muskogee Creek critic Craig Womack even goes so far as to state that "Tricksters do *not* originate in Native American cultures," but in "ethnographic" discourses on Indigenous literatures, reflecting a "laziness" on the part of critics who want to define the character as a "trope rather than a reality within Native cultures" (*American Indian Literary Nationalism* 70, original emphasis). With due respect to these critics, I acknowledge that the term "Trickster" comes with much baggage, and express that it is my interest to use the term with attention to cultural, historical, and political particulars in this work. I am also interested in taking up their concerns as well. As I argue in this essay, it has been particular specificities that are lacking in most critical endeavours of tricksters and trickster stories. Lenses with a focus on these, perhaps, may lead to more responsible, respectful, and Indigenous-centred models of literary analysis.

3   Wisdom, love, respect, bravery, honesty, humility, and truth—there are several areas where this is cited, but my father used *The Mishomis Book: The Voice of the Ojibway,* by Edward Benton-Banai, to teach us (64).

4   For more on traditional histories of *Anishinaabeg* storytelling practices and their contexts, see George Copway's *The Traditional History and Characteristic Sketches of the Ojibway Nation* (London: Charles Gilpin, 1850), Basil Johnston's *The Manitous: The Spiritual World of the Ojibway* (St. Paul, MN: Minnesota Historical Press, 1995), Larry C. LeBlanc's *A Compendium of the Anishinabek: An Overview of the Historical Anishinabek with special reference to the People of the Three Fires Confederacy*

(M'Chigeeng, ON: Kenjgewin Teg Educational Institute, 2003), and the Saginaw Ojibwe Anishnabek tribe's *Diba Jimooyung, Telling Our Story: A History of the Saginaw Ojibwe Anishnabek* (Mt. Pleasant, MI: Saginaw Chippewa Indian Tribe of Michigan, 2005) for some good references.

5   In this I reference J. Edward Chamberlin's important 2003 text *If This Is Your Land, Where Are Your Stories?: Finding Common Ground*, where he importantly breaks down the constructed Eurocentric binaries between "oral cultures" (which are devalued) and "written cultures" (which are valued) in mainstream discourse. As he writes:

> This kind of thinking—if we can call it that—encourages people to treat other societies with a blend of condescension and contempt while celebrating the sophistication of their own. And it entrenches the misconception that there *are* such things as "oral cultures" and "written cultures." Think about it. All so-called oral cultures are rich in forms of writing, albeit non-syllabic and non-alphabetic ones: woven and beaded belts and blankets, knotted and coloured strings, carved and painted trays, poles, doors, verandah posts, canes and sticks, masks, hats and chests play a central role in the cultural life of these communities, functioning in all the ways written texts do for European societies. And, on the other hand, the central institutions of our supposedly "written" cultures—our courts and churches and parliaments and schools—are in fact arenas of strictly defined and highly formalized oral traditions, in which certain things must be said and done in the right order by the right people on the right occasions with the right people present. We are, all of us, much more involved in both oral and written traditions than we might think. And our stories and songs draw on the resources of both. (19–20)

6   To clarify, I am employing the term "nation" and "nationhood" throughout this paper not proposing that members of the Anishinaabeg nation (or other Native nations for that matter) are interested in the formation of industrialized and historically western "nation-states" (although a few are). Instead, I utilize Indigenous "nationhood" in much in the same way Justice uses it, to denote "a concept rooted in community values, histories, and traditions that ... asserts a sense of active sociopolitical agency, not simply static separatism from the world and its peoples. This idea is compatible with that of an autonomous ethno-nationalism drawn from the exercise of community self-determination, as proposed by Kahnawake Mohawk political theorist Gerald/Taiaiake Alfred" (*Our Fire Survives the Storm* 24). Crucially, Justice also points out that "Indigenous nationhood is more than simple political independence or the exercise of distinctive cultural identity; it is also an understanding of a common social interdependence within the community, the tribal web of kinship rights *and* responsibilities that link the People, the land, and the cosmos together in an ongoing and dynamic system of mutually affecting relationships" (24). Indigenous nationhood therefore is "the political extension" of "peoplehood," a concept first put forth by Cherokee anthropologist Robert K. Thomas (25).

7   I want to send out a gitchi-miigwech to my colleagues who offered thoughts, read, critiqued, and assisted in the editing of this paper (and its other versions): Deanna

Reder, Linda Morra, Keavy Martin, Sam McKegney, Neal McLeod, and members of my PhD supervisory committee who are constant influences: Daniel Heath Justice, Linc Kesler, Mary Chapman, and Margery Fee.

8   I spoke about these topics on two roundtables on Indigenous literatures at the 2007 Canadian Association for Commonwealth Literature and Language Studies (CACLALS) conference, and this paper emerged from those discussions. I want to thank my fellow panel members at the CACLALS Aboriginal Literatures 2007 roundtable: Janice Acoose, Rob Appleford, Natasha Beeds, Deanna Reder, Robbie Richardson, Judith Leggatt, Sam McKegney, and Cherie Dimaline. I also want to personally thank my colleague Armand Garnet Ruffo for his generous thoughts, which provoked my initial thoughts when drafting this essay.

9   I continue to be, in this vein and others, influenced by Linda Tuhiwai Smith's important 1999 book *Decolonizing Methodologies: Research and Indigenous Peoples*, particularly in the demands Smith makes of researchers who wish to make their careers, salaries, and life paths by studying Indigenous knowledges and knowledge systems. Interrogating the historically exploitative ways western researchers have treated Indigenous knowledge keepers, most often as "if their views did not count or their lives did not matter," Smith concludes that:

> In contemporary Indigenous contexts there are some major research issues which continue to be debated quite vigorously. These can be summarized best by the critical questions that communities and indigenous activists often ask, in a variety of ways (of researchers): Whose research is it? Who owns it? Whose interests does it serve? Who will benefit from it? Who has designed its questions and framed its scope? Who will carry it out? Who will write it up? How will its results be disseminated? (9–10)

10   This is, obviously, a large statement that one could spend books, never mind one article, backing and supporting. While I do touch upon several widely held "exploitative attitudes" in literary criticisms of Native literatures, others have commented on this trend as well. For further scholarship, see Vizenor's *Fugitive Poses: Native American Indian Scenes of Absence and Presence* (Lincoln, NB: Bison, 1998), Joanne R. DiNova's *Spiraling Webs of Relation: Movements Toward an Indigenous Criticism* (New York: Routledge, 2005), Daniel Heath Justice's *Our Fire Survives the Storm: A Cherokee Literary History* (Minneapolis: U of Minnesota P, 2006), Jace Weaver, Craig Womack, and Robert Warrior's co-written *American Indian Literary Nationalism* (Albuquerque: U of New Mexico P, 2006), and Sam McKegney's *Magic Weapons: Aboriginal Writers Remaking Community after Residential School* (Winnipeg: U of Manitoba P, 2007).

11   On this point I credit Sam McKegney, who argues in *Magic Weapons* that scholars in Indigenous literary studies need to take responsibility for how their criticism affects Native communities, and not retreat into what he calls "strategies for ethical disengagement" (39). Among these include: retreating into silence (ignoring the field completely), focusing inward (and narcissistically performing another kind of erasure), "Deal[ing] in the Purviews of Non-Native Critics," or relying on ignorant, tentative, qualified, and provisional claims (39–40). Although McKegney addresses non-Native scholars as employing some, or all, of these "strategies," Native critics are hardly immune.

12   Remarking on the influence of *The Trickster*, Vine Deloria, Jr., writes that its
"description of Trickster myths has become the predominant interpretation of
scholars" (*Spirit & Reason* 23). This trend has continued, according to Franchot
Ballinger, and the book remains the "seminal description of the American Indian
trickster (or so the frequency of citations suggests)" (21).

13   As Justice, in *Our Fire Survives the Storm*, critiques Pearce's *Savagism and Civilization*, the text establishes a set of "contrasting and conflicting binaries" which suggests a progressivist discourse in which Indians (the savages) must eventually
become Europeans (the civilized), or die. Some of these infinitely refracted binaries also divide Native communities into "fullblood vs. mixedblood, progressive vs.
conservative, assimilated vs. indigenous, Christian vs. traditionalist, savage vs. civilized" (20–1). Pearce's "conceptual model" in *Savagism and Civilization* would
influence thinkers and mainstream discourse for years following, and is widely considered one of the most disseminated studies of American Indians in the twentieth century.

14   "Termination," as Rawls writes,

> had many component parts, but it was essentially a withdrawal by the fed-
> eral government of all relations with the Indian tribes. It sought to "detrib-
> alize" or "individualize" Native Americans by phasing out tribal governments
> and subjecting Indians to the laws and taxes of the states in which they
> lived. Federal trust protection of Indian lands was to be removed, tribal
> assets would be transferred or sold, and individual Indians would be granted
> title to their lands ... Indians would thus take their place in American soci-
> ety alongside their fellow citizens with the same rights, privileges, and
> responsibilities. (38)

15   Radin's *The Trickster* continues to have widespread influence. The Smithsonian
Institute, arguably an "authority" on Indian culture and history in the American
mainstream, cites the book on its "recommended reading" list for "Literary Criticism" of Native American Literatures. Schocken Books, a division of Random
House, continues to republish *The Trickster* to meet demands from universities. The
text also continues to be translated and sold in countries throughout Europe.

16   By 1969 in the U.S., Termination had resulted in widespread erasures of federal
recognition for tribes, the integration of Native students from boarding schools
into public education systems continued to result in "perpetual cycle[s] of academic failure," and the denial of Indian land and resource claims undermined
sovereignty and self-determination practices (Champagne 8, 317, 320–1). In
Canada, the draconian Indian Act continued to dictate, control, and stifle First
Nations' economic practices, land claims, membership, and treaty rights (and
deny virtually all Inuit and Métis claims), the residential school system maintained an assimilationist cultural and political federal agenda, and—as in the
U.S.—the blatant misrepresentation of Native cultures, stories, and discourses
continued to be produced and disseminated, gaining national attention and noto-
riety (Champagne 338–59, Petrone 95–6).

17   In *The People Shall Continue*, Ortiz beautifully describes the process of Native peoples meeting and sharing their stories of culture and colonization during the
period of Red Power cultural revitalization, writing, "Everywhere, the People on

the reservations, in small towns, in the large cities—they were talking, and they were listening. They were listening to the words of the elder People who were speaking, 'This is the life that includes you. This is the land that is yours. All of these things that were pushed away from us and broken by the American powers and the government, they are alive, and we must keep them alive. All of these things will help us to continue'" (21).

18   See uses of post-structuralism and post-colonialism in the following works: Andrew Wiget, ed., *Critical Essays on Native American Literature* (Boston: G.K. Hall, 1985); Gerald Vizenor, ed., *Narrative Chance: Postmodern Discourse on Native American Indian Literatures* (Albuquerque: U of New Mexico P, 1989; rpt. Norman: U of Oklahoma P, 1993); Vizenor, ed., *Survivance: Narratives of Native Presence* (Lincoln: U of Nebraska P, 2008); Brian Swann and Arnold Krupat, eds., *Recovering the Word: Essays on Native American Literature* (Berkeley: U of California P, 1987); Hertha Dawn Wong's *Sending My Heart Back Across the Years: Tradition and Innovation in Native American Autobiography* (New York: Oxford UP, 1992); Krupat, *The Turn to the Native: Studies in Criticism and Culture* (Lincoln: U of Nebraska P, 1996); Louis Owens, *Other Destinies: Understanding the American Indian Novel* (Norman: U of Oklahoma P, 1992), and *Mixedblood Messages: Literature, Film, Family, Place* (Norman: U of Oklahoma P, 1998); James Ruppert, *Mediation in Contemporary Native American Fiction* (Norman: U of Oklahoma P, 1995); Susan Berry Brill de Ramírez, *Contemporary American Indian Literatures and the Oral Tradition* (Tucson: U of Arizona P, 1999); A. Robert Lee, ed., *Loosening the Seams: Interpretations of Gerald Vizenor* (Bowling Green, OH: Bowling Green State U Popular Press, 2000); Elvira Pulitano, *Toward a Native American Critical Theory* (Lincoln: U of Nebraska P, 2003); and Ben Carson, "The 'Cosmopolitan Consciousness' of Gerald Vizenor and Native American Literary Separatism," *English Studies Forum* 3:1 (Fall-Winter 2007), <http://www.bsu.edu/web/esf/3.1/Carson.htm>.

19   After years of reflection and further reading, I assert that this is a one-sided use of Vizenor's "Trickster Discourse" anyway. Even critic Arnold Krupat, one of his earliest proponents, has altered his position, writing in his 2002 book *Red Matters: Native American Studies* that "the identity Vizenor has elaborately been defining and redefining has at base the deep and unmistakable roots of 'tribal' values—which can and indeed must be taken along wherever one may go—to the cities, to Europe, to China, anywhere.... In these regards, Vizenor may well have provided *Indian* versions of cosmopolitan patriotism" (112). One can make similar claims in the work of King and Owens.

Works Cited

Akiwenzie-Damm, Kateri. "Erotica, Indigenous Style." *(Ad)dressing our Words: Aboriginal Perspectives on Aboriginal Literatures*. Ed. Armand Garnet Ruffo. Penticton, BC: Theytus, 2001.

Babcock, Barbara, and Jay Cox. "The Native American Trickster." In *Handbook of Native American Literature*. Ed. Andrew Wiget. New York: Garland, 1996. 99–106.

Ballinger, Franchot. *Living Sideways: Tricksters in American Indian Oral Traditions.* Norman: U of Oklahoma P, 2004.

Benton-Banai, Edward. "The Great Flood." In *Wisconsin Indian Literature: Anthology of Native Voices.* Ed. Kathleen Tigerman. Madison: U of Wisconsin P, 2006. 92–4.

———. *The Mishomis Book: The Voice of the Ojibway.* Hayward, WI: Indian Country Communications, 1988.

Blaeser, Kimberly. "A Gathering of Stories." In *Stories Migrating Home: A Collection of Anishinaabe Prose.* Ed. Kimberly Blaeser. Bemidji, MN: Loonfeather, 1999. 1–7.

———. *Gerald Vizenor: Writing in the Oral Tradition.* Norman: U of Oklahoma P, 1996.

Bright, William. "The Natural History of Old Man Coyote." In *Recovering the Word: Essays on Native American Literature.* Eds. Brian Swann and Arnold Krupat. Berkeley: U of California P, 1987. 339–87.

Brooks, Lisa. *The Common Pot: The Recovery of Native Space in the Northeast.* Minneapolis: U of Minnesota P, 2008.

Canby, William C., Jr. *American Indian Law in a Nutshell.* 3rd ed. St. Paul, MN: West Group, 1998.

Cardinal, Harold. *The Unjust Society: The Tragedy of Canada's Indians.* Edmonton: M.G. Hurtig, 1969.

Chamberlin, J. Edward. "From Hand to Mouth: The Postcolonial Politics of Oral and Written Traditions." In *Reclaiming Indigenous Voice and Vision.* Ed. Marie Battiste. Vancouver: U of British Columbia P, 2000. 124–41.

———. *If This Is Your Land, Where Are Your Stories?: Finding Common Ground.* Toronto: Alfred A. Knopf Canada, 2003; rpt. Toronto: Vintage, 2004.

Champagne, Duane. *Native America: Portrait of the Peoples.* Detroit: Visible Ink, 1994.

Deloria, Barbara, et al., eds. *Spirit & Reason: The Vine Deloria, Jr., Reader.* Golden, CO: Fulcrum, 1999.

Deloria, Vine, Jr. *Custer Died for Your Sins: An Indian Manifesto.* New York: Macmillan, 1969.

Deloria, Vine, Jr., and Clifford M. Lytle. *The Nations Within: The Past and the Future of American Indian Sovereignty.* New York: Pantheon, 1984.

Douglas, Mary. *Purity and Danger: An Analysis of Concepts of Pollution and Taboo.* London: Pelican, 1970.

Eagleton, Terry. *Literary Theory: An Introduction.* 1983. Rpt. with new preface. Minneapolis: U of Minnesota P, 2008.

Episkenew, Jo-Ann. "Socially Responsible Criticism: Aboriginal Literature, Ideology, and the Literary Canon." In *Creating Community: A Roundtable on Canadian Aboriginal Literature.* Ed. Renate Eigenbrod and Jo-Ann Episkenew. Penticton, BC: Theytus; Brandon, MB: Bearpaw, 2002. 51–68.

Fagan, Kristina. "'What About You?': Approaching the Study of 'Native Litera-
    ture.'" In *Creating Community: A Roundtable on Canadian Aboriginal Literature*.
    Ed. Renate Eigenbrod and Jo-Ann Episkenew. Penticton, BC: Theytus; Bran-
    don, MB: Bearpaw, 2002. 235–54.

hooks, bell. "Postmodern Blackness." In *The Norton Anthology of Theory and Criti-
    cism*. Gen. ed. Vincent B. Leitch. New York: Norton, 2001. 2478–84.

Johnston, Basil. "Is That All There Is? Tribal Literature." In *An Anthology of Cana-
    dian Native Literature in English*. 3rd ed. Ed. Daniel David Moses and Terry
    Goldie. Toronto: Oxford UP, 2005. 98–105.

———. "One Generation from Extinction." In *An Anthology of Canadian Native Lit-
    erature in English*. 3rd ed. Ed. Daniel David Moses and Terry Goldie. Toronto:
    Toronto: Oxford UP, 2005. 92–7.

Josephy, Alvin M., Jr. "The New Indian Patriots: An Introduction." In *Red Power:
    The American Indians' Fight for Freedom*. Ed. Alvin M. Josephy, Jr. New York:
    McGraw-Hill, 1971. 1–8.

Justice, Daniel Heath. *Our Fire Survives the Storm: A Cherokee Literary History*. Min-
    neapolis: U of Minnesota P, 2006.

———. "Renewing the Fire: Notes Toward the Liberation of English Studies."
    ESC: English Studies in Canada 29:1–2 (2003): 45–54.

King, Thomas. "Godzilla vs. Post-Colonial." *World Literature Written in English* 30:2
    (1990): 10–16.

Kroeber, Karl, comp. and ed. *Traditional Literatures of the American Indian: Texts
    and Interpretations*. Lincoln: U of Nebraska P, 1981.

Krupat, Arnold. *Red Matters: Native American Studies*. Philadelphia: U of Pennsyl-
    vania P, 2002.

Lawrence, Bonita. *"Real" Indians and Others: Mixed-Blood Urban Native Peoples and
    Indigenous Nationhood*. Lincoln: U of Nebraska P, 2004.

Lévi-Strauss, Claude. *Structural Anthropology*. Trans. Claire Jacobson and Brooke
    Grundfest Schoepf. New York: Doubleday, 1967.

Maracle, Lee. "Oratory: Coming to Theory." In *By, For, and About: Feminist Cultural
    Politics*. Ed. Wendy Waring. Toronto: Women's Press, 1994. 235–40.

McKegney, Sam. *Magic Weapons: Aboriginal Writers Remaking History after Residen-
    tial School*. Winnipeg: U of Manitoba P, 2007.

McLeod, Neal. *Cree Narrative Memory: From Treaties to Contemporary Times*. Saskatoon:
    Purich, 2007.

Murray, David. "Translation and mediation." In *The Cambridge Companion to Native
    American Literature*. Ed. Joy Porter and Kenneth M. Roemer. Cambridge: Cam-
    bridge UP, 2005. 69–84.

Norman, Howard. "Wesucechak Becomes a Deer and Steals Language: An Anec-
    dotal Linguistics Concerning the Swampy Cree Trickster." In *Recovering the
    Word: Essays on Native American Literature*. Ed. Brian Swann and Arnold Kru-
    pat. Berkeley: U of California P, 1987. 402–21.

Ortiz, Simon J. *The People Shall Continue.* San Francisco: Children's Book Press, 1977.

———. "Towards a National Indian Literature: Cultural Authenticity in Nationalism." *MELUS* 8:2 (1981): 7–12.

Pearce, Roy Harvey. *Savagism and Civilization: A Study of the Indian and the American Mind.* Baltimore: Johns Hopkins P, 1965. [Rev. ed. of *The Savages of America: A Study of the Indian and the Idea of Civilization.* Baltimore: Johns Hopkins P, 1953.]

Petrone, Penny. *Native Literature in Canada: From the Oral Tradition to the Present.* Toronto: Oxford UP, 1990.

Preston, Jennifer. "Weesageechak Begins to Dance: Native Earth Performing Arts Inc." *The Drama Review: A Journal of Performance Studies* 36:1 (Spring 1992): 135–59.

Radin, Paul. *The Trickster: A Study in American Indian Mythology.* 1956. Rpt. New York: Schocken, 1972.

Ramsey, Jarold. *Reading the Fire: The Traditional Indian Literatures of America.* Rev. and expanded ed. Seattle: U of Washington P, 1999.

Rawls, James J. *Chief Red Fox Is Dead: A History of Native Americans since 1945.* Orlando: Harcourt Brace College Publishers, 1996.

Ruffo, Armand G. "Why Native Literature?" *American Indian Quarterly* 21:4 (Autumn 1997): 663–73.

Shohat, Ella. "Notes on the 'Post-Colonial.'" *Social Text* 31/32 (1992): 99–113.

Smith, Linda Tuhiwai. *Decolonizing Methodologies: Research and Indigenous Peoples.* London: Zed, 1999.

Swann, Brian, and Arnold Krupat, eds. *Recovering the Word: Essays on Native American Literature.* Berkeley: U of California P, 1987.

Teuton, Christopher B. "Theorizing American Indian Literature: Applying Oral Concepts to Written Traditions." In *Reasoning Together: The Native Critics Collective.* Ed. Janice Acoose et al. Norman: U of Oklahoma P, 2008. 193–215.

Toelken, Barre. "Life and Death in the Navajo Coyote Tales." In *Recovering the Word: Essays on Native American Literature.* Ed. Brian Swann and Arnold Krupat. Berkeley: U of California P, 1987. 388–401.

Turner, Victor W. "Betwixt and Between: The Liminal Period in *Rites of Passage.*" In *The Forest of Symbols: Aspects of Ndembu Ritual.* Ed. Victor W. Turner. Ithaca, NY: Cornell UP, 1967. 93–111.

Vizenor, Gerald. "A Postmodern Introduction." In *Narrative Chance: Postmodern Discourse on Native American Indian Literatures.* Ed. Gerald Vizenor. Albuquerque: U of New Mexico P, 1989; rpt. Norman: U of Oklahoma P, 1993. 3–16.

———. *Manifest Manners: Narratives on Postindian Survivance.* Lincoln: U of Nebraska P, 1999.

Warrior, Robert. *Tribal Secrets: Recovering American Indian Intellectual Traditions.* Minneapolis: U of Minnesota P, 1995.

Weaver, Jace. "From I-Hermeneutics to We-Hermenutics: Native Americans and the Post-Colonial." In *Native American Religious Identity: Unforgotten Gods*. Ed. Jace Weaver. Maryknoll, NY: Orbis, 1–25.

Weaver, Jace, Craig S. Womack, and Robert Warrior. *American Indian Literary Nationalism*. Albuquerque: U of New Mexico P, 2006.

Winnebago Tribe of Nebraska. "History of the Winnebago Tribe of Nebraska." <http://www.winnebagotribe.com>. Accessed 12 October 2008.

Womack, Craig. *Red on Red: Native American Literary Separatism*. Minneapolis: U of Minnesota P, 1999.

The Trickster Moment, Cultural Appropriation, and the Liberal Imagination in Canada

Introduction

Writing about the trickster or about a specific incarnation, such as Nanabush, the Ojibwa trickster, can be dangerous. As Drew Hayden Taylor points out in "Academia Mania," literary critics tend to overinterpret. About a critic who was sure that a crow in one of his plays represented Nanabush, Taylor writes: "If he thinks a crow is Nanabush, let him. There's a whole flock of Nanabushes living around my mother's house. He'll have a field day" (87). Taylor goes on to quote Daniel David Moses about academic literary critics: "They all like to play 'Spot the Trickster'" (88). As an academic, I am fated, paradoxically, to take the trickster seriously—and Taylor has promised to humour me: "I'm not responsible for these views and criticisms; the trickster is at fault here. The trickster made me do it. Yeah, they'll buy that" (88). The trickster may have become a hermeneutic fad, but the sudden visibility of the trickster in mainstream Canada in the 1980s came from the need to open up a space for Indigenous cultural production.[1] The trickster provided a strategic rallying place for Indigenous artists across Canada to make strong political points in a way that was healing for them and their communities, while (somewhat) dampening the backlash against their revelations of continuing colonial abuse and oppression to a mainstream audience in denial. Indigenous writers closely associated with the trickster made the point that Indigenous people were tired of being stereotyped in mainstream Canadian cultural production, tired of having traditional stories used without permission or even acknowledgement of the storytellers, and tired of being excluded from national and provincial institutions that regulated access to education, grants, and cultural capital.

59

The Committee to Re-establish the Trickster (CRET)

According to Moses, the idea for the Committee to Re-establish the Trickster (which they abbreviated to CRET, apparently, so they could call themselves "the CRETins"; cf. Sherman) came to him in late winter or early spring in 1986 in Toronto ("Trickster's Laugh" 107).[2] He and his allies in the project—Tomson Highway and Lenore Keeshig-Tobias—were at that time all extremely active in the city's literary and performing arts world, particularly with Native Earth Performing Arts (1982–). One reason for establishing this Committee was to get attention for their work and that of other Indigenous artists. Moses observed that he had "seen what we are all doing, that it is good and worthy of attention" (107). He remembered three people with "differences in cultural values, assumptions and behaviours" who were "at odds often, but laughing almost always" (107): the issue was "what can a meeting between a Cree musician and playwright (Tomson), an Ojibwa storyteller (Lenore) and a Delaware poet with Iroquoian roots [Moses] agree to agree on?" (108). He saw their "area of agreement"—the need to re-establish the trickster—as a "rather rich irony," since they were planning to use this traditional figure to combat stereotypes, which often freeze Indigenous culture in a traditional past. Moses remarks that "the Trickster as we know or rediscover him, as Coyote or Weesageejak or Nanabush, as Raven or Glooscap is as shifty and shiftless, as horny and greedy, as lucky, as funny, as human as any of us" (109–10). What they were looking for was something that could be taken seriously enough to "open up a space for a little bit of the strange but true about us" (109). The choice of the trickster could be seen, then, as the work of compromise, as what has come to be known as a branding exercise; it could even be regarded as an act of cultural (re-)appropriation or repatriation:

> What we choose to lever open that space with is a tool some anthropologist or ethnologist came up with—digging around through our stories, taking them apart, sorting those parts and slapping labels on them, one of those labels being the category "archetype," with a subheading "Trickster." It is in us to hope that if this Trickster character was strange enough to a scientist to be marked and remarked upon, then it might also be true enough to get us all beyond the scientific attention span. (109)

The scientist referred to here is most likely Paul Radin, a student of Franz Boas, who began fieldwork with the Winnebago in 1908 and published *The Trickster: A Study in American Indian Mythology* (with a commentary by Carl G. Jung) in 1956. The trickster as an abstract concept came to Canada, then, with some anthropological and some psychological baggage. The label, invented by a non-Indigenous social scientist, was appropriated because it facilitated cross-cultural work among Indigenous cultural producers with different perspectives, it focused efforts on reviving tradition, and it attracted some non-Indigenous attention long enough to subvert the stereotypes. Indeed, Highway's play *The Rez Sisters*, which featured a trickster hero, Nanabush, was already in rehearsal when Moses had the idea for the Committee; the play's runaway success cemented the popularity of the trickster. Intense work began on cultivating Indigenous writing: the new Indigenous canon in English was under construction.[3]

Appropriation of Voice

One of the most memorable battles for the Indigenous arts community was called the appropriation of voice debate. Mainstream writers who wrote from the position of minority cultural insiders began to be seen as exploitative imposters who were using foreign subject matter without considering the cultural or political impact on the communities from which they took it. Indigenous writing entered the awareness of the mainstream audience in the 1980s as part of a larger surge of writing by visible minority and recently immigrated Canadians, a surge marked by frustration with narrow, stereotypical, and even racist definitions of who is Canadian. Just as the Canadian nationalists of earlier eras had struggled to establish provincial and national institutions that would support Canadian culture, such as the Canada Council for the Arts (1957), these new writers struggled to found new institutions and to achieve equity of access to the resources of existing ones so that they could get their vision out. The Indigenous intellectuals involved in this struggle articulated Indigenous experiences of colonization and appropriation, and used traditional Indigenous protocols about the ownership and telling of stories to mark Indigenous difference. The insistence on control over speech and writing about Indigenous issues was a political move, even though it was made in the "soft" area of culture. Indigenous people were tired of having things done to and "for" them by government bureaucrats: to insist on a place at the table after the near-disaster of the White Paper of 1969 was essential. But some felt that to deal with the state and with the wider Canadian society rather than with their own cultures was a mistake. Jeannette Armstrong's *Slash* deals with the debates about whether Indigenous people should be involved in the patriation of the Constitution Act (1982). The hero argues that getting legal recognition was unnecessary: "We don't need anybody's constitution, what we have is our own already. We hold rights to the land and to nationhood" (241). Winning money or even land in court would be a wasted effort without a living culture; what was important was that "[t]here were young people who were ... rebuilding a world view that had to work in this century, keeping the values of the old Indian ways" (232).[4] Most of the Indigenous writers who emerged during this period were consciously working on this project, albeit from different cultural and political perspectives. As Tomson Highway made clear in his *Kiss of the Fur Queen*, music, dance, theatre, writing, and the other arts—based on traditional roots—were to be the magic weapons with which Indigenous people would make a new world. The trickster—the transformer—became central to this movement.[5]

At the Third International Writers' Conference in 1988, Lee Maracle asked Anne Cameron to "move over" to permit Indigenous writers space to speak. At issue was Cameron's extremely successful novel, *Daughters of Copper Woman* (which has sold over 200,000 copies since first published in 1981, with all royalties going to Indigenous women's projects).[6] Part of the problem was that, in the novel, Cameron told traditional stories without public permission to do so, as was customary. Cameron, in her account of this event in "The Operative Principle Is Trust," writes: "I have not been censored or stifled, or denied any freedom of speech or expression; I have been asked to take a step or two to one side. Not down. To one side...." (69). Cameron's reaction was relatively mild. Maracle (in the same collection) noted, "I am told by a host of the [CBC program] *fifth estate* (who has yet to air the interview with Anne Cameron and myself) that Timothy Findley, among others, is categorizing my objection ... to such abuse and appropriation of our cultural heritage and sacred ways as fascist" (186). She concludes, however, that "[w]hat is ... important is that women of colour are entitled to author their own stories. I do not hear any outcries from any corner of the publishing community about the penchant that women's presses have for publishing books about (white) women, written by (white) women and not men" (186).

Keeshig-Tobias, founding chair of the Racial Minority Writers' Committee of The Writers' Union of Canada (TWUC), raised the issue of cultural appropriation at an AGM in 1989 and argued "that the stories and cultures of the First Nations (and, by extension, other minorities) should not be appropriated by non-native writers" (Moore).[7] This argument was in line with the stated goal of the Committee to Re-establish the Trickster: "to consolidate and gain recognition for Native contributions to Canadian writing and to reclaim the Native *voice* in literature" (*The Magazine* 2, emphasis mine). This imperative brought a debate that had been ongoing in feminist (cf. Niedzwiecki), ethnic minority, and Indigenous literary circles into the mainstream, where it generated a great deal of heated comment that continued to the Writing Thru Race Conference in 1994 and beyond. Later commentary on this conference, which took place when Roy Miki was Chair of the

Racial Minority Writers' Committee, shows that it profoundly shook mainstream notions of Canadian culture. TWUC and other cultural institutions also underwent a transformation in thinking because of this debate. As Monika Kim Gagnon and Scott Toguri McFarlane point out,

> in its sponsorship of the conference, TWUC's leadership began to articulate a different sense of literary production that challenged the dominance of pluralistic notions of Canadian literature. The pluralist, multicultural understanding of what is good about literature argues that it should show that, underneath, we are all the same and that different Canadian stories reflect this certain "Canadian essence." By giving itself over to others and by sponsoring a site of cultural difference, TWUC, if somewhat hesitantly, supported the notion that different cultural locations are just that—different. They produce different needs and require different forms, both literary and sociopolitical. There is a need, the conference insisted, for other ways of writing through race.

Change came over time, but Keeshig-Tobias and her allies did not find their struggle easy; speaking in 1989, she told Hartmut Lutz that "Dan Moses and I belong to the Writers' Union, we are the only 'Indians' there.... You know this issue of voice came up, this issue of racism in writing and publishing. The motion didn't pass!" ("Lenore" 83).[8]

The Liberal Imagination

Although TWUC was a bastion of left liberal writers, those on the Racial Minority Writers' Committee raised an array of issues that many found unpalatable or incomprehensible. The debate epitomized "the general liberal dilemma," which is "that there will always be a moment at which liberalism will illiberally turn against those whom it perceives as not (yet) liberal (enough) in order to convert them into its own image" (Pels 153). The debate tricked many mainstream writers into exposing a systemic problem of access to the public: freedom of speech is certainly worth protecting, but, as Lorne Simon put it, you should not "use the excuse of freedom of speech to hog the conversation" (47). Discourse constructs the meanings of events, and the discourse around the debate fell into the pattern that has been described as "democratic racism": "The central discourse of democratic racism is denial, the failure to acknowledge that cultural, structural and systemic racism exists in a democratic liberal society" (Tator 3). The negative reaction of those in the mainstream media and writing community revealed the power of dominant liberal ideas about the creative process, intellectual property, and artistic quality to exclude cultural minorities who wanted to assert a collective presence in the Canadian arts scene.

The media quickly focused on a perceived threat to freedom of speech, and reduced any potential for subtlety in the debate to near-zero. Despite many attempts to turn the discussion to the issue of access to media attention, publication, and grants, it became caricatured as a shootout between racial minority writers who were depicted as would-be censors and mainstream writers who argued the claims of the minority writers were a threat to freedom of speech. Many routes through this discursive phenomenon were possible, which burgeoned as controversies erupted around the 54th Congress of PEN held in Toronto in September 1989, and continued through the release of the Report of the Racial Minority Committee to the Canada Council in January 1992 (cf. Tator for other related controversies of the time). One could point out, as does Allan Hutchinson, that "the [Canada] council is ... in the business of allocating public funds to support the work of writers and artists. As such, it is surely appropriate for it to channel its scarce resources to those Canadians whose cultural voice has been less often heard" (A16). But this sort of statement was rare. Moses summed up the polarization of the debate this way:

> Journalists have asked me if I condone censorship, if I don't want my stories to be told, as if my only choices were to be lied about or to be ignored. I wish to exercise a third option: I can and will tell my own stories myself. You too can try to tell Native stories if you dare, but you better be prepared to go Native, to own and be owned by these stories as we are, to do them justice. ("Whose Voice" 15)

A news release from the Writers Guild of Canada (22 April 1992),[9] which represented around 950 writers, stated that "actions that in any way restrict freedom of expression are simply a form of censorship." This assertion sounds noble enough until one realizes that, for some members, the action of complaining that someone's writing contains racial stereotypes may have counted as censorship. Neil Bissoondath[10] agreed: "I reject the idea of cultural appropriation completely. I reject anything that limits the imagination. No one has the right to tell me who I should or should not write about, and telling me what or how I do that amounts to censorship. I don't believe anyone can steal the culture of another" (quoted in Godfrey C1). Bissoondath here equates critique with censorship, and appears to be asking that anyone who criticizes him for what he writes ought to be censored. Of course, it is a common reaction to want freedom of speech for oneself and those who share one's opinions, while wanting the differing opinions of others to be stifled. These writers appeared to be reacting to the threat of criticism rather than to the threat of censorship. Their reaction was not an attempt to admit new voices to the debate, but to ensure that only the same old voices would continue to dominate. The cry for freedom, in fact, was an attempt to stifle dissent. Here, for example, is Timothy Findley on the Canada Council: "So they're not going to impose guidelines [on appropriation] ... but just look at their response! They are 'distributing information.' Just a quiet little reminder to the juries, right? It's 'Censor thyself, before we have to.'... It's creating an atmosphere of intimidation" (quoted in Hurst H11).

Mainstream writers compared the minority writers to the fascist South African government that supported apartheid. Bissoondath commented that "[w]hat has frightened and saddened me ... is that ... while in South Africa you have people recognizing that apartheid is evil and unworkable, that we seem to have groups in this country who are trying to institute a certain apartheid of the mind based on culture" (*Morningside* 37). Fascism and Nazism were also used as analogies for the approach of the minority writers. Findley, for example, said that "[i]n 1922 they burned 10,000 books at the gate of a German university because those books were written in unacceptable voices" ("Letter" D7). A column by Erna Paris, headed "A Letter to the Thought Police," suggested that "as a pleasing, tidy gesture, the Canada Council may also wish to draw up blood purity charts for jurors and hopeful authors and scholars, since everyone will need to demonstrate their biological fitness before qualifying for grants" (A16; cf. Groening 4–13 for more on the history of the debate). While positioned in the media as Nazis and white South African supporters of apartheid, however, most of those arguing against appropriation were members of visible minorities and often they were women. (It's worth noting that Bissoondath is of Indo-Trinidadian origins, Findley gay, and Paris, Jewish—and can be understood, if not necessarily forgiven, for reacting so strongly. They had more to lose than most by being categorized as "minority" writers.) The framing of the debate othered the protesters in the public eye, turning them into unreasonable bullies rather than what they were—fellow writers trying to get a legitimate point across about the failure of that wonderful liberal imagination to produce much beyond stereotypes and the failure of major institutions to treat their work equitably.

In 1990 Keeshig-Tobias wrote "Stop Stealing Native Stories," a one-page opinion piece in the *Globe and Mail* with a title that launched a thousand uncomprehending tirades. The problem for Keeshig-Tobias was that the liberal imagination could only imagine as far as its own ingrained opinions:

Stories are much more than just the imagination, and Canadian writers might research circumstances and events, artifacts and history, but why bother if it's fiction? And whether it is fiction or non-fiction, the fact is, stories have power. With non-fiction, non-Native authors have a better chance of 'getting it right,' but with fiction, God help us, here we go again, these people haven't learned. ... And so a few canoes, beads, beaver ponds and a buffalo or two are used to prop up the whore, the drunkard or the shaman. These romantic clichés and stereotypes, however, serve only to illustrate how they, the outsiders, see or want to see Native peoples." ("The Magic" 176, 174)

And these people really had not learned. Pauline Johnson had said much the same thing almost a hundred years earlier in the same newspaper (*Toronto Sunday Globe*, 1892), under the title "A Strong Race Opinion: On the Indian Girl in Modern Fiction":[11] "The term 'Indian' signifies about as much as the term 'European,' but I cannot recall ever having read a story where the heroine was described as 'a European.' The Indian girl we meet in cold type, however, is rarely distressed by having to belong to any tribe or to reflect any tribal characteristics" (178). The Indian girl as depicted in fiction, she complains, is always the same, in love with the white hero, but always dying, usually in some self-sacrificing way. She concludes that novelists are not interested in discovering anything about the people about whom they write: "half of our authors who write up Indian stuff have never been on an Indian reserve in their life, have never met a 'real live' Redman, have never even read Parkman, Schoolcraft, or Catlin; what wonder that their conception of a people that they are ignorant of, save by heresay, is dwarfed, erroneous and delusive" (183). And critics who have surveyed English-Canadian representations of Indigenous people all conclude that these representations are stereotypical and almost always serve the purposes of the mainstream rather than revealing or attempting to change misconceptions about Indigenous peoples (cf. Coleman, Emberley, Fee, Francis, Goldie, Groening, and Monkman).

Why do many Canadian writers, for the most part, never learn? What stabilizes these stereotypes? And, more interestingly, how does the dominant ideology manage to exclude the Other without open racism? Neil Bissoondath describes the creative process thus:

how my stories come about is not easily explained, for the truth is that I don't find the stories, they find me. Characters emerge unbidden ... and I follow them into their worlds, grateful for their generosity.... If the characters live, they will at times do and say things I dislike or with which I disagree, but this, far from detracting from their validity, lends them a greater integrity, for literary characters should be fully developed individuals with minds and lives of their own existing in the imaginative world of the writer. They must be true only to themselves and their circumstances. They owe allegiance neither to the writer nor to the social groups to which they belong.... To oblige a character to adopt a preordained stance is to kill that character; it is to take away his or her individuality, to remove freedom of choice. ("I'm Just a Writer" C1)

This passage is compelling, but it is not Bissoondath's original creation; it is part of a long-lived Western discursive formation promulgated widely in the education system of the former British Empire. Let's look at it more closely. Characters arrive in Bissoondath's head unbidden; he writes down everything that they tell him, even if he doesn't like it; and, in effect, he runs a little democracy in his head, in which everyone has freedom of speech. Here is a truncated version of the same idea from Findley, another writer who hears voices: "The subject of voice appropriation, as it applies to fiction, is a non-starter ... writers do not *steal* stories—they *hear* them. And what I hear, I will write. *This is my job*" (emphasis in original, "When You Write" 13). But where are these voices coming from? Well, usually from the often-limited experiences of the writer and from the dominant discourse, which explains why Keeshig-Tobias says, "I think the most important thing for a non-Native writer to do when they write about Native issues is to have respect—respect means research and talking to the people" (as cited in Williams).

This vehement insistence by two important writers that the voices to which they should listen are those in their heads, rather than those of the contemporary people about whom they are writing, can be traced to the German Romantic nationalist notion of the *Volksgeist*, or the spirit of the people (cf. "Volksgeist"). For J.G. Herder (1744–1803) and other later European thinkers, national legitimacy is founded on the spirit of the people, but the *Volk*, in his view, is a metaphysical entity as much as a real community. The great poet was in touch with the *Volk* at the spiritual level, which served as a kind of conduit for the national voice. This model is a useful way of justifying the activity of "speaking for" others, others who are portrayed as unable to speak because they are inarticulate, illiterate, unselfconscious, and inartistic. This idea became foundational to Romanticism and is closely tied to ideas of representing the people politically as well as culturally.

This belief that it is legitimate, even virtuous, to represent others is ingrained in Canadian culture; it's hardly surprising that it recurs so often in the debate. What is interesting is that it requires one to insert oneself into the position of the Other without really thinking about it, because, after all, one is just a conduit. To think about it is to fake something that should happen at a spiritual rather than a rational level. So Bissoondath argues: "Pulling a story together is in many ways an act of the unconscious. I do not, as a writer, sit down and think: Today I will write a story about a black woman or a Jewish man—for this would be journalism. I do not write a story to score points about racism or socialism or capitalism—for this would be propaganda" ("I'm Just a Writer" C1). In other words, one cannot, as a serious creative writer, honestly do research or even plan ahead as one writes. Neither can one think about political issues. Authenticity is not based on the knowledge of a particular community, but on resistance even to the idea of gaining such knowledge—a version of imaginative objectivity, as it were. And Bissoondath was not alone in his ideas. The Writers Guild press release put it this way: "This extraordinary capacity of human beings to explore what they do not 'know' but can only imagine, to examine the unimaginable ... is a right and privilege so precious and so essential to the development of all culture and all cultures, to the whole life of man, that every attempt to limit, regular, censor, tidy, to manage it, is a real and present danger" (n. pag.). The release continues to exhort the Canada Council to protect "the freedom of our creative people and especially our writers." The effect of this sort of rhetoric is to convince readers that writers are some sort of untouchable priesthood. Findley, asked by minority writers to be sensitive to issues of appropriation, asked "who the *hell* do they think they are?" (quoted in Hurst H11). Moses and Keeshig-Tobias and the others involved in the struggle thought they were writers too. But perhaps they were not "our writers" as defined by the Writers Guild.

The ideology of the free liberal imagination separates the aesthetic from the political and the economic, in the process reducing the power of art (since art that makes political points can be dismissed as "propaganda" and art that makes money can be dismissed as pandering to vulgar tastes). Once that is done, then elite evaluation decides what is and is not aesthetically "good." Those who resisted the idea that juries should contain appropriate numbers of minority artists argued that ethnic background was irrelevant, because the juries made their judgments on literary quality alone. Those with cultural capital provided by upbringing and education in the dominant class, when they reinscribe the status quo, appear not to be "political" at all. Further, as Pierre Bourdieu points out, dominant artists and intellectuals "have always practiced that form of radical chic which consists in rehabilitating socially inferior cultures or the minor genres of legitimate culture" (84). Finally, cultural appropriation in settler colonies is driven by a need to cover up the theft of the land. Usually, non-Indigenous immigrants to Canada do not want to learn about Indigenous people: they want to *be* indigenous, to belong here without question, not to have to deal with the most problematic form of appropriation, that of the land (Fee 24; cf. Coleman). Despite mainstream Canadians' resistance to facing the fact that much of their power and privilege is based on this founding act of theft, land claims are still in the courts because Indigenous land claims have merit, although they are constantly being denied or obscured by a combination of cultural appropriation and the refusal to listen to Indigenous voices.

Morningside

Keeshig-Tobias was given space on the influential CBC radio show *Morningside*, along with the host, Peter Gzowski; Joyce Zemans, head of the Canada Council; authors Neil Bissoondath, Heather Robertson, and Rudy Wiebe; Michael Bliss, a historian; and Patricia Smart, a literature professor. Keeshig-Tobias said, "I don't think that things like cultural appropriation can be legislated and I'd be loath to do that. I think what has to happen is a real awareness, a waking up of *privileged*, to date *privileged* artists" (*Morningside* 35). After a long discussion in which Bissoondath reviewed his ideas, she finally declared, "your imagination comes right up to my nose, and if you try to get inside my head then I have the right to push back" (46); she described fiction about the cultural Other as "trying to crawl inside someone's consciousness before they have even vacated their physical bodies" (48). At that moment, she turned around Bissoondath's metaphor of characters freely entering his mind unbidden: she described it as a kind of violent intrusion, even a kind of vampirism. This is the Indigenous experience of the "wannabe," someone who wants to be a conduit for exotic knowledge, someone who wants to be Indigenous magically—or to channel Indigeneity—without any of the pain or learning. This explains one of Keeshig-Tobias's article titles, "The Magic of Others." Over and over again, Indigenous writers pointed out that what they needed was political solidarity and support, not to be spoken for but to be heard; however, their words were repeatedly seen as exclusionary along racial lines. In 1990, Keeshig-Tobias wrote that, "as Ms. [Maria] Campbell said on CBC Radio's Morningside, 'If you want to write our stories, then be prepared to live with us.' And not just for a few months.... Be there with the Lubicon, the Innu. Be there with the Teme-Augama Anishnabai on the Red Squirrel Road. The Saugeen Ojibway. If you want these stories, fight for them. I dare you" ("Stop Stealing" A7).

Minority writers rarely make the move of speaking for others in favour of trying to get stories about their own misunderstood and stereotyped cultures into the public eye. Heather Robertson walked directly into this difference when she said, "What I think would be much more creative and interesting is if Lenore had a whack at writing as Heather Robertson, in my voice, as a white, middle-aged woman. I think that would be fascinating"; Keeshig-Tobias responded, "I don't" (*Morningside* 42). And why would it be fascinating for Keeshig-Tobias to do what practically everything in the environment off the reserves presses her to do—that is, to assimilate? Notice, however, that Robertson assumes it is more creative to write about someone from a culture other than one's own. Members of minority groups who write about their own situation are seen as inherently unoriginal and over-political in this liberal model of creativity, and thus their writing is judged as qualitatively inferior. And, as Sneja Gunew has discussed, those minority writers who cannot be read as simply "representing" their own presumed homogeneous cultures are seen as stepping out of line in their violation of the expectation of the dominant culture of a realist narrative of Otherness (57–60).

Keeshig-Tobias sees appropriative writers as imposing just one more form of social control: "for how many more decades are we going to have Indian agents and missionaries speaking for native people?... and how many times are we going to become the mission of some white-Canadian writers?" (*Morningside* 41). She notes that there is a void in which Indigenous stories might have been expected to exist, and points out that writers don't think to ask about "why the void exists in the first place and I'll tell you why it exists. It exists because this country, this place called Canada, outlawed native cultures. *Outlawed* the ceremonies. *Outlawed* the dances. *Outlawed* the clothes. *Outlawed* the languages. And with that the stories. That's why those voices are not there" (*Morningside* 41).

She also raised the issue of protocol around Indigenous stories: "You know, in our culture, people own stories. Individuals own stories. Families own stories. Tribes own stories. Nations own stories. And there is a protocol if you want to tell those stories: you go to the storyteller. And if you don't and you start telling those stories, then you are *stealing*" (*Morningside* 42). Michael Bliss argued that "she is trying to create a property right in the stories and a property right in cultures in which you would sue people for doing that and, would you . . ."; she interrupted to assert, "Well, it happens all the time. Isn't that what copyright is all about?" (*Morningside* 42). Her attempt to discuss the idea of an Indigenous copyright did not get her anywhere. But the year after she failed to convince Bliss, and possibly others on this panel of eminent Canadians, the UN passed a declaration "that the intellectual property of Indigenous peoples is theirs to own and control" (Nason 252; cf. Brown).

Things were changing, however slowly. Certainly, the trickster was overdetermined in this process. Marie Annharte Baker opens up some of these uncomfortable issues when she points out that, "[i]f the trickster is determined to be a multiple personality (not just half fool, half hero), we are talking corporate being, generic brand Trickster. McDonald's clown is not simply enticing us in to a hamburger parlour, we are incorporated into a global disaster. Because it is so difficult to define the Trickster (some even say it is the Whiteman), we always need to define the moment of the Trickster. Then sometimes we don't know the presence of the Trickster unless we trip up and over our very limited human undertakings" (48). To define the moment of the trickster is to consider the trickster not as an icon— something to be "spotted" like a rare bird—but as part of a historical process of rearranging social relations, a true transformation. The trickster increased Indigenous power, and this explains some of the backlash of the appropriation debate. And, although the debate about appropriation included many more voices than Indigenous ones,[12] theirs were prominent. The debate, however painful, opened up access to grants and legitimacy that enabled Indigenous artists to do their work, work designed to provide Indigenous people with a sense of cultural identity, to provide material for school and university curricula, and to explain Indigenous peoples to other Canadian communities. The willingness of Keeshig-Tobias and many others to face hostile questions, reiterate their points, hold meetings, run magazines, publish press releases, talk to reporters, and write poems, articles, plays, and novels created an alternative to the assumption that there was only one way to be Canadian—one defined by the mainstream—and that they and other minorities would have to assimilate to it or forever remain Other. The founders of the Committee to Re-establish the Trickster and those who supported them can look back on the transformation they worked at with pride— although they might just say that the trickster made them do it.

Acknowledgements

I would like to thank Deanna Reder for inviting me to write this paper, and the Writers' Union of Canada, Renate Eigenbrod, Daniel David Moses, and especially Lenore Keeshig-Tobias for helping me with access to materials and information related to the appropriation debate, including *The Magazine to Re-establish the Trickster*. SSHRC provided a grant that allowed me and Sneja Gunew to interview several of the writers closely connected to the debate. Susan Crean, President of TWUC during much of the debate, helpfully commented on a version of part of this paper that I gave in 1993 as "Free Speech or Prison House: The Debate about Cultural Appropriation in Canada," at the conference "Post-Colonialism: Audiences and Constituencies" in Edmonton. Lally Grauer told me about the Taylor reference which starts the essay.

Notes

1   Perhaps the critics are to be forgiven, because, for a while, everyone who was anyone wrote at least one trickster story, play, or poem. Here is a sampling: Beth
Brant published a lesbian Coyote story in *Mohawk Trail* (1985); King's trickster
story, "One Good Story, That One" appeared in 1988, and "The One about Coyote Going West" in 1989; Jeannette Armstrong contributed an ecologically focused
Coyote story to King's *All My Relations* (1990); Lee Maracle used Raven as a muse
in "Native Myths: Trickster Alive and Crowing" (1990), in *Ravensong* (1993), and
elsewhere; Moses produced a play, *Coyote City*, in 1990; Keeshig-Tobias wrote a
long poem, "Running on the West Wind," published in 1992; and Marie Annharte
Baker's *Coyote Columbus Café* (1994), illustrated by Rebecca Belmore, featured a
coyotrix with coyotisma.

2   The founding of the Committee to Re-establish the Trickster is not originary, but
provides a useful moment to anchor the discussion. See Allan Ryan for a more
comprehensive trickster reading list.

3   To be represented in a canon is not the same thing as having equitable access to
cultural capital, that is, to an education that leads to social, political, or economic
power (cf. Guillory). New writing was showcased in *The Magazine to Re-establish the
Trickster* (1988–89), edited by Keeshig-Tobias. As well, Alootook Ipellie edited
Kivioq: Inuit Fiction Magazine, associated with the Baffin Writers' Project (1990)
and named after an Inuit trickster figure, while *Gatherings* was founded in 1990
at the En'owkin Centre in Penticton, BC. In 1991, Moses, with Terry Goldie,
compiled *An Anthology of Canadian Native Literature in English,* which became the
first university teaching anthology.

4   In 1986, Armstrong became Director of the En'owkin Centre with a closely related
mandate: it is "an Indigenous cultural, educational, ecological and creative arts
organization ... taking a lead role in the development and implementation of
Indigenous knowledge systems, both at the community and international levels"
(En'owkin Centre).

5   The House of Anansi, founded in 1967 by Dennis Lee and Dave Godfrey to construct and speak to a Canadian nationalist audience, is named after a West African
trickster, but this borrowed trickster had none of the traditional cultural or ethnic links of the Indigenous ones. Non-settler writers turned to traditional mythic
creatures as characters and inspiration, too. For example, Hiromi Goto's use of
the tengu in *Chorus of Mushrooms* (1994) and the kappa in *The Kappa Child* (2001),
and Larissa Lai's fox in *When Fox Is a Thousand* (1995), assert a connection to
ancestral culture in the face of an assimilating white settler Canadianness. Ironically, this singular Canadianness was in part constructed in publications from
the House of Anansi, such as Northrop Frye's *The Bush Garden: Essays on the Canadian Imagination* (1971) and Margaret Atwood's *Survival: A Thematic Guide to
Canadian Literature* (1972).

6   See Christine St. Peter's two articles, "'Woman's Truth' and the Native Tradition:
Anne Cameron's *Daughters of Copper Woman*" (*Feminist Studies* 15:3, 1989), and "Fem-
inist Afterwords: Revisiting Copper Woman" (in *Undisciplined Women: Tradition and
Culture in Canada,* 1997); see also Jonathan Dewar's "From Copper Woman to Grey
Owl to the alterNative Warrior: Exploring Voice and the Need to Connect" (in
(Ad)dressing Our Words: Aboriginal Perspectives on Aboriginal Literatures, 2001).

7 Keeshig-Tobias was the only non-white member of the first ad hoc committee to discuss issues of racism in publishing by the TWUC, formed in 1988 (Godfrey). She was the first chair of the Racial Minority Writers' Committee, founded in 1990. See Fee's "Who Can Write as Other" for discussion of the similar debate in New Zealand/Aotearoa around Keri Hulme's *the bone people*.

8 It took TWUC a decade to process some of the issues raised by the Committee: "To ensure that the Union itself would be neither exclusionary nor negligent about the needs of writers outside the mainstream, the Union formed the Social Justice Task Force and adopted the report that grew out of its discussions in 1998" (Moore).

9 Note that the Writers Guild of Canada is not the Writers' Union of Canada, which is always referred to here as TWUC.

10 Bissoondath, a novelist and short story writer, wrote *Selling Illusions: The Cult of Multiculturalism in Canada* (1994), which gives a good outline of his ideas.

11 Gerson and Strong-Boag, editors of Johnson's work, suggest that this somewhat sensational title might have been supplied by the newspaper (323), and, of course, this might also have been the case with the Keeshig-Tobias piece.

12 Marlene NourbeSe Philip, for example, spoke and wrote extensively on the issue, and was severely criticized for protests around minority representation at the 54th PEN Congress held in 1989 in Toronto (cf. NourbeSe Philip).

Works Cited

Armstrong, Jeannette. "This Is a Story." In *All My Relations: An Anthology of Contemporary Canadian Native Fiction.* Ed. Thomas King. Toronto: McClelland and Stewart, 1990. 129–35.

———. *Slash.* Penticton, BC: Theytus, 1985.

Baker, Marie Annharte. "An Old Indian Trick Is to Laugh." *Canadian Theatre Review* 68 (1991): 48–9.

———. *Coyote Columbus Café.* Winnipeg: Moonprint, 1994.

Bissoondath, Neil. "'I'm Just a Writer'—That's the Voice That Matters." *Globe and Mail* (Toronto), 18 April 1991. C1.

———. *Selling Illusions: The Cult of Multiculturalism in Canada.* Toronto: Penguin, 1994; rev. and updated, 2002.

Bourdieu, Pierre, and Loïc J.D. Wacquant. *An Invitation to Reflexive Sociology.* Chicago: U of Chicago P, 1992.

Brant, Beth. "Coyote Learns a New Trick." In *Mohawk Trail.* Ithaca, NY: Firebrand, 1985. 31–5.

Brown, Michael F. *Who Owns Native Culture?* Cambridge: Harvard UP, 2003.

Cameron, Anne. *Daughters of Copper Woman.* 1981. New ed. Madeira Park, BC: Harbour, 2002.

———. "The Operative Principle Is Trust." In *Language in Her Eye: Writing and Gender.* Ed. Libby Scheier, Sarah Sheard, and Eleanor Wachtel. Toronto: Coach House, 1990. 63–71.

Canada Council. *Recommendations of the Advisory Committee to the Canada Council for Racial Equality in the Arts and the Response of the Canada Council.* January 1992.

Coleman, Daniel. *White Civility: The Literary Project of English Canada.* Toronto: U of Toronto P, 2006.

Emberley, Julia V. *Defamiliarizing the Aboriginal: Cultural Practices and Decolonization in Canada.* Toronto: U of Toronto P, 2007.

En'owkin Centre (Penticton, BC). <http://www.enowkincentre.ca/>. Original website accessed 2 January 2008.

Fee, Margery. "Romantic Nationalism and the Image of Native People in Contemporary English-Canadian Literature." In *The Native in Literature: Canadian and Comparative Perspectives.* Ed. Thomas King, Cheryl Calver, and Helen Hoy. Toronto: ECW, 1987. 15–33.

———. "Who Can Write as Other?" In *The Post-Colonial Studies Reader.* Ed. Bill Ashcroft, Gareth Griffiths, and Helen Tiffin. London: Routledge, 1995. 242–5.

Findley, Timothy. "When You Write about This Country." Excerpt from the 1992 Margaret Laurence Memorial Lecture, sponsored by the Writers' Development Trust and the Writers' Union of Canada. Delivered at the National Library of Canada, Ottawa, 5 June 1992. *Canadian Forum*, September 1992: 8–14.

———. Letter to the Editor. *Globe and Mail* (Toronto), 28 March 1992. D7.

Francis, Daniel. *The Imaginary Indian: The Image of the Indian in Canadian Culture.* Vancouver: Arsenal Pulp, 1992.

Gagnon, Monika Kin, and Scott Toguri McFarlane. "The Capacity of Cultural Difference." 22–23 April 2003. Department of Canadian Heritage. <http://www.pch.gc.ca/special/dcforum/info-bg/05_e.cfm>. Accessed 2 January 2008.

Godfrey, Stephen. "Minority Writers to Raise Their Voices." *Globe and Mail* (Toronto), 23 May 1992. C1.

Goldie, Terry. *Fear and Temptation: The Image of the Indigene in Canadian, Australian and New Zealand Literatures.* Montreal: McGill-Queen's UP, 1989.

Groening, Laura Smyth. *Listening to Old Woman Speak: Natives and alterNatives in Canadian Literature.* Montreal: McGill-Queen's UP, 2004.

Guillory, John. *Cultural Capital: The Problem of Literary Canon Formation.* Chicago: U of Chicago P, 1993.

Gunew, Sneja. *Framing Marginality: Multicultural Literary Studies.* Melbourne: Melbourne UP, 1994.

Highway, Tomson. *The Rez Sisters.* Saskatoon: Fifth House, 1988.

Hurst, Lynda. "Can(not!)lit." *Toronto Star*, 11 April 1992. H1, H11.

Hutchinson, Allan. "Giving Smaller Voices a Chance to Be Heard." *Globe and Mail* (Toronto), 14 April 1992. A16.

Johnson, E. Pauline (Tekahionwake). "A Strong Race Opinion: On the Indian Girl in Modern Fiction." In *Collected Poems and Selected Prose*. Ed. Carole Gerson and Veronica Strong-Boag. Toronto: U of Toronto P, 2002. 177–83.

Keeshig-Tobias, Lenore. "Lenore Keeshig-Tobias." Interview with Harmut Lutz. In *Contemporary Challenges: Conversations with Canadian Native Authors*. Ed. Harmut Lutz. Saskatoon: Fifth House, 1991. 79–88.

———. "The Magic of Others." In *Language in Her Eye: Writing and Gender*. Eds. Libby Scheier, Sarah Sheard, and Eleanor Wachtel. Toronto: Coach House, 1990. 173–7.

———. "Running on the West Wind." In *An Anthology of Canadian Native Literature in English*. Ed. Daniel David Moses and Terry Goldie. Toronto: Oxford UP, 1992. 238–41.

———. "Stop Stealing Native Stories." *Globe and Mail* (Toronto), 26 January 1990. A7.

The Magazine to Re-establish the Trickster 1.2 (1989).

Maracle, Lee. "Native Myths: Trickster Alive and Crowing." In *Language in Her Eye: Writing and Gender*. Ed. Libby Scheier, Sarah Sheard, and Eleanor Wachtel. Toronto: Coach House, 1990. 182–7.

Monkman, Leslie. *Native Heritage: Images of the Indian in English-Canadian Literature*. Toronto: U of Toronto P, 1981.

Moore, Christopher. "The Writers' Union of Canada, 1973–2007." <http://www.writersunion.ca/au_history.asp>. Accessed 23 December 2007.

Morningside (CBC Radio). Transcript of broadcast. 1 April 1992. "The Public Face of the Cultural Appropriation Debate: Who Speaks for Whom?" *Textual Studies in Canada* 2 (1992): 30–48.

Moses, Daniel David. *Coyote City*. Stratford, ON: Williams-Wallace, 1990.

———. "The Trickster's Laugh: My Meeting with Tomson and Lenore." *American Indian Quarterly* 28:1/2 (2004): 107–11.

———. "Whose Voice Is It, Anyway?: A Symposium on Who Should Be Speaking for Whom." *Books in Canada*. January–February 1991. 15.

Moses, Daniel David, and Terry Goldie, eds. *An Anthology of Canadian Native Literature in English*. Toronto: Oxford UP, 1992.

Nason, James D. "Native American Intellectual Property Rights: Issues in the Control of Esoteric Knowledge." In *Borrowed Power: Essays on Cultural Appropriation*. Ed. Bruce Ziff and Pratima V. Rao. New Brunswick, NJ: Rutgers UP, 1997. 237–54.

Niedzwiecki, Thaba. "Print Politics: Conflict and Community Building at Toronto Women's Press." MA Thesis, U of Guelph, 1997.

NourbeSe Philip, Marlene. *Frontiers: Selected Essays and Writings on Racism and Culture, 1984–1992*. Stratford, ON: Mercury, 1992.

Paris, Erna. "Letter to the Thought Police." *Globe and Mail* (Toronto), 31 March 1992. A.16.

Pels, Peter. "The Trickster's Dilemma: Ethics and the Technologies of the Anthropological Self." *Audit Cultures: Anthropological Studies in Accountability, Ethics, and the Academy.* Ed. Marilyn Strathern. London: Routledge, 2000. 135–72.

Radin, Paul. *The Trickster: A Study in American Indian Mythology. With Commentaries by Karl Kerényi and C.G. Jung.* London: Routledge and Kegan Paul, 1956.

Ryan, Allan J. *The Trickster Shift: Humour and Irony in Contemporary Native Art.* Vancouver: U of British Columbia P, 1999.

Sherman, Jason. "Making a Bid to Reclaim the Native Voice in Literature." *Toronto Star*, 25 March 1989 [SA2 edition]. M8.

Simon, Lorne. "Freedom of Expression?: Are Native Voices Being Silenced in the Name of Artistic Freedom?" (Final report on the forum "Telling Our Own Story: Appropriation and Indigenous Writers and Performing Artists.") *Canadian Forum* (July/August 1993): 46–7.

Tator, Carol, and Frances Henry. "The Role and Practice of Racialized Discourse in Culture and Cultural Production." *Journal of Canadian Studies* 35:3 (2000): 1–14. <http://findarticles.com/p/articles/mi_qa3683/is_200010/ai_n8912544/pg_1>. Accessed 2 January 2008.

Taylor, Drew Hayden. "Academia Mania." In *Funny, You Don't Look Like One: Observations from a Blue-Eyed Ojibway.* Penticton, BC: Theytus, 1996. 84–8.

"Volksgeist." *Dictionary of the History of Ideas.* <http://etext.virginia.edu/cgi-local/DHI/dhiana.cgi?id=dv4–66>. Accessed 5 February 2008.

Williams, Kenneth. "Cultural Appropriation and Aboriginal Literature." Aboriginal Multi-Media Society. *Windspeaker.* Classroom Edition, Issue #3. <http://www.ammsa.com/classroom/CLASS3appropriation.html>. Accessed 19 May 2008.

LINDA MORRA

The Anti-Trickster in the Work of Sheila Watson, Mordecai Richler, and Gail Anderson-Dargatz

In this chapter, I wish to consider three works by non-Native writers, specifically those by Sheila Watson, Mordecai Richler, and Gail Anderson-Dargatz, who have shown themselves to be fascinated by specific incarnations of Indigenous tricksters. In so doing, I would like to examine some of the secondary criticism that has proliferated around their respective literary works, particularly the kind of attention that has been paid to their use of the trickster, as I also tentatively suggest some other possible critical avenues. When I began to recognize the sheer number of authors who have employed the trickster within the evolving corpus referred to as "Canadian literature"— or, to put it in terms set by Daniel David Moses, when I rather pathetically engaged in the game of "Spot the Trickster"—I began to wonder not only *why* these writers had made use of that figure, but also how faithful they remained to the original trickster's characteristics and how closely allied their narratives were with the tales from which they had borrowed. I also wanted to know if I might track some changes temporally in terms of their respective approaches—why I finally selected Watson, Richler, and Anderson-Dargatz, who were largely writing in different decades—and of the criticism that has evolved in response.

Part of the challenge for me, as a non-Native, Euro-Canadian female academic is that, quite simply, I do not have sufficient nationally specific knowledge about each of the Indigenous trickster figures under scrutiny—Coyote (Nlaka'pamux) and Raven (Haida)—nor about the specific contexts from which they emerged in order to determine the extent to which these writers have drifted from the original tales; future critical engagement, I hope, will be able to redress this lack of information better than I am able to do here. I have read, for example, Robin Bringhurst and Bill Reid's largely disparaged collection of stories, *The Raven Steals the Light* (1984), which informed Richler's own book. It was therefore easy to determine how far Richler drifted from his original text (insofar as one can refer to Bringhurst and Reid's text as an "appropriate source") because there is so little about his use of the Raven that resembles its counterpart; in the case of both Watson and Anderson-Dargatz, it was considerably more difficult. The focus of my discussion below, limited by my lack of authority on the subject, will therefore focus on what the authors seem to be doing with the figures, as I also, at least, call attention to some of the currents in writing and in literary criticism.

Although it would be a form of considerable hypocrisy on my part to impugn the writers whom I have chosen for their employment of the trickster when I am not altogether familiar with the Indigenous epistemologies from which these figures arise, and although there is no need to re-enter the "appropriation debate" of the 1980s, since so much has been said on the subject, I would still like to draw attention to what James (Sakej) Youngblood Henderson refers to as "the anti-trickster" for the purposes of my discussion:

> Among colonized peoples, the cognitive legacy of colonization is labelled "Eurocentrism." Among some Indigenous peoples, Eurocentrism is known as the twin of the trickster or imitator, or the "anti-trickster." Similar to the trickster who emphasizes Aboriginal thought and dramatizes human behaviour in a world of flux, the "anti-trickster" appears in many guises and is the essence of paradoxical transformation. The "anti-trickster" presents a cognitive force of artificial European thought, a differentiated consciousness, ever changing in its creativity to justify the oppression and domination of contemporary Indigenous peoples and their spiritual guardians. (58)

Henderson here highlights how the "anti-trickster" may take on similarities or likenesses to its original Indigenous counterpart, but ultimately embodies Eurocentric ideas. As Homi Bhabha observes of colonized subjects who "mimic" their colonizers, the colonizing subjects and the objects they render are, in this instance, the "*almost the same, but not quite*" (86) in a manner that belies that "differentiated consciousness." So, in the case of Richler, Watson, and Anderson-Dargatz, it is not the colonized who mimic, but rather the colonizers; as Youngblood would suggest, these three authors are thus implicated in the process of creating anti-tricksters.

When I began to consider the figure of the "anti-trickster" as it appears in non-Native Canadian writing, I also could not help but be reminded of the third part of *Monkey Beach*, titled "In Search of the Elusive Sasquatch," in which Eden Robinson makes one of the only two explicit references to the trickster figure to appear in the novel:

> Weegit the raven has mellowed in his old age. He's still a confirmed bache-lor, but he's not the womanizer he once was. Plying [sic] the stock market—instead of spending his time being a trickster—has paid off and he has a comfortable condo downtown. He plays up the angle about creating the world and humans, conveniently forgetting that he did it out of boredom. Yes, he admits, he did steal the sun and the moon, but he insists he did it to bring light to humankind, even though he did it so it would be easier for him to find food. After doing some spin control on the crazy pranks of his youth, he's become respectable. As he sips his low-fat mocha and reads yet another san-itized version of his earlier exploits, only his small, sly smile reveals how much he enjoys pulling the wool over everyone's eyes. (295–6)

I take this passage to be an indictment of mainstream consumer culture's appropriative tendencies, although there are likely other interpretive possi-bilities (such as, for example, the consequences of assimilation, even as the passage also playfully shows how Weegit has not "lost" many of his original traits, but uses different means for somewhat different ends). It struck me that Weegit might be seen as an emblem of Western culture, or, at least, a figure that may be seen as less definitive of Indigenous nationalities when removed from appropriate contexts and more in the service of persistent Western col-onizing processes. By placing this reference at the beginning of a chapter that gestures towards the search for the "Sasquatch," a Western term for the Haisla B'gwus, I think Robinson is suggesting the complicity of a Western audience in pursuit of Indigenous mythology that is not only elusive for that audience, but also altered as the object of the prying, intrusive gaze (he becomes "Sasquatch" rather than "B'gwus") by the very perceptual frame-works used.[1] When used by non-Native writers, the sacred trickster (in what-ever incarnation it appears) becomes far removed from its original function—in Robinson's novel, for example, even participating in the read-ing of "sanitized" versions of his exploits that are more digestible or palatable to an undiscerning yet demanding public.

For me, Robinson's novel offers an instance of how the trickster, its prevalence in mainstream Canada by the 1980s at once a "hermeneutic fad" and a register of "the need to open up a space for Indigenous cultural pro-duction," might be seen to have been co-opted by non-Natives for their own purposes (Fee 59)—these purposes, in turn, may become a reiteration of col-onizing tendencies or a tool for further colonization. Cultural appropriation, in these terms, thus continues to be "the strategy by which the dominant imperial power incorporates as its own the territory or culture that it surveys and invades" (Ashcroft, Griffiths, and Tiffin 19). Specifically, as I will discuss in this paper, the trickster as depicted in the works of such writers as Watson, Richler, and Anderson-Dargatz thus demonstrates the crux of ethical conflicts in which questions come into play about what writers may depict, how such depictions are affected by the contexts from which one writes and for whom one is writing, and how to approach the resulting works critically and responsibly.

Sheila Watson: Indigeneity vs. Cosmopolitanism

Sheila Watson's novel *The Double Hook* (1959) is considered by critics to be the quintessential modernist novel in terms of technique (cf., for example, Bowering and Willmott), especially for her insistence upon the removal of the omniscient narrator. The action of the novel takes place in a small community, set in Cariboo country, the interior of British Columbia, over which the figure of Coyote presides and to which he is instrumental. His "omnipresence" is suggested by the description of the community's locale "[i]n the folds of the hills/under Coyote's eye" (11). As many critics have noted, his likeness to Judeo-Christianity's God is also evidenced in a number of the assertions that characters make; so one character, William, asserts that "I don't know about your God [...] Your god sounds only a step from the Indian's Coyote" (66). For this novel, Watson made three key aesthetic decisions that are central to the purposes of my discussion. The first relates to the authorial voice—or lack thereof—to which I have already alluded. She was deliberate in her decision to "get rid of reportage, the condescension of omniscience" that is invoked by an intrusive narrative voice (Untitled interview, 354). About a decade later, also in an interview, she declared that "I had to get the authorial voice out of the novel for it to say what I wanted it to say. I didn't want a voice talking about something. I wanted voices" ("It's What You Say" 158). And yet again, in another interview, she recalled that she could "hear the voices beginning" that would inform the novel, in a manner that recalls what Margery Fee observes earlier in this collection as a "German Romantic nationalist notion" (67; cf. also "What I'm Going to Do" 183). As Fee notes, this model of thinking "requires one to insert oneself into the position of the Other without really thinking about it, because, after all, one is just a conduit. To think about it is to fake something that should happen at a spiritual rather than a rational level" (67). This belief is informed by the "ideology of the free liberal imagination" (68), which implies that the aesthetic impulse is separate from political and economic ones.

Watson's disengagement from the authorial voice, her removal of an omniscient narrator, I believe, is related to a second aesthetic decision—the deliberate erasure of any identity markers in relation to ethnicity or Indigenousness. In an interview, she noted that she was preoccupied by "the problem of an indigenous population which had lost or was losing its own mythic structure, which had had its images destroyed, its myths interpreted for it by various missionary societies and later by anthropologists—a group intermarried or intermingled with people of other beliefs" ("It's What You Say" 159). She argued that, ultimately, she chose to do so because she "didn't want it to be an ethnic novel—not a novel about Indians or any other deprived group, but rather a novel about a number of people who had no ability to communicate because they had found little to replace the myths and rituals which might have bound them together" ("It's What you Say" 159). The lack of ethnic or Indigenous identity markers and the use of such abstract language underscore a community that has problems engaging in meaningful relationships and that suffers from isolation (cf. Morris 2002, 55–6) and from a sense of dislocation. In terms of more recent scholarship, Anca Raluca Radu argues that this "absence" suggests that "ethnicity has become immaterial, while human relationships have become central": "In this way," she adds, "the colonial binarism of the oppressor and the oppressed is dismantled, and the creative and resurrecting potential of hybridity underlined" (126). This kind of celebratory discourse, which I will take up again when examining the work of Richler, sidesteps some fundamental issues in relation to accountability or responsibility to Indigenous nations. At the very least, I might observe now that issues of land ownership are evaded because causation or the colonization process are not the focus of the novel but rather the dislocation engendered by that process.

The removal of the omniscient narrator and of references to ethnicity and Indigenousness means that Coyote's representation is meant largely to stand apart from the other characters' interpretive framework, although they also somewhat contribute to how he is represented within the parameters of the book; yet, when he speaks, it is clear that he stands very much within a tradition that has less to do with the Nlaka'pamux tales from which he emerges than with a Judeo-Christian tradition (cf. Mitchell 64). When he speaks and even when many of the characters speak, the discourse employed recalls biblical patterns of expression. And this feature is the third aesthetic decision Watson makes that many critics have elsewhere noted—this "recognition" has much to do with my and other critics' academic training, which, until recently, largely excluded Indigenous literatures (a "catch-all" phrase that, as Jennifer Kelly notes in this volume, demonstrates a political bias), as it also does with

Watson's own literary background and intimacy with Catholicism. In an interview with Watson, for example, Daphne Marlatt points out that Watson gives Coyote at least one speech "that is Christian. It comes out of Biblical reference, Christian liturgy" (354), an idea with which Watson concurs: "There are many references to the Old Testament—expressions of fear" (354). And so many critics have made similar observations. John Watt Lennox, for example, sees Coyote as part of a "trinity" with Mrs. Potter and Kip, and as an all-seeing figure, one who "suggests a God or power of great strength" (70). Although Coyote is "initially associated with Old Testament power of fear and vengeance," he is, for Lennox, associated with "the New Testament god of reconciliation" after Lenchen's baby is born (72). Leslie Monkman suggests that Coyote stood in "Satanic opposition to Old Testament Jehovah" (64). And Beverly Mitchell argues that he has "his prototype in the Old Testament": "Many of his speeches are either explicit or implicit allusions to words spoken by God to the Chosen People and can be identified in the Scriptures" (67).

Mitchell also recognizes the inadequacy of contemporary approaches in terms of critiquing literature (specifically, she identified Canadian and "other" literatures), although she returns to Northrop Frye's theories related to mythopoeia and to his "The Theory of Myths" (63) to analyze Watson's novel. She also quite uniquely locates Coyote in the "legends of the Okanagan, Thompson [Nlaka'pamux], and Shuswap tribes" (only a handful of critics, including Barbara Godard, identify so particularly the origins of the Coyote to which Watson refers). Although her source for these narratives is the more dubious *Indian Legends of Canada* (1960) by Ella Clark, she at least suggests in more specific terms from which narratives this Coyote figure arises (64).

Godard, another critic who identifies Coyote's origins within Thompson [Nlaka'pamux] tales, suggests that his misapprehension by characters in the novel is related to their increasing distance from their own cultural origins:

> One level of narrative and allusions refers to the mythological trickster god, Coyote, of the Thompson Indian tribe of which Kip is a member and the Potter family are descendants. [...] Although Watson has made use of the belief that Coyote is a mediating god, a helper to the Old Man, to structure her narrative and to show the movement within the community to greater wisdom, she allows only fragments of this myth to be retained by the community. No meaningful pattern of culture exists. (175–6)

Godard seems to imply here that the varying interactions with Coyote are related to the "fragments of this myth retained by the community." In part, it is so—Watson surely means to allude to an Indigenous culture that is being "badly translated" to characters who inhabit this community and who have little sense of Coyote. Even those characters who, as Glenn Willmott puts it, are "apparently but certainly Native character[s]"—his own tentativeness related to Watson's removal of traces of ethnicity and Indigenousness—seem to be uncertain about Coyote, certainly also a result of the process of assimilation that those imputed to be Indigenous in the novel would have experienced (111).

But I must note that Watson is part of that culture that misapprehends Coyote, which is "badly translated" not just for her characters, but also for her. The ambiguity she deliberately creates, the removal of the authorial voice, the lack of specificity about characters' ethnicity or Indigenousness, the inability of the said characters to connect with each other because of the cultural distance from their own and others' mythologies, also creates ambiguity for critics and further contributes to the loss of Indigenous narratives and to the mystification of a trickster figure that largely represents how a non-Native audience responds to the said figure.[2] So whose trickster figure is this? Ultimately, in terms of both depiction and critical interpretation, Watson's Coyote might be characterized as the "anti-trickster," the figure who is "a cognitive legacy of colonization," an expression of Christian rather than any specific Indigenous mythology.

Mordecai Richler: Multiculturalism

During Canada's changing mid-twentieth century socio-political and cultural climate, one that valorized multiculturalism and responded to the country's changing demographics (the last racial and ethnic barriers to Canadian immigration, for example, were lifted in 1967), Mordecai Richler wrote *Solomon Gursky Was Here* (1989). In part, Richler's novel constitutes a part of a larger ethnic and racial protest that challenged older policies of assimilation and that demanded new models of national citizenship. In response, he invites a rereading of the dominant historical record that includes revisionist accounts of the Franklin expedition; the novel thus seeks to redress the problems engendered by a dominant Anglo-Canadian vision of the country, which is primarily embodied through the narrator Moses Berger's attempts to forge protagonist Solomon Gursky's biography. In so doing, Moses—and Richler through Moses—demonstrates how history has been written to the exclusion of those who did not previously fit the exclusively constructed English- or French-Canadian viewpoint. So, countering such Anglo-Canadian prevailing historical records and modes of thought, Moses argues that Canada's soul might actually be found in "thousands of bars like [The Caboose] that knit the country together" rather than in "Batoche or the Plains of Abraham or Fort Walsh or Charlottetown or Parliament Hill" (66); in other words, Canadian identity revolves around working-class minorities, not "historic defeats, military battles or the parliamentary process" that are governed by a select few (Brydon 104). At the same time, Richler shows how those who were omitted, such as Solomon, often participated in the historical record in very meaningful ways. His novel is about the recovery of lost narratives—in Solomon's case, saving some Jews from Hitler's ravages, and, in Ephraim's case, surviving the Franklin expedition and intermingling with the Inuit who teach him how to survive.

For the above purposes, Richler makes explicit use of the Haida's Raven, informed by his reading of Bringhurst and Reid's *The Raven Steals the Light.* This figure appears throughout the novel in relation to the protagonists, Ephraim and Solomon, who, by virtue of their connection to Raven, are to be regarded with greater respect, who are associated with Richler's evolving moral code, and who are thus meant to operate as resistant to existing hegemonic political and social structures. In using Raven to voice his concerns about political historical accounts and social values, he seems to suggest that there is a moral authority that in part emerges from Indigenous culture— except that, within the confines of the novel, Raven is not associated with the Haida, but both with the Inuit and with the Jewish figures, Ephraim and Solomon. Such apparently laudatory mingling appears at other moments throughout the novel, one key example being when Ephraim introduces Jewish customs and practices to the Inuit, as they in turn teach him about survival in the Arctic (310–11).

Criticism of the 1990s celebrated "hybridity," as Richard Todd's and Diana Brydon's responses to the novel indicate: Todd appreciates how various cultural traditions "combine and intermingle to place legitimacy and bastardy in a delicate balance" (318), while Brydon celebrates Richler's cultural intermingling as an ideal and as an attempt to subvert prevalent notions of cultural purity.[3] Richler does seem quite consistently to mock those characters who refuse any "mixing" with other races or cultures—the naïvely immovable Bert Smith, the racist Professor Hardy, and the discriminatory Stu MacIntyre who claims that "your people are such confirmed city-dwellers, and would usurp positions that could be filled by the native-born, or immigrants from the Mother Country, that we simply cannot open the flood-gates" (366). These figures represent Canada's anti-Semitic immigration policy of the period and its attitudes towards those who are considered "native born." Initially, then, it seems that Richler's purpose is less suspect than that of other mainstream writers; he is not, after all, part of mainstream Anglo-Canada and, it may be argued, Raven seems to occupy a role within Richler's work that conforms with its generalized purpose—a boundary-breaker, a survivor whose sense of mischief and sexual voraciousness are evidenced within the novel by the various antics in which its assigned progenitors, Solomon and Ephraim, engage.

The problem with this celebration of hybridity is that, if Richler is endeavouring to recover lost narratives, he subsumes Indigenous narratives that have yet to be fully recovered; we still do not have sufficient information about the original stories in order to be so haphazard with them. I know enough to suggest that the Haida Raven is not so necessarily or explicitly associated with justice and vengeance—as this figure most certainly is throughout the course of Richler's novel. Wherever images of Raven appear, there instances of swift justice follow. One instance includes Hollis's purportedly suicidal hanging, which is linked to having shot Ephraim's raven (5); another occurs at Sir Hyman's (that is, Solomon's) lavish supper, in which blood-filled matzoh is given to his dinner guests, notable anti-Semites (377–8), directly upon the heels of his retelling of "Raven and the First People" (370–1) to Moses. Richler did indeed research the Haida Raven, his knowledge apparently deriving from the decried version of *The Raven Steals the Light* (see "Author's Note" 415), yet he departs considerably even from these versions to use it to serve his own literary purposes.

Whatever one might say about Richler's use of Raven, I think its shortcomings become more apparent in the manner in which he portrays the Inuit, which is far from being either positive or well informed. Ephraim is able to deceive them so successfully and to elicit their servility because of their apparent utter gullibility. While acting in apparently trickster-like fashion by enjoying "women lying with him under caribou skins" (327–8), he issues a set of commandments that suggests an overlapping of Christian and Judaic traditions. In his parodic declaration of the Old Testament God's commandment—"I am Ephraim, the Lord thy God, and thou shalt have no other gods before me. Thou shall not bow down to Marssuk, whose prick I have shrivelled, or to any other gods, you ignorant little fuckers" (327)—he creates an entire "Arctic adherent" who are depicted as sufficiently primitive and naïve as to remain faithful for generations to come (328). Richler has here significantly departed from his earlier novel, *The Incomparable Atuk* (1963), in which, at the very least, one Inuit figure, Ignak, staunchly opposes the "imperialist baubles" that do not compensate for their exploitation.

I would contend that, while it is worthwhile to resist rigid notions of cultural purity that may further perpetuate racism, as both Todd and Brydon suggest and as this novel shows in such figures as MacIntyre and Hardy, Richler's counter-discursive narrative denies the particular vulnerability of Indigenous cultural tales and even reconstitutes notions of "cultural purity" by depicting the Inuit as he does—although it may also be true that very little escapes his satirist's gaze. Also, whereas his mingling of Jewish and Native narratives is clearly the work of the imagination and works to his larger purpose of demonstrating how effective cultural "impurity" may be, he also clearly privileges a Jewish minority; instead, to use Raven in the manner he does is to duplicate the very colonizing processes he attacks within the confines of the novel. In other words, Richler accomplishes much for the Jewish minority, but little for the Inuit and little for the Haida culture and mythology upon which he constructs the framework for the novel's system of justice and retribution. From the point of view of criticism of the 1990s, Richler's use of Raven may be seen as for the greater good and value of "cross-cultural contamination"; from a more recent point of view for the call for greater responsibility to Indigenous narratives, he would not.

Gail Anderson-Dargatz: Regionalism

Of the three novels under scrutiny, Anderson-Dargatz's novel, *The Cure for Death by Lightning*, is the most recently published. Nominated for the Giller Prize in 1996 and winner of the Ethel Wilson Prize for fiction, *The Cure for Death by Lightning* generally received favourable reviews and was even compared to Sheila Watson's *The Double Hook* for its "evocation of small-town, rural British Columbia and its respect for First Nations myths and traditions, particularly those having to do with the enigmatic figure of Coyote" (Rose 112). Anderson-Dargatz focuses upon Turtle Valley, a farming town in British Columbia during the Second World War, and, also like Watson, upon a Nlaka'-pamux region in which Coyote reigns as the primary trickster figure. The narrative is told from the limited perspective of fifteen-year-old Beth Weeks, who recounts the challenges and difficulties of her coming of age in Turtle Valley and whose narrative is thus concerned with her growing sexual awareness; a coming-of-age story, a *Bildungsroman*, there are not only tests involved in her maturation process, but rather real sexual threats to Beth's person from male figures, including her father, from whom her mother utterly fails to protect her.

At the same time, Beth's story is located within a larger framework, divided between an (unidentified, although presumably Salish) Indigenous community and Euro-Canadian settlers; as the title indicates, it explores how much indeed these communities are in need of "cures" for various kinds of illnesses, especially those related to sexual aggression and repression. Herein apparently lies the importance of Coyote to Anderson-Dargatz's novel. Many of the men who suffer from unbridled sexual desires are also related to the Coyote figure and are characterized as being "possessed" by that figure, which comes to be seen as a scapegoat for unrestrained and violent male sexuality. Presented as a hostile and malevolent presence, Coyote is associated with at least three primary figures: Coyote Jack, whose very name suggests his identification and who, as a liminal character, is isolated from both communities because of his lack of self-control; Beth's father, whose war-related traumas are reactivated by his encounter with a bear and induce his subsequent cruel, aggressive, and irrational behaviour; and Filthy Billy, who takes a range of precautions to avoid complete "possession" by Coyote. In spite of the fact that many men have apparently gone off to fight in the Second World War, the sheer number of men who populate the narrative and who exact control over women is daunting and perhaps indicative of the legacies of a patriarchal system that remains intact even when there are few men present.

So, Coyote Jack, who seems to be most allied with the trickster Coyote and who disappears and reappears from the woods that surround the community, speaks of how his sexual impulses overpower him, and how he tries "to stop it," that is, those impulses that make him pursue the women of the community. The manner in which Beth describes him when he attempts to assault her is also surely meant to recall the Coyote trickster figure:

> He looked laughable, a clown. I turned once again towards home and his footsteps crunched behind me. He threw me down in the snow and fumbled with his clothes. Suddenly he got up. He twisted, batted the air, and screamed, and the scream became a howl. His body flitted back and forth between man and coyote, then the coyote dropped on all fours and cowered away from me. He bristled and growled. I stood slowly and clapped my hands, as I would to scare off any wild animal. The coyote turned and trotted off and disappeared in to the bush. (272)

Although Coyote Jack may "look" laughable, the scene is anything but humorous; instead, Anderson-Dargatz seems to use Coyote to suggest a form of "possession" rather than to refer to a Secwépemc tale of sexual licentiousness.

Anca Raluca Radu thus approaches Anderson-Dargatz's novel from a feminist perspective and suggests that both Christian and Native myths are used to respond to that patriarchal system—her narrative "represent[s] a decentralized, female comment on and re-evaluation of two myths that look at the base of western and Native cultures, namely the Christian God and Coyote, the helper of the Old Man" (121). She argues that the novel parodies and deconstructs the "traditional figure of Coyote": "The white appropriation of the myth situates Coyote in the context of cultural transgressing of national and ethnic boundaries" (131). Her tribute to such "transgressing" allows her to espouse a feminist point of view that, as she asserts, in turn permits a critique of the legacies of a patriarchal structure. Thus, as Radu observes, women repress their sexuality, as is figured in Beth's initial hiding of evidence of her own sense of growing maturity—red lipstick and a scrap of red velvet that are concealed at the base of a tree stump whose leaves turn "flagrantly, shamefully red" every autumn. Bertha, the symbolic bearer of the scrap of red velvet, represents the Native community, and is presumably used by Anderson-Dargatz to articulate a point of view that opposes and counterbalances a male-oriented and aggressive one. As a midwife to both the women on the reserve and the white women of the community, she is seemingly a pivotal character who holds a larger community of women together (9). Bertha is the bearer of many of the stories of Coyote that abound; yet Bertha herself, who is the apparent spokesperson for the community, is estranged from and shunned by that community because she lived outside the reserve and was married to a white man.

Beth (whose name suggestively reverberates with Bertha's) learns of the stories of Coyote through Bertha and learns to interpret the events around her through the narratives she has heard. So Radu writes that "Coyote, as an exotic, elusive figure from a western perspective, provides Beth with a perfect surface upon which she can project her trauma. [...] Due to *its mutability and elusiveness, Coyote lends itself to the ambiguous expression of trauma*" (130, italics mine). I might be persuaded that Beth's limited perspective controls how we see and what we come to learn about Coyote—she selects details for the purposes of telling her own story. A demonic figure that not only represents sexual violation, but also allows male figures to be absolved of their sexual aggression and violent misdeeds, Coyote is indeed reshaped within Anderson-Dargatz's novel for entirely new purposes. Yet there is no concession built within the framework of the existing narrative to assist the uninformed reader with stories about Coyote; claims like those that Radu makes about Coyote as an "elusive" and "mutable" figure only exacerbate the problem. Coyote is elusive only because we have much to learn about the actual stories from which he originates—and instead of burdening that figure with other layers of meaning that are of our own invention, we might perhaps open ourselves up to and learn about what the figure means for an Indigenous community (and, yes, I am aware that, in making this kind of assertion, I am flying in the face of the postmodern dismissal of "originary meaning," a dismissal that conveniently allows critics to side-step ethical commitments).

As Gerald Vizenor notes, traditional tricksters will evolve in response to new cultural forms and changes, even those introduced by Western aesthetics. And, as Diana Brydon notes, some cultural mixing may have positive implications by avoiding dependence on "myths of cultural purity or authenticity" and instead "thriv[ing] on an interaction that 'contaminates' without 'homogenizing'" (99)—so, she argues, insistence upon notions of cultural purity will be self-defeating because they reinforce binary conceptions that will engender "continued marginality and an eventual death" (99). Yet aesthetic depictions must at least be driven by an ethical imperative of accountability, by greater familiarity with Indigenous epistemologies. Ultimately, although non-Natives might work co-operatively on their side of the cultural divide to change the terms of appropriative tendencies, the use of tricksters in an unspecific context or in a manner that belies their original purpose contradicts the very resurgence and uses of culturally specific tricksters in the first place—the retelling of narratives meant to allow for the reassertion of agency and for the restoration of Indigenous national identities.

Notes

1   I should add that Robinson, in an interview, also declared that she herself was castigated by her own community for disclosing sacred aspects of Haisla culture in the novel.
2   Glen Deer demarcates himself from these other critics by suggesting that Watson's novel works "*against* rational analysis" (26) and questioning Watson's objectives: "[T]here is a tension here between the epistemological uncertainty that is promoted in the text and the vatic aspirations and authority of the implied author: if the world is resistant to human understanding, then upon what basis can the implied author claim to be speaking authoritatively? Can the human writer speak about epistemological uncertainty from the perspective of an omniscient God? By appropriating the authoritative discourse of the prophet, Watson opens herself to the charge that she is contradicting the message of her own text" (41).
3   And this is precisely the kind of critical temptation to which I also succumb in another article addressing Mordecai Richler's *The Incomparable Atuk*.

Works Cited

Anderson-Dargatz, Gail. *The Cure for Death by Lightning.* Toronto: Alfred A. Knopf, 1996. Rpt. Toronto: Vintage Canada, 1997.
Ashcroft, Bill, Gareth Griffiths, and Helen Tiffin. *Post-Colonial Studies: The Key Concepts.* New York: Routledge, 2000.
Bhabha, Homi. *The Location of Culture.* London: Routledge, 1994.
Bowering, George, ed. *Sheila Watson and* The Double Hook. Ottawa: Golden Press, 1985.

Brydon, Diana. "'The White Inuit Speaks': Contamination as Literary Strategy." In *Past the Last Post*. Ed. Ian Adam and Helen Tiffin. Calgary: U of Calgary P, 1990. 191–203.

Clark, Ella. *Indian Legends of Canada*. Toronto: McClelland and Stewart, 1960.

Deer, Glen. "Miracle, Mystery, and Authority: ReReading *The Double Hook*." *Open Letter* 6:8 (1987): 25–43.

Fee, Margery. "The Trickster Moment, Cultural Appropriation, and the Liberal Imagination in Canada." In *Troubling Tricksters: Revisioning Cultural Approaches*. Ed. Deanna Reder and Linda M. Morra. Waterloo, ON: Wilfrid Laurier UP, 2009. 59–76.

Godard, Barbara. "'Between One Cliché and Another': Language in *The Double Hook*." *Studies in Canadian Literature* 3:2 (1978): 149–65.

Henderson, James (Sakej) Youngblood. "Postcolonial Ghost Dancing: Diagnosing European Colonialism." In *Reclaiming Indigenous Voice and Vision*. Ed. Marie Battiste. Vancouver: U of British Columbia P, 2000. 57–76.

Lennox, John Watt. "The Past: Themes and Symbols of Confrontation in *The Double Hook* and "Le Torrent." *Journal of Canadian Fiction* 2 (1973): 70–2.

Mitchell, Beverly. "Association and Allusion in *The Double Hook*." *Journal of Canadian Fiction* 2 (1973): 63–9.

Monkman, Leslie. "Coyote as Trickster in *The Double Hook*." *Canadian Literature* 52 (Spring 1972): 70–56. Rpt. in *Sheila Watson and* The Double Hook. Ed. George Bowering. Ottawa: Golden Press, 1985. 63–9.

Morriss, Margaret. "The Elements Transcended." *Canadian Literature* 42 (Autumn 1964): 186–201.

———. "'No Short Cuts': The Evolution of *The Double Hook*." *Canadian Literature* 173 (Summer 2002): 54–70.

Putzel, Steven. "Under Coyote's Eye: Indian Tales in Sheila Watson's *The Double Hook*." *Canadian Literature* 102 (Autumn 1984): 7–16.

Radu, Anca Raluca. "'More Like a Devil': Coyote in Sheila Watson's *The Double Hook* and Gail Anderson-Dargatz's *The Cure for Death by Lightning*." *Open Letter* 13:2 (2007): 120–33.

Reid, Bill, and Robin Bringhurst. *The Raven Steals the Light*. Vancouver: Douglas and McIntyre, 1984.

Richler, Mordecai. *Solomon Gursky Was Here*. Toronto: Alfred A. Knopf, 1989.

———. *The Incomparable Atuk*. Toronto: McClelland and Stewart, 1963.

Robinson, Eden. *Monkey Beach*. Toronto: Alfred A. Knopf, 2000.

Rose, Marilyn. "Auspicious Beginnings." *Canadian Literature* 165 (Summer 2000): 112.

Todd, Richard. "Narrative Trickery and Performative Historiography: Fictional Representation of National Identity in Graham Swift, Peter Carey, and Mordecai Richler." In *Magical Realism: Theory, History, Community*. Ed. Lois Parkinson Zamora and Wendy B. Farif. Durham, NC: Duke UP, 1995. 305–28.

Vizenor, Gerald. "Crossbloods." In *Shadow Distance: A Gerald Vizenor Reader*. Hanover, NH: Wesleyan UP, 1994. 227–46.

Watson, Sheila. *The Double Hook*. Toronto: McClelland and Stewart, 1959; rpt. 1966.

———. "It's What You Say." Interview with Sheila Watson by Bruce Meyer and Brian O'Riordan. In *In Their Words: Interviews with Fourteen Canadian Writers*. Toronto: Anansi, 1984. 157–67.

———. Untitled interview (with Pierre Coupey, Roy Kiyooka, and Daphne Marlatt). *Capilano Review* 8/9 (1975–76): 351–60.

———. "What I'm Going to Do." *Sheila Watson: A Collection*. Special issue of *Open Letter* 3:1 (1974–75): 181–3.

Willmott, Glenn. "Sheila Watson, Aboriginal Discourse, and Cosmopolitan Modernism." In *The Canadian Modernists Meet*. Ed. Dean Irvine. Ottawa: U of Ottawa P, 2005. 101–16.

RAVEN

RICHARD VAN CAMP

Why Ravens Smile to Little Old Ladies as They Walk By ...

I wanted to record an erotic story I heard from the Dogrib Nation. I heard it one summer when I was working with kids on a fishing island in the middle of Great Slave Lake, north of Yellowknife, NWT. This was before I met my wife, Pam, and before the death of our daughter, Isabell. The story is about how Raven acquired such a beautiful, flaming red tongue. When a Raven opens its beak towards you, look in. You will see a beautiful pink pussy in its mouth.

Really.

The story goes like this. A long time ago the Dogrib people had kicked the shit out of Raven. They had it with the fucker. He had tricked, shamrocked and shananagined them one times too many. The Dogrib are magnificent fighters. Executing cowboy kicks, bannock slaps and aerial maneuvers, they are acrobats of destruction when they battle and I'm so proud to be one. Anyway, this wasn't the first time they kicked the shit out of Raven, but they wanted it to be their last. As Raven buckled, his face swollen, his left eye rammed shut, the people decided to rip off his beak. They did, too, the bastards. They pulled it right the hell off and ran back to town. With his black body ruined and crushed, Raven fell inside a coma.

How the Dogrib hid Raven's beak was they gave it to a blind, old woman. They told her what they had done and she agreed to hide it. She was a powerful medicine woman and they trusted her. She knew what to do. The woman hid it under her dress, placing it between her thighs, pointing down. The long dress she wore prevented anyone from seeing the hard, black beak. With the beak, came Raven's tongue.

The tongue, lonely for a mouth, sought her sunshine spot, tasting and wiggling itself all the way in, as far as it would go. The old woman jumped when she first felt this, but soon loved what she felt.

It felt delicious.

From that day on, the old woman experienced such intensity that she was dizzy and lost and wonderful all at the same time. Well, she just had to stay home. Why leave the house? Thinking their mother was sick, her daughters would bring her food. The old woman insisted that she was all right and smiled for the first time in years. All day she would bounce, bend over, wiggle and rock back and forth. The tongue loved its newfound mouth and this reborn woman loved her newfound, secret friend!

This went on for weeks. The old woman had never been happier.

Raven, however, was on the lookout for his beak and tongue. Because Raven's sense of taste was gone, the nose behind his beak had developed an excellent sense of smell. He walked into Fort Rae and demanded the Dogrib people return his beak at once. No one knew anything; that's what they told him. Raven said he wouldn't leave until he found his beak. He had grown skinny and people asked if he had a tapeworm. He told them all to fuck right off. He sat and glared, watching everyone in the community.

It wasn't long before he overhead the old woman's daughters talking about their mother. They were concerned that, being blind, their mother was no longer coming outside to visit. They were concerned that perhaps she was wanting to die. They said they had heard her moaning all hours of the night, sometimes crying out with a heavy voice.

"Perhaps," one said, "she is depressed. "

"No, no," the other daughter said. "She's never looked happier."

The Raven's senses tingled! Raven shot up and ran toward the old woman's house. He walked straight in and the old woman was on all fours, rocking herself and arching her back. She shot up and straightened out her dress, "Who is it?"

Raven changed his voice, "It is me, your daughter. I have come to do your laundry."

"I'll do it myself," she said. "Leave me alone."

"Are you sick, Mother?" the voice asked.

"No," she answered, "just tired."

Suddenly, Raven jumped the old woman and pulled her dress up. There was his beak between her thighs! He pulled but his tongue wouldn't let go. He pulled and pulled with all his might, and finally it came loose. He placed his beak snuggly back on and was about to walk out the door but stopped to drink what was in his mouth. "Holy lick!" he said.

Raven looked at the old woman and smiled. She winked and smiled back! She had strong medicine and could still feel his tongue inside her. Raven licked at the inside of his beak, and enjoyed his newfound friend, which was now secured in his mouth, and flew back, beak intact, to the sky to plot more tricks on the Dogrib People.

And I know he was smiling all the way.

That is why, even to this day, when you see a raven open its mouth towards you, you will see a flaming red tongue and a beautiful pink pussy inside. And this, too, is why we ravens smile to little old ladies as they walk by.

Mahsi Cho!

Gasps, Snickers, Narrative Tricks, and Deceptive Dominant Ideologies

The Transformative Energies of Richard Van Camp's "Why Ravens Smile to Little Old Ladies as They Walk By ..." and/in the Classroom

Richard Van Camp's "Why Ravens Smile to Little Old Ladies as They Walk By ..." is such an unforgettable piece of writing. It is so multi-layered, produces so many ripples (and gasps and snickers), and leads to so many critical trajectories that I scarcely know where to begin discussing it. At once funny, bawdy, and seriously thought-provoking, the story plays with a multiplicity of assumptions—about Indigenous literatures, trickster figures, narrative authority, language, sexuality, and the elderly, among many others. In my experience as a non-Dogrib, non-Indigenous, white euro-Canadian instructor in "Indigenous Literatures" classrooms, I find that this story never fails to elicit shock, embarrassed giggles, confusion, consternation, indignation, outright laughter, running jokes throughout the remainder of the term (many, no doubt, out of the range of my hearing), more than a little "instructor trepidation," and some of the most productive critical questioning, my own included, that I have been privileged to observe and engage in.[1]

Ooh, this story is crazy. I can't believe Van Camp published this. Geez.
   —Tim Munro, Siksika Nation

In what follows, I offer a discussion of "Why Ravens Smile to Little Old Ladies as They Walk By ..." in terms of some of the responses the story has generated in my classroom experience, my strategies for facilitating discussion of the story to date, and some of the many critical trajectories the story offers. Among these is a consideration of how some aspects of the published stories about Raven by Dene elder George Blondin, whose support and influence

Van Camp has publicly acknowledged, may further enrich the appreciation of this remarkable story and its representation of Raven. (And here I address the risks involved in considering such questions of "influence" and "use of tradition" as well.)[2]

There is a surprising absence of critical attention on Van Camp's remarkable work, which includes the novel *The Lesser Blessed* (1996) and the collection *Angel Wing Splash Pattern* (2002), in which "Why Ravens Smile ..." appears.[3] Knowledge of Dogrib narratives of Raven, trickster figures, and analytical paradigms that have been produced by or received the support of the Dogrib community have yet to become prevalent in mainstream academic literary study. Yet, without community/nationally specific knowledge, how can one assess to what extent an Indigenous writer, such as Richard Van Camp, has—or has not—drawn on a *specific* tradition of storytelling and of trickster figures? How can that delicate balance between authorial independence *from* tradition, *from* the burden of representation placed on writers of Indigenous ancestry, and the use or transformation *of* tradition be discerned without such, or, at the very least, some knowledge? It is my hope that this discussion of "Why Ravens Smile to Little Old Ladies as They Walk By ..." demonstrates thoughtful and appropriate engagement, and, more importantly, the necessity of the transformation of academic structures and practices (even in its limitations) towards accountable and nationally specific critical analysis of Indigenous literatures.

My broader critical target (for I am not critiquing or "criticizing" the story at all), then, is how readers, students, critics, and teachers of "Indigenous Literatures" have been deceived, "tricked," by institutional structures and dominant nationalist ideologies, including multiculturalism, that claim inclusiveness and support of Indigenous perspectives. In fact, the very structures in which we work constrain us—for example, the catch-all category of "Indigenous Literatures" set against the numerous and very specific and in-depth national, period, and genre studies of the British literary tradition.[4] These shape our labour and limit critical practices that truly acknowledge the depth of literary histories in First Nations, Métis, and Inuit communities. It is my hope that integral to the transformation towards National Indigenous literary studies will be questions of pedagogy and the opening for discussion, scrutiny, and accountability the often-problematic privacy of the classroom, in which "meanings" are produced, reproduced, authorized, and rewarded, but not always accounted for.

Trick: 1. a cunning act or scheme intended to outwit someone; an illusion 2. a skilful act performed for entertainment or amusement; a clever or particular way of doing something.
    —Oxford English Dictionary

The theoretical "death of the author," lingering notions about objectivity and the assumed necessity of "critical distance," and suspect attachments to notions of literature as purely "imaginative" work removed from ideologies, politics, racism, and land rights, have often worked together and rather too comfortably *with* the notion of the private classroom and *against* accountability to Indigenous communities, even as we publish about and "teach" Indigenous literatures. Further, rarely in academic publishing[5] are full literary texts included in "analyses" of them. Rather, the critic's voice/view is typically placed in a position of authority vis-à-vis the "absent" text (absent writer, absent community). The "text" appears only in fragments, in selected quotations that function to "illustrate" the critic's position. Typically, only those who have previously read the literature in question in its entirety are in a position to challenge the critic's perspective.

It is for these reasons that I would like to acknowledge and thank Richard Van Camp: thank you for your remarkable gift of writing. Thank you for so generously agreeing to have your story appear here for each reader to enjoy and engage with, for celebrating the agency of "students," and for resisting some of these academic practices that create distances and hierarchies among writers and teachers/critics and readers/classroom participants.

It is also with my deepest appreciation that I acknowledge Shon Stimson and Tim Munro: thank you for sharing here your thoughtful and insightful and funny responses to "Why Ravens Smile to Little Old Ladies as They Walk By ..." from our course in Indigenous literatures, and for your commitment to collaborative learning. I have learned from you.[6]

The raven was the first bird on Earth. All animals respected Raven because of this, and believed him to be the most powerful of animals. All strong medicine people had raven medicine and were able to communicate with ravens. Ravens had the ability to foretell the future and to find game for people.

Some claimed that Raven, although powerful, was not entirely to be trusted. In fact, it was said that he often played tricks on others.
    —George Blondin, *When the World Was New: Stories of the Sahtú Dene* (5)

I share with many non-Indigenous people what I would call a generalized—and grossly simplified—understanding of trickster narratives as both entertaining and pedagogical, with each story part of a much broader cycle or series of stories, and of tricksters as imperfect figures with incredible abilities, from whose foibles and successes listeners learn fundamental values and ways of knowing.[7] Important distinctions, however, need to be made regarding notions of "tricking" as "deception" and the culturally specific histories and representations of trickster figures and the epistemologies used to appreciate these appropriately—even as these may incorporate broadly understood notions of tricking and deception. "Why Ravens Smile to Little Old Ladies as They Walk By ..." is enriched by how Van Camp so masterfully intertwines and utilizes multiple denotations and connotations of tricking and tricksters.

Prior to preparing this piece, I had facilitated classroom discussion about "Why Ravens Smile to Little Old Ladies as They Walk By ..." primarily in terms of a pedagogy of unpacking assumptions. This discussion focused on explorations of what constitutes, or is assumed to constitute, Indigenous literatures and "Indigeneity"; what is or isn't considered "appropriate" subject matter for literature; deconstructing oppressive silences around the body and sexuality (not without my own silences as well), opening up consideration of "Indigenous erotica"; and exploring how gaps in knowledge constrain appreciating Indigenous literatures in their culturally specific contexts. This is, in many ways, productive and important. Aware of my lack of knowledge of Dogrib/Dene histories and perspectives of Raven and trickster stories, I have until now introduced in the classroom only this generalized information I have about trickster figures, and I have used the generalization as an example to raise the issue of the institutional/dominant national reasons for the lack in academia of specific Indigenous national studies.

But it is precisely this lack of knowledge—this stopping point, based on my awareness of my lack of knowledge, in fact—that to me epitomizes the historical, systemic problems that this anthology is exploring. This is not to suggest that critical self- and collective-reflexivity are not crucial, in theory and in the classroom, as I hope to show, but that such reflexivity is part of the process, not the sole goal, in addressing these concerns.

I put *Angel Wing Splash Pattern* on course readings fairly early in the term for several reasons, primary among these being the richness of Van Camp's work. Each piece in the collection is distinct and worthy of detailed discussion, yet the collection as a whole also has a remarkable cohesiveness.[8] Many classroom participants list Van Camp's work as among their favourites.[9] My other primary reason for introducing Van Camp's writing early in a course, admittedly, is my attachment to a certain level of shock value, not so much regarding the erotic content of a single story in Van Camp's work, although this effect is considerable, but regarding how his collection as a whole disrupts confining assumptions about what constitutes "Indigenous literatures" and "Indigeneity."

Someone somewhere is shaking their head in shame. I enjoyed it though.
   —Tim Munro

There are, of course, multiple entry points for the teaching and critical appreciation of literary texts. In my classroom experience, it is the sexual/erotic content of "Why Ravens Smile to Little Old Ladies as They Walk By …," which really only informs part of the piece, that seems almost instantly to produce a fascinating and enormous elephant in the classroom. (Okay, I'm euphemizing.) Specifically, it is the use of the word "pussy" (I cringe as I type it), the representation of oral sex and sexual pleasure—in an *Indigenous* story, no less—that seems to produce an intrigued, questioning, and critically productive pedagogical space and opportunity.

A person could reach puberty, live her entire adult life, go through menopause and still not have stumbled across a single erotic poem or story by a First Nations writer. Or, to make it even more depressing, I realized one could live and die as an Indigenous person and not come across a single erotic poem or story by an Indigenous writer from Canada, the US, Australia, Aotearoa (aka New Zealand) … I know, I looked.
   —Kateri Akiwenzie-Damm, "Erotica, Indigenous Style" (143)

The plot of the central story of "Why Ravens Smile to Little Old Ladies as They Walk By …" involves the characters playing tricks and developing schemes to outwit each other. Less explicit, or at least perhaps less obvious to readers (even after the first and second reading), are the numerous narrative "tricks" the story plays on at least some readers' assumptions. The title does not initially indicate the sexual content of the story, but instead evokes the tradition of explanatory tales: "why the turtle has a shell," "why mouse's teeth are brown," and so on. The phrase in the title, "little old ladies," likely suggests a far different image than that implied later in the story. Rather, what I believe emerges for many readers are references to other homogenized "traditional myths and legends" encountered or filtered primarily through the mainstream and which, if including heterosexual relationships at all, vaguely represent "romance" but certainly not specific sexual acts and pleasure. Images of Disney's Pocahontas seem to hover here.

Further, the reference in the first sentence to an "erotic story" may or may not come as a surprise to readers who, if reading *Angel Wing Splash Pattern* chronologically, would have already enjoyed/been challenged by the preceding, "Let's Beat the Shit Out of Herman Rosko!" A stunning and funny deconstruction of masculine bravado and a compassionate exploration of male fears of and desires for intimacy in heterosexual relationships, the story makes an unforgettable, although never explicitly described, connection between yellow Halls cough drops and the successful performance by men of oral sex on women. I discuss this particular story in further detail below. In the introductory paragraph of "Why Ravens Smile to Little Old Ladies as They Walk By ...,", I would suggest that the connective statement—that the narrator heard this story "from the Dogrib Nation"—functions to ameliorate the potential shock of the mention of "erotica," even perhaps to override it, by calling upon other assumptions: the reference to the Dogrib Nation provides "authorization" for the story and calls up mainstream notions of what constitutes traditional (i.e., definitely *not* erotic) Indigenous stories. I do not suggest that traditional stories in their own contexts and epistemologies did not and do not have "erotic" or "sexual" content; indeed, the point here is that, without appropriate training in such traditions, it is impossible for me to make any valid comment on them. In other words, I don't think readers register "erotic" at first, despite the clear use of the term. Such was my own reading as well.

In conjunction with this assumed suggestion or reading of cultural authority and authorization in the title "Why Ravens Smile to Little Old Ladies as They Walk By ...," the use in the introduction of the first-person voice, combined with the narrator's reference to a wife, and to a daughter who had died, can work to reinforce assumptions about autobiography as reflective of "truth." (After all, how could, or why would, anyone make up a child who had died?) Even the sentence that states that this "is a story about how Raven acquired such a beautiful, flaming red tongue" does not signal anything unusual within a reading paradigm of "traditional explanatory stories." It is the next sentence, with its explicit comparison—no, *equation*—of a Raven's tongue with women's genitalia ("a beautiful pink pussy") that starts the shock waves that reverberate throughout the remainder of at least initial readings of and immediate thinking about the story.

Richard Van Camp wastes no time in giving the reader a dose of what they are in for as he discloses towards the ending of the first paragraph: "'When raven opens its beak towards you, look in. You will see a beautiful pink pussy in its mouth'" (24). It was like a car accident; you don't want to look but curiosity gets the best of you. My initial reaction was most likely shared by all other people who had read this story. The reaction was that there could not be a story in the histories of Indigenous culture that

can contain so much disrespect for elders, women, and sexuality. But as I pondered Richard Van Camp's rationality behind the writing of this story, a number of realities surfaced ...
—Shon Stimson, Siksika Nation

In my classroom experience, the narrative shift in the final paragraph, from the first-person to the first-person plural, and the identification of the narrator as one of many ravens—"And this, too, is why *we ravens* smile to little old ladies as they walk by" (26, emphasis added)—initially tends to go unnoticed. Most of us, I suspect, would still be processing the content of what precedes this narrative shift. Moreover, the next narrative "trick" regarding narrative authority occurs in the Afterword, which may be completely overlooked altogether. There is no particular footnote at the end of "Why Ravens Smile ..." to direct readers specifically to the "Afterword."[10] This in itself is a fascinating strategy, in that Van Camp seems entirely comfortable in allowing readers to engage with the piece with or without the added twist of the "Afterword":

> I heard a variation of this story on a fishing island outside of Edzo on the Great Slave Lake. We were at a science camp with a dozen kids, scientists and Dogrib elders. The lake dropped so fast one afternoon, we were stranded out there. We weren't expecting this at all, but it didn't matter. We had lots of grub, a full moon, a great fire, and a small army of great storytellers out there. I'm sorry if the story tricked you, but the raven is a trickster and I'm such a goddamned liar ... (103)

In the "Afterword," we are told fairly explicitly that a trick has occurred, that the narrator/writer has deceived "us" readers. Statements such as "I'm sorry if the story tricked you" and "I'm such a goddamned liar" (103) throw into doubt not only the reliability or even the existence of the "I" of the "Afterword," but also that of the narrator of the story, his wife, their child,[11] and the entire piece—as one clever, funny, surprising deception, and an extremely thought-provoking and entertaining one at that. This final sentence of the Afterword, in suggesting that Van Camp (or is that his narrator?) is performing the role of raven as trickster (or *is* a trickster), opens up even more questions: does this playful invocation of the trickster as "explanation" in fact function as an excuse, or, indeed, a rather unapologetic apology, for the deception? After all, the sincerity of the apology—"I'm sorry if the story tricked you"—is rather reduced by the conditional, explanatory phrases that follow: "but the raven is a trickster and I'm such a goddamned liar ..." Is this kind of qualified explanation (sorry, but not sorry) a characteristic of raven in Dogrib epistemologies? Is this, literally, nothing more than writerly play-ing? Or is the invocation of raven (writer) as trickster here another engage-ment with (messing with, playing with and challenging) readers' assumptions and expectations about Indigenous writers, literature, trickster narratives, and "tradition"? Indeed.

It was to my understanding that most people enjoyed the work but could not bring themselves to admit it…. I wanted to challenge myself in further exploring the attitudes behind my own reactions and what it means for native expression as a whole.
    —Shon Stimson

The sexual content of "Why Ravens Smile to Little Old Ladies as They Walk By …" makes the initial discussion of the story in the classroom scary, and risky, for instructor and students, although for different reasons, of course. It is with naming some of these risks and challenges that I try to begin.[12] To begin consideration of the text, I share some of my own initial responses to the story, and my own processes of working to interrogate their cultural and his-torical foundations and limitations. I do speak personally—of the silences around the body and sexuality I experienced as a young, white Catholic girl/teen in small-town Ontario, of the Judeo-Christian inheritances of the binarism of body-versus-soul, of the shame attached to the body, of the equa-tion of sexuality and sin. I try to discuss this as openly as I can, to search for a balance that acknowledges the seriousness of the effects of the silencing and denigration of sexuality (who knows who in a classroom has experienced sex-ual abuse, for example?); it perhaps relieves some of the uncertainty and dis-comfort around addressing and naming these issues in the classroom.[13] I may share, for example, my conviction as a Catholic child who had recently learned about "sex": "I am the youngest of six children. My parents had sex a total of six times, and the sole purpose was the creation of me and my sib-lings. Pleasure definitely was *not* involved." I refer to the *Vagina Monologues* and to strategies of wresting terms for women's bodies from their denigrating contexts and reclaiming them as positive assertions of sexuality and identity. I share my own inability to reclaim some terms that I personally experienced as damaging, oppressive, the "p"-word and the "c"-word, and a number of other terms that I do not name directly—nor do I need to do so, considering their continuing circulation in popular sexist discourse. I will not (cannot) repeat in class the "p-word" used in the story (and I even struggle to repro-duce it in print here as well). Indeed, some may experience the story as "offen-sive," and here I am reminded further of my ethical responsibilities as instructor with authority in the classroom.[14]

I may point out the significant correlation between mainstream derogatory terms for women and women's bodies, and terms naming or related to animals. I may indicate how this process is related to the historical processes of racist stereotypes of Indigenous peoples, and of Indigenous women. I discuss mainstream assumptions about the elderly and sexuality and the assumed incompatibility of the two; I raise questions about societal attitudes towards the treatment of the elderly, and the effects of the transformations from extended to nuclear families, with the elderly placed in care facilities rather than cared for by families. And this can open discussion of Indigenous perspectives on the "elderly" and "elders" as well. I try to stress a distinction between rampant media representations of anatomy and sexuality-as-commodity and, much more important, seemingly rare expressions of healthy sexuality and intimacy.[15] This is to introduce the suggestion, too, that Van Camp's collection as a whole offers a compassionate and often funny critique of confining constructions of both sexuality and masculinity.

And I also ask students if they think this story would ever be included in their high school curriculum. (This usually generates eye-rolling, chuckles, and vigorous head-shaking.)

When the people got a hold of Raven's beak, they thought they hid it well. But even the Raven's beak was mischievous as he found ways to erotically pleasure an old medicine lady. By the sounds of it, the lady didn't seem to mind.
—Tim Munro

It seems to me that the repression of erotic art is symptomatic of our oppression and signifies a deep psychological and spiritual break between a healthy and holistic tradition and an oppressed, repressed, shamed and imposed sense of reality.... The silencing of our erotic expression says our sexuality is not "permissible," that its expression is unacceptable, that we must remain unseen and ignored, that we must accept the dehumanizing impacts of being oppressed and colonized.
—Kateri Akiwenzie-Damm ("Erotica, Indigenous Style" 147)

Essentially, I frame the discussion this way in order to introduce and demonstrate how our own cultural and historical positioning, personal experiences, and previous exposure to Indigenous literatures and trickster narratives shape and perhaps limit our responses both to Indigenous literatures generally and to this piece in particular. Indeed, the story and responses to it work effectively to introduce and explore one possible thread of investigation, reading, and study—Indigenous erotica, the absence of which signals, in Akiwenzie-Damm's view, the history of colonization rather than any historical or even current absence of erotic stories in Indigenous communities.

Real life medicine people could see the portrayal of the medicine woman as blasphemous and wrong. Nevertheless, I do not see why an old woman should not enjoy the pleasures of oral sex. Evidently Van Camp felt this way too when he wrote this peculiar tale of the Raven.
—Tim Munro

... had the story been expressed the same way by a mainstream noted author, would there have been the same response? Mainstream society is familiar with the concepts and methods that have been used by authors over the generations to add erotic gestures to a piece of literature or story to enhance it. This is apparent in the seedy novels created by contemporary writers and even in the writings of Shakespeare. What is not familiar to today's society are the relatively new findings and dealings with Aboriginal expression. Modern societies have only recently begun to accept other forms of the indigenous ability to express their circumstances. With that in mind, mainstream society has only started to touch the surface of First Nations' narratives....

Somewhere in the back of Richard Van Camp's mind was his intent to assault the perceptions of the stereotypical nature of the native experience. It may be the wish of Van Camp to break down the romanticizing of native peoples to open up avenues for Aboriginal expression.... By the end of this story there would be the changing in perspectives of an open minded person in regards to the contexts of Aboriginal stories. It may give the reader a chance to see more in the way of the complexities of Aboriginal peoples, not just as the noble savage ...
—Shon Stimson

We need to see images of ourselves as healthy, whole people. People who love each other and who love ourselves. People who fall in love and out of love, who have lovers, who make love, who have sex. We need to create a healthy legacy for our peoples.... [I]n a broad sense Indigenous erotica speaks about the healing nature of love, about love that celebrates us as a whole people, about love that is openly sexual, sensual, emotional, and spiritual. Love, and the expression of it, is a medicine to heal the pain of oppression, hatred, lovelessness, and colonization. It is a way for Indigenous writers and other artists to freely express themselves and their ideas about love and sexuality, without being constrained by imposed moral codes or definitions.... To reclaim and express our sexuality is part of the larger path to de-colonization and freedom.
—Kateri Akiwenzie-Damm (148, 149, 151)

I have attempted in the classroom, with some success within the constraints, to introduce my generalized knowledge of trickster figures, to suggest a reading of "Why Ravens Smile ..." in relation to this generalized knowledge, and to stress the limitations in this reading regarding the lack in mainstream academia of culturally, nationally specific understandings of Dogrib literary traditions and trickster stories. In other words, I raise questions about the possibility that Van Camp may be drawing on or transforming such traditions—that, as a writer, he may or may not be *performing* the role of trickster, even as he represents Raven as a trickster figure. ("I'm sorry if the story tricked you, but the raven is a trickster and I'm such a goddamned liar ..." [103]). This suggestion is not intended to confuse students by offering an interpretation, then immediately undercutting it, but to point to the systemic reasons for this lack of knowledge and the need for more culturally specific, nationally focused analyses of trickster figures, even if, in terms of this particular story, the result is to say that Van Camp's Raven is not drawing on "tradition" at all.

In my understanding, traditionally, each trickster story is part of a much longer, complex, and integrated system of narratives. In some trickster stories, the trickster emerges as rather heroic, as helper, for example; in others, the trickster's foibles and errors become an object lesson in how *not* to behave. In either case, the stories have both an entertainment and pedagogical function; they may be shared with a broad audience, including adults and children. The pedagogical effects of each narrative and its telling, then, are profoundly dependent on levels of knowledge regarding the larger cycle of stories, with these levels of knowledge possibly but not necessarily related to the age of the listener.

The story gives a contemporary twist on old legends of the Raven. The Raven is a legendary trickster figure in many Native cultures. Raven is responsible for countless tales of how he tricked the Aboriginal peoples. Van Camp reveals his wittiness and humour throughout this text.... On the last lines of the story, Van Camp stated this was all a big trick. And this is too is why "we" Ravens smile at little old ladies as they walk by. He is continuing the whole trickster theme.
—Tim Munro

With this text, I would suggest that it is possible with close reading (and without much, if any, education in "traditional" knowledge) to discern in the text a particular pedagogical narrative. Here, at the conclusion of this particular round of back-and-forth "tricking" between the Dogrib people (one might assume Dogrib men) and Raven, Raven and indeed the medicine woman emerge as the winners: the elderly woman with her strong medicine is still able to feel Raven's "tongue inside her," with the implication being that she will continue to experience the sexual pleasure the tongue has provided even after her "separation" from the beak. And Raven, the story implies, emerges with knowledge of pleasuring women that the Dogrib people, at least in the time frame of the story, apparently do not: "Raven looked at the old woman and smiled. She winked and smiled back!" It could be suggested, then, that there is within this narrative a "lesson" after all, insofar as the Dogrib people perhaps went too far in tearing off Raven's beak—"They did, too, *the bastards*" (24, emphasis added)—and their punishment, or loss, is their lack of knowledge of the pleasures Raven and the medicine woman will continue to enjoy. The power of the medicine woman and of the Raven, in other words, is not diminished by the end of the story but, rather, reinforced.

There are other textual details often overlooked in the surprise of initial readings, yet worthy of note. Van Camp's temporal play, not only between the framing commentaries set in the present and the central narrative set a "long time ago" (24), is also a play of language. Here, ostensibly, we have a story set in the past, but which is told in English, using such terms as "shamrocked," "shananagined," "bastards," and "fuck right off"—hardly traditional Dogrib words. One could suggest, then, without specific knowledge of Dogrib epistemologies regarding the construction of time and how this relates to Western "time" (or not), that there is a literal *and* symbolic significance to this temporal, linguistic interplay. The past merging with, or into, the present suggests and demonstrates the resiliency, maintenance, and transformation of Dogrib perspectives. At the same time, and, I would argue, more importantly, the use of contemporary language in a story set partly in the past, in "a time long ago," can be read to signal *not* the imposition of the English language and its ideologies, but rather the remarkable ability of Dogrib epistemologies to *incorporate* and integrate the English language and "the West" into itself.[16]

The language and descriptions used may have offended some people as they read the story. But to use any other form will not have the met the desired effect that the writer wished to portray. When Van Camp uses "pussy," "... kick the shit out of," "fucker," and "... bastards" (24) it not only connects with the reader but it also gives the reader the "shock and awe" effect. Words like "private part," "beat up," "sucker," and "idiots" just do not carry the same weight; it would be to the same effect as beating around the bush. There would be the absence of not giving his talents or the audience any credit for their abilities. To some the downplay in expression may be an insult more than the use of the story's current terms.
—Shon Stimson

It is precisely because our tribal stories are comical and evoke laughter that they have never been taken seriously outside the tribe.... But behind and beneath the comic characters and the comic situations exists the real meaning of the story ... what the tribe understood about human growth and development.
     —Basil Johnston, "How Do We Learn Language?"

Holy lick!
     —Richard Van Camp (26)

There are multiple risks in reading "Why Ravens Smile to Little Old Ladies as They Walk By ..." in relation to the published stories of Dene elder George Blondin, even as Van Camp acknowledges in a very general way Blondin's influence on his writing. Will classroom participants, presented with Blondin's Raven stories either before or after reading Van Camp's text, too quickly and easily "apply" Blondin's story onto Van Camp's? Blondin's Raven stories, at least the ones with which I am familiar, after all, do *not* refer to medicine women and oral sex. One of my biggest concerns has been the apparent or assumed ease with which some, or a little, understanding of trickster traditions in general, or of Raven, can lead to a traditional or "First Nation-al" paradigm being imposed upon a text inappropriately, or unilaterally. My concern has been that in introducing to a class (and I would say here that I am assuming non-Indigenous students) *some* information, filtered as it is, even some of Blondin's Raven stories, some students will assume that Van Camp's story is "traditional": that is, "Raven is magical; medicine power is powerful; sexual repression was not necessarily traditional; therefore, Dogrib medicine women enjoyed oral sex with Raven as part of their traditions ..."[17]

With what interpretive approaches, then, can we attend to Blondin's texts, published versions of oral stories for which most non-Indigenous critics have no epistemological frame of reference? And then, how might we proceed in understanding the relationship between Blondin's Raven stories and Van Camp's "Why Ravens Smile to Little Old Ladies as They Walk By ..."? In the historical, oral context from which Blondin draws, there are variations in the stories from storyteller to storyteller; there are the differences between oral and published versions, and between the original language and the English versions.[18] There are considerations to be made regarding the audience's level of knowledge, as Blondin states:

> It used to be that every family with a living grandfather or grandmother possessed a storyteller from another time. The duty of storytellers was to tell stories every day. That is why Dene tradition is so complete, as far back as the days when Naácho—giant now-extinct animals—roamed the world. Since

it's difficult to keep track of things if you try to tell a long story from one day to the next, each day's story was complete in itself. These short tales, put together, made up complete stories. ("Introduction: Storytelling Among the Dene," *When the World Was New: Stories of the Sahtú Dene*, i)

And there is the critical fact that Richard Van Camp is a contemporary, creative writer who, in his own words, "blazed his own trail" in his writing. So he writes in his Foreword to Blondin's *Trail of the Spirit:* "When I met George Blondin, I was humbled because I was shaking hands with someone who has dedicated his life to documenting the stories, beliefs, and philosophies of the Dene people of the Northwest Territories, and he has inspired me over the years *to blaze my own trail with my writing*" (1, emphasis added). This leaves the question of influence rather open-ended, to say the least: "you may have to work out the meaning of some of these stories for yourself. Dene legends don't all have a nice beginning, middle, and end like on television" (George Blondin, *Yamoria the Lawmaker: Stories of the Dene*, viii). And yet, the more I consider some of Blondin's work, the more *possibilities* of influence of Dogrib/Dene stories of Raven I think I discern. Although these are not one-to-one direct correlations, I find them intriguing, and pedagogically and critically inviting of nationally specific learning. On my initial readings, I completely glossed over specific details. Indeed, in the classroom, neither participants nor I addressed these concerns: the fact that a *blind* medicine woman registers Raven's smile and that she "winked and smiled back!" (26), and the question of how the old woman "had strong medicine and could still feel Raven's tongue inside her" (26) after their "separation." I suspect that, on my initial readings, I fell into—or deposited these details—into what now seems like an oddly contradictory place. I realize now that I continued to read the story quite literally, the image of bird beak and female body rather locked in my mind, a Western inheritance of human versus animal firmly in place. On the other hand, I unquestioningly relied on a homogenizing trap of "medicine mysticism" that infers I need not explore further out of "respect" for (the assumed unknowable and unlearnable) tradition: "*of course,* with her medicine," I assumed, "the blind woman would be able to see and wink" (noting the exclamation point and the "surprise" of the narrator as well); "*of course,* she would still be able to feel Raven's tongue"; "*of course,*" even as I am faced with a narrator/writer who challenges me to challenge everything I think about this story.

Medicine power is very complicated. These stories do not explain everything; they are short versions of much longer stories. They do touch on the most important things that

these medicine people did. I hope, because the stories are short, they will be read by many people, young and old, Dene and non-Dene.
—George Blondin, "Introduction," *Medicine Power* (n. pag.)

Knowing how to communicate with animals came through medicine power. Each medicine person had this communication, but in a different way and with a different animal. If a person owned a strong medicine on the raven, this person could talk to ravens and ravens could talk to the person, sometimes predicting the future. And if this person had a strong enough medicine, he could transfer himself into a raven and stay with the raven for a while. Later, he could come back to being human again. Some people stayed with an animal and came back to human form able to tell the Dene how various creatures made a living and raised their families in the animal world. Many of our stories describe this.

Medicine people could also understand the things animals communicated to one another. In fact, certain strong medicine people were able to disguise themselves as animals ...
—George Blondin, *When the World Was New: Stories of the Sahtú Dene* (ii)

Blondin's descriptions of medicine power and of Dene storytelling are quite explicit insofar as they make it very clear that there is an entire epistemology involved, and that individual stories are hardly representative of and do not contain that "tradition." Indeed, assumed in the context of telling the story is the awareness of varied levels of contextual, culturally specific knowledge (or the complete absence of it): "I hope, because the stories are short, they will be read by many people, young and old, Dene and non-Dene." And even as I cringe at and resist students' characterizations of literature as having "surface" and "hidden" "meanings," I would suggest that Blondin's and Van Camp's stories do share a balance of both literal, denotative, "accessible" elements (the plot, the "lesson," the humour) as well as culturally specific references. That is, those familiar with Dene traditions and language will/may be more likely to connect a single story to the larger cycle of stories and their epistemological significances; there may be moments of "recognition" lost on the untrained. In other words, since reading the Raven stories in Blondin's *When the World Was New*, and considering Blondin's description of medicine power, I sense in my own responses to "Why Ravens Smile to Little Old Ladies as They Walk By ..." interpretive shifts, shifts not only in terms of unlearning previous ethnocentric assumptions, but also in terms of seeing elements of the story differently, or perhaps for the first time.

This is *not* to suggest that any of Blondin's published Raven stories include references to oral sex, or to any sexual content at all. The eight explicitly Raven stories at the beginning of *When the World Was New*, for example, are in part explanatory stories—why Raven is black, why Raven has three long toes, why fox doesn't walk straight. Together, they describe various characteristics of Raven. He has exceptional abilities, is clever and vain, is helpful at times, but at others selfish and driven by his appetite (for food) at the expense of all else, and is not to be trusted. There are elements of some of these narratives that seem quite accessible to me: in "Why Raven Is Black," Raven insists that, as the birds are "painted beautiful colours" (7), he be painted last so that he will be "more beautiful than everybody else" (7). The birds and animals play a trick on Raven as a lesson about his vanity, and he ends up black rather than the brilliant colours he had expected. Other stories are both accessible in terms of plot, and more challenging in terms of the appreciation of particular historical/cultural contexts and references: "The Brothers-in-Law," about two whiskeyjacks and two woodpeckers who lived together (the "woodpecker's sister was married to the whiskeyjack and the whiskeyjack's sister was married to the woodpecker" [8]), appears to me to be a commentary on proper relationships but clearly requires further knowledge to assess any possible correlation properly. In "The Man and the Raven," the following statement is at once clear denotatively and quite complex epistemologically: "Once there was a young man whose medicine was the raven. Since ravens cannot be trusted, the man had trouble with his own medicine" (11). And, even in "Why Raven Is Black," there is a reference in the first paragraph to "strong medicine people [who] changed themselves into animals" (7). My point here is that it has historically been very convenient, I think, for non-Indigenous readers of such narratives, even those that appear to be "explanatory tales," to locate references to complex epistemologies rather too easily and simplistically within the realm of the "unknowable," "unlearnable," and even the inexplicable "magical," and to do so in the guise of cross-cultural respect.

I do not have any training in Dogrib/Dene epistemologies. Yet here I would like to indicate, even in a small way and with two short, specific examples, how Blondin's stories have at least opened up new, and to me, suggestive avenues for further critical thinking on Van Camp's "Why Ravens Smile to Little Old Ladies as They Walk By ..." Blondin refers several times to the abilities of medicine people, particularly "[w]hen the world was new," to communicate with and transform themselves into the animals whose medicine power they held: "If a person owned a strong medicine power on the raven, this person could talk to ravens and ravens could talk to the person, sometimes predicting the future. And if this person had a strong enough medicine, he could transfer himself into a raven and stay with the raven for a while. Later he could come back to being human again. Some people stayed with an animal and came back to human form to tell the Dene how various creatures made a living and raised their families in the animal world" (*When the World Was New* ii). Blondin stresses that this ability provided an important way in which the Dene came to understand and learn from the animals. These stories, then, offer not only accessible lessons about communication, co-operation, and the importance of humanity's respect for "nature" and the environment but are suggestive (although by no means accessible to the untrained) of an entire epistemology that includes, but is not singularly focused on, what may be referred to as traditional ecological knowledge.[19]

Keeping in mind, as we are told, that Van Camp's narrator is "a god-damned liar," that "raven is a trickster," and that the story may have "tricked" us on multiple levels, and, at the same time, trying to avoid the simplistic application of Blondin's description of the transformation of medicine people into animal form *onto* Van Camp's medicine woman, I find it nonetheless intriguing that learning of this ability also transforms my reading of the story. At a literal, denotative, level, I can still "see" a reference to a sexual act between an elderly woman and, well, a beak (not even an entire bird), that is both surprising and funny. And now I also see a connotative, culturally specific possibility that the medicine woman in the story *becomes* a raven. The two ravens then communicate and transfer knowledge—quite pleasurable knowledge at that—even as others, including the woman's daughters, do not see the medicine power at work.

I am not, of course, suggesting that I would "teach" this reading as definitive in any way. Pedagogically, however, it could be productive in inviting consideration of how this possibility may open readings regarding non-hierarchical, co-operative relationships; and, in working to resist often simplistic and romanticized assumptions, this consideration could be linked to discussions about the significance of culturally specific traditional ecological knowledge and the need for Aboriginal studies, and to questions of Aboriginal sovereignty. In other words, I would hope classroom participants would start to feel cheated, "tricked," by the deceptions of homogenizing academic structures that leave us recognizing gaps in knowledge but seemingly unable to fill them, and that they would advocate for nationally specific courses and programs of study.

Another interpretive thread that emerges for me comes from Blondin's brief description of Raven's ability to "foretell the future." I do not, in fact, find any particular explicit evidence of this characteristic in Blondin's Raven stories aside from Blondin stating this ability; nor do I think there is *explicit* reference to this characteristic in Van Camp's representation of Raven in "Why Ravens Smile ...," even though the linguistic and temporal interplay discussed earlier could be suggestive of this possibility. I would like to consider how the intertextual play between "Why Ravens Smile ..." (ostensibly set in the past—at least the explanatory narrative per se) and "Let's Beat the Shit Out of Herman Rosko!"—both of which make explicit reference to oral sex performed on women by men/male figures—could be read ("provocatively") as suggestive of Raven's ability to foretell the future. If, for example, "Why Ravens Smile ..." is a playful explanatory story, or a play on such stories, or a play on assumptions about such stories, it explicitly "explains" how Raven came to have the knowledge of how to pleasure women orally and how/why the Dogrib men (who had "kicked the shit out of Raven," and ripped off his beak [24]), in the time frame of "a long time ago," did not have such knowledge. In turn, "Let's Beat the Shit Out of Herman Rosko!," which directly precedes "Why Ravens Smile ..." in *Angel Wing Splash Pattern*, is set in a contemporary community. Herman Rosko, a university-trained counsellor, has returned to the community. His listening and communication skills have won the trust of women, and therefore he is the object of both jealousy and admiration from the men. Initially, those most caught in expectations of masculine bravado, and threatened by Rosko's ability to communicate with women, posture about beating him up. (There are pickup trucks and plenty of swearing involved.) What begins to win over the men, or so it seems at first, is Herman's apparent sexual knowledge, which involves how to perform oral sex successfully on women: "Herman says if you don't usually go down on your woman, just use yellow Halls" (20). This, however, is as explicit as the story gets—one man won over by Herman refuses to reveal the "secret" of the "four ice cubes" and instead states that there is a "code of conduct, man" (19) that forbids the disclosure of more personal detail. Ultimately, humorously and insightfully, "Let's Beat the Shit Out of Herman Rosko!" is not about the secrets of sexual knowledge but a compassionate exploration of the male characters' need for, fear of, and lack of experience with intimacy, and, at the end, their willingness to risk vulnerability. It is a self-contained narrative that functions independently (and deserves thorough discussion on its own).

Considering, then, how "Why Ravens Smile ..." follows this story, how both have references to the performance of oral sex on women, or to the lack of such knowledge, and how one of Raven's characteristics is the ability to foretell the future, it is possible to enjoy a reading of "Why Ravens Smile ..." as, in part, an explanatory story in relation to "Let's Beat the Shit Out of Herman Rosko!" In other words, "Why Ravens Smile ..." explains why Raven, but not the Dogrib men, has the knowledge of how to pleasure women orally. This lack of knowledge is the men's punishment for stealing Raven's beak. "Let's Beat the Shit Out of Herman Rosko!" explores the contemporary effects of this lack of knowledge in relation to a range of other factors as well, including bravado and fear of and desire for intimacy. Raven's wink to the medicine woman, in this way, can be read as an acknowledgement of the future, when this knowledge will re-emerge, be shared, and enjoyed.... And lest readers unfamiliar with all the pieces in *Angel Wing Splash Pattern* think this suggestion is rather extreme, I would point to the explicit intertextual play and referencing between "Sky Burial" and "Snow White Nothing for Miles." Although the two stories again function independently, "Snow White Nothing for Miles," which comes after "Sky Burial" in the collection, in fact functions as the "prequel" to "Sky Burial," and explains how and why it has come to pass that Icabus, in "Sky Burial," ends up in a shopping mall, where he transfers his medicine to an adopted Cree girl, before dying.

Not a Conclusion

Prior to embarking on the (fun) challenge that has been the writing of this piece, I have rather adamantly refused to entertain in print a reading of author/Van Camp "*as trickster*" in relation to "Why Ravens Smile to Little Old Ladies as They Walk By ..."[20] My own experience with this characterization is a vexed one: I am concerned that it has been called upon by non-Indigenous critics as a shorthand, albeit well-intentioned, attempt to acknowledge narrative traditions outside of our own histories and experiences, and to acknowledge rightly the significant impact of individual Indigenous writers, particularly when these writers have used trickster figures and narrative structures in their work. For me, the characterization has carried a suspect element of delighting in the exotic, the funny, the ribald, the *not* "us." I have been concerned that its *shorthand* use can function to put the focus on us, the reader being taught, the non-Indigenous reader being taught by Indigenous text/writer. I think this raises the spectre of asymmetrical power/race relations, the burden of representation, the onus on Indigenous people to teach non-Indigenous people, again, *still* ("teach me about your culture"), and the focus of the critical gaze remaining on the dominant ("this is what I learned from the story"; "yes, it really is all about me"). And this characterization/dynamic can circulate, unchecked, in the private classroom, at the expense of nationally focused, culturally specific analysis accountable to specific First Nations communities and their concerns—as perhaps it has in classes I've facilitated, as I have at times raised the question.

And yet, through several (*several*) drafts, this characterization has hovered, undeniably. I have learned from this story. I have witnessed classroom learning from this story, and this learning has involved more than the learning of self- and cultural critique. If, even at a grossly generalized level, I understand

trickster narratives as pedagogical and culturally specific, then, as I continue
to question (and question) this multi-faceted story and its myriad effects and
possibilities, I have to own that this narrative teaches me, catalyzes further questioning, learning, and unlearning.

What emerges, then, is the need for critical and culturally specific understandings of the role of the reader/listener of trickster narratives, and what
impact culturally specific understandings of this role might have on interpretive and pedagogical approaches and institutional and systemic transformation as well. Indeed, just as I would argue that there is an inherent risk in
the generalization of "writer-as-trickster" regarding reinscribing particular
power relations ("teach me about your culture"; one text as representative of
an entire nation), there are also risks in *not* allowing ourselves to learn and
change from our reading of Indigenous literatures—or in not admitting that
we do. What are the risks, or the power relations involved, if we do not include
in our analyses the agency and strategies of Indigenous writers in knowingly
placing their work in the public realm, as public discourse—knowingly, and
despite the risks of misinterpretations? And how does our adherence to
notions of "objectivity" reassert itself through our failure to explore also culturally and nationally specific perspectives on the roles and *responsibilities* of
readers/listeners of Indigenous literatures? How is our failure to learn this
crucial aspect of storytelling and trickster stories an abdication of our responsibilities as listeners/readers—a responsibility we may not even realize and with
which we have been entrusted, as yet another effect, and deception, of dominant nationalism's "multiculturalism"?

Popular discourses of multiculturalism, of "tolerance" and "respect" for
cultural difference, tend to stop here, which is why they are so popular, unfortunately ("That was a fun story. Let's move on to the next."). They tend to
assume and assert that silent acknowledgement of cultural specificity ("difference") is sufficient, and that such "difference" is not learnable, not wished
to be learnable, but rather conveniently placed in a box of unknowability
where it cannot (is not allowed to) teach us, transform us, or how we see and
act in the world—and where it cannot affect land rights legislation, social
justice movements, or the protection of the environment.

Take it. It's yours. Do with it what you will. Tell it to your children. Turn it into a play.
Forget it. But don't say in the years to come that you would have lived your life differ-
ently if only you had heard this story.
　　You've heard it now.
　　—Thomas King, *The Truth About Stories: A Native Narrative,* 151

It is my hope, then, that this discussion has indicated Richard Van Camp's gifts as a writer deserving of extended critical and pedagogical attention, and has also supported the views shared in this anthology regarding the need for genuine institutional commitments to Indigenous *national* studies as rich, complex, rewarding, and transformative fields of study. It is my hope that what has emerged here has been a critique of dominant national ideologies and structures, as they troublingly shape academic practices in their homogenizing of the specific national traditions of First Nations, Métis, and Inuit communities. I would hope that this piece has been successful in at least generating further discussion on the need to open for scrutiny and accountability the often-problematic privacy of the classroom, in which "meanings" are produced, reproduced, and authorized, but not necessarily accounted for.

Thank you.

Notes

1   I would like to acknowledge the engagement with this story, and the contributions to their colleagues' learning, and to my own, of the participants of the University of Calgary's ENGL 385—Fall 2005, Winter 2006, and Fall 2007, the latter held at Old Sun Community College, Siksika First Nation.

2   I would like to thank and acknowledge Dr. Deanna Reder for directing me to Blondin's works, about which I was also previously unaware, even in my previous "teaching" of Van Camp's work. In addition to the texts by Blondin listed in the Works Cited is *Yamoria the Lawmaker: Stories of the Dene* (Edmonton: NeWest Press, 1997).

3   Prior to hearing Richard Van Camp read "Mermaids" at the "For the Love of Words" conference in Winnipeg in 2004, I had never heard of Richard Van Camp nor of the Dogrib Nation (and I had only generalized knowledge of the Dene people). I am not exactly comfortable putting this into print. And yet I also know that I am not alone in this circumstance, not alone bearing vast gaps in knowledge about specific nations and histories and traditions and yet teaching university Indigenous literatures courses. Such is my particular history; such is a collective, national inheritance that is not mine alone. And it is for this latter reason that I write of it.

4   This is most obvious when considering the time assumed to be required to become a "specialist" in, say, Victorian literature, in relation to the ways in which the institution seems to expect that one instructor somehow can "cover" all of Indigenous literatures, in all genres, and for all time periods (perhaps even in a single course). This has been my experience in the Department of English at the University of Calgary, which to my knowledge has no required course in Indigenous literatures as part of its degree requirements, and offers only one half-credit course in ENGL 385: *Topic in Aboriginal Literatures*, the latter on an occasional basis. Granted, within this requirement, an instructor could, theoretically, focus on one genre, one nation, one theme, or one time period, but, to my knowledge,

this generally does not occur; as in my experience teaching the course, it is usually structured as a "survey" course and usually it focuses on contemporary literatures.

5   Yet in academic publishing, critical accountability to and dialogue with the (varied) communities from which Indigenous literatures come remains constrained by a number of factors regarding accessibility—availability and dissemination of the material, language, methodology, and so on.

6   Mr. Van Camp, Mr. Stimson, and Mr. Munro independently reviewed this article prior to agreeing to have their work included here. I approached Mr. Stimson and Mr. Munro requesting their consideration of agreeing to include their work here after the completion of our course and the submission of final grades. Mr. Van Camp was approached by the editors, Deanna Reder and Linda Morra, following initial submission of this article. The article has been revised slightly since the initial submission, and each contributor has had the opportunity to review it again prior to publication. To a certain extent, I think it is fair to suggest that their consent indicates support for what follows. However, I do not consider this to mean full agreement with or "authorization" of what I have written—nor do I want it to be read as such—but rather as a commitment to collaborative learning and dialogue.

7   My own academic training occurred in an institutional and "theoretical" climate that Niigonwedom James Sinclair aptly describes as one of "cultural relativism," which implies (or even asserts) that a trickster is "a figure that knows no home, no responsibilities and transgresses all boundaries" (28). This seemingly contradictory combination of limited knowledge and an overarching, homogenized, and de-historicized theory has functioned (disturbingly efficiently), as Sinclair so forcefully argues, in a reinforcement of colonial discourse and power.

8   While I do put the collection on course readings early in the term, by the time classes read it, I have worked to introduce some critical questions regarding expectations about what constitutes Indigenous literatures, and this in turn leads to productive questioning regarding assumptions about Indigeneity and identity as well. While we usually have discussed the pressures on Indigenous writers to conform to dominant and internalized expectations, and I have often introduced critical self-reflection and journaling as part of the course, this story none the less comes as a surprise.

9   Participants comment on the fullness and "relatable" qualities of his characters and their experiences and perspectives, the accessibility of his language (with the swearing and humour an apparently welcome change from previous experiences in some literature classes), and finding the various pieces funny, engaging, moving, refreshing (and interesting insofar as they too are unfamiliar with Dogrib/Dene literatures), and definitely thought-provoking. In terms of subject matter, there appears to be no holds barred for Van Camp, and his range is stunning, as he seamlessly weaves AIDS and suicide, grief, and traditional medicine in "Mermaids," for example. For my own part, I would rank Van Camp's profound and compassionate exploration of the limitations and often devastating effects of constructions of masculinity particularly engaging and astute.

10   In the "Afterwords" section of *Angel Wing Splash Pattern,* Van Camp provides background context for each piece in the anthology, explaining, for example, the historical exploitation of the Dene in the uranium mining industry ("the uranium leaking from port radium and rayrock mines is killing us"), or an experience that catalyzed the writing process: "I was at a dance one night ..." ("Let's Beat the Shit Out of Herman Rosko!"); "When I went for my degree at UVIC ..." ("The Night Charles Bukowski Died"); and "I received a call one night from a friend ..." ("Mermaids"), for example. They all read autobiographically, and there is no apparent reason, except for the case of "Why Ravens Smile ...," to doubt the veracity of the narrative voice (i.e., Van Camp is sharing a bit of history about the creation of the story, which is interesting but not necessarily crucial in the appreciation of the stories). This is not to espouse the idea of the "the death of the author" (and in ways that, as Sinclair suggests, deny the "continuance" of Aboriginal people), but to suggest that the Afterwords function productively in providing both context and in raising questions about the role of the "author's" views in the processes of "interpretation."

11   Van Camp dedicates *Angel Wing Splash Pattern* "with love" to his "wife, Michelle Reid." This dedication does not, of course, invalidate the possibility of a previous marriage and a child who died (though the information currently available on Van Camp via standard research methods is sparse). The point here, though, is much less about Van Camp's personal life than it is about the disruption of assumptions about first-person narration, autobiography, fact, and "truth."

12   In my classes, at the outset I address ethical concerns that may arise regarding sensitive course content—literature dealing with residential school histories, for example, which may trigger painful memories for survivors (first-, second-, and third-generation)—and create guidelines with the class regarding confidentiality, the right to leave the class as needed (with subsequent checking in), and the value of the choice to not speak.

13   And of course, each classroom is a unique community of racialized, gendered, classed, beings; in each course where I've introduced this text there have been both men and women; two classes comprised Indigenous students and non-Indigenous students, and one was comprised entirely of Indigenous students. And (rather obviously), my location, as a white, middle-class straight woman—and instructor—influences the discussion, including what is and isn't shared by classroom participants.

14   This was brought home to me in one class in which we considered Marilyn Dumont's "Squaw Poems" and listened to a CBC documentary by Carol Morin (Northern Cree/Chipewyan) on "Reclaiming the Word 'Squaw'" regarding the efforts of a group of Aboriginal women to reclaim the word "squaw" from its derogatory connotations and to celebrate its origins in (at least two) Algonkian languages as a signifier of women's roles, strength, and leadership. It was only much later in the term that a young Indigenous man shared with me how painful it was for him to listen to the documentary due to the effects the derogatory term had on women in his family. I remain grateful to this man for sharing this with me, for sharpening my awareness of ethics in the classroom.

15   This discussion has been met variously—with engaging discussion, albeit primarily with white students, and critique of both the media and "sex education" courses, which, the students report, are all about "plumbing" and "biology," but not about relationships, trust, or intimacy—and with respectful silence. I do not doubt, however, that active listening was occurring.

16   This can be seen also in "Mermaids," when the elder, Snowbird, states that "Jesus was a medicine man" (8).

17   And, although I may seem somewhat facetious here (and I am certainly underestimating Van Camp's writing savvy, and my own abilities as classroom facilitator to forestall such assumptions), I have also seen/read/heard enough problematic statements regarding Aboriginal peoples, literatures, and issues, to be, I think, appropriately wary.... Indeed, as I reviewed this section of the article, I reflected on the fact that this is how I may have read the story at one (earlier) time in my own process of learning/unlearning ...

18   The Foreword to *Medicine Power* stresses these variations, noting as well that the publication of Blondin's stories in this particular publication does not indicate "formal approval" of Blondin's versions of the stories. Joanne Barnaby, Executive Director of the Dene Cultural Institute, writes:

> It is important to understand that in our oral tradition there are differences in how stories are told. This happens for several reasons. Sometimes there are language differences. Sometimes people from different places may tell a story differently. Differences can also be simply due to the personalities of the storytellers. Our publication of these stories from George's perspective is not a formal approval of these versions. Rather it represents the Institute's great appreciation of George's dedication to sharing what he knows with all of us. (n. pag.)

In his acknowledgements in *Medicine Power*, Blondin writes, "These stories belong to the Dene. I have put these stories on paper, but they are not mine" (n. pag.).

19   In "Yamoria Lives with the Beavers," for example, Blondin states that "[t]he great medicine man [Yamoria] once decided to stay with the beavers for a year. He made himself into a beaver and went to live with a beaver family in early fall. Yamoria was powerful enough to work on the beavers' minds so that the animals would accept him. He wanted to find out how the beavers make their living, so he could report it to the people" (39).

20   In my own experience, this notion emerged most specifically with the publication and performance of Tomson Highway's plays, the appearance of Thomas King's *Green Grass, Running Water,* and Highway's *Kiss of the Fur Queen.* This is not to suggest, however, that there has not also been careful and thoughtful critical work done regarding these texts; I am, indeed, generalizing here.

Works Cited

Akiwenzie-Damm, Kateri. "Erotica: Indigenous Style." In *Ad(dressing) Our Words: Aboriginal Perspectives on Aboriginal Literatures.* Ed. Armand Garnet Ruffo. Penticton, BC: Theytus, 2001. 143–51.

Barnaby, Joanne. "Foreword." In *Medicine Power*. By George Blondin. Hay River, NT: Dene Cultural Institute, 1996. N. pag.

Blondin, George. *Medicine Power*. Hay River, NT: Dene Cultural Institute, 1996.

———. *When the World Was New: Stories of the Sahtú Dene*. Yellowknife: Outcrop, 1990.

Johnston, Basil. "How Do We Learn Language?" In *Talking on the Page: Editing Aboriginal Oral Texts*. Ed. Laura Murray and Keren Rice. Toronto: U of Toronto P, 1999.

King, Thomas. *The Truth About Stories: A Native Narrative*. Toronto: Anansi, 2003.

Morin, Carol. "First Voice: "Reclaiming the Word "Squaw."'" Radio documentary. *Sounds Like Canada* (CBC Radio 1). Bernard St. Laurent, host. 19 March 2003.

Munro, Tim. Reflective Reading Journal. ENGL 385 (University of Calgary; Fall 2007). Old Sun Community College, Siksika Nation.

Sinclair, Niigonwedom James. "Trickster Reflections: Part I." In *Troubling Tricksters: Revisioning Critical Approaches*. Ed. Deanna Reder and Linda M. Morra. Waterloo, ON: Wilfrid Laurier UP, 2009. 21–58.

Stimson, Shon. "English 385 Assignment #2." ENGL 385 (University of Calgary; Fall 2007). Old Sun Community College, Siksika Nation.

Van Camp, Richard. *Angel Wing Splash Pattern*. Cape Croker Reserve, ON: Kegedonce, 2002.

———. "Foreword." In *Trail of the Spirit: The Mysteries of Medicine Power Revealed*. By George Blondin. Edmonton: NeWest, 2006. 1–3.

———. "Why Ravens Smile to Little Old Ladies as They Walk By ..." In *Angel Wing Splash Pattern*. Cape Croker Reserve, ON: Kegedonce, 2002. 24–6, 103.

A Conversation with Christopher Kientz

Christopher Kientz traces his Native ancestry back to the Eastern Cherokee nation of Tennessee and the Dawes Rolls. For the past ten years,
Kientz has worked as an independent producer and animator, developing
multimedia projects for commercial clients in both Canada and the United
States. He has scripted, produced, and directed award-winning video, animation, interactive media, and website projects for numerous clients. Growing up among the Navajo, Zuni, and Hopi people of New Mexico gave Kientz
a great respect for North American Indigenous art and culture. *Raven Tales*
represents the culmination of this interest. *Raven Tales* is both an animation
and production company founded in 2004 by Kientz and Simon James, and
the name of a cartoon series, the first six stories with Raven as the central character. In subsequent episodes that shifted from Raven, Kientz and Simon
have consulted with First Nations elders to develop stories from respective
Indigenous groups.

Linda Morra interviewed Kientz via the Internet in November 2007.

LM Might we begin with a brief history of the inception of *Raven Tales*? How
did the idea come about?

CK I grew up surrounded by fairy tales, either in book form or as told to me
by my mother and father. For the most part, these stories were in the
usual pan-European tradition. However, since my mother is half-Chero-
kee, I was also introduced to a number of traditional Native American stories and characters. All of these stories had a profound and lasting effect
on me, but the most memorable were always the stories of the Cherokee
people, which my mother had told me and which she had learned from

her father. Quite a few of these stories featured tricksters of one kind or another, like Rabbit and Water Beetle. Even as a child, I always found their adventures more interesting than those of, say, Aesop or the Grimm brothers.

There was something liberating in the idea of a central protagonist who wasn't necessarily or always moral and certainly not an innocent à la Snow White, Cinderella, and Pinocchio, but a character driven by self-interest, especially because his or her self-interest almost always served a greater good. For example, Rabbit inadvertently ends up giving fire to the First People out of a wish to smoke them out of his home. He succeeds in smoking them out, but they end up with fire, which makes their lives better and advances their culture. In the same way, Water Beetle begins the creation of the whole world by tricking other animals to bring earth up from below the ocean that, at the time, covers all things. He tricks them because he wants a place where he can rest for a bit. From self-interest and trickery comes the beginning of all things. These trickster stories were in stark contrast to the very direct moralizing of so many of the other fairy tales with which I grew up, and seemed richer somehow in their moral complexity. As a child, I couldn't know this complexity was part of the attraction, but I know I was always drawn to trickster stories.

I also grew up in New Mexico, so traditional Native American stories and sacred objects like Katsina and Navajo weavings and sand paintings were simply a part of day-to-day life. A number of my friends were also Native American, primarily Apache, so growing up in New Mexico I learned more about Kokopelli and Coyote, who were central creation figures in the southwest, and also about our tricksters. Coyote especially fascinated me because he was both a physical reality—actual coyotes skulked around our orchard—as well as a spiritual being responsible for the birth of the First People, the scattering of the stars, and so much more. The day-to-day experience of dealing with coyotes informed part of this fascination. My Apache friend Richard made sure that I knew to avoid the stare of a coyote, to turn around and take another road if one crossed my path, and to gather up its scat and bury it around the house so spirits wouldn't come in and so forth.

When I moved to Vancouver, I was introduced to the central character of the Northwest folklore, Raven, and I knew immediately that I wanted to tell not just his stories, but all of the stories I remembered from my childhood—stories of Coyote and Rabbit and the Rough Faced Girl and so on. The main reason for wanting to tell these trickster stories was to give them a central place alongside pan-European stories and to introduce the trickster, generally denigrated to second-rate status as a character of folklore, to a new audience who could see the figure as I did—as a bringer of light, an embodiment of life in all its complexity. A big part of this initial impulse came from talking to other people in the Vancouver area who had no idea that Raven was such an important character of folklore. They knew all of the pan-European stories and characters—but none of the local ones such as B'gwus, Dzunukwa, Kolus, and many more. Yet these stories and characters were every bit as compelling. Even though they were surrounded by masks and carvings with these characters present, they had no idea who they were, or what larger role they played in communities that lived in their presence.

LM So what became the driving impulse of this project?

CK Part of what drove me was the idea that these stories were generally only to be found in anthropological journals or books, and that most of these retellings lacked the humour of the originals or oral versions I remembered. I also thought the stories were perfect for animation, given the fantastical nature of the medium and the young audience. I wanted other children to know these stories as I had, as something different, with all of the moral ambiguity and humour intact. So I guess the initial idea was to do two things: tell the stories of Raven and his ilk as characters central to a rich and fascinating tradition, and to put them into a format that would be accessible to young children and general audiences.

LM In terms of satisfying the impulse to create in "a format that would be accessible to young children and general audiences," might you elaborate on your audience? Do you have priorities in terms of for whom you create this animation series? Might you elaborate on your (or your team's) objectives?

CK Ultimately, we found a studio in Calgary called New Machine Studios, which already had about twenty percent of their staff with Indigenous status. They were also willing to work with us in relation to hiring some specific talent we had found, such as animator Caleb Hystad, now one of our directors and editors.

We create largely for an audience that comprises six- to eleven-year-olds, which is the major demographic for animation. Our first hope was to ensure that Indigenous children in Canada, and Native Americans in the United States, would have a show that would be based on stories from their own communities with Native-based characters that were positive. We even went out into the community at friendship centres and hogans and asked the children what stories they wanted to see and wrote scripts based on those requests. But we also hoped for a wider audience that would embrace these stories much like the folklore from Europe and Asia. So, in addition to Native American children, children from all cultures could see and appreciate these stories.

LM How did you begin the process?

CK I roughed in the general concept of retelling traditional folklore from the point of view of a few major characters—Frog, Eagle, and Raven. Then, by happenstance, I met Simon James, a Native American animator who was also working along the same lines. He and I worked together to generate the first six stories we wanted to tell. All of the stories had Raven as a central character who, by his actions, helps the First People to progress towards one kind of enlightenment or another. After that, we approached First Nations Chiefs to ask permission to tell the stories as we'd told them.

LM How might you characterize your interactions with the First Nations Chiefs when you and Simon approached them to ask permission to tell the stories? Obviously, their response was ultimately positive because you are proceeding with the animation series, but was it consistently so? Were there reservations expressed? Did they have—or do they continue to have—input in the process?

CK Our interactions with First Nations councils and hereditary Chiefs have been uniformly positive, although they were all initially somewhat puzzled by our approach. Traditionally, First Nations councils and Chiefs are not asked permission by authors or television producers to have their stories told. Since all of the material is already in the public domain (via anthropological texts), First Nations no longer have any legal control over their oral traditions or artwork. That's why you find so many knock-off prints and masks that are not Native American in origin but made in China.

We were actually advised by a lawyer not to ask permission from the councils, as that might imply some legal ownership on their part. But we felt it was the right thing to do—they did own these stories—so we asked anyway. The Haida were especially happy to have us ask for their input because, in the past, government groups like the National Film Board created adaptations of Haida stories without any of their input. We also made sure to create some revenue streams back to the community in the form of various donations to American Indian Study programs.

In addition to getting permission, we've also worked with Indigenous representatives to help shape the scripts and, just as with the process of getting permission, this part has been a great experience, keeping us honest, really. It's also helped us solidify support for *Raven Tales* as a cornerstone for Indigenous education in Canada.

LM Does that mean that there are plans in the works to do animated trickster stories that are Cherokee in origin? Please, correct me if I am wrong—the animated stories I have seen thus far seem to be Haida in origin. What are the plans for future animations vis-à-vis the trickster?

CK The first four stories were all Haida, so your sense of that is correct. All of that had to do with the affiliations of the major producers. We knew from the start we wanted to feature folklore from across North America, but we wanted to establish a base first. The second part of the first season, episodes ten and twelve, are both Cherokee stories. Episode ten, for example, is the story of how sickness entered the world. This story features designs and words in Cherokee; it is book-ended with the regular characters being told the story via Frog. So we stay in the same Northwestern setting with the same major characters, but we move around geographically as part of the story being told. We've done this with episodes eight to thirteen actually, so we're expanding our base of stories and are moving across North America as we tell them. We even have two Coyote stories, so we will feature other tricksters as the series continues. As for future animation, I am working with Gerald McDermott, a famous children's author, to create some animation based on his own series of trickster tales.

LM Aside from Simon James and Gerald McDermott, how did you develop your current production team?

CK Simon and I spent a long time trying to pitch *Raven Tales* to existing studios in Canada, but none was interested. They didn't think there would be demand from broadcasters. Even after we found a broadcaster willing to put the show on the air nationally, studios still didn't want to do the show. They felt like we couldn't find enough foreign broadcasters. Studios also felt our wish to have a studio willing to hire at least a good proportion of the animation talent from the Indigenous population was out of line. We found there were quite a few Indigenous artists and animators, but few were working steadily in the business, and we wanted to change that.

LM If one of the challenges you faced was trying to persuade or locate willing broadcasters, what would you say have been other challenges? How did you resolve these?

CK Even before we got to the stage of seeking broadcasters, we found it very difficult to find financing. When we first started out creating *Raven Tales*, we sought funding as a non-profit agency from groups like the Ford Foundation, CPB/PBS, the National Film Board of Canada, the Gates Foundation, and the National Indian Education Association (NIEA), among others. They all suggested that the medium of computer animation wasn't something they could support because it didn't reflect the authentic or traditional standards for Native American art. My belief, and Simon's as well, is that the stories, the people who tell them, and the quality of the final piece are the most important aspect of the work, not the medium, so it was perplexing to us as Native American artists to be told we should self-censor our work to meet the demands of a group of non-Natives so they could be assured that what they were supporting was "authentic." So we turned to private finance and became a for-profit company. We ended up leveraging our personal equity to get loans to make the show.

We also found it hard to find production companies actually willing to produce the show. Even with full financing in place, production companies saw the show and the market as too limited to invest their time and production team. I don't blame them really, since classically Native American or First Nations programming is ghettoized to time slots or channels with a limited audience. Eventually, we found a production company who could see that there might be a larger audience if the show was designed and produced to be mainstream while it still avoided homogenization. We resolved all of these issues through sheer will and perseverance. Both Simon and I felt strongly enough about telling these stories not to give up. We also had the support of First Nations communities who were eager for a show that would tell their stories.

LM Although, as you said earlier, you believe animation appeals to children (one of the primary audiences targeted), what do you think are the implications of using this form, especially when we consider the original oral transmission of the said trickster stories?

CK Simon and I thought a great deal about the use of animation to tell these stories and the differences between an oral tradition and the medium of animation. Clearly, there are some major differences—an oral presentation allows the teller of the story to improvise, elaborate, and interact with the audience. It is a more egalitarian and immediate form of storytelling, fluid and interactive. Animation, on the other hand, is a fixed medium with the creator and the audience removed in space and time. Animation also forces upon the audience a more passive role, much more than both an oral retelling or even a written transcript. It's pretty much impossible to form a direct parallel between the two mediums.

Among non-Natives, especially anthropologists, there is a sense often that the removal of a story from the oral tradition and adaptation to another medium, especially a contemporary one, invalidates the experience. This response may be valid; however, it assumes that the oral tradition of storytelling is the only way Indigenous populations tell stories that can be adapted, which is far from the reality. Indigenous people also have dance, sculpture, and the visual arts, with which we may draw closer parallels to more contemporary mediums like animation. Ultimately, Simon and I felt like the medium of animation had more in common with traditional carving and dance; both of these mediums require a great deal of craftsmanship and preparatory work, allow less for improvisation, and require a more rigid, formal sensibility. Carving and dance, like animation, also remove the creator from an interactive relationship with the audience. In the case of dance, the audience is involved only as a spectator; the audience is a passive participant for the most part. In the case of a totem, the audience reads the work from bottom to top, but otherwise the work is more spectacle than narrative.

So, in the case of *Raven Tales*, we placed an emphasis on adapting carved and dance works in forging the animated series. For example, we modelled the characters to look like traditional Northwest Coast carvings and also created walk cycles and character movements to mirror Raven or Eagle dancers. We also placed an emphasis on dialogue, as in dance performances in which the dialogue is sung, as well as an overarching narrative voice, which is also present during dance presentations.

On a final note: in creating the series, our hope was to make *Raven Tales* a starting place for children, not a capstone to their experience of Indigenous stories. The ideal response to seeing *Raven Tales* would be to seek out more cultural resources, including elders who can tell these stories in their original language and form.

LM Might you track for me the manner in which you and Simon—and perhaps other members of the production team—negotiate amongst yourselves about the stories you select and how you choose to represent them (for example, a character's voice)?

CK Generally, Simon and I suggest the stories first with the idea of concentrating on a particular character with the story somehow impacting his or her life. The idea is to give each character in *Raven Tales* a chance to grow and learn. Since this is a children's show, most of the lessons we concentrate on relate to basic value lessons—for example, the importance of honesty, or believing in yourself, or helping others and working together. So, in the case of Sea Wolf, for example, we reworked a Coast Salish story about the first totems to be about a character named Gwai, who learns an important lesson about keeping promises and finding his own particular skill. Once Simon and I agree on the general outline, I write the story, then I work with the cast members to finalize dialogue and narration. Then we go to the appropriate First Nations council—in the case of Sea Wolf, the Cowichan—and make sure we aren't doing anything out of step with the original intent of the story. With their approval, we write the final script. The animators also work to give each character its own individual quirks. Once we move into production, the script rarely changes, but we give the cast some latitude in relation to how they do their voice work. Overall, the whole process is highly collaborative and also pretty rewarding.

LM Let's talk about your most recent work. How does your new partnership with Atomic Cartoons and the development of *Task Force Shaman* relate to or fit into the ideological parameters of *Raven Tales*?

CK *Task Force Shaman* was something I came up with as we travelled around the world as part of the National Geographic All Roads Film Project and showed *Raven Tales* to various Indigenous communities. Each time we'd show *Raven Tales*, whether it was in New Zealand with Maori children watching, or in Norway with Sami children, they all talked about wanting a show about their own culture, or a show with characters from their communities. I also noticed that many children outside the immediate Indigenous community knew more about American superhero characters than local folklore. For example, a group of children from an Australian school in Sydney had never heard of the Rainbow Serpent or Dreamtime, two amazing folklore elements from the Aboriginal communities that were part of their own country's heritage. I found the same thing in British Columbia, where schoolchildren could tell you all about Batman or Superman, but had no idea who Dzunukwa was, or Kolus, or any number of local folkloric characters. One school in Campbell River actually had a totem with a Sea Wolf design across the street, yet most of the students had never heard the story of Sea Wolf or knew the connection to Campbell River. So, I got it in my head that what I'd like to do after *Raven Tales*, albeit along the same ideological line, is to create a series that puts a group of Indigenous children from across the globe in a contemporary setting and make them the heroes of the series. I thought such a series would have a broader appeal and find a larger audience than *Raven Tales*, even as it remained a celebration of Indigenous folklore. That led me to talking to people like Cliff Curtis, a Maori actor, as well as contacts I'd made from my travels, to see what they thought. All of them loved the idea. I also got to thinking about commonalities in terms of Indigenous cultures and came up with the shaman angle. All of these cultures still have elements of shamanistic rites and still abide by shamanistic ritual. I thus created a backstory that would bring together these different characters and give them a reason to be heroes in a contemporary setting, while still using folkloric elements from each culture. As with *Raven Tales*, we're still going to work with Indigenous communities to craft the stories and make sure we aren't fudging anything—only, this time, we're going to move the action from the past to the present, and give the whole series a more global focus.

LM And give us something more to which to look forward. Thank you very much, Chris.

CK Thank you.

Personal Totems

I was born a poor, black child
—Steve Martin, 1977

The absurdity of that comic statement, from Steve Martin's stand-up routine, is realized by the fact that he wasn't actually born a poor, black child. Obvious, I know. Then again, you may not who Steve Martin is; however, his racial identity did become a central plot point behind his 1979 movie, *The Jerk*. In the movie, Martin was raised by a poor, black family in the southern United States. Sheltered from the world outside him and from the fact that he isn't black, he decides to leave the nest, so to speak, to experience the world around him, and to live in a world in which he belonged—a white world.

The fundamentals within the story (I won't deconstruct them further) can be seen in a number of different stories throughout the ages, most notably as a pop culture reference—Superman. A Kryptonian boy crash-lands on earth and is raised by human parents. From the get-go, Superman (Clark Kent) is strong and aware of his powers at an early age. Steve Martin's character in *The Jerk* isn't aware he isn't black, a fact he doesn't realize until his adoptive mother finally has had enough of his lack of rhythm and lets him in on the obvious secret.

In a way, I think *The Jerk* relates to my own childhood. For a brief stint, I actually thought I was blue. Blue, you ask? Yes, blue. Grover from *Sesame Street* was, back then, my best TV friend. And, as a child raised on TV programming, I was presented with a model that my four-year-old brain couldn't really grasp.

That which is presented to you on TV isn't always the truth—obviously. Not that thinking I was blue for a while was a morally changing experience for a four-year-old, but it does mirror another interesting part of my history.

Growing up at the pinnacle of television pop culture, I was blissfully unaware of the rich cultural heritage to which I belonged. Born in May of 1975, I was the product of my mother's summer love when she was quite young. Luckily, I was born into a family and a culture that valued keeping adoption within the family, so I was raised by my grandparents. By the time I began to realize I wasn't blue, I began to form memories of relationships. And the strongest I had and still have is of my sister, who, in fact, came memorably to my aid one fall afternoon.

I had come home from school to discover, in an era of rarely locked doors, that the side door was locked. Puzzled, I walked around to the back to check out the sliding door, which was also locked. Being the crafty kid that I was, I noticed that the kitchen window was open, so I slid my (then) small frame through. I was either bewildered as to why my Mom and Dad weren't home or I was hungry, so I picked up the telephone and dialed the only number I could think of—that of my sister.

I can't recall the details of the conversation, but I'm sure it had something to do with both my inability to open up a can of Chef Boyardee and her questioning me about why my parents weren't home. When you're seven, falling into a predictable routine is commonplace: get up, go to school, come home. Also: Mom wakes you up; Mom makes you breakfast. Then: you rip your pants on the fence; you go through the day not caring that the said pants are ripped; you hop the same fence again; you come home. Finally: Mom gives you a snack, then dinner; you sleep. Repeat the next day. So I was also a bit worried as to why neither my Mom nor my Dad were home. Shortly after our telephone call, Dani, my sister, came to see me.

Our subsequent conversation is one that I clearly remember. It's one of those memories that someone is likely unable to forget. After learning that I was left alone, Dani had come over with her boyfriend and his incredibly cool car (I credit him and *The Dukes of Hazzard* for my love of 1960s–1980s muscle cars. But I digress). I remember that I must have been sitting on the floor, possibly playing with some toys, when she came up behind me. She told me that she was there to get me and that I was going to come live with her and Jerry because Mom and Dad were having some issues. There was a pause, as I could imagine I must have been upset and acting like any seven-year-old would: a bit overcome with emotion, wanting it all to be normal again.

Cue: the sappy 1980s *Days of Our Lives* music.

"I am your Mom," she finally said.

As I play it all out in my head, I imagine myself utilizing the greatest of all actors' tricks, perhaps something the Haida Raven himself perfected long before he coaxed the first man from the clamshell. I'm conjuring up how the scene must have gone down—and I credit it to one part overactive imagination and one part obligatory soap opera watching for an entire spring break. So, after the scene is played out in my head in the vein of cheesy daytime soaps, I figured, as a seven-year-old, that it was common-place for the people with whom I lived to be my parental units. Woman, man, kid = family. It wasn't until I was about twelve that I finally clued into the fact that our strong resemblance was more than just a brother/sister simi-larity. I don't recall what it was that finally helped me clue into my slightly skewed lineage. I just remember being twelve and finally figuring it out. Maybe it took my brain those five years to put all the pieces together, but when I look back on my life I notice some displacement. The year when I was eight was a huge transition for me. It was the start of the school year, and I went from the familiar to the unfamiliar—from a suburb and ele-mentary school to an inner-city school. I guess one could look back and figure I might have had it a bit rough. But the only thing that I see as neg-ative in those years was the fact that I must have liked grade three so much, I wanted to do it again.

Yes, being uprooted and made to repeat a grade could be seen as nega-tive—but I went along with it. I never rebelled in my teenage years and I never used it as a crutch to gain sympathy. I was just being me: a happy 1980s kid going through the motions of the week and waiting for my Saturday morning cartoons.

I dissect my life for the sake of my art and, within that dissection, I dis-cover a lot about myself and about how pop-consumerism works. I have learned that my generation was bred to consume: Saturday morning cartoons were thirty-minute advertisements for various toys that we just couldn't live without. The 1980s set up the framework for contemporary consumerism. You can ask me if my uprooting and the discovery of my biological mother were traumatic all you want—some might even get off on dissecting the inner workings of how it affects me as an artist and as a person. But ask me what was *really* traumatic to me at that point in my life and I'll tell you it wasn't the discovery that the person I thought was my sister was actually my mother. No—it was the fact that I never got to have a Megatron Trans-formers action figure. Fuck, what I would not have done for that shiny transforming gun. This was the holy grail of Transformers—what kid from the 1980s wouldn't want to whip out one of those Mo-Foes in a dusty Vancouver alley gunfight?[1]

If a thirty-minute episode of the Transformers isn't a thirty-minute toy advertisement, I don't know what is. Kids have a powerful inclination towards adapting. And I see these childhood memories of my life as a story about adapting to fit in with what I was about to become. It was a big year of change for me: living seven years of my life in one house, and finding out that the people whom I thought were my parents actually were my grandparents and that the person whom I thought was my sister was, in fact, my mother. It makes for a very special episode of *Jerry Springer*. But, as with every good episode of *Jerry*, there comes a twist.

A year later and I celebrated my eighth birthday in my new life. Tensions between my grandparents only allowed for one to attend the party. But, within that year, we had moved to the lower level of the duplex we lived in and soon my grandfather, who at the time was living in a hotel, moved into our old suite upstairs. I then became known as Ronnie's shadow, a seeming aside to the story I'm telling but relevant to my lineage nonetheless. With the minor hiccup of where I was living and with whom I was living finally tucked neatly away in the recesses of my mind, I began to settle into the normal existence of being an eight-year-old child. I was living in the city and growing up in an age that can only be described as the beginning of contemporary pop culture.

That year for my birthday I received a strange new gift from my mom, a.k.a. my grandmother—a Walkman! It might as well have been a Volvo, the thing was half the size of my torso and heavy as hell. I tried to hide the shame of the large brick that I lugged around to school back in the good old days. I did feel safe that it wasn't about to get stolen anytime soon. After all, the school bully, who was only slightly bigger than I was, would probably get about five feet away before discovering he would be unable to make a clean getaway with an additional eighty-pound kid strapped onto the seemingly only twenty-pound Walkman. Now there is no way I looked even accidentally cool with a small country hanging from my neck; and there was no way in hell I was even going to attempt a moonwalk with this thing throwing off my balance. Top off the image with ridiculously large orange foam earphones and I stood out more than the almost abnormally tall tubby kid in the class picture who was held back a year. Mind you, it didn't help that *I* was the almost abnormally tall tubby kid in the class picture that was held back a year. I would lug this brick around with a shoulder strap astride me, listening to my first tape, Michael Jackson's *Thriller*. 1982 was a good year for me, not just because of the Walkman (the early versions of the thing should have been dubbed "back-problems-man"), but also because, while consumerism was being marketed to me via my favourite Saturday morning cartoons, I discovered something about myself that would later shape my chosen path in life as an artist.

"I always was the cowboy"

I had come running home from school one day, super-excited over what I had just learned about: Indians. Of course, this was the time before political correctness, and before we referred to this group of people as the First Nations[2] (or First People). So, I burst in through the front door, out of breath and excited. I blew past my dog, Skipper, in my excitement, and flung off my shoes as I normally did: with such enthusiasm that I tried to hit the ceiling with them. I ran towards the kitchen and slid in, Tom Cruise *Risky Business*–style (before he went crazy). I was unaware that I had just blasted by Dani as she tried to nap on the couch. I'm sure my door-slamming, shoes-hitting-the-ceiling, Skipper-barking-like-crazy antics put an end to her afternoon siesta.

I enthusiastically told her about the people we had learned about that day—told her the art that was shown to me was similar to that which her boyfriend, Jerry, did. I repeated my lesson with great detail, told her about the art and culture and about how these people once lived on the coast where we spent our summers in commercial fishing: "Today, we learned about the Kwakiutl people."[3]

She propped herself up on the couch and looked at me with a half-smile: "That is who you are, Sonny." Being eight, I really didn't understand the ramifications of what it was like to be part of a minority. After all, I was just some little white kid from the 'burbs, although living in the city, a kid playing "Cowboys and Indians" in the alley, blissfully unaware that I was actually a double agent.

We all have stories that make up who we are. I try and delude myself in thinking that this "double agent" status is just the normal run of things. But when I explain my lineage to people, I might as well just tell them I arrived on earth one day from a planet that exploded, or that I grew up a poor black child in the deep South. But those events in my early life lead to the inspiration towards the artwork I make today. I see it as an important step in deconstructing who we are as purveyors of pop culture. Do I think I am unique? I'd be lying if I said, "No." But the fact of the matter is that my generation and the generations after me have felt the effects of consumer culture since we began to walk. And this is why I believe that, as the pop culture generation, we have the right to use these icons as our own personal totems: we are so inundated by items and imagery of pop culture, we also have the right to use it as a way to dictate our own lineage. Yes, we are the Pepsi Generation.

The Family Biz; or, "Sonny's a whiny B****"

I guess one could hold onto the romantic notion of what it is like to be an artist. I could spew out typical crud like, "Oh, I've been an artist all my life," which is pretty much bullshit if you ask me. It's almost like saying I got involved in the arts because I showed my early talent in kindergarten by eating paste. It's one of those clichés we artists like to implore. It gives our chosen profession a bit of a romantic sheen. I've recently seen a documentary in which the subject was a five-year-old abstract painter. But, really, what five-year-old isn't an abstract painter? The parents were proud that their child was starting to rake in thousands of dollars per painting, but they were scared to death that their child was a prodigy, which, for these parents, was tantamount to being a "freak."

I could argue that I've been an artist all my life because I would rather have been doodling in the margins than actually getting "hooked on phonics." However, calling yourself an artist isn't about selling your first work or landing some big project. Art, for the most part, is a personal thing. And calling yourself an artist isn't something you do just willy-nilly. It takes time to build yourself up and to be aware of what it is exactly to be an artist—which is something that is needed to be discovered on a personal level. At first, calling myself an artist was a hard thing to do. Even in art school, I'd blurt out every so often that I was an artist and I felt like I had to explain myself—like I had just told the whole room I was radioactive. But it wasn't the completion of art school that made me want to call myself an artist. It was the realization that I was doing something I loved. This wasn't my hobby: this was my path in life. It was when I figured out that I had a voice in what I was creating that I felt I could shed the inhibitions revolving around my label. And, ultimately, it was when I was able to make people question the fabric of "what is Indian art or what is art" that I considered myself a creative thinker.

I come from a long line of fishermen[4] that included my grandfather—a.k.a. "dad"—and his son Ted, which through the rather *Jerry Springer* version of my life, was known to me as "my brother"—a.k.a. "Uncle." Okay, so the line isn't that long, but take into consideration that colonization in B.C. happened under 200 years ago and also that I come from a culture whose main food source is salmon. So, yeah, I come from a long line of fishermen. My grandfather was the youngest captain in the commercial fleet during that time; add to the fact that he was an Indian man, and that's truly something to consider, especially given that, back in the early 1940s, the First People were badly oppressed. But he beat the odds and proved himself to be a valuable asset to the fleet. So I spent every summer between the ages of five and seventeen on a commercial seine boat. I grew up on the W#4 and my grandfather wanted to groom me to take over the reins one day, much like how he groomed Ted. For the most part, I spent the early years in the galley doodling, lying in my bunk reading comics, or sitting on the top deck from which I could look down and watch the crew work. This is where I probably picked up my knack for colourful language. When I got a little older, I'd venture down onto the deck to help put the fish in the hatch. Around the time I hit my teenage years, my grandfather would start to remind me what he had in store. He wanted me to be a captain: one day I'd work side by side with him, eventually taking over the big chair, even if it was more like an uncomfortable stool.

The summer before my grandfather passed away, I started to venture onto the deck a little more. At that point in my life, I was more immersed in art and theatre than I was in becoming a fisherman. Maybe it was the hard work; maybe it was the slimy working conditions. Something in me knew I wasn't going to be able to fulfill my grandfather's dreams of becoming the next seine boat sensation. One afternoon in particular, I got up rather late. I wasn't an integral part of the crew, so my sleeping past four in the morning was okay. Anyway, I was mostly just along for the ride, so I tried not to get in the way. But, after the guilt of laziness set in, I'd usually pop on the deck to help out a little. Nothing big—coil some ropes, put fish in the hatch, or pump out the bilge. What I really wanted to do was run the drum or the winch. I was allowed to run the winch once, but nearly "fucked some shit up," as I remember it being put to me. This one afternoon, I made my way out onto the deck at pretty much the end point of the set. I wandered to the stern to help remove salmon from the webbing. My grandfather had manned the drum and had put it in idle for me to remove a sockeye caught by the gills in the webbing—usually a simple task, but I stood there, trying as hard as I could to get that sockeye loose. Pulling on the tail, as it wiggled in a last fight for breath, I grabbed the web and tried to snap the salmon loose, but nothing was budging. I was frustrated, so I began to deploy some of that previously discussed colourful language. I swore like the devil himself took hold of me. It wasn't my proudest moment; to save you the gory details, as no one likes to be on PETA's naughty list, the sockeye was flung from the net, *sans* head.

My grandfather stopped the drum altogether to allow the crew on the mid-deck to do some work. I wiped scales from my face and kicked the sockeye head over board. Some say that the head of a salmon is a delicacy, but I just couldn't take those cold, lidless blue eyes staring up at me from the deck. Dad walked over to me and said, "You're going to law school."

I laughed that comment off pretty quick. I wasn't the best student during my high school days, as I much preferred to draw or to be on stage. I believe I was destined to be in some sort of creative field, and, if it weren't for the lack of love for hard work, the lure of good fishing money would have surely sucked me in. But I knew my life wasn't meant for something as labour-intensive as fishing, let alone law. But I think at that point he knew I was on my own path. My frustrations with a simple fish sealed the deal for him. Regardless of my path, he just wanted the best for me. Even with his flaws, he was able to inspire other generations to step up to the plate and forge a new path—or one that happened to be the same as his. He knew I was meant for something else and he had a message for me—find my own path. No matter what I did, he knew I'd be forging my own way. Save for a few tantrums.

My grandfather helped shape me into the person I am today—a little more so than in the traditional ways you could imagine. He helped shape my obsession with pop-consumerism and helped shape my mindset with personal totems: what we own dictates our lineage. When my grandmother and he split, for reasons that were their own, for which I know now had nothing to do with me, they started a mini-battle for who might be the coolest— a.k.a., "Who can spoil Sonny the most?" It seems silly, really, and, at that point in my life, I never really saw it as a battle—I just saw it as a way to get new shit I didn't really need. It was their split that helped fuel my obsession with becoming a collector of pop culture. It also gave me the stigma of what some would call a spoiled brat. But that's another story. Their guerrilla warfare of who could give me the most crap was at the pinnacle of 1980s consumerism. I never really saw their over-giving to me as a way to buy my love. It was just cool to get new toys every couple of weeks. So why the hell didn't I get that Megatron Transformer I so desired? I was the envy of my friends and I became the centre of attention to the kids who just wanted to play with my new toys. I became a casualty of consumerism in their battle—which led not only to the dissection of my childhood through my art and my dissection of pop culture but also to my consideration of how it affects us as a whole and as a First culture that is the complete opposite to the hoarding culture that has become our society.

Challenging Tradition

When I first began my post-secondary exploration of art, I did so without reference to the culture that I learned of at the age of eight. That was more of a last step in finding out where I fit within the world and what I was going to do with my life. I knew who I was and where I came from, but I never really explored the options that were open to me. I never grew up in the culture, so I was never exposed to the same cultural experience as my many cousins were. I was blissfully unaware of my lineage, and when I decided to forge my own path, I went in blind, clinging to something I just loved to do.

As a kid, I read comic books; now I'm a collector. Comics were my escape and provided me with more entertainment than a television ever could. It was that love for superheroes that propelled me to create my own. Anyone in my family could look back fondly on my childhood and teen years and say they never saw me without a pencil in my hand. It was that love of drawing that propelled me into pursuing a post-secondary education. My high school years were filled with artistic expression. I was heavily involved in theatre and, at the time, when I decided to go to school, I was faced with a choice: pursue theatre or pursue art. Sometimes the choice is made for you; as my future luck would have it, the choice for me was art.

The path that was laid out for me was the path of an artist. Jumping ahead a few years, I transferred into one of Canada's most prestigious art institutions. It was at the Emily Carr Institute in Vancouver where I really started to delve into who I was. And, in doing so, I had to look into my past to discover what fundamentally made up "Sonny." I was bored in the studio late one night, quite possibly coming down off a high from a quick Hacky Sack session, and more than likely licking the salt off my fingers from the bag of chips I inhaled while giggling through the empty halls of the school. It was on that late fall evening that I discovered a new direction for my work. I wanted to come up with something that was uniquely my own and that was more representative of both who I was and how I fit within my culture.

My base mandate for most, if not all of my work, is to forge something new out of the old. At the time, I was toying with using new media to tell old stories. I was successful in my technique, but what failed me was the message. I was more content with trying to fight the stereotypes of what was "Indian art" than actually trying to come up with something uniquely my own. My work, iconically West Coast, was based more in theory than image. At the time, what I was creating was no different in my eyes than what was already created. Whether it was work being created by a master carver of the past, the most sought after contemporary master carver, or some dude sitting on the corner of Robson and Howe carving up five-dollar plaques for the tourists, it was all the same—it promoted a stereotype of what that Indian art should be, a stereotype that not only dictated what Indian art should be, but what a "real Indian" is. For me, the challenge was, and has been since then, to overcome the wall of stereotype, to extend the boundaries of First Nations art, to push contemporary art and ideals in a new direction.

My Indian-ness is not made up of the stereotypical notions that some hold onto. I don't live in a tipi and, even though my great-grandfather was a chief, that doesn't make my grandmother a "real Indian princess." My hair isn't long, my skin is not red, and my Indian-ness is not dictated by my status card. What dictates my Indian-ness is my knowledge of the past, the fact that I know who I am and where I come from. It's with these notions that I can challenge the stereotype of the perceived Indian identity. I decided, that late fall evening, that it was best to drop what I was doing and try to come up with something truly new—rooted in the culture, but completely different from anything that anyone else had done. I thought about how I got involved with art in the first place: Super Heroes. I thought that maybe if I just got back into drawing the way I used to, it would free me up and provide me with a new direction. I was fuelled by sugar and weed, so I set out to look back to the past to find a bit of inspiration.

A main focus of my work over the past few years has been trying to fig-ure out how pop culture affects us through a direct exploration of how it affects me. Moreover, I'm trying to figure out how it affects the First People of Canada. It's no secret that the First Peoples have had a bit of a rough go: it's a tad demoralizing to have your culture and home ripped away from you. Not that I understand this from first-hand experience: how could I know when I look like your seemingly average white guy? But that is one of the things I enjoy doing, although it is a bit hard to take. I don't have first-hand experience of what it is like to lose your culture; I am the by-product of that loss. My lineage wasn't exactly hidden from me, but neither was it explained to me until I discovered it. Some could call me a "born-again Indian," but that just tempts me to grow my hair out: trust me, my days of long hair are best left to bad high school photos.

Before This Turns into an "Angry Indian Rant"

But I must digress: Who is a First Nations person? Who is an Indian? Why am I using the word "Indian"? Are the factors that determine culture or race made up of skin colour? Or is it cultural upbringing that makes you who you are and who you become? I ask these questions because these questions are constantly asked of me. I mention them because of who I am and how I was raised. I mention them because the "angry Indian" is not me, although I did break into those rants from time to time. I've heard the "angry Indian" rant too many times to care and, like most people who tend to be at the receiv-ing end of the said rant, tend to glaze over. I soon realized the truth of the old adage, "you'll catch more flies with honey."

For me, humour is honey. I found that the best way to draw people into the political side of my work was to sugar-coat it, much like the sugary cereals of pop culture and much like any functioning government would. I lure people in with a bit of humour to make the politics easier to swallow. It's all about education and, for the most part, it's received well. I use subliminal advertisements, although my message isn't as bad as an ad for KFC (*go and get a bucket of chicken!*). To me, the angry Indian rant is dead. Why do I need to be angry? Me—white boy incognito from the 'burbs? How could I have had it rough at all? In the history lesson about Sonny's life in this essay, some might see that my life was a little upside-down for a few years. Some might even think I'd be a prime candidate for being a bit off-kilter. But I'm resilient: I constantly look to my past to find answers. When I first started off as an artist, I constantly looked to the past for guidance. And what I found angered me. I found the atrocities that afflicted my people and became socially angry for the first time. And I used to deploy the "angry Indian rant." On occasion, I still do, but it's usually with my friends, and, in that case, I'm just preaching to the choir.

I began to explore the rich cultural heritage to which I belonged. I was influenced by Bill Reid and his mission to have his work and First Nations art hung alongside other masterful works in an art museum, instead of an anthropology museum. Bill's work was a stepping stone for me. His work helped define my direction as an artist. And I began to explore the issues that came along with being a First Nations person. I knew that there were events in Canadian history that were a blight, but I wasn't fully aware of those issues until I started to learn of them while at the Emily Carr Institute. In my early work, I tried to build a concept of what I'm doing, which is furthering the exploration and the understanding of my culture.

Sugar-coated Lies and Sugar-coated Cereal Share Similarities

First Nations culture in Canada is defined by the stereotypical notion of what or who a real "Indian" is. I follow in the belief of many that, with the eyes of the world coming to us, specifically in Vancouver in 2010, Canada has chosen to reiterate this stereotype and to deliver this view to its audience. Vancouver is located in the territory of the Coast Salish. And their aesthetic is something uniquely representative of West Coast iconography. So what did the organizers of the 2010 Olympics choose as the logo? One would assume a totem pole, or some sort of totemic image—a welcome figure or perhaps the image of the Raven. Nope: Inukshuk. Something clearly representational of the Inuit people, thousands of miles away. Welcome to Vancouver, home of the cultural stereotype. Vancouver is using this "ideal" stereotype from the North. I can't wait to see all the tourists coming into Vancouver, geared up for parka weather, when they should be gearing up for a raincoast climate. But hey, it's not my call to promote to the world what it's actually like here on the "wet coast." The world is seeing us as fur-clad, ice-dwelling, seals-as-pets people, which is fine by me because it gives me something to complain about and fuels a new direction for my work: consumerism.

We belong to a culture of consumerism; we choose objects of mass production to represent our identities. With brands such as Coke, iPod, Nike, and McDonald's, it's no wonder that that overall trademark loyalty is seemingly growing by leaps and bounds. With every new generation that comes into its own self-awareness, corporate association is bringing the world together in a weird clash of globalization and anti-conformity.

Over the past twenty years (at least in the realm of contemporary pop culture), branding has become a way of life for many. I'll even admit that I am part of that conformity. And for those immersed in the pop culture aesthetic, choosing a particular brand to represent yourself is a way to communicate to the world where your affiliations lie. It states, "I'm different, but I'm still just like you." In essence, it's choosing conformity to speak for individuality.

Breakfast Series, installation view: *Cereal Boxes*, 2006 (Treaty Flakes, Lucky Beads, Salmon Crisp, Salmon Loops, Bannock Pops). Digitally printed, 12 x 7 x 3 inches each.

My current body of work, the Breakfast series, Personal Totem series, and Urban Totem series, examines how we allow everyday consumer items and icons of pop culture to define our lineage—how branding, brand loyalty, and technology relate to the idea of totemic representation. I too am a product of pop culture. I grew up in the age of mass media advertising, subliminal advertisements, and the stories/mythos of Saturday morning cartoons. I am able to combine my pop roots with my learned traditional Laich-kwiltach heritage. Learning of my dual identity at the age of eight, I began to explore and understand that identity by the age of twenty-one. In the past eleven years, I've been able to juxtapose two seemingly un-combinable cultures and then to speak about how we choose icons and objects to define ourselves. By creating the personal and urban totemic representation imagery, laden with a sense of ironic wry humour and informed by social, economical, and environmental issues, I speak to the idealistic notion of conformity by *not conforming* to the notion of the "Indian identity."

"We are Canadian"

What is the problem with Canada? We have this pristine preconception of us: we're awesome. *We are Canadian.* But as I sit here and write this essay, I'm confronted by something that usually happens to me on a daily basis. I'm a crazy magnet. Not only has my love life been plagued by women who were clearly off their rocker, but I'm approached on an almost daily basis by people whom most would consider crazy. But, in a city as affluent as Vancouver, you would assume that we have measures in place to help out the people who need help. We don't; we're just like any major Western city. We have problems we'd much rather ignore.

As I sit here in this café, surrounded by people sipping on their lattes, writing papers, chatting, including that one dude sitting in the corner with a guitar plucking the same strings in ADD fashion, I'm confronted by a Native man. I'm tucked neatly behind a pane of glass, staring out at the street, and giving my eyes a break from the screen. I look out the window when this person obstructs my peripheral vision for too long; I slowly raise my head. He is a little dishevelled, not completely down and out, but someone I probably would not want to run into in a dark alley. I look over and do what most do when they notice a "crazy" person in public—I ignore him. But, as I look up, he starts to talk at me through the plate glass window. What he was saying, I'll never know. As I said, I see people like this on a daily basis rambling at me, telling me tales of how they lost their shopping bag and so forth. My problem, apparently, is compassion.

When I look up at this man in the process of writing this essay about myself and my work, I begin to question why we as a society have shunned this man. And it only proves my point: we much prefer to bury the problems our ancestors have created. The settlers of what is now called Canada chose to decimate a race; they made First People the dregs of society. We—"Canadians"— are not a pristine example of humanity. We like to pretend we are—and people see us as such—but we show them what we want them to see. We break out our First People as totems of this land. We use them to promote a harmonious society. But here I am, sitting in a small café in the urban jungle, being yelled at through the window by a man who clearly needs attention. This man is the epitome of what is wrong with our society—we ignore those who need help, whose very situation we've directly or indirectly created, but instead we spend resources on a two-week parade that will only exacerbate these problems in the long run.

Death Blanket and To the Indians ...

Two of my works, *Death Blanket* and *To the Indians* ..., are my comments about the ugly stain on the pristine white carpet that is known as Canadian history—and, as with any other stain, the couch has been moved around to hide it from view. Not everyone knows of this stain, and most are content with keeping it that way. Admit it or not, there was a genocide that occurred here in Canada, that dramatically reduced the size of the Indigenous population. I call it the world's forgotten genocide. Something tells me it's probably not the first, but it is the largest in our Western history. It far outnumbers those who died in the Holocaust, but no one is willing to acknowledge the fact that it happened. Most would rather see it merely as sour grapes rather than an actual crime against humanity.

First People had no immunity to the industrial diseases brought over from Europe: measles, influenza, whooping cough, and, most notoriously, smallpox. These diseases had already wiped out a large number of people within the early years of first contact. Those who didn't die right away were shipped off to reserves, and eventually residential schools, to be stripped of their humanity and, paradoxically, to be assimilated into "civilized" society. Treaties and agreements were beginning to be ignored in the hopes that, with assimilation and attempted genocide, the land would eventually belong to the government and the Hudson's Bay Company. Eventually, the decimation of the people led to the adoption of the Indian Act (1876), which rendered every Native in Canada a ward of the state: infantile white guilt at its finest, really. Realizing that we've caused a problem, now we must try and rectify the problem. How? By adopting an Act that forced the people to become dependent on a handout by the government. Removing oneself from the confines of the Act meant one lost a connection to one's resources; assimilation was the only other alternative. It was the hope of the Act that the people would assimilate, give up, and walk away from any claim they could have held to their own culture and resources.

Some hold to the misconception that the Act dictates that I get a house, that I get free education, and that I get free health care. It does not. If I want a house, I have to move to an area that won't provide me with the resources that I need to sustain myself, and, if I did, the house wouldn't be free. My education is not free. And I, just like everyone else in Canada, take part in the joke known as "Universal Health Care." The Act only had one goal, to assimilate the First People fully, to remove the "Indian" from the Indian. I think the writer of *Star Trek: The Next Generation* must have been doing some research into world history before coming up with the idea for the Borg, which is associated with the phrase "Resistance is futile." In the words of Lt. Cmdr. Worf, "Assimilate this!"[5]

How Does the Trickster Relate to these Politically Heavy Pieces?: Trickster, oh Trickster, When Did You Go?

I've never been one for being overly heavy-handed or prone to the "angry Indian rant." But, from time to time, it can and will be conjured up. When I talk about these pieces, I usually prefer to place these rants between humorous pieces. Exploring the notion of the trickster is a subtext in my work. I make reference to Raven in the vast part of my works; however, sometimes it's not blatantly obvious that what you are looking at is indeed Raven. But Raven is a transformer, and I see him "keeping up with the Joneses," so to speak. Raven, in my work, transforms into these objects/icons of pop culture to stay in the loop. After all, he is the creature that brought light to the world by knocking up the Chief's daughter after turning himself into a pine needle. A win–win situation, if you come to think of it: he gave us light and got the virtue of the daughter at the same time. Very *James Bond.*

My work is the embodiment of Raven's transformation, his ability to adapt. I feel like saying, "I embody the trickster," but I have this weird feeling that if I do that, this essay might turn into some sort of manifesto that I write from a cave with a typewriter that has a sticky "T" key.

It's all about survival: Raven as iPod, Raven as a can of Coke, and so on. But these objects of pop culture lack Raven's finesse and charm, which is why I put them in the context of "Personal Totems": to explore our fascination

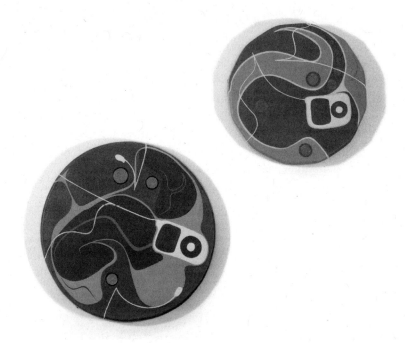

Personal Totems #1 (left) and *Personal Totems #2* (right), 2008. Acrylic on deer hide, diameter 20 inches and 16 inches.

with these objects and how we use them to dictate our personal pop lineage. We are a culture obsessed with items. Some say it's the design aesthetics or the functionality that makes us crave these things. But really, it's just stuff we don't really need, which detaches us from the world around us. We ignore others by drowning them out with the latest album ripped to some sort of media device. But, even though some of these objects remove us from society, we are still able to relate to each other because we all have the same sort of crap. Whether it's a Blackberry (aptly nicknamed "Crackberry"), iPod, laptop, digital camera, or any other object of pop-consumerism, we can relate to these items like figures on a totem pole. You might not have anything in common with the Goth-chic on the bus you see each morning on the way to your job, but, regardless of the blood-curdling screaming coming out of her iconic white ear buds, you may relate to her based on the fact that you have those same buds rammed in your ears. Even if you're listening to Barry Manilow, you have something in common: you share the same personal totem.

Raven's iDrum, 2007. Acrylic on deer hide, diameter 16 inches.

The Cola Wars

The Cola Wars of the 1980s brought consumerism to the forefront—which carbonated sugar water you chose to drink told the tale of whose side you were on. I'm sure that, ten years from now, if anyone from my generation mentions "Cola War" to someone in their twenties, that same twenty-year-old will ask who won, what was the casualty rate, and did it have something to do with the Cold War? Were there nuclear weapons? Were there casualties? One could answer in this way: yes, the nuclear fallout could be thwarted by a pair of Levi's jeans and there was death—to individuality. Bringing pop culture and the Cola War to Cold War Russia could be considered the first step in creating a democracy. Giving a voice to the people via consumerism: democracy through pop culture.

When the 2010 Olympic bid was awarded to Vancouver, the majority of the public sighed with relief and joy. Bringing the world to Vancouver would surely help, not hinder. If you ask anyone on the Downtown East Side if the

Olympics have benefited them in a positive way, I'm pretty sure you'll get a resounding "no!" I was pretty disappointed in the bid being awarded to Vancouver. After all, we have (much like any major urban centre) problems that the money could be better spent on, instead of a two-week parade: hospital beds, housing for the homeless, and the treaty process in B.C. But, as any good governmental mandate, all those things are being "addressed" in the coming of the Olymp-apocalypse. For example, the athletes' housing will be turned into a combination of low-income/social housing and luxury condominiums. But I beg the question: Who would want to spend from nearly half a million to over two million dollars for a condo to live in the same building as someone on social housing? I bet you one ridiculous Olympic mascot that the social housing aspect gets axed and the luxury condo owner can live in peace knowing that he won't have the bane of society living three floors below.

Okay—so how the hell does this all relate to the trickster? Ah. Art—you have so many levels. In the history of the Olympics, this is the first time that leaders of a host city, in this case the Vancouver Organizing Committee for the 2010 Olympic and Paralympic Winter Games (VANOC), have tried to include the local indigenous communities in order to avoid conflict. After all, with the treaty process in full swing, the four nations that reside in the Vancouver/Whistler area could have a dramatic impact on the Games and, through protest, leave an ugly stain on the pristine reputation of the Games. Now, it seems that there has always been some element of protest to the contemporary Olympics. Mostly because, as I stated before, the money could be better spent on aspects of our society that need fixing. But the Games promote themselves as a fix, and bring in revenue and infrastructure. All of which is a band-aid, really. Canada promotes itself as a caring, understanding culture—one that embraces multiculturalism and welcomes all with open arms. And the government will implore the First People to put a friendly, sometimes stereotypical face to Canada. Canada is the friend to the Indian when it wants something, but, for the most part, this country tries to hide the shame that is its past. The strategy, to bring the Four Host Nations to the table and allow them a voice, automatically curbs some of the potential controversy.

The trickster makes a subtle subtextual appearance in "Enjoy Coast Salish Territory." I created this piece to speak to the notion that the Games, and the world, will be visiting Coast Salish Territory—a reminder that the land and the original people need to be respected. Heavy politics aside, the piece also has more of a personal connection to it as well. I think back to the day when I learned who I was—the temporal pinnacle of pop culture, when the war between Coke and Pepsi was a dominating force in all modes of pop communication. "Hands across America" was pop advertising at its finest. It proved that there were people with the inspiration to think outside the box, as it was also a valiant attempt at "one love":

> I'd like to buy the world a home and furnish it with love
> Grow apple trees and honeybees and snow-white turtledoves
> I'd like to teach the world to sing in perfect harmony
> I'd like to buy the world a Coke and keep it company.
> It's the real thing. Coke is what the world wants today.[6]

I'm what is classed as an "Urban Indian";[7] I'm pretty serious about respecting this land that I inhabit. This piece not only brings political awareness to this area, but it is a tribute to the fact that I reside in Coast Salish territory and that I pay respect to the Four Nations that make up this area. I thank and honour them in my contemporary-traditional way in the creation of this piece.

I love how the piece is invisible in the right context and how it speaks to the notion of how we are aware, yet unaware, of how pop advertising affects us. One of the best comments I've heard on the piece was, "I walked into the gallery and immediately said, 'What the fuck is a Coke sign doing in here?' Then I went up to it. Brilliant!"

The Anatomy of the Trickster

On the West Coast, the trickster stories (in the form of the Raven) usually have a moral which the audience can pick up. The outcome for the trickster could be considered negative, but its interactions provide valuable insight or a valuable lesson in morality for the audience. A simple "trickster story" of my life as an artist would go something like this: one day, Raven was presented with a choice, either pursue a path that he loves or work in a shoe store smelling feet all day. The choice for Raven was quite clear—pursue that which he loves and become the Creator. A year later, he was pursuing that which he loved, but he had to go back to smelling feet to be able to afford to do so.

Raven has adapted to fit in within in our society, and he bombards us with what we think we need. Where is the moral in the contemporary retellings of the trickster? Will it be an awakening one day that what we need is driving us to destroy our environment? I really don't know; Raven likes to let the audience decode his message. Until we get it, he still continues to get away with whatever he wants. I'm still in the lucid dream-state in which Raven is telling me to paint iPods. iPods—this little white box that I convinced myself I needed is making its way into everything I paint. Why? Because it is part of who I am. My technology relates me to you: it is my personal totem.

Notes

1   Playing guns. I remember that back in the day, toy guns used to look like real guns. So much, in fact, that I freaked out some dude ripping through the alley one day. The neighbourhood I grew up in was along the lines of what was to be later known as the SkyTrain—built to bring the 'burbs out for Expo 86. There was an open construction pit down the block from my house, when construction sites were not being fenced off. I spent hours in those pits with my friends, sliding down the dirt hills in boxes we took from the back of the drugstore. Anyway, one day I was playing in the open pit by myself. The construction crew placed a nice, big pile of dirt by the alley. Perfect for a pop-gun sniper. I took aim at the speeding truck from my perch and fired the pop. No projectiles came out, but the dude in the truck slammed on his brakes and backed up to give me an earful about the safe use of a gun—which is odd, because I can't think of any eight-year-old having a real gun. But that is just how real-looking the toy guns used to be. When toys were toys …

2   I've just been informed that we are now to call ourselves Aboriginal. But wait a week—there will be another definition of who we are supposed to be.

3   Now referred to as the Kwakwaka'wakw.

4   To be politically correct, it is "fisher." But "fisher" sounds like some ridiculous looking long-billed water bird who sits on rocks all day looking for the next opportune moment for food. I will entertain "fish-fighters" or "fish entrapment officers," if you like. Don't get me wrong: I'm not belittling the women who work in the industry. My grandmother worked on commercial fishing boats all her life and her sister was one of the first female captains in the fleet. Even they called themselves "fishermen." It's the whole Indian/Aboriginal thing on another level.

5   The movie *Star Trek: First Contact* has some interesting comparisons with the discovery of the new world and colonization of North America. Not to go into too much of a nerd-gasm over probably one of the best Star Trek movies—this particular quotation was from a climactic scene in which there is a battle to regain control over the starship Enterprise, almost lost to the evil Borg. Lt. Cmdr. Worf readies his trusty phaser rifle and blasts the Borg out of the sky.

6   "The 'Hilltop' Ad: The Story of a Commercial." From *Fifty Years of Coca-Cola Television Advertisements: Highlights from the Motion Picture Archives at the Library of Congress.* <http://memory.loc.gov/ammem/ccmphtml/colaadv.html>.

7   "Urban Indian" is a term used to describe Indigenous people living off their home reserve in a major urban area.

RIGOUREAU, NAAPI, AND WESAKECAK

Dances with Rigoureau

"Uncle Morris was a *rigoureau*, a mixed-blood shapeshifter."
When I first read the above sentence in a story called "The Republic of Tricksterism" by Paul Seeseequasis (470), I hesitated at that word—
rigoureau. Just a little hitch of recognition and disquiet. I had nearly forgotten
it, and perhaps I would have forgotten it altogether if I hadn't encountered
it again there, in that uncanny context. Uncanny because it reminded me
that *my* uncle, too, was a rigoureau. His sister, my auntie, told me so.

"He's got the rigoureau in him, that Eli," she said to me once, when I was
twelve or thirteen. I forget what occasioned the label: perhaps another of his
wins at cards, or a bingo bonanza—or maybe another debt cleverly evaded,
or possibly more of his legendary shenanigans with women. Eli's luck and his
shiftlessness were perennial subjects of family gossip. Some of my relatives
shook their heads at his various misadventures, but I know this particular
aunt had a soft spot for him, as did all of his nieces and nephews.

"Those rigoureaus," my aunt went on, "they know how to change. Change
their luck, change their voice, change their face. Their bodies too, I hear.
They can make themselves into a coyote, or a dog, or even a wolf."

"You seen Uncle Eli do that?" I said. "You seen him be a werewolf?"

But she explained that, no, a rigoureau was not a werewolf, not an unwilling full-moon transformer, but someone who could change himself at will. And
that a rigoureau was not someone to be afraid of, really, unless you made the
mistake of lending him money—because then he would metamorphose into
a gopher or something, and you would be out of luck.

And no, she hadn't seen this transformation happen, not to Uncle Eli or
anyone else. "But I know one thing," she said. "I know it runs in our family.

Uncle Alcide was a rigoureau too, they used to say. And now Eli, he's just the same. Changing, changing. You watch him, the way a dog will come to him. They all come running up to him like he's a long-lost brother, like he's got pork chops in his pockets. It's because they know."

I did watch Uncle Eli after that, not with fear but with a sense of identification, of idealization even. I wanted to be like Uncle Eli, to be able to change myself to suit any situation, to mingle with whomever or whatever I wanted. Because I saw that Eli *was* able to make himself at home with everyone in the area, no matter what their background, and I associated that talent with what my auntie had said: he knew how to change himself. Although he couldn't read or write in any language, he spoke in snippets of Ukrainian and Cree and German and French. His jokes were almost always ethnic jokes, generally considered to be atrocious ones even back then, but the interesting thing about them was that he changed them slightly each time he told them, so you never knew if it would be the Frenchman or the Ukrainian or the Indian or the Englishman who would end up as the butt of the joke. He seemed to fit in with any and all of these ethnic groups in our community. For a long time, I had thought this was just because he worked for a brewery and he distributed gallons of free beer to the Saskatchewan countryside every weekend, but then he quit drinking, and the brewery closed down; yet, he continued his multicultural chameleonism without any apparent problem. It was only when Auntie Marie told me about the rigoureau that it started to make sense.

Dogs did come to him from everywhere, I noticed, and always with their heads held low, their tails sweeping the ground. He had no dog of his own, but everyone else's dogs seemed to think they belonged to him. And there was even something doglike about Eli himself: his smile, simultaneously ingratiating and hungry. I used to practise that smile myself, just as I practised card-playing and joke-telling—because, to my mother's abject horror, I wanted to be Uncle Eli when I grew up. After all, it ran in the family.

Two or three years after I heard the rigoureau story, Uncle Eli got his first real job in at least a decade. He was appointed the dog catcher for the town and reserve community of Loon Lake, where he had lived for a number of years. It was the perfect job for him, since even the most feral of the local dogs would walk right up to him, heads bowed, listening to his jokes and cajolings. He got paid ten dollars a dog, and there were dozens of strays on this reserve and in the neighbouring town—enough to keep Eli in cigarette money for a long time. He impounded the dogs in an old chicken coop that one of the villagers had donated, and he went out to feed them and play with them twice a day. He spent hours with them, even though he wasn't paid to do it.

But eventually the impromptu dog pound filled up, and not one single owner had showed up to claim a dog. Of course, Uncle Eli knew the dogs didn't belong to any single person, but the village council had forgotten about that, or they hadn't bothered to tell Eli what would be required if nobody stopped in at the pound to rescue their pets. Eventually, when the howling of the dogs in the chicken coop became audible even in the town office, the village administrator told Eli the plan: he would be required to euthanize the dogs. He would be paid a hundred-dollar bonus every time this was necessary.

He thought this over for a couple of days, and he even came to our place and told us about the injustice of it, the underhandedness of his employers. We were pretty sure he would quit, or find a way to get himself fired. But when I went to visit him a week later, he was still employed, and the chicken coop was empty. He never spoke about how he had accomplished his task.

After this, Loon Lake was known to be inhabited by packs of ghost dogs. They returned to the scene of the chicken coop night after night, and they howled at the outskirts of town, so eerily that even the coyotes refused to answer. And when people asked Uncle Eli about these apparitions they had seen—particular ghosts of particular dogs they had known in the community—he said he knew nothing about them. He could only catch the flesh-and-blood dogs, he said, and after that it was none of his business.

He continued to do a booming trade as the dog catcher, gathering up strays and then euthanizing them once a month. But the townspeople began to notice that no matter how many dogs were dispatched each month, their population continued to increase. Uncle Eli was so busy, he started saving up for a new truck.

It ended when the town administrator caught Uncle Eli feeding a pack of ghost dogs on the outskirts of town. They weren't ghosts at all, of course. And, after an investigation into Eli's accounting procedures, it was discovered that some of the dogs had been caught and released half a dozen times, to the tune of ten dollars per capture.

"It's not my fault if they keep escaping," Uncle Eli said. And soon he also escaped, to a different town, where he began another of his many lives.

When I first heard Aunt Marie's rigoureau story, I didn't know what cultural tradition it came from. I thought it might be specific to our family, a narrative that explained our collective peculiarities and probably wouldn't make sense to anyone else. But, of course, now I realize it's a Michif word, deriving from the French "loup-garou," the frightening figure in a series of werewolf folk tales that are common in Quebec, France, and Louisiana. In Margaret Atwood's *Surfacing*, the Québécois Catholics are said to believe that "if you don't go to church, you'll turn into a wolf" (57), and indeed when the narrator encounters the spiritual form of her father at the end of the book, he seems to have at least partially made that transformation: "it gazes at me for a time with its yellow eyes, wolf's eyes.... I see now that although it isn't my father, it is what my father *has become*" (187, my emphasis). And the narrator herself has also clearly changed by this point in the novel, because she is no longer afraid of such a composite human-animal figure. She even imagines that she herself is growing fur.

In *Surfacing*, the werewolf represents that which Euro-Canadians (and "Americans") must suppress if they are to continue their imperialistic domination over natural creatures. Any recognition that humans are part animal would short-circuit the colonial paradigm of maximizing profit through the utilization of land and animals. I think there are also some other related reasons that the loup-garou is virtually always a symbol of terror in European cultures. The loup-garou, like the werewolf, is obviously a manifestation of a fear of giving into irrationality. But it also represents a fear of an unstable humanity, a humanity that is subject to periodic fluctuations—and also a humanity that is hybrid. The lycanthrope (from *lukos*, wolf, and *anthropos*, man) is a composite being, an entity in the transition zone between the animal and the human. Such instability is almost always figured in Western discourse as a curse, an affliction which must be kept secret at all costs. Werewolves are driven out of communities because their very existence threatens the cohesiveness and uniformity of the group, as Giorgio Agamben points out: "What had to remain in the collective unconscious as a monstrous hybrid of human and animal, divided between the forest and the city—the werewolf—is, therefore, in its origin the figure of the man who has been banned from the city" (105).

The loup-garou is also implicitly about race. European ideas of lycanthropy are manifestations of a tropism for purity and a commensurate stigmatization of all kinds of hybridity (whether it be racial or inter-species hybridity). It is no coincidence that so many stories of lycanthropy are highly sexualized: the erotic depravity of the lycanthrope is represented as the possibility of miscegenation or bestiality, which might introduce a curse or a stain, or a hereditary disease, into the general population. This is, of course, all the more reason to drive a stake through their werewolf hearts before they can accomplish their nefarious destabilization of humanness.

Much has already been written about the stigmatization and exoticization of Métis people in relation to this rhetoric of purity and the pathologization of hybridity.[1] There is the famous nineteenth-century description of the Métis as "the one-and-a-half men," meaning half white, half Native, and half devil.[2]

In this conception, the fact of the Métis' hybridity is thought to be much more than the sum of its parts. It leads to an excess of depravity, of shiftiness, of traitorous tendencies. This is nowhere more visible than in the multitudinous depictions of Louis Riel as an inherently untrustworthy, changeable, impulsive figure. During Riel's trial, the prosecution made much of the "lurking presence" of Indian heritage in him (quoted in Racette, 47). "What do we see?" the prosecutor asked. "In the *changing light* of his *dark* Indian eye we see the civilized man struggling with the Indian" (quoted in Racette, 47; my emphasis). This struggle might be considered one of the primal scenes of colonialism, which Derek Walcott would later describe as "the gorilla wrestl[ing] with the superman" (l.25). The "changing light," the instability of Riel's racial identity, is what the prosecutor identifies as the most dangerous thing about him. Riel may seem "light" but he is changing; he is "dark" and yet also still changing. This mercurial quality was what most terrified the prosecutor. In this colonial mindset, it appeared that Riel could take on the appearance of a civilized man, but he was also liable to transform into a savage without warning. And, even worse, by Riel's very existence, he threatened the idea of the distinction between the civilized and the savage. The only way Euro-Canadian society knew how to deal with such composite beings was to kill them and to hope that they stayed dead.

Of course, they never do. Not even after the invention of silver bullets. Riel's hundreds of posthumous incarnations provide ample evidence of this.[3]

As you will have gathered already, the rigoureau story is different from the loup-garou tradition in at least one important respect. In Métis stories, the rigoureau is often a heroic figure, or, if it is a villain, this villainy is positioned in such a way that it might still be seen as heroic. I believe this is at least partly because Métis people can identify all too well with the plight of this transspecies being, the rigoureau, but it is also probably because the rigoureau stories are connected to Cree and Anishinaabe transformation stories, in which people are gifted with the ability to change themselves into certain creatures and sometimes animals are able to turn themselves into humans.[4] The activity of transformation in such cases is often far from being an affliction; it is, in fact, usually a highly desirable power. In rigoureau stories, the putative instability of hybrid identity can come to be connected with these much more positive Indigenous understandings of transformational power, so that the rigoureau's hybridity can be seen not as a curse but as a source of strength: the power to shift one's own identity, the power of bodily self-determination. Thus, Seeseequasis says of his Uncle Morris, "They envied his power, his ability to turn into a dog, a bear, or almost any kind of rodent he chose" (470). Morris's power, as a "compassionate trickster" (471), is always turned towards upsetting paradigms of racial purity, which in this case are set up by both colonial authorities and by "status" Native politicians, who seek to protect their status by defending colonial definitions of Aboriginal authenticity and purity. Morris says to all urban Native people, "Burn your status cards ... and throw away your colonial pedigree papers. Don't let the white man define us. Let's define ourselves" (470). However, his pleas for a free-form, inclusive definition of indigeneity are not accepted by everyone in the urban Indigenous communities.

Morris becomes a folk hero of non-status Indigenous people, which includes the Métis but also what Seeseequasis calls "the urban orphans and mixed-bloods" (470). His situation as a mixed-blood shape-shifting folk hero of the dispossessed hybrid people makes him a contemporary version of Riel himself. And Morris, like Riel, pays the ultimate price for his ongoing campaign against the ideologies of purity and status. He is beaten to death and his body is dumped in a grain chute. But because Morris is a rigoureau, he cannot be killed so easily. He comes back to life after five days, now as a wheelchair-bound paraplegic. After this, he goes on to lead a rebellion of the "mixed bloods and urban orphans" (471) who take over the Friendship Center, declare a "Republic of Tricksterism" (472), and destroy the status membership rolls, thereby creating "a world of merging colours" (472)—a world which might be compared to Riel's provisional government of 1869–70. However, this uprising is short-lived, and, after Morris and his followers abandon the building, he is once again caught by his enemies and killed. This time he comes back to life more drastically transformed: turned into a termite, he goes into the Indian Affairs offices where he "gnaw[s] at the bureaucrats' desks" (473). Clearly, he will continue to work at undermining the ideology of purity that Seeseequasis describes as an invention of colonialism.

My Uncle Eli and Paul Seeseequasis' Uncle Morris fit in well with the image of the rigoureau as cultural hero of mixed-blood and/or Métis people, but there are other representations of the rigoureau which are not so unambiguously positive. Maria Campbell records one rigoureau story in her *Stories of the Road Allowance People* that might seem to be closer to the colonial traditions of the lycanthropy narrative, since at least some of the Métis people in the story are terrified by the rigoureau, or "Rou Garou," as Campbell calls it. Campbell's narrator says:

> Dese Rou Garous
> dey was differen
> Dey was bad tings from dah dark side of dah eart.
> Lees I tink dey was from dah dark side.
> Maybe I tink dat cause dats what dah Prees he tell us (29).

This vilification of the Rou Garous is clearly different from Seeseequasis' depiction, but the narrator's mention of the priest and "what [he] tell us" about the Rou Garous provides a crucial level of distance between the tale and its received meanings in the community. The narrator's mother, in fact, provides a commentary on the Rou Garou story in which she suggests that this demonization of the Rou Garou is an insidious method of colonial coercion.

The Rou Garou in question here is a woman, called "Josephine Jug of Wine," not because she drinks but because she lived "in dah big city for a long time" (30). Josephine is a loner in the community, except for her connection to her husband Chee Kaw Chee. She is also noteworthy in that she doesn't subscribe to Catholic beliefs, which seem to be the most common ones in the community. As a former urbanite, a loner, a disbeliever, and a strikingly beautiful woman, she is marked in the community as an outsider, and the narrator's mother points out the injustice of such scapegoating: "My mudder he say / jus cause Josephine he don believe in dah Virgin Mary / dat don give us dah right to call him a name like dat" (that is, like Josephine Jug of Wine) (30). Despite this warning, the community's men continue to call Josephine by this name, and they later go on to tell and retell the story of Josephine as a Rou Garou who terrifies the community by her nocturnal howling and her eventual appearance in wolf form.

The Rou Garou in this story might well be a trickster of sorts, because when she first appears to George L'Hirondelle, his car loses its brakes on a treacherous downhill slope. However, as in many of the Coyote stories, the trick ends up being visited upon the trickster herself, because George's careening Hudson ends up hitting the wolf-woman at the bottom of the ravine. When the Rou Garou is seriously wounded, George is able to get a clear look at her, and this is when he recognizes that she is Josephine.

The men of the community then organize a ruse to entrap the Rou Garou while she is in her human form, and George is sent over to her house while her husband is kept busy with a poker game. George spies on Josephine and he sees that "dat woman was all black an blue" (46). This marking of her body is taken as proof that she is the Rou Garou. This second encounter with the Rou Garou is also, strangely, the occasion of George's conversion to Catholicism. He has been a stubborn unbeliever up until this point, but when he is confronted with the "evil" (46) presence of the Rou Garou, he makes the sign of the cross and calls on Jesus and the Virgin Mary for help. And, in keeping with European lore of lycanthropy, the Rou Garou woman disappears from the community just after this moment. She is apparently vanquished by George's invocation of Christian icons.

This might seem to be quintessential werewolf-movie fare: the cross drives away the Rou Garou and the community is made safe again. But the interjections of the narrator's mother make the story something altogether different. She points out that this particular view of the Rou Garou—as something to be feared and to be driven away by Christian belief—is, in fact, a construction of colonialism, which is designed to effect the conversion of Native people to Christianity. The narrator says:

> But you know my Mudder
> he was real mad when I tell him what Tommy he tell me.
> > He say dah Prees he win again an he give anudder woman a bad name
> jus to make good Catlics out of dah peoples. (48–9)

The function of the narrator's Rou Garou story is to encourage what amounts to a witch hunt, his mother says. The Rou Garou is the token outsider who must be sacrificed in order to preserve and even enhance a sense of uniformity and cohesion in the community. Because the Rou Garou here is a figure of female power and of changeability—as opposed to priestly authority—she must be driven out. The story of the Rou Garou in this case is essentially performing the function of the priest, persuading community members to embrace Catholicism.

And readers have already learned a very interesting thing about the narrator's mother earlier in the story, which gives us further leverage in interpreting her critique of the narrator's view of the Rou Garou story. The narrator says:

> I never tell many peoples dis
> but my Mudder you know
> he was never a Catlic. Hee jus preten all hees life
> an dat way
> dah Prees he don know dat some of dah peoples dey was
> fooling aroun wit dah ole way. (31)

So the mother has, in fact, been playing the role of a good Catholic, but only in order to practise "dah ole way" in peace. In other words, the narrator's mother sees that her own religious practices make her very similar to Josephine. This makes me think the Rou Garou/rigoureau is still very much a figure of Métis identity in this story, but this time in the role of the scapegoat—representing perhaps the internalized self-hatred of Métis identity that

Campbell also writes about in *Halfbreed*.[5] By driving out the Rou Garou and taking on the Catholic beliefs, these men are unwittingly divorcing themselves from an important part of their own cultural traditions. The Rou Garou definitely does represent the ethos of "dah ole way," as the narrator himself notes at the beginning of the story, when he says:

> My ole granfawder he could turn hisself into a bear;
> An I knowed dis ole woman when I was a boy
> dat one he turn hisself into a kiyote. (29)

The narrator's mother points out that the narrator has developed a double standard, not fearing such transformations when they occurred in "dah ole time" (28), but fearing them in the present moment. He has unwittingly adopted a colonized mindset in relation to the old ways. The mother's comments suggest that he should perhaps think of Josephine as something more like a hero than a pariah.

What the Seeseequasis story and the Campbell story share is the movement of ejection, the attempted banishment or extinguishment of the rigoureau figure. One story overtly identifies with that figure, even in his defeat, whereas the other one partly identifies with the Rou Garou hunters, and then reflects obliquely on the wisdom of such an identification. In both stories, the rigoureau is the central figure in the drama of othering and self-identification in the community.

My Uncle Eli seems to be familiar with that drama of ejection, too. He has moved from place to place, from job to job, whenever his welcome has worn out. Yes, he's still alive, long after any of us would have predicted, and he's still changing, changing. Some people say he has changed himself into a black sheep, but, of course, that's no change at all. No, the change this time is that he has been cast out of another town. That's how it always works with him: everyone loves him for a while, and then gradually the people get so tired of his little tricks that he can no longer go back. But that's okay; he has found another town a little distance down the railway line. He'll stay there for as long as they let him.

I stopped in to visit Uncle Eli last summer for the first time in years. We sat at his kitchen table drinking de-alcoholized beer and Clamato juice, and we played a few games of cribbage like in the old days. He won every game, of course. As we played, he unleashed his usual barrage of terrible ethnic jokes, and he made fun of my city clothes, my urban accent. He told me I should write a book about him someday. Then he reminisced about a few of his adventures in his various temporary hometowns, and eventually he worked his way back to the story of his dog-catcher days in Loon Lake. I knew it was time to ask the question I had come there to ask.

"Hey Uncle," I said when he paused to roll a cigarette. "You ever hear any stories about the rigoureau?"

He raised an eyebrow, leaned down to lick his cigarette paper. "Could be. Why?"

"Well I seem to remember Auntie—one of the aunties—telling a story about rigoureaus. She said that you . . . knew something about them."

He didn't say anything for a long time. He just looked at me with that smile, the hungry dog smile—the one that sometimes flashed onto his face when he told a joke that we didn't get.

And then a sound came out of him, a delicate keening from somewhere behind his grin, and gradually it opened up, and he lifted his face towards the dingy ceiling and gave forth an enormous, ululating howl. His whole body quivered with it. And when the sound had finally disappeared, he took a long breath and turned back towards me, almost smirking.

"You know, Bunyok," he whispered. "It runs in the family."

Notes

1   For example, in the two most famous books by Métis writers, Maria Campbell's *Halfbreed* and Beatrice Culleton Mosionier's *In Search of April Raintree,* Métis girls and women are constantly being shuttled between the twin poles of stigmatization and exoticization. In Gregory Scofield's *Thunder Through My Veins,* the young Scofield yearns to be "Cree—not some forgotten half-breed who didn't belong anywhere" (117).

2   Murray Dobbin's biography of Jim Brady and Malcolm Norris, *The One-and-a-Half Men,* explains the history of this term, and goes some distance towards recuperating it into a label of heroic strength rather than a racial slur.

3   The most comprehensive study of the many stories, poems, and plays in which Riel appears as a character is Albert Braz's *The False Traitor: Louis Riel in Canadian Literature.*

4   Human–animal transformations are very common in Cree and Anishinaabe storytelling traditions, as in many other Indigenous cultures. Two particularly good examples in the Cree tradition, illustrating the positive and negative potential of transformation powers, are Coming-Day's "The Bear-Woman" and Louis Moosomin's "The Bearsark Woman" in Leonard Bloomfield's translated collection *Sacred Stories of the Sweet Grass Cree.*

5   At one point in the memoir, Maria imagines Cheechum (her great-grandmother) "standing beside me with a switch saying, 'They make you hate what you are'" (103). *Halfbreed* is an extended meditation on the ways in which scapegoating can be internalized by its victims.

Works Cited

Agamben, Giorgio. *Homo Sacer: Sovereign Power and Bare Life.* Trans. Daniel Heller-Roazen. Stanford, CA: Stanford UP, 1998.

Atwood, Margaret. *Surfacing.* 1972. Rpt. Toronto: McClelland and Stewart, New Canadian Library, 1994.

Braz, Albert. *The False Traitor: Louis Riel in Canadian Literature.* Toronto: U of Toronto P, 2003.

Campbell, Maria. *Halfbreed.* Toronto: McClelland and Stewart, 1973.

———, trans. "Rou Garous." *Stories of the Road Allowance People.* Penticton, BC: Theytus, 1995. 28–49.

Coming-Day [Kā-kīsikāw-pīhtukäw]. "The Bear Woman." In *Sacred Stories of the Sweet Grass Cree.* Ed. and trans. Leonard Bloomfield. Saskatoon: Fifth House, 1993. 57–61.

Dobbin, Murray. *The One-and-a-Half Men: The Story of Jim Brady and Malcolm Morris, Métis Patriots of the Twentieth Century.* Vancouver: New Star, 1981.

Mosionier, Beatrice Culleton. *In Search of April Raintree.* Critical ed. Ed. Cheryl Suzack. Winnipeg: Portage & Main, 1999.

Moosomin, Louis [Nāh-nāmiskwākāpaw]. "The Bearsark Woman." In *Sacred Stories of the Sweet Grass Cree.* Ed. and trans. Leonard Bloomfield. Saskatoon: Fifth House, 1993. 61–5.

Racette, Sherry Farrell. "Métis Man or Canadian Icon: Who Owns Louis Riel?" In *Rielisms.* Catalogue of an Exhibition held at the Winnipeg Art Gallery, 13 January–18 March 2001. Catherine Mattes, curator. Winnipeg: Winnipeg Art Gallery, 2001. 42–53.

Scofield, Gregory. *Thunder Through My Veins: Memories of a Métis Childhood.* Toronto: HarperCollins, 1999.

Seeseequasis, Paul. "The Republic of Tricksterism." In *An Anthology of Canadian Native Literature in English.* 3rd ed. Ed. Daniel David Moses and Terry Goldie. Don Mills, ON: Oxford UP, 2005. 468–74.

Walcott, Derek. "A Far Cry from Africa." In *The Broadview Anthology of Poetry.* Ed. Herbert Rosengarten and Amanda Goldrick-Jones. Peterborough: Broadview, 1993. 754.

ELDON YELLOWHORN

Naapi in My World

Naapi always lived just beyond my perception. He was like the whistling I heard whenever the wind blew across the pile of pop bottles my father had collected by the road. I was too young to have known him, so all I heard were the stories about him. My imagination created a skinny old man with long grey hair who wore buckskin clothing and tied a band around his forehead. I imagined he might still be around, and I had my own impressions of his presence. Naapi is the old man in Oldman River. Going to the river was my "safari" because a trip to the woods in the valley always meant adventure for a prairie boy. Every time I heard the grouse drumming I thought of Naapi. I learned why certain trees looked like they were struck repeatedly with a knife, or why bullberries had thorns. Every question beginning with "Why?" got the response "Because Naapi made it like that!"

For some unknown reason, my query, "Where is Naapi now?" only received a vague reply that he had gone north. He had his reasons for deciding to live elsewhere, but he promised to visit periodically. This means that he comes back every year with presents, which he leaves for you if you have been good.

Somewhere in the process of converting to Christianity, I learned, Naapi gained an alter ego. I discovered that, to the old people of my reserve who could not speak English, Naapi was just the Blackfoot Santa Claus. "Omahka-toyiiksistsikoo" is how Blackfoot speakers say Christmas. "Naapi aakootoowa Omahkatoyiiksistsikoo" means Santa Claus is coming at Christmas.

Like everyone else, I looked forward to Christmas because it meant a visit from Naapi—especially since he brought me presents, all wrapped up in shiny paper. Beyond my instant gratification, I was oblivious to whom I dedicated my good behaviour.

When I stopped believing in Santa Claus, I found I had no need for Naapi either. When I became a teenager, television replaced the church as the centre of my life. I stopped going to mass when I discovered mass media. I grew indifferent to the holidays I had celebrated earlier in my childhood.

Through my studies in anthropology, however, I revived my interest in those old Blackfoot stories I had ignored for so long. I searched my memory for details about the events and consequences that made these stories so entertaining. In retelling them, we transmit information that our ancestors first learned in their time, even if their meaning may change for and in each generation. Still, one thing is certain: Naapi stories made facts memorable.

Blackfoot people still ponder the character called Naapi. His identity and relationship with Sun, the chief of heaven, are still subjects of speculation. Of course, he was famous for his foibles. He could be rowdy, randy, and risible all at once. These qualities made him the archetypal trickster. In retrospect, I should have known all along, since I always got a present from him—but never what I asked for.

"Niitakksikaitaapitsinikii" (I will tell stories of ancient times) starts every Blackfoot story about Naapi. Woven into these Naapi stories are the details of how the present world came to be and how life on earth appeared. Some events that occurred in those ancient times left tangible reminders that explained the origin of conditions of the current era. Blackfoot people believe that the world was destroyed and recreated by the action of Sun. What follows is the story of Naapi and how he survived the destruction of the former world to become the creator of the present one.

The World According to Naapi

A long time ago, the sky and the earth were joined. There was no day or night during that time. Humans and star-people walked side by side and held daily conversations on all manner of subjects. Unlike the snakes, whose treachery doomed their kind, humans and star-folk had no aspirations to overthrow their creator. Mostly, they lived harmoniously with each other, sharing in all the experiences they encountered. But their idyllic community ended when a star-boy joined some human children at play in the forest near a river. At first, everyone enjoyed their games, but then the human children began to tease and taunt the star-boy. The human boys led the teasing until everyone threw their insults at him. Their hysteria built to violence as they picked up stones and hurled them at the star-boy. When he lay helpless on the ground, one of the older boys picked up a cobble, walked up to him and dropped it. The human children came to their senses too late. They stood stunned knowing that they had done a terrible wrong.

They fled the scene, running in different directions. As they disappeared into the forest, the star-boy exploded. Baubles of light streamed about in chaotic frenzy and hit against trees or landed on the ground nearby. Like embers fading to ash, the star-boy's remains dimmed and solidified. Where they hit the trunks of trees, bracket fungus grew out of the bark, and where they landed on the ground, puffball mushrooms appeared. For that reason, Blackfoot speakers make no distinction between fungi and stars when they say "kakato'siiksi" (sing., "kakato'si"). This story reveals the connection between the two meanings. When ceremonialists build a sacred fire, they use the dried punk of bracket fungus. Its combustibility, old Blackfoot people would say, is the residual heat of the star-boy being released into the fire.

The human children who witnessed the explosion trembled in terror, as they wondered how they were capable of such a deed. They shuddered to think of what would happen next. They said nothing as they drifted away from each other and glumly stumbled back to their camp. Although their parents might have wondered about their silent children, nobody noticed anything awry. At least the human parents were unconcerned by the sudden flight of merriment from their camp.

The mother of the star-boy, on the other hand, knew something was amiss. She had cooked a meal earlier and still her son had not returned. So she went looking for her husband, in case they were together. She found her husband visiting with some humans and interrupted their conversation to inquire if he knew about their son's whereabouts. He answered in the negative and asked why she was concerned. She said their son was missing and grew apprehensive as she wondered where he might be. She recognized a human boy peeking out from inside a tipi and then remembered her son saying he was joining his friends by the river.

She thought he might still be there, and, with her husband, they decided to go and look for him. They went to the places where they usually found him. They grew wary as they approached the river's edge. Something was out of the ordinary. Even the trees looked different. Then they came to the place where their son had been murdered. There they saw the small crater marking the place where he had exploded. They realized that the bracket fungus on the trees and the mushrooms on the ground were what remained of their son. They cried out in anguish as they raced back to camp, all the while blaming themselves for not being more vigilant. They wondered who would carry out such a heinous act. Someone had to know! They wondered if the human children had something to do with what happened.

The star-people convened a meeting with their chief, Sun. The parents told him of a suspicious death. They described how their son had gone off to play with some human children directly before he went missing. They were able to describe his usual playmates. Sun said that he would go to the humans and ask if their children were responsible. Sun went to the humans and told them of the suspicious demise of the star-boy and of how he was last seen playing with some human children. Sun demanded that the humans hand over their children for interrogation by the star-people. Fearing the fate of their children, the human parents denied any connection between the two circumstances.

Sun became exasperated with the humans' refusal to deal with the crime and went back to his tipi, where he met a mob of angry star-people. He told them of human denials and they chimed together that the humans could not go unpunished for their stubborn evasion of justice. After some more deliberation, the star-people decided that, if they could not get justice, then all the humans should share the fate of the criminals. They agreed that humans could not be trusted as neighbours anymore. Their safety could only be gained by putting distance between their villages. They decided to create a separate sky country well removed from the earth. Their parting gesture would be clouds raining constantly upon the earth until it was drowned by water.

Sitting at the back of the conference tipi was an elder star-man named Naapi. His thick, white mane was evidence of his age. He was the last of his star-family and no one paid any attention to him. All his kin had grown old and lost their light and energy. Afterwards, he lived alone in his tipi; the only visitors who ever stopped by and broke his loneliness were the humans. His favourite task was giving names to the children the humans brought to him. He felt a special attachment to the humans and loved them like the family he once knew. When he heard what the star-people were planning, he decided to warn the humans. After the meeting, he left the tipi and went over to the human families and told them they were in danger. The world would soon be visited by cataclysms because the star-people were angry and were threatening to peel the sky away from the earth. They were planning to inundate the world with water and drown them all.

He described the approaching calamity and said there might be a safe haven in the mountains. He instructed them to follow him there and to climb with him to the lofty heights of Ninaiistako, the chief mountain. He told them they had no time to strike their camp or pack their food. They had to go immediately. Nobody doubted his words, since they all considered him their grandfather. They left their camp behind and made haste to get to the mountains. As they were crossing the plains, a strong wind blew in and great clouds of dust billowed in the air. Naapi told them the star-people were pulling the sky away from the earth. People looked about in confusion as everything blue seemed to lift off their world. They strained against the wind as they watched the blue float over their heads until it was above the highest trees. Soon they could see the star-people walking about and rising higher and higher. Finally, they appeared only as points of light as they disappeared with the blue. Then the world was cloaked in darkness, as swollen rain clouds closed off all sight of the blue. Water burst down from the clouds and washed the earth. Hailstones pelted the people as they ran for cover under the trees. They found no shelter there because the lightning seemed to track down those huddling under trees and fry them to cinders.

Naapi urged them to keep walking. They left the trails in the valleys because the riverbanks could not contain all the water. They started marching faster when even the river valleys were overflowing. Lakes were forming or getting deeper right before their eyes. Those who tarried too long in one place were lost in the deluge. The band seemed to grow smaller with each step they took. Only a few reached Ninaiistako, the chief mountain, where Naapi led them. Anyone who looked behind saw the plains disappearing fast under a sheet of water. Anything they ever owned was now rolling in the muddy waters. They could not waste any time on regret, however, because the flood waters were lapping at their heels. One or two people lost their footing as they clambered up the steep slopes and disappeared instantly in the undercurrent foaming up behind them. Naapi reached the top of the mountain and looked behind to see only a few people desperately seeking the summit. He knew their chances were slim, but he encouraged them to climb faster.

Knowing that he too might drown if he did nothing, Naapi reached into his carrying pouch and withdrew a wondrous lariat. Every colour imaginable shimmered off its length as he twirled it over his head. He threw the rope in the direction of a passing cloud to capture it within the noose. He pulled it taut and anchored his end to the top of Ninaiistako, so the cloud could not rain down anymore. To this day, when Blackfoot speakers see a rainbow, they still say the rain will stop soon because Naapi has let fly his lariat and has captured the clouds. For the few souls who made it near the summit, Naapi quickly made a raft from the logs that floated nearby. However, nobody survived the deluge to join him on it. At last, the star-people had gotten their revenge because all the humans drowned in the flood. Like the snakes, the humans brought on their fate with their treachery.

Naapi had not acted fast enough in tying down the clouds, as the rising water soon inundated the mountain. He climbed aboard his raft and floated with his regret for a long time after the clouds stopped sending rain. When the clouds broke apart, they revealed a brilliant blue sky above the open water. Naapi could see Sun sitting bright in the middle of it; nearby was his wife, Moon, and barely visible was their son, Morningstar. Naapi surveyed the water all about him and could not see a mote of dry land. Because Sun had been keeping watch over the inundation of the world by rain, he was close by and could hear Naapi speak. Naapi's tone was respectful, but reflective, when he revealed his thoughts to Sun. Naapi said he understood why the world was destroyed, but he added that creating humans had not been a mistake in the first place. He found them to be endlessly fascinating and their companionship to be a constant source of amusement. Sun told Naapi that he could join the other star-people in the sky country that they had just made. However, Naapi declined their offer because he now felt more out of place than ever. He said he might as well float on the water until his light and energy expired. Sun could not accept that option. So he gave Naapi the power of creation and told him to make a new world so he could fulfill his desire to re-create humans. Naapi learned that creation would be his choice and dilemma, but the power to destroy it was reserved for Sun. He also learned that Sun and his family would watch over it closely and not interfere. Sun said that, at times, he would retreat to his lodge in the sky country so that the other star-people could watch over this new world created by Naapi.

Infused with the power of creation, Naapi suddenly felt vigorous and rejuvenated. He could do anything, since he was a creative force with only his imagination to limit him. That is when he first understood the dilemma of creation. Fortunately for Naapi, not everyone was destroyed in the flood. While he was pondering his priorities, Loon suddenly swam by and asked Naapi if he could rest on his raft. Loon ululated his affection for water, but he thought that too much of a good thing was not so good. He told Naapi how he survived the flood by swimming on the rising water. He was certain that some other water-people had survived, but he was not sure where they were at that moment. Just then, Muskrat came paddling along and also climbed on board the raft. He was too short of breath to talk, so he only gasped and pointed to a driftwood log where Otter and Beaver clung for safety. Naapi directed the raft towards them and brought them on board. No one was injured, but they were all cold and tired, so they huddled beside Naapi. While they recovered their wits, Naapi thought of what he had to do.

The small cadre of survivors rested and recovered; when they finally awoke, Naapi announced to them that he had a plan. He told them that if he wanted to create a new world, he would need a handful of mud from the old one. He would need one of them to dive into the water, find the bottom, and retrieve some earth. Once he had the mud, he could use it to create a solid, new world. Muskrat was rested and volunteered to go first. Before anyone could object, he was in the water. Many heartbeats later, he came to the surface, gasping for air. Muskrat recovered his breath and apologized for his failure. Naapi assured Muskrat that his apology was unnecessary. He had not failed because they had discovered that the water was far deeper than they expected.

While everyone was preoccupied with Muskrat, Loon jumped into the water. He was long gone before they could object. All they could do was wait and see if he had any success. They waited and waited. Finally, Loon broke the surface of the water and gulped in air as if it were a particularly large trout. Once he regained his composure, he too apologized for not succeeding. Naapi told him not to worry; they were just glad he could still breathe. Naapi told them that the flood water was deeper than he thought and that he might have to reconsider his plan. With a single voice, they objected and said his plan could work. Otter said he would try next. He hyperventilated for a few seconds and dove into the water. An instant later, he disappeared into its murky depths. For a long, long time he remained submerged, as they waited with bated breath for him to surface. Suddenly, he cried from the water as his aching lungs filled with air. He was aided aboard the raft and he told Naapi of his failure to reach the bottom.

Naapi was seriously rethinking his plan. He confided his uncertainty to Beaver, who persuaded him that his plan could work. Beaver convinced Naapi to let him make one more effort. So Beaver jumped into the abyss and slapped his flat tail on the water in furious bravado. He was gone far longer than any of his mates. Muskrat chewed his claws, while Otter darted around the raft and studied the water. Loon warbled nervously that Beaver might be lost. Just as Naapi reassured him that everything would be fine, Beaver's lifeless body floated to the surface. They choked back their cries so they could pull him aboard the raft. Beaver's body lay on the raft. As his friends began to mourn, Naapi said he could revive Beaver by sharing with him the spirit of breath. His friends waited anxiously as Naapi pulled open Beaver's mouth and breathed into him. Instantly, he revived, and his companions cheered in delight. Beaver began coughing up the water he had swallowed. They cheered even louder when Beaver opened his paw to reveal a clump of mud. They all agreed that, in the new world, Beaver should be chief of the water-people. Naapi concurred and said he had much work to do.

He accepted the mud from Beaver and proceeded to demonstrate his creative powers. He rolled the mud in his palms, all the while breathing over it.

When it formed a ball, he threw it back in the water. Rather than sinking, the ball of mud bobbed in the water and began to grow. First it grew to be the size of their raft, then an instant later it was the size of a small island. It continued to increase in size until it grew to be a big island. Soon the castaways no longer felt marooned on their raft, which they abandoned on the first beach they spied. They stood on dry land for the first time since the flood. Naapi had created the world anew and none of his companions could contain their joy.

As water retreated from view, Loon fretted that he might soon perish because, despite everything, he was still a diving bird. Muskrat chimed in that he too liked water around; not having any would pose serious problems for him. Otter echoed Muskrat and Loon's concerns, but he said he liked flowing water, so a river or stream would be nice. When Naapi saw their predicament, he etched in some river valleys and formed some shallow land where water could collect. Since Beaver was declared the chief of the water people, Naapi instructed him about how to control flowing water, so that he could create a home for himself, and for Muskrat, Otter, and Loon. Naapi set about creating mates for his companions by forming them out of clay and sharing with them the spirit of breath. Then he created the trees in the forest and all the animals that lived on the land.

He made this world because he had enjoyed the company of humans. He felt his world would remain forever empty if he did not create them again. He picked up some clay and shaped it into the image of a man. Then he shared with his creation the spirit of breath and instantly the man began to breathe on his own. He shaped some clay into the image of a woman and brought her to life with his breath. Naapi told the couple who they were and then taught them how to live in the world he had created.

Before he left, he had one last piece of advice for his people. He warned them that the star-people could be vengeful. When Sun retreated to his lodge and darkness closed in, the star-people would appear to keep watch over the world. For eons, the ancestors of Blackfoot people inhabited the world Naapi had created for them. They enjoyed all its benefits, as they also faced its obstacles. However, they were always mindful of Naapi's warning to respect it, otherwise the star-people might destroy it again if human actions caused them anger.

DEANNA REDER

Sacred Stories in Comic Book Form
A Cree Reading of *Darkness Calls*

I have listened to many Cree interpretations of the Wasakaychak creation story, and each time the storyteller has insisted on including his or her own twists and experiences into the adventures of Wasakaychak.
—Geraldine Manossa (169)

On the cover of Steve Sanderson's *Darkness Calls* stands a young man slouching, holding his backpack, seemingly unaware that behind him and slightly to the left is a monster with formidable abdominal muscles whose gigantic claw-like hands are about to close around him. The young man also seems oblivious to the other fierce-looking being, grim-faced and stern, who is looking on intently. The fact that this scene graces the cover of a comic book, with its accompanying set of generic expectations, gives the reader clues to the possible storyline.

At first glance, the young man appears to be a hapless victim, but he must in fact be central to the story, if for no other reason than that he occupies a central position on the cover. Given the size and somewhat otherworldly nature of the two figures on either side of him, it is easy to guess that the one on the left, with the wild grimace, flowing grey hair, and threatening gesture, is a menace, and most likely a supervillain. The figure on the right looks less aggressive, although distinctly determined and ready for battle, a stoic foil for the grey-haired figure who is obviously enraged. Although this figure to the right does not have the obvious markings of a superhero, he is costumed, with what looks to be an eye mask, but could be face paint, concealing his identity. By all appearances, in the vernacular of the comic book,

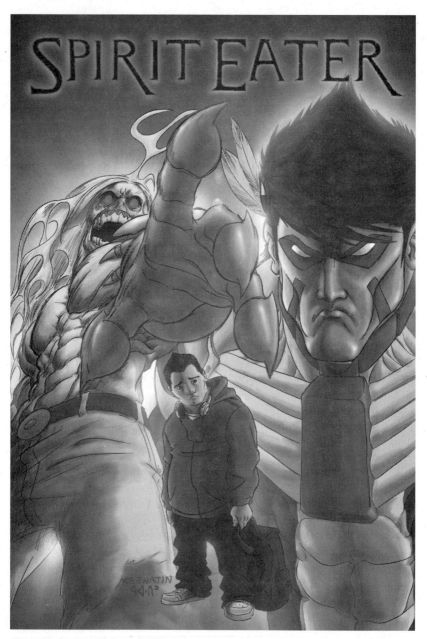

Steve Sanderson, *Darkness Calls*, cover art.

it seems as though there is about to be the archetypal fight between villain and hero, between evil and good. It appears that the fate of the pensive young man rests upon that outcome.

Until the story unfolds, there is no way to identify the ominous figure on the left as the Cree cannibal, Wihtiko.[1] Even should the reader recognize the name, it is possible that he or she would consider him to be a pop culture icon. After all, the Wendigo, as he is more commonly called, is a character who appears in the video games *Final Fantasy* and *Warcraft*, in the role-playing game *Dungeons and Dragons*, and in Stephen King's novel *Pet Sematary*. In fact, there is even a comic book version in the Marvel universe, in which Wendigo is a foe of, among others, the Incredible Hulk. Likewise, it would be difficult to identify without being told that the figure on the right is the Cree trickster, Wesakecak. Certainly, references in popular culture to Wesakecak are rare. However, what is commonplace are explicitly non-Cree shape-shifters, characters who are able to change themselves from human to animal, to plant or inanimate object, or to shift gender or race (e.g., Marvel's Wolfsbane, DC Comics' Chameleon Boy).[2]

Just as it is impossible to identify Wihtiko and Wesakecak from the comic book cover alone, it is equally impossible to know from the image alone that the young man is Cree, any more than one could know that his name is Kyle. One clue that this storyline might not be conventional is the three characters' somewhat dark complexions, since white characters dominate the world of comics and any character of colour is unusual.[3] Of course, the logo "C.A., Certified Aboriginal" in the lower right-hand corner, and the artist's signature (taken from Sanderson's middle name, Keewatin), rendered in both English and Cree syllabics, are more explicit indicators.

Even so, even after reading *Darkness Calls*, it is not obvious to the reader that the Healthy Aboriginal Network has both produced and distributed this work. Although its anti-suicide message is clear, *Darkness Calls* does not read like a public service announcement because it is not preachy and its storyline is not simplistic. In fact, the comic has received so enthusiastic a reception that its first run of over 40,000 copies has sold out. It is only from media interviews with Sanderson, a member of James Smith Cree Nation in Saskatchewan, that one could know he was inspired to write this story when he found out that his younger cousin had contemplated suicide.[4]

Clearly, *Darkness Calls* can be read as a tool in a suicide-prevention campaign. It also can be examined using a host of critical approaches devised by literary critics who regularly study representation in comic books and graphic novels. But as a Cree-Métis academic living at a time when Indigenous scholars are pressed to contribute to the intellectual health of our nations, I wonder how I can best discuss this text.[5] It is not that I need to make the case that comics are worthwhile objects of study—cultural theorists have already laid the groundwork for me in this capacity; neither do I need to argue that *Darkness Calls* is socially relevant, as it is directly working to eliminate suicide rates for Aboriginal youth that are roughly five times the national average.[6] Instead, the question with which I am grappling, so urged by contemporary Indigenous theorists, is to understand my relationship to the text and responsibilities to my community. How can I, as a Cree-Métis person situated in my own particular context, celebrate and contribute to Cree intellectual traditions so often neglected in conventional literary study? Implicit to this question is the assertion that Cree intellectual traditions exist and continue to flourish. How can I participate in a conversation that would welcome, respect, and be accessible to not only Aboriginal people in general but Cree and Métis people in particular?

In order to participate in Cree-centric inquiry, I discuss *Darkness Calls* as specifically Cree, a contemporary retelling of âtayôhkêwin, a sacred story that usually features the Cree trickster. Historian Winona Wheeler describes âtayôhkêwina as "the foundations of Cree spirituality/religion, philosophy and world-view [that] contain the laws given to the people to live by" (202). As a part of this tradition, *Darkness Calls* is no mere comic, but rather a sacred story about Wesakecak. Admittedly, this assertion is somewhat of a stretch. To begin with, this comic book narrative is not an explanation of creation, nor does the story focus directly on the exploits of Wesakecak; it is Kyle who is the main focus of the narrative. As well, although Wesakecak is typically described in âtayôhkêwina as amusing, lustful, boastful, and arrogant, these aspects of his character are absent in *Darkness Calls*. He is, however, a shape-shifter. As the elder who visits Kyle's school states: "The way [Wesakecak] looks is really up to the imagination of the storyteller. Sometimes he is an old man, sometimes he's young. He can be a raven or a coyote. Anything he needs to tell us his story" (9). What is significant about this statement, besides providing useful information, is that it is a moment of double meaning, not only in the one narrative line of an elder speaking to the school audience but also in reference to the story within the story, in which Wesakecak as action hero is in the form that the storyteller "needs to tell us his story." What we as readers do not discover until later is that the elder is, in fact, Wesakecak in the form of an old man who at the end of the story transforms into a raven and flies away.

Key to the story are four distressing moments within the plot when: (i) Kyle is insulted by his teacher; (ii) he is bullied by his classmates; (iii) he is publicly disrespected in front of the school community; and (iv) he is belittled at home. The aspects of this comic that resemble sacred stories and mark it as specifically Cree are the four basic values that this story articulates in response to these moments:

- responding to (iv): that the concept of one's relations is greater than the notion of the typical nuclear family, and includes not only extended family members but also spiritual relations;
- responding to (iii): that respect is fundamental for the health of the person and of society;
- responding to (ii): that stories about violence have healing potential and are appropriate for all ages;
- responding to (i): that conflict must be faced not just in the physical but also the metaphysical realm.

(i) First distressing moment: Kyle is insulted by his teacher

Although the first incident is not immediately apparent in the first frame of the comic, it is clear that the scene is glum. Even though it is sunrise, the sky is cloudy and the landscape is awash in muted tones. The second frame focuses on a collection of buildings easily identified by a large sign in the foreground as a high school. Less noticeable is the school's name, "Chief Hubert Smith," and a medicine wheel inscribed in the centre, the first hint that the story is either located on a reserve or in a rural and predominantly Aboriginal community.

Sharing the same visual line is frame three, depicting the empty hallways of the school, illuminated by large florescent lights that draw one's eye to the voice bubble that points around the corner. The dialogue, "how to divide algebra into the triangular isosceles," signifies both that a math class is in progress and that nonsense is being taught. When the following line shows us a fatuous, pasty, middle-aged male teacher droning on and a series of bored, confused, or sleeping youth, it is confirmed that the classroom teaching is ineffective and irrelevant.

But at this point Kyle is not struggling. In fact, at the bottom frame of the first page, he is the only student in class who is engrossed in his work, his back hunched over and his pencil in motion. Given the pose and dialogue of the teacher up at the front, his back to the class, writing on the board, and his admonition to "apply this to your daily lives," it seems unlikely that Kyle is writing notes on the lesson.

Instead, Kyle is drawing. On page 2, frame 1, we see the cartoon of an action figure, an ammo belt slung across one shoulder, a machete in one hand and a machine gun in the other; in frame 2, we see the excited eyes of the cartoon's creator. It is another moment that resonates on multiple narrative lines, when the artist of *Darkness Calls* draws an image of Kyle as artist who is also drawing.

At this point, in frames 3 to 5, the teacher turns from the board, notices the student's intense concentration in contrast with the other disaffected youth, and pauses, his hands on his hips signalling that he is about to speak directly to Kyle. In frame 6, on the bottom line of page 2, we get our first glance of the young artist. He has dark hair, skin and eyes, and is dressed in a black hoodie. The headphones that rest around his neck and his hairstyle, a modified version of a Mohawk, indicate that he listens to punk music.[7] A word bubble hangs in the air next to him—clearly, the teacher calling out his name. Kyle looks up, both surprised and concerned to be called upon, his pen still in hand, still poised on the paper.

Juxtaposed next to this, in frame 7, which is drawn from the back of the class, is the view of his classmates who have turned around to see what he is doing. The teacher is in front of the classroom, his arms crossed, sternly asking, "What have I told you about drawing during class?" It is this frame that situates Kyle as the misunderstood artist and loner, isolated from his peers. But it is on page 3, after his classmates have left the room, that real damage is inflicted. After the teacher accuses Kyle of "doodling his whole life away," he states, "Are you even listening to me? What's the point?" and, without allowing Kyle to answer, dismisses him, both literally and metaphorically: "Just go for lunch … that's all you're good at anyway" (3). This moment replicates the current public school system, in which the teacher of Native students is often non-Native and, given dismal graduation rates in Canada for Aboriginal students, regularly fails to inspire Aboriginal youth. In this story, Kyle is subject, as well, to the teacher's open scorn.

(ii) Second distressing moment: He is bullied by his classmates

Although Kyle finds solace in the school library, where he is able to listen to music and read comic books while eating his lunch, it becomes clear that Kyle is not only hiding from his teacher. In the middle of page 4, he exits from the library at the same time three students enter from outside, their language, gestures, and clothing identifying them as fans of gangsta hip hop. Kyle pauses, knowing that he is unable to avoid a confrontation. The three circle and pester him ("Hey, how come you do your hair like this? Are you gay?") before asking him what he is listening to: "Sounds like punk music"; "Guess that means your [sic] a punk, huh?" At this point, they trip Kyle and step on his headphones before leaving.

(iii) Third distressing moment: He is publicly disrespected in front of the school community

Later on in the afternoon, after rejecting the comfort of a friend, Kyle goes to the school auditorium for a special assembly. The palette for this scene is brighter and, as Kyle participates in the smudge, he seems, if not happy, at least more peaceful. The visiting elder is first seen on page 8, frame 6, standing relaxed and with his hands in his pocket. Upon introduction in frame 7, he smiles broadly and infectiously. He tells the students on page 9 that he wants to talk "about respect and about the old ways," "about Wesakecak, the trickster, and what he teaches us about ourselves."

As the elder speaks, Kyle reaches into his knapsack and begins to draw. Instead of drawing in order to ignore what is being said, Kyle is inspired by the stories and, on page 10, frame 1, he draws Wesakecak as a cartoon superhero, vaguely reminiscent of Marvel Comics' Thunderbird, with the same mask and similar features. This is the only time in the storyline, other than in one-on-one conversations with a comforting friend, that we see Kyle interact positively with his classmates as they watch him approvingly as he draws.

It is at this time that the third distressing moment takes place. The math teacher disrupts the assembly in order to reprimand Kyle for drawing: "You obviously don't respect [the guest] or your own culture enough to be here. Go to the office" (page 10, frame 9). Kyle tries to act disinterested but when he gets outside, fights back tears, especially when he sees his friend who follows him.

It is at this point in the story, as the boys talk outside, that the extent of Kyle's despair is understood. Although his only friend reminds him that he is a great artist and that his drawing is his future, Kyle responds: "My future? What do you mean by that? I'm just trying to get through today" (14). But Kyle also knows that he is not the only one to feel despair. He remembers two of their peers who have committed suicide, and the hopelessness, accompanied by alcohol abuse, in the community: "That's all people want to do is drink and die. That's all I have to look forward to" (15).

(iv) Fourth distressing moment: He is belittled at home

Despite his friend's support, Kyle returns home discouraged. As he sees his house in the distance, he experiences another moment of distress that stops him in his tracks. He thinks about the criticisms and insults he experiences at home, alongside the anger and unhappiness, and he sits down on a large rock, immobilized. It is at this point that Kyle begins to repeat,

"I want to die … I want to die" (18). A dark shadow looms behind him in the forest and, at the top of page 19, calls out his name. Frames 2 to 4 are a succession of shots, first of his face frightened, then the shadow calling out to him, and Kyle's face again; in frame 5, the call of a raven distracts him. This is the first hint that Kyle is being beckoned, first by Wihtiko and next by Wesakecak, and foreshadows the subsequent battle between the two.

As Kyle looks up he sees a truck in the distance coming up the road towards him and, by page 20, the sense of foreboding has passed as Kyle realizes that the driver of the truck is the affable elder who had been at his school. This is a pivotal moment in the narrative when the distresses of the first half of the story are resolved through the presence and work of the visiting old man.

Kyle hesitatingly approaches the new arrival and when the guest knows his name, Kyle asks him, "Do we know each other?" (20). The man identifies himself first as Kyle's grandfather and then clarifies that he is "your grandfather's brother on your mom's side" (21). Based on this relationship, Kyle invites the man into the house and they begin to talk over a cup of tea. This is partly because Kyle appreciates his culture's definition of family. To paraphrase Jo-Ann Episkenew: "In the Cree kinship system, extended family relations are more important than blood relations … all of [his grandfather's] brothers would be [Kyle's] grandfathers. Relatives are wealth" (68).[8]

Cree Teaching in Response to (iv)

The concept of one's relations is greater than the notion of the typical nuclear family

The wealth that the elder brings offsets the poverty of Kyle's home life. In his moment of despair, Kyle remembers his mother telling him to "lose some weight" and his father telling him that he is "useless" (17). But rather than demean Kyle, the elder praises and encourages him: "I'm glad to see you're drawing and taking an interest in the old ways.… It's a really good idea using your art as a way to keep the stories alive" (22). (This is another moment of multiple narrative lines in which the elder's words affirm not only Kyle's art but Sanderson's, too.)

But there is also another way in which to read the connection between Kyle and the visiting elder, who is Wesakecak in disguise. Neal McLeod, who like Sanderson is also from nihtâwikihcikanisihk, the James Smith Reserve, is author of *Cree Narrative Memory: From Treaties to Contemporary Times* (2007). He emphasizes the close familial relationship between Wesakecak and Cree people:

The proper term is *kistêsinaw*, which denotes the notion of the elder brother. This instantly assumes a state of kinship and relationship between humans and the rest of creation. It also moves beyond the intersubjective limitations of human-based discourse which has dominated the West. It moves beyond the conceptual straitjacket that the term "trickster" puts *wîsahkêcâhk* in: the term suggests to some that this sacred being is little more than a buffoon. (97)

This visit by Kistêsinaw reminds Kyle that his family, and therefore his wealth, is greater than the dysfunction that he experiences at home. He is related to a much wider circle of being, including sacred relations in the spiritual realm.

But Kistêsinaw also brings another form of support. He states: "I was kinda upset at your teacher interrupting me and treating you so poorly. So tomorrow your teacher is going to have an apology for you" (22). According to this grandfather, it is not Kyle who has broken the rules, but rather the teacher, who does not understand the core value of respect. In an interview in the 1980s, elder Peter Vandall discusses the social controls in traditional Cree society that functioned in place of an elaborate legal system. He explains that, even though it seemed as if the Crees "were not subject to any formal law, … [they] had their own rules[:] always to treat one another with respect and for the young people to pay heed to the elders" (51). The teacher was not only rude to Kyle; he also showed disrespect to the elder in front of all the schoolchildren. The elder freely admits that he was upset by the teacher, obviously expressed it at the school, and, by his intercession, gets the promise of an apology for Kyle. This validates Kyle's experience that he had been ill-treated and that his emotions matter.

Cree Teaching in Response to (iii)
Respect is fundamental for the health of the person and of the community

The elder is not simply being a kind advocate. He is responding to a Cree belief that the community is in danger when someone suffers abuse. At its most extreme, according to Swampy Cree storyteller Louis Bird, a severely abused person might turn into a wihtiko:

> There is a certain point when the mind can not tolerate any more and when that limit is reached it turns chaotic, and then it turns really crazy. A person turns crazy. Sometimes the person actually became an other-than human and he was not normal anymore. Automatically such a person would want to retaliate and hurt or kill someone. A person who got that way was very dangerous. (112)

When the elder begins to talk to Kyle over the kitchen table, he compliments Kyle on his art and states, "Too bad you left so early. I didn't get to tell you about the Wihtiko" (22). It is his kindness that protects Kyle, just as much as his warning about the spirit-devouring monster.

When, on page 23, the old man begins to tell his stories, there is a narrative switch. While the style that best describes the drawing up to this point is realism, thereafter the graphics become more cartoon-like. The "story within the story" is in some sort of alternate universe in which Wihtiko takes on a terrifying shape. Because we have already seen Kyle's drawing of Wesakecak, we understand that this is a story as Kyle would illustrate it.

Pages 25 to 40 are elaborate depictions of Wesakecak determined to stop Wihtiko from eating the spirits of young people. He leaves his high-rise apartment, described as his lodge, and flies by motorcycle to the darkest parts of the city, an industrial wasteland. Intermittent frames show Wihtiko in a large warehouse, slowly advancing on an anonymous youth. When Wesakecak arrives he and Wihtiko begin to fight, with very little dialogue but with typical sound effects for comic book battles: "Pow," "Thud," "hhuuck" (36).

In "Conventions of the Superhero Narrative" (2005), Mila Bongco argues that there are two common ways to interpret these obligatory fight scenes. At first glance, it appears that comic books support the status quo. Chaos might erupt, but the hero generally wins and peace is always restored: "There are elaborate fight scenes whose winner is almost inevitable" (46). However, there is a less conservative interpretation that suggests that comic books portray the anarchic potential of society, that "the outcome of the fights is often only secondary to the unfolding of the disruption and its effects [and] the ensuing confrontation with the villains" (47). According to these interpretations, the popularity of comic battles is either the satisfaction that good trumps evil or the visceral thrill of the looming threat. But this analysis offers little to Sanderson's story precisely because, in Cree cosmology, Wesakecak does not represent the powers of good, just as good and evil are not considered to be polar opposites. In Cree cultural stories, good does not necessarily trump evil and the hero is not always triumphant.

Sanderson's battle scenes are not indulgent episodes of violence but rather a restaging of the initial confrontation in the school hallway, when Kyle is criticized and mistreated by his classmates. In the context of the story, it is Kyle who is completing the drawings, as he reimagines moments of conflict. Rather than a fight between good and evil, it is a testing of courage in the face of fear of tangible threats.

This tradition of telling graphic stories full of serious subject matter to everyone, regardless of their age, was something that impressed Steve Sanderson. He notes that in his own experience the elders in his community would tell stories that were:

> very raw and very real. They never watered them down, never dumbed them down, never softened them up ... never sugar-coated the stories. They thought enough of their audience, children included, that they didn't shy away from the scary.[9]

It is partly this storytelling model that inspired Sanderson to take subject matter that is taboo and form it into a story that is accessible and understandable to young adults.

Cree Teaching in Response to (ii)
Stories about violence have healing potential and are appropriate for all ages

According to Louis Bird, the inclusion of acts of violence or wrongdoing is often an integral part of the story:

> Even though some of them sound horrible and terrible to different cultures, for the [Swampy Cree] culture it is a necessary type of teaching system. It saves lives. It saves the families. It saves the children. It allows people to have a serious understanding about where they live. These stories are about shamanism (in English) [or spiritual powers]. As humans, when we listen to the exciting part of a story—whether the story is bad or good—we always listen to parts that are horrible and terrible. We remember them vividly and we like those kinds of stories. (4)

The battle scene in *Darkness Calls* could be understood as a mnemonic device, to help the listener/reader remember the story vividly. The fighting also makes the story exciting, the pleasure encouraging learning. Including the horrible and terrible is key to the story's pedagogical value and its ability to save lives. According to Bird, the violent story has redemptive potential.

The fact that Wesakecak does not win the battle contravenes the conventional outcome of a superhero narrative, especially as he makes statements full of bravado. He declares to Wihtiko: "I told you, I'm not going to let you kill any more young spirits" (39). Moments later he is captured in Wihtiko's grip and forced to admit that "You're right. I can't stop you. You're more powerful than me" (41). But hope is not lost. Wesakecak declares that the one who can stop Wihtiko is the anonymous teenager who has been Wihtiko's prey.

After this declaration, there is another narrative shift. Suddenly it is possible to identify the youth in the "story in the story," and it is Kyle, seemingly transported from the kitchen table of his home to the abandoned warehouse. At first, he is mystified and frightened, but once he begins to fight back, he becomes stronger, louder, and more assertive: "I don't wanna die. I don't believe in the things you say about me. I'm sick of people criticizing me and everything I do! You don't get to choose that for me! You have no power over me" (44). It is not Wesakecak who saves Kyle from destruction. There is no appearance of a superhero to save the day. Instead, Kyle's words vanquish the Wihtiko.

Cree Teaching in Response to (i)
Conflict must be faced not just in the physical but also the metaphysical realm

In a 2001 article, Saulteaux and Métis critic Janice Acoose writes that her grandmother, her Coochum, told her that "the *Wiintigo* would disappear if … we were brave enough to chase it away with a big stick" (46). In accordance with Coochum's counsel, Kyle knows that he cannot avoid, be saved from, or run away from this monster. He uses his bravery and his words to lash out at and chase away Wihtiko. Although his show of courage and strength could be dismissed as self-assertiveness, in the context of *Darkness Calls* it is a spiritual epiphany.

At Kyle's moment of triumph, he is suddenly transported back to his home, sitting across the kitchen table from his elder. The graphics are once again realistic in style, although the palette is brighter than the first kitchen scenes because the sun streams in at the end through a side window. His facial expression is one of shock, as he is possibly amazed at this adventure, possibly uncertain about the mechanics that brought him from one story and back into another. The elder praises him and counsels him: "Now you know the power inside of you. Now you know how much you're worth. Now it's your responsibility to pass it along to someone else. I know you can with your drawing and your wisdom. You have a strong spirit inside of you" (46–7). This is a full-circle return to early passages in the narrative, when the teacher admonishes him for doodling his whole life away. While belittling him, the teacher had told Kyle that he needed to learn to focus (3). By the end of the story, Kyle discovers his strength, and from this his focus and sense of purpose, rather than the other way around. Again, this transformation is grounded in Cree cosmology and is spiritual in nature. Neal McLeod argues that the sacred stories, the narratives of wîsahkêcâhk, "point to relationships between humans and other beings, and to the possibility of radically reimagining constructed social spaces" (98). *Darkness Calls* is an example of this reimagining.

Even the narrative shifts in Sanderson's comic, from the story to "the story within the story" and back again, are in keeping with Cree storytelling style. In "Honoring Ni'Wahkomakanak" (2008), Janice Acoose discusses a contemporary Cree short story with words that aptly describe *Darkness Calls*: "When Nêhiyawak mythological figures spirit onto the page, narrative/storytelling voices shift shape, story seams bust wide open as truth turns into fiction, and myths spill into each other" (229). There is more than one way that this description applies to Sanderson's work. On one hand, the appearance of the elder telling Kyle Wesakecak stories shifts shape and busts open story seams as the elder becomes Wesakecak and Wihtiko's prey becomes Kyle; on the other hand, it also shows Sanderson's use of the Cree imagination, and Wesakecak and Wihtiko as concrete manifestations of this tradition, accompanied with the inherent power of Cree sacred stories that is the truth turning into fiction, spilling into each other. The storyline could not be possible had this been a showdown between Superman and some super villain.

That being said, I do not suggest that only Cree readers can appreciate this work. In fact, the Healthy Aboriginal Network has taken Sanderson's comic and turned it into a short film with added narration. What is remarkable is that this narration is not in English—presumably viewers can read the English dialogue in the word bubbles; neither is it in Cree or even Michif, at least at this time. Instead, the storyline is narrated in Gitxsan. The Gitxsan-Wet'suwet'en Education Society commissioned the DVD as an attempt to help youth in Hazelton, B.C., who in recent years have suffered a spate of suicide attempts.[10] There has been an unexpected benefit to distributing the film throughout the region, a benefit thought to help young people value themselves and their culture. Richard Van Camp, an editor for the Healthy Aboriginal Network, has reported that it is not only the power of the story that is shared[11] but also the fact that Aboriginal youth are able to learn their language by watching the DVD.

But the youth of Hazelton are not the first to learn about their culture from a mix of cartoon and film. While Sanderson himself remembers stories about Wesakecak from storytellers in the community, he also remembers a children's CBC television show in the 1980s. Tantoo Cardinal would introduce each episode, and then the story would be based on adventures with Wesakecak. "It wasn't exactly animation," Sanderson states. "It was paper cutouts that had that traditional Cree art look to them."[12]

Although Sanderson is certain that for the Cree, "our strength is in our storytelling," it is clear that the form is not rigid or resistant to innovation. As the elder tells the school audience in *Darkness Calls*: "The way [Wesakecak] looks is really up to the imagination of the storyteller. Sometimes he is an old man, sometimes he's young. He can be a raven or a coyote. Anything he needs to tell us his story" (9). Wesakecak can even take the form of a comic book hero. Anything Sanderson needs to tell us his story.

Notes

1   There are many ways to spell Wihtiko and Wesakecak. I have chosen to use the spelling as it is in the comic book, but when I quote other authors, I maintain the spelling they have chosen.
2   In the comic book canon, shape-shifters destabilize social categories. For example, X-Men's Mystique, one of the few bisexual characters in comics, is able to turn herself into the shape of any human, giving readers the opportunity to consider the role of gender in her identity and sexual orientation.
3   For example, Brad Mackay writes in an article for the *Toronto Star* that even though "the Marvel universe contains more than 5,000 characters ... only 100 or so of these are black—less than two per cent of their fictional population. This pales in comparison to the nearly 14 per cent that the U.S. Census says makes up American society at present [and 12 per cent if you include all of North America]." See "Hero deficit: Comic books in decline" (18 March 2007), <http://www.thestar.com/sciencetech/article/193167>.
4   See "Revamped Cree Legend Fights Teen Suicide in New Comic," CBC website, <www.cbc.ca/arts/story/2006/06/21/cree-comic-hero.html> (accessed 9 May 2008).
5   See the essay by Niigonwedom James Sinclair in this volume, as well as works by Craig S. Womack, Daniel Heath Justice, Jace Weaver, and Robert Warrior.
6   See Health Canada, *Acting on What We Know: Preventing Youth Suicide in First Nations*, <http://www.hc-sc.gc.ca/fniah-spnia/pubs/promotion/_suicide/prev_youth-jeunes/index-eng.php> (original website accessed 1 May 2008).
7   I want to thank the Simon Fraser University class of FNST 322–2008 (Indigenous Popular Fiction), who immediately recognized the meaning in this hairstyle and defined for me what "that's tight" means.
8   Episkenew is actually explaining how, in *Halfbreed*, all of Grannie Dubuque's brothers would be Maria Campbell's grandfathers.
9   Personal communication, 21 May 2008.
10   See "B.C. Community Pleads for Help to Halt Suicide 'Epidemic,'" CBC website, <http://www.cbc.ca/canada/british-columbia/story/2007/11/22/bc-hazelton suicides.html> (accessed 21 May 2008).
11   Personal communication, 25 March 2008.
12   Personal communication, 21 May 2008.

Works Cited

Acoose, Janice. "A Vanishing Indian? Or Acoose: Woman Standing Above Ground?" In *Ad(dressing) Our Words: Aboriginal Perspectives on Aboriginal Literatures.* Ed. Armand Garnet Ruffo. Penticton, BC: Theytus, 2001. 37–56.

———. "Honoring Ni'Wahkomakanak." In *Reasoning Together: The Native Critics Collective.* Ed. Craig Womack, Daniel Heath Justice, and Christopher B. Teuton. Norman: U of Oklahoma P, 2008. 216–33.

Bird, Louis. *The Spirit Lives in the Mind: Omushkego Stories, Lives, and Dreams.* Comp. and ed. Susan Elaine Gray. Montreal: McGill-Queen's UP, 2007.

Bongco, Mila. "Conventions of the Superhero Narrative." In *Comic Books.* Examining Pop Culture Series. Ed. David M. Haugen. Detroit: Greenhaven, 2005. 43–56.

Episkenew, Jo-Ann. "Socially Responsible Criticism: Aboriginal Literature, Ideology, and the Literary Canon." In *Creating Community: A Roundtable on Canadian Aboriginal Literature.* Ed. Renate Eigenbrod and Jo-Ann Episkenew. Penticton, BC: Theytus; Brandon, MB: Bearpaw, 2002. 51–68.

Manossa, Geraldine. "The Beginning of Cree Performance Culture." In *Ad(dressing) Our Words: Aboriginal Perspectives on Aboriginal Literatures.* Ed. Armand Garnet Ruffo. Penticton, BC: Theytus, 2001. 169–80.

McLeod, Neal. *Cree Narrative Memory: From Treaties to Contemporary Times.* Saskatoon: Purich, 2007.

Vandall, Peter. "Social Control." In *Stories of the House People.* Ed. Freda Ahenakew. Winnipeg: U of Manitoba P, 1987. 46–51.

Wheeler, Winona. "Reflections on the Social Relations of Indigenous Oral Histories." In *Walking a Tightrope: Aboriginal People and Their Representations.* Ed. Ute Lischke and David T. McNab. Waterloo: Wilfrid Laurier UP, 2005. 189–214.

COYOTE AND NANABUSH

Coyote Sees the Prime Minister

Coyote went east to see the
PRIME Minister.

I wouldn't make this up.

And the PRIME Minister was so HAPPY
        to see Coyote
        that he made HIM a member of
        cabinet.

Maybe YOU can HELP us solve the
        Indian problem?

Sure, says that Coyote,
        WHAT'S the problem?

When Elwood tells this story, he
        always LAUGHS and spoils
        the ending.

Coyote Goes to Toronto

Coyote went to Toronto
        to become famous.
It's TRUE
        that's what she said.

She walked up and down those
        FAMOUS streets.
And she stood on those
        FAMOUS corners.

Waiting.

But nothing happened.

so.
Coyote got hungry and went
into a restaurant
to EAT.

But there was a long line
        and Coyote could see it was
        because the restaurant was
        painted a BEAUTIFUL green.

so.
Coyote painted herself GREEN
        and she want back to the rez
        to show the people what an
        UP-TO-DATE Coyote she was.

And she STOOD on the rez
        and waited.

So that RAIN came along.
So that WIND came along.
So that HAIL came along.
So that SNOW came along.

And that PAINT began to peel
        and pretty soon the people
        came along and says,
HEY, that's Coyote, by golly
        she's not looking too good.

And the women brought her FOOD.
And the men brushed her COAT
        until it was shiney.
And the children PLAYED with
        their friend.

I been to Toronto Coyote tells
        the people.
Yes, everybody says,
We can SEE that.

JO-ANN ARCHIBALD (Q'UM Q'UM XIIEM)

Excerpt from Indigenous Storywork: Educating the Heart, Mind, Body, and Spirit

First Nations/Indigenous stories about Coyote the Trickster often place her/him in a journeying mode, learning lessons the "hard" way. Trickster gets into trouble when she/he becomes disconnected from cultural traditional teachings. The Trickster stories remind us about the good power of interconnections within family, community, nation, culture, and lands. If we become disconnected, we lose the ability to make meaning from Indigenous stories.

I took a long journey with Coyote the Trickster to learn about the "core" of Indigenous stories from Elders, to find a respectful place for stories and storytelling in education, especially in curricula. I also learned how to do story research with Elders. I worked intensively with three Coast Salish Elders and thirteen Stó:lō Elders, who either were storytellers or were versed in the oral traditions. They shared both traditional stories and personal life-experience stories about ways to become a storyteller, cultural ways to use stories with children and adults, and ways to help people think, feel, and "be" through the power of stories.

The Elders taught me about seven principles related to using First Nations stories and storytelling for educational purposes, what I term storywork: respect, responsibility, reciprocity, reverence, holism, interrelatedness, and synergy. Experiential stories reinforce the need for storywork principles in order for one to use First Nations stories effectively. These seven principles form a Stó:lō and Coast Salish theoretical framework for making meaning from stories and for using them in educational contexts. I learned that stories can "take on their own life" and "become the teacher" if these principles are used.

During the journey Coyote and I learned that these storywork principles are like strands of a cedar basket. They have distinct shape in themselves,
but when they are combined to create story meaning, they are transformed
into new designs and also create the background, which shows the beauty of
the design. [...]

The storybasket that I, and maybe Coyote, have learned to make comes
from living stories and making meaning from them based on interactions
with others, particularly with Elders. My first storybasket, which started from
my dream, is not perfect. There are flaws. The next one may be better because
I have learned some storywork principles and methods that I didn't know
when I started this one. I need to keep coming back to the Elders to learn
more and to have them check my storywork weaving process in order to see
whether I am doing it in the "right" way.

In Stó:lō tradition, a basket maker gives her first basket away to someone
who may find it useful. I give this storywork basket to you.

DANIEL MORLEY JOHNSON

(Re)Nationalizing Naanabozho
Anishinaabe Sacred Stories, Nationalist Literary Criticism, and Scholarly Responsibility

Consider the arrogance of a culture that believes in outside experts, the experts who create simulations, and consider a culture that believes in such experts over natives, over the wit and wisdom of native stories, and the cultural predators who reduce the original, mythic, and ironic perceptions of natives to mere material evidence.
　—Gerald Vizenor (Anishinaabe)

By continuing to tell our sacred stories and controlling the telling of those stories, we are sustaining our cultural sovereignty.
　—Lawrence W. Gross (Anishinaabe)

The present essay is a humble attempt to survey some of the stories about what we most familiarly know as Northern Woodland tricksters. Not trickster stories—but stories about tricksters, that is, theorizing as a mode of storytelling. These theory-stories will not exactly be about "tricksters," although many of the authors we will explore employ the word. In keeping with the philosophy behind this collection of essays, however, I agree with Nêhiyaw (Cree) scholar Neal McLeod's recent comments about the inaccuracy of the label "trickster" in Nêhiyaw tradition:

> The proper term [in Nêhiyawêwin or the Cree language] is kistêsinaw, which denotes the notion of the elder brother. This instantly assumes a state of kinship and relationship between humans and the rest of creation. It also moves beyond the intersubjective limitations of human-based discourse which has dominated the West. It moves beyond the conceptual straitjacket that the term "trickster" puts wîsahkêcâhk[1] in: the term suggests to some that this sacred being is little more than a buffoon. (97)[2]

For McLeod, the English word trickster shares a similar dynamic with the colonialist notion of *terra nullius* (empty land) employed by colonial governments via their own courts to argue that Indigenous lands have been empty of laws and government structures, the British North American attempt to codify legally the white man's burden. He writes, "[t]he term 'trickster' is part of this same trickery, making Indigenous narratives conceptually empty and potentially devoid of truth" (97). He argues that what are usually termed trickster stories in the Northern Woodlands context should rather be seen as part of the genre of sacred stories (âtayôhkêwina in Nêhiyawêwin), thus highlighting their centrality to the culture and beliefs of Indigenous nations.

McLeod's reconceptualization of the terminology opens possibilities for our present discussion of "the trickster," and challenges what we may have come to know about such figures in works of anthropology, folklore, and literature. The first part of this essay will briefly articulate an Indigenist literary criticism based on humility and reciprocity, which will be followed by an examination of the theoretical work of Gerald Vizenor (Anishinaabe), particularly his writing on "trickster hermeneutics" in conversation with recent critical work on Indigenous literary nationalism. Like McLeod, Vizenor has been critical of the ways academics, particularly non-Indigenous social scientists, have misrepresented Anishinaabe tricksters; instead, as we will see, his theorizing supports the work of the nationalist critics. Keeping with literary nationalist theory, we will read Vizenor's theoretical work in the context of Anishinaabe culture, literature, language, history, and theory. We will also gesture towards the implications of literary trickster hermeneutics for disrupting the dominating colonial-historical narrative.[3] (Recall that, etymologically, hermeneutics derives from the Greek trickster, shape-shifter, and messenger Hermes, who was an intermediary between the gods and mortals.) This essay is an attempt to avoid the trickiness of colonial-power-knowledge and reproductions of dominative social science discourse that describes, delineates, and defines "the trickster" without regard for Indigenous epistemologies.[4]

In his essay on public memory in Canada and the forced removal of the Sayisi Dene from their sacred homelands in Northwestern Manitoba to the shores of Hudson Bay, education theorist Roger I. Simon writes, "What might it mean to live our lives as if the lives of others truly mattered? One aspect of such a prospect would be our ability to take the stories of others seriously, not only as evocations of responsibility but as well as matters of 'counsel'" (62). If we think of Indigenous stories and theories as matters of counsel for all of us who live in the Americas, the relationship between the storyteller and the

listener implies that, as a result of hearing the story, some action will be taken
and transformation will take place. Real transformative action requires more
than sympathetic listening; it demands taking responsibility for the stories
we have been told. Simon continues thus:

> What might be the substance of a point of connection at which I am touched
> to respond to the memories of others, not in the sense of some meaningless
> sentiment, a too-easy sympathy, or the false nostalgia of a late imperialism,
> but rather as means of experiencing certain events as part of ongoing rela-
> tions of power and privilege, the legacy of which I participate in and I am
> called to transform? (65)

He alerts us—particularly those of us who are descendents of Amer-European colonizers—to the ongoing colonial dynamics that we must confront
when listening to Indigenous stories, a confrontation that must necessarily
lead to the transformation of the colonialist legacies we have inherited. I recognize my complicity (as a result of my power and privilege) in the ongoing
colonization and occupation of Indigenous lands by the British Crown via its
proxy state, the Dominion of Canada. I position myself as a settler who has
been called upon to transform the current reality of oppression. I hope to do
so by allying myself with those warriors, like Taiaiake Alfred (Kanien'kehaka),
"who want to beat the beast into bloody submission and teach it to behave"
(37). Many scholars reveal their ignorance by the assumptions they make; I
would rather admit up front my relationship to the knowledge about which
I am writing.

The "obviative" or fourth person is a grammatical concept in Anishinaabemowin (the Ojibwe language) and related Algonkian languages, such
as Nêhiyawêwin. J.R. Valentine describes the obviative in linguistic terms:
"Within a given clause, only one third person animate referent can be in the
foreground at one time; all other third person referents are backgrounded
by making them obviative," which is marked by particular suffixes on animate nouns and inflections on verbs in Anishinaabemowin (623). The proximate form indicates the centre of attention in a discussion, whereas the
obviative form marks a person who is less important (Wolfart and Carroll
25). The foregrounded referent is said to be proximate, and all other referents are obviated, or, in other words, *not* the focus of the sentence or conversation. The obviative form is used to distinguish between third persons,
notably to "disambiguate the participants in subordinate clauses to those in
a main clause" (Valentine 625). For example: Wgii-waabamaan dash niw zhiishiiban niibna bbaa-gomod [He (Nenabozh) saw many ducks as he floated
about] (Valentine 625). The ducks (zhiishiiban) are obviated and Nenabozh

is proximate; we know it is he who is floating about, not the ducks, as the verb bbaa-gomnid is also proximate. The key for our current discussion is the way obviation differentiates proximate and distant third persons, such that peripheral subjects are marked by the obviative form. This concept from Anishinaabemowin can be instructive for those of us who are non-Natives studying Indigenous literatures. I position myself as peripheral to the conversation, not as an expert, but as an obviated visitor sharing what I have been taught.

According to Dr. Donald Blais (Penobscot-Métis), my Indigenous Spiritualities instructor at the University of Toronto, trickster stories teach humans about humility; we learn to abandon our arrogance and egocentrism in the presence of the Creator through such story cycles. Because the Creator's morality is beyond being conceived by humans, as evidenced by these spiritual stories, we are left with a sense of wonderment at Creator's playfulness. Similarly, Vizenor has written that self-reflection is an essential attribute of non-Natives doing work in Indigenous studies, and he is critical of those scholars who have studied Anishinaabe culture "from secure carrels in libraries" to produce endless theses and monographs that "reveal more about the cultural values of the observer than the imaginative power of spiritual tribal people" (140–1).[5] Therefore, part of identifying the place of my voice in this conversation is to distance myself from the work and attitudes of other shaaganash Indigenous Studies academics.[6]

What if literary theorists were to question our responsibilities to communities? The recent scholarship of North American Indigenous literary nationalist critics has emphasized the need for work that responds not only to the intellectual paradigms of Indigenous nations, but also to the needs of Indigenous communities. Unlike some Native Studies academics, I do not take this call for accountability to mean that only Native people can write about Native literature. In fact, nationalist critics explicitly state the opposite—they simply and rightfully demand a meaningful, informed engagement with Indigenous peoples and their texts. This approach, according to Daniel Heath Justice (Cherokee), "is not a necessarily exclusivist act that seeks an idealized cultural purity," but rather "a deeply realistic and life-affirming act" (*Our Fire* 10). A reading based in intellectual-national sovereignty "privilege[s] an understanding of community as being important to a nuanced reading of [a] text" (*Our Fire* 10). As such, Osage scholar Robert Allen Warrior calls for an approach "that defines people not on what they are, but on what they do in relation to what our communities need" (210). Nationalist criticism has challenged the trendy hybridity theories that are currently in vogue in literary studies, and, in this regard, these critics differ somewhat from Vizenor's "mixedblood" theorizing. Craig Womack (Muskogee/Oklahoma Cherokee) offers his writing as an antidote to globalized homogeny and the hegemony of dominative Amer-European nation states:

> Radical Native viewpoints, voices of difference rather than commonality, are called for to disrupt the powers of the literary status quo as well as the powers of the state—there is a link between thought and activism, surely. Such disruption does not come about by merely emphasizing that all things Native are, in reality, filtered through contact with Europe, that there is no "uncorrupted" Indian reality in this postcontact world we live in. This is an assimilationist ideology, a retreat into sameness and blending in. (*Red on Red* 5)

Jace Weaver (Cherokee) elaborates with reference to hybridity theory: "In a new multicultural version of the discarded melting pot hypothesis, some non-Native critics desire Natives to dissolve into a soup of hybridity (in which, they too, of course, can share), embracing our mixed-blood identities" (29). Weaver suggests that in our "mult-cult" society, Amer-Europeans want Natives "to rend the Buckskin Curtain for them, and they [non-Natives] are wounded when we say we have grown to like it just fine as a way of maintaining a demarcation, much like a border between nation-states" (37).

Maintaining separateness does not mean severing contact altogether. Womack wants Native literature to be taught *as* American literature: "It is our America, after all, and our canon, and we should stay put since it is our home. Rather than withdrawal, the solution is seeking greater and higher quality literary autonomy" (163). This method, rooted as it is in intellectual autonomy, appears to be grounded in responsibility and the practice of strengthening self-determining Indigenous nations; it provides a useful alternative to theories that would rather see separate and distinct groups mashed together in a multicultural form of homogenous McCulture, in which the Big Mac is made out of bison—it's still the same fast food hash as everywhere else.[7] In "The Necessity of Nationhood: Affirming the Sovereignty of Indigenous National Literatures," Justice alerts us to why dominative readings of Native literature in North America tend to stress culture over politics: "Cultural readings, by themselves, distract us, and they fix our attention on shallow surfaces. Culture alone cannot change the world. The power—and danger—of nationhood is that it *can*" (151).[8] No wonder it appears that some non-Native scholars are so resistant to recent nationalist literary studies, and choose instead to continue wrestling over who can say what about whom, or to contend the non-viability of Indigenous perspectives, all apparently in order to enhance their respective careers. Our purpose here is not to engage in this sort of useless monologue, but rather to contribute to the spread of Anishinaabe theories in the context of Indigenous nationalism in order to weaken the whitestream[9] grip over both academic discourse and the land on which this discourse takes place. The remainder of this essay will illustrate the power and danger of nationalist tricksters to the dominating cultural narratives of discovery.

(Re)Nationalizing Naanabozho: Gerald Vizenor from a Literary Nationalist Perspective

Vizenor has invented a postmodern vocabulary to articulate his vision of Indigenous identities, with terms that highlight the "blendedness" of post-contact Indigenous worlds (i.e., crossblood, mixedblood) and the Baudrillardian difficulty of differentiating a simulation (or worse, simulacra) from the "real thing(s)"; his terms include "postindian," "invented indians," "fugitive poses," "double others," and so forth. Although some scholars use this terminology to suppose that Vizenor rejects "an Indigenous identity" in favour of one that is hybridized, Weaver argues in "Splitting the Earth" that "the identity Vizenor has elaborately been defining and redefining has at its base the deep and unmistakable roots of 'tribal' values ... Though Vizenor champions what he calls 'crossbloods,' he nonetheless champions them as Natives rather than 'hybrids'" (21–2).[10] Vizenor identifies himself as an enrolled member of the Minnesota Chippewa Tribe, White Earth Reservation, and asserts that his "life story started with an anishinaabe family history" (*Postindian Conversation* 61). In *The People Named the Chippewa*, he writes with specificity about Anishinaabe culture and literatures, and argues against simplified or uncritical pan-tribalism and the misnomer *indian* in the documents of discovery and ethnographic texts: "The cultural and political histories of the Anishinaabeg were written in a colonial language by those who invented the Indian, renamed the tribes, allotted the land, divided ancestries by geometric degrees of blood, and categorized identities on federal reservations" (19). Still, Vizenor does write that "in the language of the tribal past ... [t]ribal people used the word Anishinaabeg to refer to the people of the woodland who spoke the same language. The collective name was not an abstract concept of personal identities or national ideologies" (13). However, a common name, language, and homeland are three aspects of Indigenous peoplehood, as recently defined by scholar Jeff Corntassel (Tsalagi [Cherokee]).[11] Again, although Vizenor may not be a separatist, his writing does in many ways complement sovereigntist assertions made by nationalist scholars.

Vizenor's writing on Anishinaabe aatihsoohkewinan (sacred story cycles) relating to Naanabozho is scattered throughout his many books and articles. From the outset, I acknowledge that aatihsoohkewinan are not to be told at certain times of the year; therefore, I have no desire to learn sacred stories out of context, nor do I want to disclose sacred knowledge.[12] I have chosen to limit this discussion to published theorizing on the subject, and not to repeat the stories themselves.[13] Such misrepresentations of Indigenous culture are part of the manifest manners in the literature of dominance about which Vizenor writes. Like the literary nationalist writers, he is critical of academics—mostly ethnographers and other social scientists—such as Victor Barnouw, a non-Native anthologist of Anishinaabe stories, who "delivered his interpretation in isolation" and "carried on an autistic monologue with science" ("Trickster Discourse" 198). Social scientific assertions made by academics like Barnouw "[reveal] power relations over the culture he has studied and invented" and do not reflect Anishinaabe philosophies; meanwhile, scholars "with state subsidies" have published widely and hence "been rewarded with doctorates and academic tenure" ("Trickster Discourse" 192). (Personally, I think I should stop right there; however, I also think non-Native scholars need to hear one of their own repeat such arguments against anthropologizing.)[14] Vizenor's critique of those scholars who refuse to respect Anishinaabe theories and protocols complements the work of Justice, Warrior, Weaver, and Womack above. Vizenor discusses the violence inflicted on Indigenous stories when they are appropriated by the academy:

> Foundational theories have overburdened tribal imagination, memories, and the coherence of natural reason with simulations and the cruelties of paracolonial historicism. Anthropologists, in particular, were not the best listeners or interpreters of tribal imagination, liberation, or literatures. (*Manifest Manners* 75)

Note that his focus is the tribal-national—not a blurry and limp hybridity—and the liberatory potential of stories denied by rigid academics.

In his essay on trickster discourse, Vizenor discusses how formalizing oral stories in academic print works to "burden the trickster sign, end comic discourse in a language game and demand legitimation" ("Trickster Discourse" 199). Dynamic story cycles thus become tied up in a circular series of footnotes and the textual cannibalism of quotations, citations, and endless requoting, all detached from Indigenous communities. So he asserts: "Social science theories abase the comic holotropes in trickster narratives.... [T]he humour that heals is closer to the oral tradition and bound to a specific culture" (199, 206). These are cautionary words for scholars who seek final versions (perhaps

akin to final solutions) of Indigenous oral story cycles and pan-Indigenous
trickster theories. One antidote for the stories recorded by clinical academi-
cians is Vizenor's description of the trickster as a semiotic sign: "The trickster
is a sign, a communal signification that cannot be separated or understood in
isolation," but rather must be *heard* "in narrative voices" (189). Following Baudrillard's definition, social science translations of aatihsoohkewinan are simulations of Indigenous stories; detaching "oral stories and the comic trickster"
can result only in "the naked corpse of the word," separate from the living
interaction of the author, narrator, characters and audience (191).[15] In *Manifest Manners*, Vizenor outlines how trickster hermeneutics is one way of disen-
tangling and distinguishing the simulation from the "real," the absent from
the present: "Trickster stories arise in silence, not scriptures, and are the
holotropes of imagination; the manifold turns of scenes, the brush of natural
reason, characters that liberate the mind and never reach a closure in stories"
(15). Although he criticizes social science definitions that render tricksters
inert, he approves of literary descriptions, and as he playfully tells us, *pace*
Barthes and Foucault, "the death of social science is the birth of the trickster
in modern literature" ("Trickster Discourse" 202). It would seem that literary
studies makes a better theoretical home for tricksters than anthropology: after
the death of the social science author, "the trickster author becomes the narrator" ("Trickster Discourse" 202).

After proclaiming the death of the "anthro," we might better understand
the liberatory possibilities of tricksters in sacred stories:

> The trickster is reason and mediation in stories, the original translator of
> tribal encounters; the name is an intimation of transformation, men to
> women, animals to birds.... Tricksters are the translation of creation; the
> trickster creates the tribe in stories, and pronounces the moment of remem-
> brance as the trace of liberation. (*Manifest Manners* 15)

One such liberatory moment in aatihsoohkewinan is when tribal-national
remembrances undermine the history invented and pathologically repeated
by colonizers, and, in so doing, free the Anishinaabe memory of creation
("the trickster creates the tribe in stories") from the burdens of imperialist
dominance, the slipperiness of the Bering Strait theory, and the selfish manners and myths of Manifest Destiny. The stories revoke gender dualities, the
boundaries of imperialist binarism, and invoke transformation by "liberating the human mind"—in fact, Vizenor writes that aatihsoohkewinan "are
the translation of liberation" (*Manifest Manners* 15). The story cycles—not
social scientific theories—assert the presence of Anishinaabe people, "the
shimmer of a tribal presence" in stories that would proclaim the death of

Indigenous history, celebrate the dissolution of sovereignty, rename the new world after Columbus, and replace the Anishinaabek with *indians* or hybrids rather than tribal citizens who uphold nation-to-nation treaties. Unlike disengaged academic monologues, "trickster hermeneutics is *access to* trickster stories [aatihsoohkewinan] ... trickster hermeneutics is survivance, not closure, and the discernment of tragic wisdom in tribal experiences" (*Manifest Manners* 15, emphasis mine). Again, Vizenor is referring to the tribal-national, the situated-ness of Indigenous knowledges in nations, homelands—in Anishinaabe people. The national literatures of survival and resistance, accessed in context, ideally accessed aurally, attest to the cultural and political survivance of sovereign Indigenous nations. "The Anishinaabe creation is out of water," and not across an ice bridge, as Vizenor claims in an interview: "We are water, and there is no presence without water and trickster stories of that creation" (*Postindian Conversations* 135).

What if we took peoples' stories about themselves seriously? "The words the woodland tribes spoke were connected to the place where the words were spoken," writes Vizenor in *The People Named the Chippewa*, his book of narrative histories of the Anishinaabek (24). Throughout Vizenor's writing we see his commitment to tribal-national specificity and to political rather than surface-level cultural readings of aatihsoohkewinan. Like the nationalist critics, he expresses the importance of place, language, history, and sovereignty in Anishinaabe story cycles. He insists on humour as a reason for Anishinaabe survivance, and insists that trickster hermeneutics can liberate stories that have been dominated by colonial-power-knowledge. Very briefly, we will conclude by examining humour as an aspect of survivance (survival + resistance) and trickster hermeneutics as a challenge to the dominating historical narrative.

Don't Mind Your Manners: Lessons from the Trickster of History

In *American Indian Literary Nationalism*, Craig Womack writes: "[N]o Indian language has the word trickster in it ... many people from home would not know what we were talking about if we mentioned the word trickster" (116). However, he does recognize the need for a common term to describe the trickiness that occurs in stories from many national traditions. He notes that scholars have yet to interrogate fully the "universal applicability" of certain terms and vocabulary, and yet to pay proper attention to "history, politics, language, or other factors that would move them beyond clichés" ("The Integrity of American Indian Claims" 155). It is evident that his concerns indirectly echo Vizenor's, and reflect the reasons behind the present volume of essays. Earlier in the same article Womack writes:

> Somehow, as a literary trope, we seem to have ... mistaken him or her ["the trickster"] for a role model, ignoring some of the more oppressive character-istics of this figure (look at the rapes, for example, that are sometimes part of trickster stories). (116)

Vizenor discusses this concern in *Postindian Conversations*: "The word itself, *tricky, trickster*, is resisted by many readers as a representation of cunning deception rather than chance and liberation in stories" (59). I have been taught that these sacred stories, generally speaking, reflect the virtue of game-playing as a sacred practice, in which the trickster figure plays either immorally or amorally, and reveals aspects of Creator; for example, he/she is motivated by play, values teaching over punishment, and puts evil into balance or har-mony rather than simply destroying it. Creator's way is not our way, and aatih-soohkewinan are instructive of this distinction.[16] Corroborating this point, Vizenor refers to Naanabozho as:

> The compassionate woodland trickster ... a teacher and healer ... capable of violence, deceptions and cruelties: the realities of human imperfections....
> [Naanabozho] is comic in the sense that he does not reclaim idealistic ethics, but survives as a part of the natural world; he represents a spiritual balance in a comic drama rather than the romantic elimination of human contra-dictions and evil. (*The People Named the Chippewa* 3–4)

Similarly, Theresa Smith notes, "Nanabush *balances* himself, depending upon his body, his free soul (instinct/intuition), and his ego soul (reason) at appro-priate times. He seeks *alliances* with others, exercises *caution* and *emotional restraint* and *reciprocates* for the help he has received" (179). Trickster hermeneu-tics can teach us about necessary contradictions, about being reflexive and honest (particularly about our histories), and about forming liberatory alliances. There must be the potential in these stories to turn over both the current reality and the manifest myths of the past. One way of achieving such a reversal is by taking lessons from Naanabozho: scholars should engage in free thinking, aim our word-arrows carefully, challenge established social norms, skewer sacred cows, and balance good judgment with playfully bad manners.[17]

In *Reading the Fire*, literature scholar Jarold Ramsey defines "The Trick-ster":

> [W]hose episodic career is based upon hostility to domesticity, maturity, good citizenship, modesty, and fidelity of any kind ... who is given to playful dis-

guises and shape-changing; and who in his clever self-seeking may accomplish important mythic transformations of reality, both in terms of creating possibility and in terms of setting human limits. (27–8)

Ramsey's emphasis on the trickster as hostile to domesticity and good citizenship may provide a good model for students of colonial history; after all, we do not need to accept the colonialist version as a scripture that is beyond being teased or mocked, or proven sickly absurd in its self-congratulatory worship of modernization and progress (that is, violence, genocide, occupation). Vizenor concurs with Ramsey's characterization: "The trickster suggests bad manners, at least, and deception of a kind that is not culturally acceptable in the best of families" (*Postindian Conversations* 59). I think these authors refer to tasteful anti-behaviour on the part of Naanabozho, a way of being in the world that upsets our uptight and arbitrary social and professional constructions. Personally, I have tried to pursue the concept of trickiness as an ideal attribute in a scholar, being a thorn in the side of my many professors who have been uncritical of colonialist myths. So Palestinian critic Edward Said writes that "[l]east of all should an intellectual be there to make his/her audiences feel good: the whole point is to be embarrassing, contrary, even unpleasant" (12). He calls for scholars to find a place of exile from which they should be "as marginal and as undomesticated as someone who is in real exile…. The intellectual in exile is necessarily ironic, skeptical, even playful—but not cynical" (63, 61). We should see some parallel with trickster theory. Vizenor even posits a trickster university in a passage from *Postindian Conversations*:

> Consider the possibility that students, like trickster characters, come to the campus not just for the degrees that might enhance their income and disguises in the community, but imagine that they come because they hope to hear in four years at least one last lecture, you know the last crease of tragic wisdom in a lecture. Someone who would speak about how they got to their ideas, rather than how their ideas are represented as some treasure of authority, but the mute lectures continue in many courses. The native trickster teases the ownership of ideas and history, that long history of territorial dominance, and the reduction of imagination to serve the causes of cultural discovery and possession. Imagine a university that encouraged the faculty to give last lectures, the synchronous creation of ideas, as if every lecture was the last one. Now, that would be almost a trickster university. (127–8)

Like Said, Vizenor prods us towards an understanding of the transformative power of the university and those of us who research, write, and teach within it. What if we taught with a sense of urgency and shared our methods and thoughts rather than conclusions as though they were received wisdom from high above? What if we taught as if the market did not dictate "skill sets" and, rather than having a capitalist "episodic *career*" (as Ramsey puts it), we consider "trickster" as an agitating verb rather than a passive historical noun? *What if?*

Anishinaabe scholar Lawrence W. Gross has articulated what he calls the "comic vision" of his nation. The Anishinaabe comic vision, expressed through sacred stories, is partly a response to what Gross calls Post-Apocalyptic Stress Syndrome (PASS), which takes the definition of post-traumatic stress disorder to the level of an entire culture. According to Gross, European invasion brought about the end of the Anishinaabe world:

> The loss of land, resources, relatives, and heritage all contributed to a shattering of the Anishinaabe world. Though fragments remained that would aid in the later reconstruction of the culture, the totality added up to an apocalyptic experience from which the Anishinaabe are still recovering. (452)

PASS explains an increase in substance abuse, violence, suicide, abandonment of established religious practices, loss of hope, and sense of despair on the part of many Anishinaabe survivors. So, in "The Comic Vision of Anishinaabe Culture and Religion," Gross writes that that vision "of the Anishinaabe is helping us overcome that trauma and helps explain how we are managing to survive" (437). He notes the typical features of a comic vision, some of which include complex conceptual schemes, a high tolerance for disorder, the unfamiliar and ambiguous, critical thinking, non-seriousness, pacifism, forgiveness, equality (including among genders), questioning of authority and tradition, situation ethics rather than rules, and social integration ("Comic Vision" 444–5). The parallels with Ramsey and Vizenor's insistence on the trickster being against good citizenship and domesticity are apparent. Perhaps it is this comic vision, visible in sacred stories, upon which, before invasion, Anishinaabek built their cultures; the people have continued to use this worldview as a way of dealing with PASS and in revitalizing a healthy Anishinaabe world. For example, Gross illustrates how story cycles in which Naanabozho wins a bet against the lumberjack Paul Bunyan works to explain why much of Northern Minnesota remains forested, and represents a symbolic (and playful) Anishinaabe victory over colonialist environmental destruction. When analyzed, such stories demonstrate the characteristics of a comic vision mentioned above ("Comic Vision" 452–3).

Kimberly Blaeser (Anishinaabe) has written about the important connection between history and Indigenous literatures. Like other authors, she refers to the ways in which literature can be a method of resisting the intellectual imperialism of the Amer-European dominating narrative; particularly important is the use of humour in overturning the tragic history of colonization in the Western hemisphere. According to Blaeser, humour in stories can "work to unmask and disarm history, to expose the hidden agendas of historiography and, thereby, remove it from the grasp of the political panderers and return it to the realm of story" (39). Trickster reversals (such as the one in the Naanabozho-Paul Bunyan story) overturn "enshrined accounts of history" and "arouse in a reader an awareness of the way that history can and has been possessed" (43). She articulates how trickster hermeneutics "liberates and empowers us in the imagination of our destinies" and allows us to envision "the what-ifs of story" (49, 44). Gross draws nearly the same conclusion: "Maintaining the role of cultural hero in new stories and new roles, the trickster liberates the Anishinaabe from the oppression of colonialism and opens healing vistas of the imagination" ("Comic Vision" 456). Trickster hermeneutics has a direct relation to historiographical method, and incites "the reader to an imaginative reevaluation of both the *accounts* and the *processes* of history" (Blaeser 43).

In her 1994 poem, "Coyote Columbus Café," Marie Annharte Baker (Anishinaabe) provides an example of how trickster hermeneutics can disrupt the dominating narrative of history. She deconstructs the European theft of land, the sexual violence of imperial conquest, and the popular myths of Columbus's discovery, thus turning over a tragic story and teasing it with comic wisdom. Take, for example, the following historical excerpt, attributed to Cristobal Colon's log book, 14 October 1492: "[S]hould your Highness command it all the inhabitants could be taken away to Castile or held as slaves on the island, for with fifty men we could subjugate them all and make them do whatever we wish. Moreover, near the small island I have described there are groves of the loveliest trees I have seen" (cf. Cohen 58–9). The Admiral's thoughts drift from forced relocation, slavery, and subjugation to the beautiful landscape he already covets. Baker tries to find the connection between Columbus (with his yearning gaze) and the subsequent violent conquest by Spanish explorers and soldiers, and attempts to locate these in terms of the religious foundations of European colonization:

> ever wonder if Colon confessed
> to a priest? what did he say
> to turn on church officials
> start a catholic Rambo trend. (73)

Baker raises an important question: how did the Admiral convince his Catholic patrons to pursue the violent holocaust of Indigenous peoples? In other words, the colonization of the Americas was not inevitable; we must remember this was a Christian conquest that has been at times deliberately brutal and genocidal *in the name of the faith.* Vizenor, who has written a great deal about Columbus, describes *indians* as "the romantic absence of Natives" in the literatures of dominance (*Fugitive Poses* 14). In the colonial-historical record, Columbus's *indians* silently surrender their land, perhaps in sign language: "[They] were extremely sorry that they could not understand me, nor I them," wrote Columbus's son in the reconstructed journal of the Admiral. Despite this admitted lack of understanding, in the same sentence Columbus claimed he "understood" one particular Chief who made it known, "that if there was anything, I wanted, the whole island was at my disposal" (Cohen, *Four Voyages,* "The Life of the Admiral by His Son, Hernando Colon," 89). To counter the silent anonymous *indian* who gave away the hemisphere, Natives are once again made present when the speaking roles are reversed in Baker's Coyote poem: "Colon would get comforted / by a kindly Native who'd say / *Don't feel bad bro. / You're lost like the rest of us*" (73). On one level, Baker's lines disarm the narrative of colonial "progress" and grant compassion to the figure who set Amer-European colonialism in motion, but also provoke us to think—it could have been different. Allan J. Ryan refers to this as "serious play, the ultimate goal of which is a radical shift in viewer perspective and even political positioning" (5).

Baker's narrator, "a poor coyote girl" at the Coyote Columbus Café, plays with history while the poet plays with language, as when the narrator approaches a guy at the end of the bar: "Boozho Dude. Hey, I'm talking / to you, Bozo Dude. My name is / Conquista. Come on adore me" (71). She teases the Anishinaabe greeting "Boozho" (related to Naanabozho), and reverses the genocidal sexual violence of the Conquistadors and other colonizers. The coyote girl explains: "[M]y optimism looks good on me / in my territory my favourite bar / & grill I bar none grill some" (71). The narrator playfully weaves between teasing Columbus and asserting Indigenous sovereignty with multiple expressions of survivance and non-conformity: "I am the landlord around here," and "I am too damn direct / for the colonized coyote / poor oppressed critter" (71–2). Note the narrator's resistance to being co-opted and oppressed. Baker re-visions Columbus through a Woody Allenesque "squirmy spiel":

> The map I made shows the Indies
>   beyond the curve in the earth.
>   Most of the crew are already
> around the bend. (73)

Again, she plays with the idea of Columbus being lost, and with the fact that he doctored his maps so as not to discourage his crew if they failed to locate land; it is well known that a day or two before landfall, his crew was leaning towards mutiny. The coyote trickster girl teases the documents of discovery, and, in doing so, provides a moment to decentre the West's canonized stories about itself and to laugh at the shortsightedness of the invaders and their descendants, such as the Canadian government's Indian Affairs department ("had an Indian affair lately?"). Towards the end of the poem, the coyote girl makes reference to the re-educational potential of Vizenorian trickster hermeneutics:

> when I'm having an Indian taco day
> I discover it's just about too late
> not to educate the oppressor
> but am I ever good at doing it. (75)

At once, the poet is able to mock Amer-European historicizing (ranging from self-congratulation to denial to repentance); the poet is also able to demonstrate the necessity of expressing survivance in the face of this one-sided historiography, and the importance of teasing, reimagining, and rewriting that history.

"Only the tricksters survive"

In *Custer Died for Your Sins: An Indian Manifesto* (1969)—parts of which originally appeared in *Playboy*—Vine Deloria, Jr. (Standing Rock Lakota) uses humour to skewer U.S. policy and whitestream perceptions of First Peoples. Deloria also writes of the liberatory potential of humour: "Often people are awakened and brought to a militant edge through funny remarks," he writes in his chapter on Indigenous humour. "I often counseled people to run for the Bureau of Indian Affairs in case of an earthquake because nothing could shake the BIA. And I would watch as younger Indians set their jaws, determined that they, if no one else, would shake it" (149). Sure enough, in 1972, hundreds of radical Indigenous activists did just that—they occupied the BIA office November 3–9, which coincided with Nixon's landslide second presidential victory. While occupying the BIA offices, activists set up a War Room in which they revised the Bureau's existing map of Indigenous (reservation) land to include the whole of the United States.[18] In addition to destroying much of the inside of the building, activists removed artwork, typewriters, office supplies, and more than 20,000 pounds of BIA documents, including restricted files (many of the documents and artworks were later recovered by

the FBI). Quite humorously, BIA office equipment was found in D.C. and
Oklahoma, whereas books, paintings, and artifacts were found in Lawrence,
Kansas (cf. Smith and Warrior, 171–3). I have heard stories of one or two of
those typewriters turning up in North Carolina and elsewhere. Although
Deloria criticized the theft of documents—an act he argued could have damaged land, water, and treaty rights cases—the symbolic redistribution of artifacts and office equipment is ironic in light of his 1969 comments on humour
fuelling militant activism.[19] It seems as though it *were* possible to shake the BIA,
even if not to its very foundations. As Paul Chaat Smith and Robert Warrior
write, "[p]aintings that a few months earlier had adorned government hallways now graced reservation homes. Baskets and pottery, liberated from stuffy
glass cases, had not been stolen, but rather repossessed by their original owners" (171). Or, at least, that is how it may have seemed to the activists who had
certainly been "brought to a militant edge."

Describing the Anishinaabe apocalypse, Gross argues that if the questioning of underlying social structures "reaches an acute enough level, the
world can collapse.... The supporting pillars of a given world can give way for
whatever reason, and society will come tumbling down" ("Comic Vision"
439). When he warns us that "worlds can collapse," he is referring to the
traumatic and deliberate sabotage and dismantling of the Anishinaabe world
on the part of invading Amer-Europeans. We might reverse this cycle, however, and seek the collapse of the 500-year colonialist continuum, the occupation of Indigenous lands by overseas usurpers, imperial overseers, the
breaches of international law and human rights, and the ongoing daily denial
of the American Holocaust. Naanabozho's questioning of established norms,
and the Anishinaabek tolerance for disorder and divergent thinking, provide a framework for survivance, evidenced in the work of Vizenor and Gross.
In *The People Named the Chippewa*, Vizenor quotes ethnographer Ruth Lan-
des's description of Anishinaabek as "zestful and wicked survivors.... Their
wit is cruel and startling to the white middle-class outsider, at whom it is often
directed" (28). Deloria declared that humour is "the cement by which the
coming Indian movement is held together" (168). Gross's Anishinaabe-centred reading of Louise Erdrich's novel *Tracks* concludes, "[o]nly the tricksters survive," a succinctly powerful acknowledgement of the importance of
comic wisdom (63). Trickster hermeneutics can overturn the notion that
Indigenous peoples are victims, and shift the focus to their survival and resistance. Like the recent work by nationalist critics, Vizenor's theorizing advo-
cates useful and hopeful academic work that is researched and written in the
context of specific Indigenous nations and their national traditions. As such,
Vizenor's Anishinaabe-centred criticism should be recognized alongside the

work of Justice, Warrior, Weaver, Womack, and others who are reasserting the importance of nationalism and accuracy in Indigenous studies. Further, we should observe the centrality of humour to Indigenous survivance, and employ trickster hermeneutics to dismantle the tragic narratives of colonialism in favour of a comic vision that promotes joyful coexistence and revolutionary opposition to the authoritarianism of academic experts and the colonialist oppressive reality of occupied North America. What if we dismantled that system with stories of comic wisdom?

Acknowledgements

I acknowledge the generous teachings of my Anishinaabe instructors and friends in the Aboriginal Studies program at the University of Toronto, particularly Alex McKay, Jean-Paul Restoule, Deborah McGregor, and Jill Carter. I am particularly grateful to Niigonwedom Sinclair for his generous comments on a draft of this essay, and Dr. Donald "Doc" Blais for his teachings that have informed all of my work. Miikwehc. I dedicate this article to my grandfather, Morley G. Spiker, whose comic stories and gentle teasing will be with me forever.

Notes

1   The word "wîsahkêcâhk" is here rendered in the standard Nêhiyawêwin (Cree language) Roman orthography. The elder brother wîsahkêcâhk is also known as Wisahkecahk or Weesakayjac among Northern Anishinaabe peoples, while most southern Anishinaabek refer to this being as Naanabozho, Wenabozho, or Nanabush (and various other spellings). Naanabozho is also known as The Great Rabbit, and the "-abooz" ending of the name may derive from the Anishinaabe word "wabooz" (rabbit). See Smith, 171. In his most recent work, Vizenor most consistently uses Naanabozho, and I will follow this convention.

2   Smith also refers to Naanabozho as an elder brother to the Anishinaabek (175).

3   Resistance to the dominating whitestream narrative is prominent in the work of many Indigenous literary authors, and is articulated throughout the creative and scholarly work of my teacher Simon J. Ortiz (Acoma Pueblo). See Ortiz's foundational essay on Indigenous nationalism and literature, "Towards a National Indian Literature: Cultural Authenticity in Nationalism," *MELUS* 8:2 (1981): 7–12.

4   Education theorist Michael G. Doxtater (Kanien'kehaka) defines colonial-power-knowledge as Amer-European knowledge created to authenticate Indigenous knowledges, in order to remind Indigenous people of their colonial subjugation. Colonial-power-knowledge renders Indigenous peoples (and their knowledges) invisible in their own lands. See Doxtater, "Indigenology."

5   In a critique of Kenneth Lincoln's work on Indigenous humour, Vizenor refers
to the importance of self-reflection (see his essay, "Native American Indian Identities: Autoinscriptions and the Cultures of Names," 123).

6   In his study of humour in Anishinaabe discourse, Roger Spielmann notes that a
typical non-Native response to being teased is to laugh and follow that by seriously
rejecting the tease, i.e., in order to confirm that they are not ignorant, or to indicate that they are indeed "in the know." Conversely, Spielmann notes that the
typical Anishinaabe response to being teased is playful self-deprecation and laughing, without the impulse to "set things straight" or to save face (127).

7   My comments here are, of course, informed by Jace Weaver's critique of hybridity theory in *American Indian Literary Nationalism.*

8   Sandy Grande (Quechua) has similarly questioned: "How has the focus on 'cultural' representations of Indian-ness contributed to a preoccupation with parochial
questions of identity and authenticity?... [H]ow has this preoccupation obscured
the social-political and economic realities facing indigenous communities, sub-
stituting a politics of representation for one of radical social transformation?"
(1)

9   Scholars have used the term "whitestream" when referring to the North American mainstream, in order to underscore the reality that the dominant/dominat-
ing culture (that is, the self-appointed "mainstream") remains inextricably linked
to whiteness. See, for example, Sandy Grande (Quechua), "Whitestream Feminism
and the Colonialist Project: Toward a Theory of Indigenista," in *Red Pedagogy:
Native American Social and Political Thought* (Lanham, MD: Rowman and Littlefield, 2004), 123–57. Grande uses the term to signify the differences between
white mainstream feminist theory and theorizing by radical women of colour.
Luis Urrieta, Jr., uses the word in a Chicano/a context in his article, "Dis-Connec-
tions in 'American' Citizenship and the Post/Neo-Colonial: People of Mexican
Descent and Whitestream Pedagogy and Curriculum," *Theory and Research in Social
Education* 32:4 (Fall 2004): 433–58. It is important to remember that full rights
of citizenship in the United States, and to varying degrees in Canada, are denied
to those who are not part of the whitestream. Recall that Status Indians in Canada
could not vote in federal elections until 1960, and were denied this citizenship
right in provincial elections in Quebec until 1969.

10 Weaver, "Splitting the Earth," 21–2, emphasis in original. Among those proponents
of hybridity theory in Indigenous literatures, I would include the late Louis Owens
(Choctaw/Cherokee), Arnold Krupat (especially his early writing), and Owens's
student Elvira Pulitano, whose scholarship was one provocation for the publication of *American Indian Literary Nationalism.* Craig Womack offers a thorough critique of Pulitano's writing in "The Integrity of American Indian Claims," 92–117.

11 Corntassel is contributing a great deal to refining concepts of Indigenous nationalism and peoplehood based on shared interlocking concepts of sacred history,
ceremonial cycles, language, and ancestral homelands (91–2).

12 Revealing sacred knowledge is a serious offence in many Indigenous nations.
Vizenor refers to "one [Anishinaabe] singer [who] was ostracized from the Midewiwin lodge because he disclosed religious secrets and allowed sacred songs to be
recorded." See *The People Named the Chippewa*, 27.

13 Vizenor lists several "burdens" on Indigenous oral tradition and memory, includ-
ing "the uncertainties of stories out of season." See Vizenor, *Manifest Manners:
Narratives on Postmodern Survivance*, 2nd ed. (Lincoln and London: U of Nebraska
P, 1999), 52.

14 Education theorist Donaldo Macedo repeats the words of an African-American
community centre staff member, who said to a white woman colleague, "Ma'am,
if you really want to help us, go back to your white folks and tell them to keep the
wall of racism from crushing us." See Macedo's foreword to Paolo Freire, *Pedagogy of Freedom: Ethics, Democracy, and Civic Courage* (Lanham, MD: Rowman and
Littlefield, 1998), xxix.

15 Vizenor, "Trickster Discourse," 191. "The naked corpse of the word" is Vizenor
quoting from a translation of Mikhail Bakhtin in *The Dialogic Imagination*.

16 The previous sentences are based on the oral teachings of Dr. Donald Blais.

17 I borrow the term wordarrows from Vizenor's book, *Wordarrows: Native States of
Literary Sovereignty* (2003).

18 The occupation of the BIA is documented in Paul Chaat Smith and Robert Allen
Warrior, especially 149–68. For the reference to the revised map, see 158–9.

19 In *Like a Hurricane*, Smith and Warrior describe the divisions created among some
people over the destruction of the building and theft of property, actions that were
apparently criticized by many. The authors provide a very balanced account of con-
troversial events during the period they cover.

Works Cited

Alfred, Taiaiake. *Wasáse: Indigenous Pathways of Action and Freedom*. Peterborough,
ON: Broadview, 2005.

Baker, Marie Annharte. "Coyote Columbus Café." In *Native Poetry in Canada: A Contemporary Anthology*. Ed. Jeannette C. Armstrong and Lally Grauer. Peterborough, ON: Broadview, 2001. 71–6.

Baudrillard, Jean. *Simulacra and Simulation*. Trans. Sheila Glaser. Ann Arbor: U of
Michigan P, 1996.

Blaeser, Kimberly. "The New 'Frontier' of Native American Literature: Dis-Arm-
ing History with Tribal Humour." In *Native American Perspectives on Literature
and History*. Ed. Alan R. Velie. Norman: U of Oklahoma P, 1995. 37–50.

Cohen, J.M., ed. and trans. *The Four Voyages of Christopher Columbus*. Har-
mondsworth, England: Penguin, 1969.

Corntassel, Jeff J. "Who Is Indigenous? 'Peoplehood' and Ethnonationalist
Approaches to Rearticulating Indigenous Identity." *Nationalism and Ethnic
Politics*. 9:1 (2003): 91–2.

Deloria, Vine, Jr. *Custer Died for Your Sins: An Indian Manifesto*. New York: Avon,
1969.

Doxtater, Michael G. "Indigenology: A Decolonizing Learning Method for Eman-
cipating Iroquois and World Indigenous Knowledge." Ph.D. diss., Cornell U,
2001.

Grande, Sandy. *Red Pedagogy: Native American Social and Political Thought*. Lanham, MD: Rowman and Littlefield, 2004.

Gross, Lawrence. "The Comic Vision of Anishinaabe Culture and Religion." *American Indian Quarterly* 26:3 (2002): 436–59.

———. "Cultural Sovereignty and Native American Hermeneutics in the Interpretation of the Sacred Stories of the Anishinaabe." *Wicazo Sa Review* 18:2 (2003): 127–34.

———. "The Trickster and World Maintenance: An Anishinaabe Reading of Louise Erdrich's *Tracks*." *Studies in American Indian Literatures* 17:3 (2005): 48–66.

Justice, Daniel Heath. "The Necessity of Nationhood: Affirming the Sovereignty of Indigenous National Literatures." In *Moveable Margins: The Shifting Spaces of Canadian Literature*. Ed. Chelva Kanaganayakam. Toronto: TSAR, 2005. 143–59.

———. *Our Fire Survives the Storm: A Cherokee Literary History*. Minneapolis: U of Minnesota P, 2006.

McLeod, Neal. *Cree Narrative Memory: From Treaties to Contemporary Times*. Saskatoon: Purich, 2007.

Ramsey, Jarold. *Reading the Fire: The Traditional Indian Literatures of America*. Rev. and expanded ed. Seattle: U of Washington P, 1999.

Ryan, Allan J. *The Trickster Shift: Humour and Irony in Contemporary Native Art*. Vancouver: U of British Columbia P, 1999.

Said, Edward. *Representations of the Intellectual: The 1993 Reith Lectures*. New York: Pantheon, 1994.

Simon, Roger I. "The Touch of the Past: The Pedagogical Significance of a Transactional Sphere of Public Memory." In *Revolutionary Pedagogies: Cultural Politics, Instituting Education, and the Discourse of Theory*. Ed. Peter Pericles Trifonas. New York and London: Routledge/Falmer, 2000. 61–80.

Smith, Paul Chaat, and Robert Allen Warrior. *Like a Hurricane: The Indian Movement from Alcatraz to Wounded Knee*. New York: New Press, 1996.

Smith, Theresa L. *The Island of the Anishnaabeg: Thunderers and Water Monsters in the Traditional Ojibwe Life-World*. Moscow, ID: U of Idaho P, 1995.

Spielmann, Roger. *"You're So Fat!": Exploring Ojibwe Discourse*. Toronto: U of Toronto P, 1998.

Valentine, J.R. *Nishnaabemwin Reference Grammar*. Toronto: U of Toronto P, 2001.

Vizenor, Gerald. *Fugitive Poses: Native American Indian Scenes of Absence and Presence*. Lincoln: U of Nebraska P, 1998.

———. "Native American Indian Identities: Autoinscriptions and the Cultures of Names." In *Native American Perspectives on Literature and History*. Ed. Alan R. Velie. Norman: U of Oklahoma P, 1995. 117–26.

———. *The People Named the Chippewa: Narrative Histories*. Minneapolis: U of Minnesota P, 1984.

————. "Trickster Discourse: Comic Holotropes and Language Games." In *Narrative Chance: Postmodern Discourse on Native American Indian Literatures*. Ed. Gerald Vizenor. Albuquerque: U of New Mexico P, 1998. 187–211.

————, and A. Robert Lee. *Postindian Conversations*. Lincoln and London: U of Nebraska P, 1999.

Warrior, Robert. "Native Critics in the World: Edward Said and Nationalism." In *American Indian Literary Nationalism*. Ed. Jace Weaver, Craig S. Womack, and Robert Warrior. Albuquerque: U of New Mexico P, 2006. 179–223.

Weaver, Jace. "Splitting the Earth: First Utterances and Pluralist Separatism." In *American Indian Literary Nationalism*. Ed. Jace Weaver, Craig S. Womack, and Robert Warrior. Albuquerque: U of New Mexico P, 2006. 1–89.

Wolfart, H. Christoph, and Janet F. Carroll. *Meet Cree: A Guide to the Cree Language.* New and completely rev. ed. Edmonton: U of Alberta P, 1981. 25.

Womack, Craig S. *Red on Red: Native American Literary Separatism.* Minneapolis: U of Minnesota P, 1999.

————. "The Integrity of American Indian Claims: Or, How I Learned to Stop Worrying and Love My Hybridity." In *American Indian Literary Nationalism*. Ed. Jace Weaver, Craig S. Womack, and Robert Warrior. Albuquerque: U of New Mexico P, 2006. 91–177.

JUDITH LEGGATT

Quincentennial Trickster Poetics
Lenore Keeshig-Tobias's "Trickster Beyond 1992: Our Relationship" (1992) and Annharte Baker's "Coyote Columbus Café" (1994)

As the essays in this collection indicate, trickster figures are ubiquitous in Indigenous literatures. From Raven on the West Coast to Glooscap in the East, First Nations trickster figures pop up in orature, literature, criticism, and theory. Most First Nations Canadian writers have at least one text that includes a trickster figure: Thomas King's *Green Grass, Running Water*; Lee Maracle's *Ravensong*; Ruby Slipperjack's *Weesquachak*; Daniel David Moses's *Coyote City*; Darrell Dennis's *Trickster on Third Avenue*; Beatrice Culleton Mosionier's *Night of the Trickster*; Tomson Highway's "Rez" plays. The list goes on and on. Highway, Moses, and Lenore Keeshig-Tobias had even formed a Native writers' group in the 1980s, which they called the Committee to Re-establish the Trickster (CRET), to emphasize the importance of the figure to Native culture. The members of CRET saw the trickster as a sign of Native culture, an alternative to the false constructions of "the Indian" under colonization. From the other side of the cultural divide, post-structuralist, post-colonial, deconstructive academics—myself included—have latched onto the figure as a way of breaking down the binary structures and logocentricity of Western discursive practice. Trickster figures break down either/or dichotomies, with their propensity for being both/and: *both* male *and* female, *both* creator *and* destroyer, *both* role model *and* cautionary figure, *both* spiritual *and* physical, *both* animal *and* human. The growth of academic interest in tricksters during the latter half of the twentieth century reflects a shift in Western thought that has taken place during the same time period. Postmodernism in literature and art, post-structuralist thought in the humanities and social sciences, and chaos theory in the pure sciences all indicate that, in academic circles at least, simplistic models, based on linear systems and binary modes of thought, are no longer considered adequate models by which to explain either the socio-cultural or the phenomenological worlds. Because tricksters cannot be contained by the linear and binary modes of thought that characterized most Western thought systems before modernism, they have been seized upon as models for more complex, non-linear, and chaotic systems.

Despite the prevalence of trickster figures in Indigenous literatures and the ways in which the figure has been used as a sign of Native culture by writers such as Highway, there is a danger that the anthropological, ethnographic, and theoretical understandings of these figures in academia unthinkingly translate Indigenous narratives into Western discourse. Anne Doueihi complains that most anthropological studies of trickster stories "have tended to focus on the trickster as a character in stories, thus taking trickster narratives only at their referential (face) value. This approach, which treats language conventionally, as a transparent medium for the communication of some meaning or another, consequently leads to the search for some univocal meaning to which the trickster and his stories might be reduced" (193–4). She goes on to note that such readings "impose their own terms on the trickster narratives instead of attending to the terms set up by the narratives themselves" (195). Doueihi's multivocal discursive approach faces similar challenges to the univocal readings she opposes. Although there are obvious similarities between the ambiguities and disconnections of trickster figures and the playful deconstruction of postmodern literature and post-structuralist theory, to read tricksters in light of such theories might be to miss specifically Indigenous modes of thought inherent in the tales. Even if it could be argued that Indigenous narrative strategies helped in the dismantling of narrative certainty that led first to modernism, and then to postmodernism, reading such narratives only through a postmodern and post-structural lens deprives them of their specific cultural contexts and ignores the differences between individual trickster figures. Similarly, the desire to play "Spot the Trickster," as Daniel David Moses puts it (quoted in Taylor 88), can lead to seeing trickster aspects in all characters, or to ignoring other aspects of texts by Indigenous authors.

In this paper I avoid analyzing oral trickster tales that might have been mistranslated, and I also do not claim authority about the ways in which the various tricksters function in their respective cultures. Instead, as a zhaanganaashiikwe (white woman) who teaches and researches First Nations literature, I examine trickster figures whose writers are deploying them explicitly at the boundaries between cultures. I am not only interested in transforming these borderlands and acknowledging the histories that have made them dangerous ground, but also in looking for ways in which cultural understand-

ing can transform political realities. The trickster figures found in much contemporary Indigenous literature also play in this liminal space; therefore, I
am positing the emergence of a cross-cultural trickster poetics, the techniques of which I will establish through examining the concept of "trickster
discourse" developed by Gerald Vizenor and reading two poems: Lenore
Keeshig-Tobias's "Trickster Beyond 1992: Our Relationship" (1992) and
Annharte's "Coyote Columbus Café" (1994). All three are Anishinaabe writers, and all three play on the boundaries between cultures to show how trickster figures and trickster discourse can be both signs of continued cultural
existence and ways of negotiating cross-cultural communication. This is not
to say that they create a hybrid culture, but that they reimagine the meeting
between worlds in a way that privileges the comic vision of Anishinaabe trickster discourse over the tragic vision applied to the meeting by most social science and other academic approaches.

Although all three texts could be read in light of postmodernism and
deconstruction, all give primacy to tricksters and Indigenous culture. Even
though there are distinct similarities and connections between trickster discourse and contemporary Western modes and theories, we should read the
imported theories through trickster discourse, and not vice versa. Vizenor's
depiction of people of mixed ancestry as tricksters emphasizes the figures' ability to play in the interstices between cultural oppositions in order to effect new
forms of cultural change. His crossblood tricksters "are the new metaphors
between communal tribal cultures and the cultures that oppose traditional
connections" (*Earthdivers* xix). He opposes academic and anthropological
emphasis on the tragic aspects of colonization, and claims that tricksters'
colonial "encounters are comic and communal, rather than tragic and sac-
rificial" ("Crossbloods" 227–8). His tricksters emphasize the humour that
exists in the playful continuation of Native cultures, humour that is central
to even the darker themes developed by Annharte and Keeshig-Tobias in
their poems. Their tricksters operate in the same ways as those of Louise
Erdrich. Lawrence W. Gross notes how, in her fiction, "within the context of
the chaos created by that apocalypse [colonization], the trickster figures find
ways to not only adapt to changing realities, but actually thrive in the new world
order" ("Trickster" 64). By reimaging both the initial meeting of Europeans
and the First Nations and the 500 years of colonization that followed in terms
of trickster discourse, these writers place the emphasis not on the devastation
that followed colonization, but on the continuation of Anishinaabe culture.

That these texts are renegotiating the boundaries between cultures is
evident in the fact that both poems were written in response to the quincentennial of Columbus's first landing in the so-called "new world." This response

is explicit in the titles of the poems: Annharte uses the figure of Columbus and Keeshig-Tobias uses the date. The titles also indicate the interrelation of trickster figures and this quincentennial. These connections between trickster figures and the first moments of colonization suggest ways in which Natives and newcomers interact both by opposing colonizing practices and, at the same time, by suggesting possible connections to colonizing peoples. "Trickster Beyond 1992: Our Relationship" could refer either to Native people's relationship with the trickster figure, and how it has changed in the 500 years of colonization, or to their relationship with white people, or both. Keeshig-Tobias, as a founding member of CRET, shares Tomson Highway's views of the trickster. His note on Nanabush accompanying *The Rez Sisters* states: "Some say that 'Nanabush' left this continent when the whiteman came. We believe he is still here among us—albeit a little worse for wear and tear—having assumed other guises. Without him—and without the spiritual health of this figure—the core of Indian culture would be gone forever" (XII). Keeshig-Tobias's poem also assumes this position. In the early sections of the poem, she suggests that Nanabush could have alleviated the pains of colonization and expresses anger at his departure: "i thought THAT / GOD-DAMN NANABUSH / WHERE IS HE WHEN / WE NEED HIM" (102). Throughout the poem, however, she discusses the new forms and transformations of Nanabush and other tricksters. Towards the end of the poem, she conflates white men and tricksters. The title of section 12 is "HOW TO CATCH A WHITE MAN / (OOPS) I MEAN TRICKSTER" (108). She ends the section by suggesting that catching the trickster/white man will pave the way to a cross-cultural understanding. She sees white women helping to control the white man/trickster and emphasizes the importance of teaching children: "Teach them the history of this land, the real history, before 1492 and since. Those stories will guide them into the next 500 years. Tell them not to do as the Trickster (I mean white man) has done" (108). Keeshig-Tobias does not specify the race of the children who must be taught, which to me suggests that *all* children must hear these stories, and that all children can learn from the cautionary tales not to replicate the mistakes and atrocities of the overreaching white man/trickster.

Similarly, Annharte's Coyote criticizes the colonizing positions of both "Columbus clones" and "Wannabes" (16), but the narrative links Coyote to Columbus, both thematically and sexually. The picture that opens the poem in the chapbook, an image of a Coyote posing in marine gear staring out of a wanted poster saying "*Wanted*: Coyote Columbus" (9) suggests that Columbus is Coyote, or vice versa. The links between Coyote and Columbus suggest ways in which people from both sides of the cultural divide can work to change the relationship. The strong narrative voice of Coyote implores "former Columbus clones" to "discover a first / nation friend lover first nation first / for keeps person" (16), suggesting that only positive personal and individual relationships can lead to genuine discovery. She discovers for herself that "it's just about too late / not to educate the oppressor" (17), echoing Keeshig-Tobias's call for cross-cultural education. These quincentennial trickster poems explicitly suggest that the problematic border between Indigenous and invader cultures is also a space in which tricksters can play and change the ground, that the next 500 years do not have to be a replication of the previous half millennium. The binary opposition between Native and non-Native becomes yet another place where tricksters can be both/and, but on their own terms, and not in specifically post-structuralist ways.

Although Annharte, Vizenor, and Keeshig-Tobias are Anishinaabeg, they do not limit their discussions to Nanaboozho (or Nanabush). Annharte writes about Coyote, and Vizenor usually refers to a more generic pan-Native trickster. Keeshig-Tobias does reference Nanabush, especially in her creation of the relationship between the Anishinaabe figure and the poetic voice as a child, but she makes a distinction between her/him and a more generic "Trickster," with which she associates both the multiple tricksters of multiple cultures and the overreaching "white man." In fact, she uses "Trickster" almost as an insult to emphasize her disgust at the figure's cowardice in the face of colonizing missionaries and politicians: "that Nanabush! That good-for-nothing Trickster" (103). Thus, she sets up a distinction between Nanabush, who is a possible source of cultural aid, and trickster, who is unreliable at best. The distinction between Nanaboozho and other tricksters might explain this apparent separation. Of all the Native North American trickster figures, Nanaboozho has the most elements of a culture hero, a mythological figure who overlaps with the trickster, but who benefits humanity in philanthropic, rather than accidental, ways. In his preface to *Earthdivers*, Vizenor explains that:

> *Wenebojo* or *naanabozho* is the *compassionate* trickster, not the trickster in the word constructions of the anthropologist Paul Radin, the one who "possesses no values, moral or social … knows neither good nor evil yet is responsible for both," but the imaginative trickster, the one who cares to balance the world between terminal creeds and humor with unusual manners and ecstatic strategies. (xii)

Given the positive nature of Nanaboozho, it makes sense that the trickster figures that Annharte and Keeshig-Tobias associate with colonizers and implicate in colonial practices are Coyote, who can be much more malevolent than Nanaboozho, and a pan-Native "trickster," who can take many forms.

In the opening and closing sections of Keeshig-Tobias's poem, a Leader charges the others to "be our Tricksters" (101, 111), emphasizing this multiplicity of Indigenous tricksters, and the distinction between these tricksters and those of other cultures. In "The Magic of Others," Keeshig-Tobias compares various tricksters' ill-fated attempts to use the magic and skills of other animals to white writers' appropriation of Native voices (176). She argues that "each Trickster has a culture. Let's be our own Trickster, eh?" (174). Even as Annharte and Keeshig-Tobias use Coyote and a more generic "trickster," their texts embody what Lawrence Gross identifies as a specifically comic Anishinaabe worldview, which "is helping us to overcome" the devastation of Anishinaabe culture under colonization "and helps explain how we are managing to survive" ("Comic Vision" 436). Rather than simply reference Nanabush in their texts, these contemporary writers take on "the characteristics of Wenabozho," as did the "old Anishinaabe" people described by Gross ("Comic Vision" 448). At the same time, the balancing between Nanaboozho and more generic tricksters, together with the arguments against cultural appropriation in both texts, reminds readers that they must remember cultural specificity, even as they are making connections between cultures.

The experimental poetics of the two texts parallel the cross-cultural trickster figures who inhabit them. Both poems exemplify the idea, first developed by Vizenor, that tricksters not only are identifiable characters in stories but also provide the form for the texts in which they appear, dismantling and decentring words, language, narrative structure, and discourse. In other words, they break down the binary distinction between form and content. Vizenor's trickster discourse combines the traditional discursive strategies of tribal tricksters with the equally shifty—and, at their best, playful—discourses of post-structuralism, deconstruction, and postmodernism. He explains his own position in terms of such Western philosophers as Bakhtin, Todorov, Lacan, Jameson, Lyotard, and Foucault. He defines "[s]ilence and separation" as "the antitheses of trickster discourse," thus indicating that trickster discourse is a vocal coming together ("Postmodern" 9). Vizenor defines "trickster" not only as a figure with specific characteristics, but also as "a comic sign, communal signification and a discourse with imagination" ("Trickster" 187), and a "comic *holotrope* (the whole figuration)" ("Postmodern" 9). He points out the ability of tribal tricksters to create new worlds by moving beyond the tragic narratives, or "*hypotragedies*," that characterize sociological and anthropological views of the meetings between the cultures ("Postmodern" 11).

Vizenor's linking of traditional Indigenous narrative forms with post-modern, deconstructive, and post-structuralist European theory might leave him open to criticisms of mistranslation of tricksters. Despite the assertion of Kimberly Blaeser that the "deep structure" of Vizenor's writing is a "mythic structure stemming from its relationship to trickster tales, and an antistructure that deliberately subverts the formal ideals of literary aesthetics" (138), his use of European literary and cultural theory indicates that this subversion of narrative is, at least in part, influenced by newer forms of Western aesthetics. Such influence is, however, consistent with Vizenor's endorsement of the use of traditional tricksters to create new culture rooted in tradition, while still taking into account the realities of colonization and the changes it has wrought. Despite the apparent similarities between Vizenor's trickster discourse and new modes of academic thought, the political implications of the two discourses are not the same. The disruptive possibilities offered by post-structuralism, postmodernism, chaos, and other such Western academic constructions grow out of modernist angst and, at the same time, react against past modes of thought. Trickster discourse, on the other hand, is an integral part of an ongoing tradition; therefore, although it seems to rebel against the same Western traditions as the academic categories do, it can act as a sign of literary nationalism in its own cultures. Gross, referencing Vizenor's concept of trickster discourse, argues that "the trickster mutates into something greater" than a single figure, and thus "liberates the Anishinaabe from the oppression of colonialism and opens the healing vistas of the imagination" ("Comic Vision" 456).

Vizenor's concepts help us to understand that, although the growing body of Native texts appears to share formal characteristics both with post-modern, experimental and avant-garde poetic movements, it is more appropriately understood as being a part of non-linear oral traditions. He points out that "[t]he trickster is never the same in oral and translated narratives; however, these differences are resolved in comic holotropes and discourse in modern literature" ("Trickster" 189). Similarly, Gross emphasizes the way in which "new myths and new presentations of old myths are helping current-day Anishinaabe deal with the effects of what I call post-apocalypse stress syndrome (PASS)" ("Cultural Sovereignty" 128). Although translations of oral tales always lose some of the elements of trickster discourse, contemporary Native writers have the ability to infuse that discourse, along with some of the flavour of Indigenous languages, into trickster narratives written originally in English. Both "Coyote Columbus Café" and "Trickster Beyond 1992" include an explicit trickster figure (or figures), but in each of the poems it is the unsettled and unsettling poetic form, rather than simply the character, that upsets a reading of the meeting of cultures as "hypotragic" and suggests, instead, that cross-cultural communication can be a method of comic resistance. The tricky forms of each of the poems unsettle fixed meaning in favour of narrative dissonance and what Vizenor would call "pleasurable misreadings" ("Postmodern" 5–6). Both Annharte and Keeshig-Tobias play with language sounds, use puns, and break down words and their multiple meanings so that they become almost meaningless. In this way, they bring the tricky character of language to the fore, showing how words can, like Annharte's Coyotrix, "lie and trick" (13). By unsettling the English language in particular, Indigenous writers are unsettling a language that has been used as a tool of domination, at the same time that they take up that tool, and shape it to their own ends. Throughout "Coyote Columbus Café," Annharte "scavenges the scraps littered around, recombines and recycles language so it does not boss *her* around" (Annharte and Grauer 117–18). She says, "I have used the Coyotrix persona (image) as a transformer of our internalized colonized mentality. The inner Coyotrix teases or tweaks meaning out of the verbiage that surrounds us. It would seem that the coyotrix is mixing it up or making it strange again. I think it is also a way of finding constituency and community with the use of words in a poem" (Annharte and Grauer 124). In the first section of the poem, Annharte's Coyote narrator looks at a potential sexual mate at the other end of the bar and says to herself "Sh Sh / be still my boogit" (11). When I teach this poem, I can always tell who speaks Anishinaabemowin (the Ojibwa language) by how they react to the line. Those who do, laugh (or at least smile behind their hands); those who don't, look confused. I invite those who don't know what the word means to guess. The context of the cliché in which the word appears ("be still my boogit") suggests that it means "heart," and this is the usual speculation (as it was my assumption the first time I read the poem). I then ask the Anishinaabemowin speakers what the word actually means, which is "fart." Although most puns are lost in translation, the punning here works *in* translation. The joke depends on the Anishinaabemowin word, the common English phrase "be still my heart," and the rhyme between the correct and incorrect translation; a knowledge of both languages is necessary to get the joke fully.

Similarly, when Coyote approaches her potential conquest, she opens with "*Boozho Dude. Hey, I'm talking / to you, Bozo Dude. My name is / Conquista, Come on adore me*" (11, emphasis in original). Again, the punning works with translation. She begins by saying "Boozho," the Anishinaabemowin greeting, meaning approximately "hello" or "how are you"; when she is, presumably, ignored, "Boozho" disintegrates into "Bozo," suggesting that the "dude" is nothing more than a clown. The language play is further complicated by the fact that "Boozho" is etymologically linked to the trickster Nanaboozho (Butling 102–3), and tricksters and clowns are related, especially as trickster figures are simplified in Western translation. The slip from the Anishinaabemowin "Boozho" to the English "Bozo" hints at everything that is lost in translation, as stories, words, and tricksters themselves move from one language to the other. "Native people often say that English is impersonal or, if used in translation, it fails to carry the spirit of what is said" (Annharte, "Borrowing" 59). The complexities of Nanaboozho become the simplicities of Bozo the clown. Annharte herself puts these playful deconstructions of language within a context *not* of postmodernism, post-structuralism, or deconstruction, but rather of Indigenous oral traditions. She says: "I've always been aware that when speaking English to a Native audience, most speakers will salt and pepper their talk with wordplay. It's a storytelling method. It's a kind of pause, to give the people time to catch up. I also enjoy working with the sounds of words" (Butling 102). Most of Annharte's wordplay is based on sound, such as the "Conquistador" pun, which puts Coyote in the dominant position, taking on the role of early Spanish colonizers, and thus dismantling their power. Although Annharte claims that she is "always searching for a simplicity and clarity in diction because English is ultimately a liar's language" ("Borrowing" 62), by emphasizing those distortions she allows a multitude of partial truths to surface.

Keeshig-Tobias, too, plays with the slippery meanings and sounds of language, most obviously in section 11 of the poem, titled "The White Man's Burden." In this section, she plays overtly with definition and language, by providing two contradictory definitions of "The White Man's Burden" and emphasizing that these conflicting definitions are based on perspective: "the white man's burden / (as he sees it)" is "to spread culture / among the primitive / (indigenous) / peoples of the world"; however, "the white man's burden," as Indigenous people know it, is "a heavy load / that he does not / have to carry" (106). She presents the white man coming up with five solutions to the white man's burden: two versions of WHITE OUT, two of WHITE WASH, and then the WHITE PAPER. The definitions refer to such contradictory sources as Collins's *English Dictionary*, Hurtig's *Canadian Encyclopedia*, and a radio script by Daniel David Moses; each plays with the formal definitions and deconstructs words through both sound and meaning. For example, in one definition of WHITE WASH, Keeshig-Tobias pulls apart words, links them to other words by sound, and shows how the language itself contains the seeds of colonization:

dye
die
die hard
di
direct direct cur
rent
(pay the rent or get out)
die out
dying race
run Indian run
dye die di
direct cur
(oh you dog you)
direct cur current
direct current
DC AC/DC
dece
ease
(easy)
dis
ease
dece
eve
deceptive
specious
(capricious)
words or act
(Indian)
actions
intended to con
ceal defects, gloss
(loss)
over over
(t) fee
lings (106–7)

What seems to be playful postmodernist deconstructive writing in fact fits
very well into the context of traditional trickster narratives, in which, as
Doueihi notes, "the story loses its solidity and breaks down into an open-
ended play with signifiers.... meaning is made possible by the space opened
between signifiers. It is in the reversals and discontinuities in the language,

in the narrative, that meaning is produced—not one meaning, but the possibility of meaningfulness" (199). Keeshig-Tobias shifts from whitewash, as the dye that attempts to whiten, to death. White governmental attempts to assimilate Native peoples, to whitewash them, or dye them white, are attempts at extermination, as is the stereotypical adage that Native people are "a dying race." Keeshig-Tobias urges her Native audience to run, but not in the dying race set up by the white man. She links both "die" and "dye" to the *di*rect current of electricity, which is further divided into "cur" and "rent": the dogs that white people see Indians as, and the rent that the landlord expects, although who pays the rent is ambiguous. Rent could be what poor Native people have to pay to their white landlords if they don't want to be evicted, but it could also be the rent that the settler government is supposed to pay in the form of treaty rights. If white people don't "pay the rent," then *they* should "get out" of the country. The Indian Act is different from the treaties, so the government's insistence on following that Act, rather than honoring the treaties, and, by implication, forcing Native people to play specific roles (to "act Indian"), is itself a form of whitewash, a deceptive/specious/capricious way of glossing over the price that must be paid in the colonial situation, both in terms of actual fees and in terms of emotions ("fee/lings").

The slipperiness of the white man's language in each of the definitions links him to the trickster, a connection that Keeshig-Tobias plays with throughout the text. Each of the first five of the "white man's" solutions to "the white man's burden" is prefaced by the same parenthetical phrase—"(as he sees it)"—that marks his understanding of the burden itself (106–7). In the sixth and final solution, however, Keeshig-Tobias cuts through all the tricky wordplay:

> the white man's solution
> to the white man's burden
> No. 6
> (as we know it)
>
> PUT DOWN THE LOAD, STUPID (107)

Where the white man *sees*, the Indigenous person *knows*. One of the main criticisms of postmodernism, from an Indigenous perspective, is that as soon as people from outside the dominant society begin to tell their stories and to tell the truth that hides behind the whitewash of colonial history, then Western academics begin to say, "Oh, there is no truth; our stories and your stories are all socially constructed." Even in a text that plays with language in order to deconstruct it, Keeshig-Tobias suggests that those very deconstructions might be part of a trick, that there is a simple truth that lies behind all the linguistic obfuscation. At the same time, that seemingly simple solution, "PUT DOWN THE LOAD, STUPID," has its own ambiguities. Since this resolution is identified as "the white man's solution / to the white man's burden," it is obviously the white man who should just "put down the load." However, back at the beginning of the section, we learned that this is "a heavy load / that he does not / have to carry" (106). In that case, the person who needs to put down the load would be the Indigenous person who has borne the burden of colonization. Taken together, the two opposing readings suggest that, in order to reach a state of decolonization, both the colonizer and the colonized need to put down burdens.

Focusing on the aesthetics and poetics of trickster discourse is, in part, an answer to the call made by Emma LaRocque, among others, who believes that "Native literature must be more about art and nuance than about ethnographic trauma and colonial discourse" (15). It might seem strange to answer this call with a reading of two poems that respond explicitly to colonial discourse, but, as these deconstructive readings of specific passages illustrate, focusing on aesthetics does not mean ignoring the political ramification of those aesthetics. As Sam McKegney points out about the semiotic play inherent in Vizenor's theories of "Trickster Discourse": "To take survivance seriously, critics must be willing to intercede in the semiotic fog of Beaudrillardian simulation and make explicit the connections between the hyper-reality of text and the political and social reality of Indigenous North America" (83). The calls to focus on Native literature as literature, to study it in terms of aesthetics rather than as artifact of culture, are never calls to be apolitical. In fact, they complement, rather than oppose, the calls to political action made by other Indigenous literary critics, exemplified by the essays in *American Indian Literary Nationalism*, by Jace Weaver, Craig Womack, and Robert Warrior. Keeshig-Tobias's exploration of "the white man's burden" is overtly political, and Annharte too makes specifically political statements in her puns. She often refers to Columbus by his Spanish name "Colon," which, as she notes elsewhere, "is part of that actual word colonized" (Butling 105), while at the same time linking him to the large intestine, the source of all shit. She also references "*Old Indian joke*[s]" which suggest that "*Indian Affairs*" is advocating having affairs with Indians, and the "*Indian Act*" makes one "*Act Indian*" (15). These playful deconstructions of repressive government agencies and policies have both simple surface and deeper political implications. The concept that the Indian Act forces people to perform Indigeneity in a manner set up by the government is hardly new; similarly, having "*an Indian affair*" is not as pleasant when one is being screwed over by the government.[1]

The shifting narrative voice of "Coyote Columbus Café" and the shifting genres found in "Trickster Beyond 1992" have a deconstructive effect like that of the language. Jeannette Armstrong notes the non-linearity of Indigenous oral narratives: "leading to all manner of side roads, cul-de-sacs, dead ends, and then leaping right back to the original path to continue the story" (24). She explains how these formal characteristics of oral literatures have moved "Aboriginal literatures away from the kind of organized little area on a page to a much more non-linear process of writing and deconstructing the linearity of organization on the page" (25). Annharte uses a counterpoint between italics and normal text on opposite sides of the page to create two different characters, or two different points of view, or an internal and an external voice. Pauline Butling distinguishes these voices in terms of tone: "One voice seems friendly and colloquial; the next one seems quite different" (104). Annharte suggests that they might represent different Native responses to colonization (Butling 105). Although these voices generally alternate, in one section they speak at the same time:

I said sweat lodge	*I shed shwatch ludge*
makes body clean inside.	*meks buddy kleen insaid.*
Keep it up. Dance pow wow.	*Kip it up. Danz pahwah.*
After this, boy. You me	*Hafta, dis, bah. You me,*
go off West German First	*go hoff big wes churman Furz*
International Wannabe Annual	*Hinter Natchinel Wanbee Annal*
Celebration. Take first; don't	*cel brayshun. Tek furz; don*
need take plastic money	*need tek plashtic monhee*
visacard. You me same team.	*vissacad. You me sam tim.*
Same team. Like hockey team.	*Sam tim. Lak hocky tim.*
Zjoonias, my boy. Think of it.	*Sch-oo—nash, my bah. Tinkobit.*
Swiss bank account, hey boy!	*Swish bank a cunt, hey bah!* (16)

One voice speaks something close to standard English, and the other a dialect that has been read variously as drunk (by Pauline Butling), as "an imitation (like Kinsella's) of the way the 'uneducated' Indian talks" (by Annharte herself; cf. Butling 206), and even as German (by some of my students). In any case, the difference between the standard and non-standard English spellings emphasizes that what one reads on the page is not what one would hear when the words are spoken aloud. The slowing down over the word "Zjoonias" (money in Anishinaabemowin) illustrates the importance the speaker places on money, while the inadvertent translation of "account" to "*a cunt*" hints at the dirtiness of this selling of culture to the highest bidder.[2]

Dual voices, however, are not Annharte's only technique for breaking down linear narrative forms. She also includes a multiple choice test:

> sure I pose baffling questions
> administer random coyote IQ tests
>
> > *what is paler than stranger?*
>
> I warn you multiple answers possible
> circle (a) the landlord comes around
> first of the month to collect rent
> wrong answer but don't pick that one
> please follow directions & circle choice
> what about (c) a landlord of colour?
> right answer is (d) I got my rights
> (b) I am the landlord around here
>
> > *how about solving the mystery*
> > *did I discover Columbus first?* (13)

This "Coyote IQ test" upsets arbitrary alphabetical order to suggest the disorder of understanding of the same landlord/tenant relationship that I have already discussed in relation to "Trickster Beyond 1992." Lally Grauer argues that the "test" exemplifies "the indigenous coyote anti-logic of 'both ... and,' of multiplicity and flexibility, right and 'wrong answer,' renter and landlord, having no rights and the oldest rights in the country" (Annharte and Grauer 123). I would add that the disjunction between question and answer upsets standard logical connections. Even if we are given the right answers, as appears to be the case, we still have to figure out how they answer the question, "*What is paler than stranger?*"

Keeshig-Tobias similarly unsettles form in "Trickster Beyond 1992." The text appears in the "essays" section of *Indigena: Contemporary Native Perspectives,* and one section of it is titled "ON TRYING TO WRITE THIS ESSAY" (105), although I have been identifying it as a poem throughout this essay. The form shifts throughout, from poetry to autobiography, to fiction, to essay, to a conversation between "M" and "E" that splits the word "me" (so that the authorial voice argues about the understanding of tricksters with herself) (109–10), to screenplay, and even to a concrete poem that turns the White Paper of 1969 into a military airplane:

                    9
                   69
                  969
                 1969
        W H I T E P A P E R
                 1969
                  969
                   69
                    9   (107)

Each genre employed by the text gives its own shape, not only to the way the words appear on the page, but also to the meaning that comes across to the audience.

Perhaps most strikingly, the first and final sections of the text tell the same story but in different genres: the first is poetry and the last is screenplay. The difference in perspective engendered by the different genres shows how the form in which a story is told affects how it is understood. The transformation of Leader into an Eagle provides an excellent example of how the same event in a story can be rendered in different ways. The poem is written in first person and works as an interior monologue:

> i change
> and soar upward through
> layers of clouds, i can
> not see, not see,
> and with the altitude
> scream, (101)

The screenplay sees the same incident through Leader's eyes, so that the reader sees what s/he sees and hears what s/he hears:

DISSOLVE TO:
LEADER'S POV
a view of the prairie rim and skyline. The
horizon BLURS and crests skyward pene-
trating cloud strata.
Over this, we HEAR the Leader shriek as if
in horror and in pain. (112)

The poetry is sparse, with few words; its use of the first-person pronoun with no clear referents confuses identity for the reader who lacks a cultural context. On the other hand, the screenplay provides more details of setting, and of visual and auditory imagery. The shifting camera angles and cuts give the reader greater understanding, but less room for the imagination. The poem works in an oral tradition, and the screenplay in contemporary technology. Both shape the story they tell; having two different versions allows the reader a more complete understanding, not only of the story itself, but also of the way genre is inextricably linked to meaning and to cultural context.

The playful language and forms in these two poems question meaning itself, reshaping the English language, which has been a tool of domination, and positing ways of achieving cross-cultural communication on a more even footing. As Anne Doueihi notes, "The features commonly ascribed to the trickster—contradictoriness, deceptiveness, trickery—are the features of the language of the story itself. If the trickster breaks all the rules, so does the story's language; it breaks the rules of storytelling in the very telling of the story" (200). The spirit and function of the trickster characters in the poems influence the texts themselves, breaking down boundaries and forcing readers to see their worlds from a new angle. The poetics used to unsettle discourse in Annharte's and Keeshig-Tobias's texts are part of a larger poetic movement in which First Nations writers play with form, style, and language in a manner that shares a great deal with postmodernism, but which has its roots in traditional forms. Marvin Francis's extended poem *City Treaty: A Long Poem* and the poems of Jeannette Armstrong that can be read either horizontally or vertically are two other examples of this movement. The difficulty and trickiness of these texts foreground the limitations of knowledge, understanding, interpretation, and language itself. Their unsettling poetics provide ways through which the ambiguities of Indigenous traditional forms can be expressed in English-language literature; more importantly, they suggest ways of negotiating the boundaries between cultures, of learning to talk to each other, to listen, and to recognize that the words we say to each other might not be heard the way we intend. Learning this kind of communication will help all of us, Native and non-Native alike, to begin the process of healing the relationship between cultures.

Notes

1   For a further discussion of the political aspects of Annharte's poem, see Daniel Morley Johnson's paper "(Re)Nationalizing Naanabozho: Anishinaabe Sacred Stories, Nationalist Literary Criticism and Scholarly Responsibility," earlier in this volume.

2   Although body parts are not used as profanity in Anishinaabemowin, or in other Indigenous languages, words for sexual and digestive organs and the acts surrounding them are profane in English.

Works Cited

Annharte, Marie Baker. "Borrowing Enemy Language: A First Nation Woman's Use of English." *West Coast Line* 27:1 (1993): 59–66.

———. "Coyote Columbus Café." In *Coyote Columbus Café*. Winnipeg: Moonprint, 1994. 9–17.

Annharte, Marie Baker, and Lally Grauer. "A Weasel Pops In and Out of Old Tunes: Exchanging Words." *Studies in Canadian Literature* 13:1 (2006): 116–27.

Armstrong, Jeannette. "The Aesthetic Qualities of Aboriginal Writing." *Studies in Canadian Literature* 13:1 (2006): 20–30.

Blaeser, Kimberly. *Gerald Vizenor: Writing in the Oral Tradition*. Norman: U of Oklahoma P, 1996.

Butling, Pauline. "'I make sense of my world through writing': An Interview with Marie Annharte Baker." In *Poets Talk*. Ed. Pauline Butling and Susan Rudy. Edmonton: U of Alberta P, 2005. 89–113.

Doueihi, Anne. "Inhabiting the Space Between Discourse and Story in Trickster Narratives." In *Mythical Trickster Figures: Contours, Contexts, Criticisms*. Ed. William J. Hynes and William G. Doty. Tuscaloosa: U of Alabama P, 1993. 193–201.

Gross, Lawrence W. "The Comic Vision of Anishinaabe Culture and Religion." *American Indian Quarterly* 26:3 (2002): 436–59.

———. "Cultural Sovereignty and Native American Hermeneutics in the Interpretation of the Sacred Stories of the Anishinaabe." *Wicazo Sa Review* 18:2 (2003): 127–34.

———. "The Trickster and World Maintenance: An Anishinaabe Reading of Louise Erdrich's *Tracks*." *SAIL* 17:3 (2005): 48–66.

Highway, Tomson. *The Rez Sisters*. Saskatoon: Fifth House, 1988.

Keeshig-Tobias, Lenore. "The Magic of Others." In *Language in Her Eye: Writing and Gender*. Ed. Libby Scheier, Sarah Sheard, and Eleanor Wachtel. Toronto: Coach House, 1990. 173–7.

———. "Trickster Beyond 1992: Our Relationship." In *Indigena: Contemporary Native Perspectives*. Ed. Gerald McMaster and Lee-Ann Martin. Vancouver: Douglas and McIntyre, 1992. 101–13.

LaRocque, Emma. "Opening Address." *Studies in Canadian Literature* 13:1 (2006): 11–18.

McKegney, Sam. "From Trickster Poetics to Transgressive Politics: Substantiating Survivance in Tomson Highway's *Kiss of the Fur Queen*." *SAIL* 17:4 (2005): 79–113.

Moses, Daniel David. "The Trickster's Laugh: My Meeting with Tomson and Lenore." *American Indian Quarterly* 28:1/2 (Winter-Spring 2004): 107–11.

Taylor, Drew Hayden. "There's a Trickster Behind Every Nanabush." *Toronto Star*, 3 June 1995. J6.

Vizenor, Gerald. "Crossbloods." In *Shadow Distance: A Gerald Vizenor Reader*. Hanover, NH: Wesleyan UP, 1994. 227–46.

————. *Earthdivers: Tribal Narratives on Mixed Descent.* Minneapolis: U of Minnesota P, 1981.

————. "A Postmodern Introduction." In *Narrative Chance: Postmodern Discourse on Native American Indian Literatures.* Ed. Gerald Vizenor. Albuquerque: U of New Mexico P, 1989. 3–16.

————. "Trickster Discourse: Comic Holotropes and Language Games." In *Narrative Chance: Postmodern Discourse on Native American Indian Literatures.* Ed. Gerald Vizenor. Albuquerque: U of New Mexico P, 1989. 187–211.

Weaver, Jace, Craig S. Womack, and Robert Warrior, eds. *American Indian Literary Nationalism.* Alberquerque: U of New Mexico P, 2006.

Trickster Reflections
Part II

Millennia later the [Anishinaubaeg] dreamed Nanabush into being. Nanabush represented themselves and what they understood of human nature. One day his world too was flooded. Like Geezhigo-quae, Nanabush recreated his world from a morsel of soil retrieved from the depths of the sea. (101)
    —Basil Johnston, "Is That All There Is? Tribal Literature"

One of trickster's primary modi operandi, *shape-shifting, the power to move fluidly beyond static definitions of cultural boundaries and taboos, is an impulse with both positive and destructive possibilities. Celebrating tricksters, it seems to me, should be done with caution. It is important to remember that shape-shifting can also be a form of witchery and that tricksters can be oppressive assholes as often as liberators—just check out the stories. (301)*
    —Craig S. Womack, *Red on Red: Native American Literary Separatism*

    Boozhoo.
    I have a Trickster story. It is my own. It is also now yours.
    It's sometimes told out loud, but for now I share it here, with you.
    You are there. So am I. I am here. And so are you.
    We're both in both, at once in this story, listening, speaking, writing, reading. We are in this together.
    That's the trick.
    It's always, for our entire lives.
    Everywhere.
    I open books and you are there. I speak and you are all I say. I write these words and you come out. Like here. And here.

You. You. You. You.

In this story.

Now.

Every morning, every day, every moment of my life you have been there. Even when I could not see you. I now know that you were around watching, listening, stalking, tricking me. Like a shadow. Like a reflection I can't walk away from.

Today you are lying right there, beside me, snoring—so loud in fact I've woken up with a headache. I stand up and you do. I scratch myself and you do. I drink some water and you do.

Luckily, you haven't woken her up. She lies with her back to us, her only movement the pulse of her steady breaths. I don't turn on the light, for fear that she might see you. Of course, I know she won't.

Ugh. Your breath is awful. What a stench. I gag. Raising my hands to my mouth, I smell your scent on my hands. I taste you on my lips. My tongue is covered by your hair. That's it. I race to the toilet. I'm throwing up, just like usual. Again. Disgusting.

I undress and get into the shower. I leave the glass door open, just a bit, hoping that you will come inside. You don't. I'm not surprised. You never clean yourself, although you badly need it. As usual, you stand outside and draw pictures in the condensation, just so I can see them. Oh yeah, there's that bird again. A tree. A man with squiggly lines coming out of his mouth. Good for you. That's what you always do—draw the same stupid pictures that make no sense.

Then I hear you opening the closet and throwing all of the clean towels onto the floor. You're pissing on them now. Oh the stink. You jerk.

Thank god I am here, in the shower, away from you. I can get away from your smell, at least for a while. I can clean myself with this fresh, hot water. I can wipe you off, close my eyes, and imagine you are gone. In the pool of my mind you don't exist, for just a second. There, I can escape you.

But I can't stay forever. I have work to do.

I step out, dripping, and see your mess. You've shit all over the sink and wiped your ass on the wall.

You've done it again. You've made a disaster. And, like always, I have to clean up, clear away the messes you create, the problems you leave behind. Every day. You infuriate me. You nauseate me. You irritate me. And, I think, with each piece of chaos, you might be killing me.

You. You. You. You.

I wipe the sink, the floor, the wall, and try not to get any of you on me. Throwing the towels in the garbage, I walk into our bedroom, leaving tiny puddles of water on the carpet. She'll be upset, but I'm in a hurry.

You're already there, of course, gazing at her peacefulness. You must have been there for a while—there's a pool of drool surrounding your feet.

Stop it. Stop looking at her. Stop touching yourself. Stop salivating, you creep. Get away from her. You will never have her. I promise you that. You don't deserve her. You don't deserve anything, nothing at all, only what you have brought to me. Anger. Hate. Pain. Tricks.

Hee hee hee heeeeeee, you moan. Hee hee hee heeeeeee. Hee hee hee heeeeeee. Hee hee hee heeeeeee.

She sighs, reaches down, and pulls the blanket around her. I hear her breathing continue.

Thank god. At least she can shut you out.

I don't want to leave. But I have to. There is no choice.

It wouldn't matter if I stayed, would it. You wouldn't leave. You are my problem. My responsibility. I must get rid of you, somehow, someday, if only to free her from you.

I open my underwear drawer and find it empty. Again. Another trick. Hearing you in the closet, I open the door and there you are, wiping pairs of my gitch on your sweaty chest. I pick up one pair and they're damp and moist, hair everywhere. Fantastic.

I put on my shirt and my tie. You, of course, stay naked, if that's what you are. With all of your long black hair it's hard to tell. Just stay over there while I put on my socks and pants. No, don't put your ass in my face. Ugh. Why don't you clean yourself? Why are you the same disgusting creature every day?

I open the hallway window, mostly to see if it is raining. You're there, of course, standing on the ledge peering back in at me. You stare at me while I look over your shoulder and avoid your eyes. It's the only way I can see anything, you're so fat.

Hmph. No clouds.

I close the glass, lock it, and put the key in my wallet. Maybe that will keep you out. Nope. There, you are, at the bottom of the stairs.

Dammit, it's like you're one step ahead of me, choosing where I will go and then pulling me along. Get lost, you. Go away. Listen, for once.

Oh, dammit. Is that the downstairs clock? It's seven o'clock. I'm late.

I race down the stairs, get to the front door, and grab my jacket. You are there, eating my shoes. Get away. I wipe your dripping saliva off and slide them on. I feel my socks squish beneath my toes.

Slamming the front door, I sprint down the path to my car. You're there, sitting in the back seat, licking the back window.

Why didn't I lock the car? Did I? Would it have mattered?

Shit. I forgot to kiss her goodbye. You did it again. You made me forget her.

Hee hee hee heeeeeee, you laugh. Hee hee hee heeeeeee. Hee hee hee heeeeeee. Hee hee hee heeeeeee.

I retreat into silence and drive. You breathe heavier and heavier as I drive faster and faster, in and out of traffic on the expressway. We pull up next to a Jeep Cherokee with three women in business suits in it. Stop it, you. I can hear you rubbing yourself, looking at them. I purposely turn down side streets, just so we don't meet any more people along the way.

Finally. Now I can get to work. Slamming the car door I reach for my briefcase and find that you've opened it and spread your filth all over my papers. Underneath, I find the remnants of you playing with yourself. I feel puke enter my throat, but hold it in.

At work I get into trouble from the man in the white pressed shirt. He doesn't want to hear why but I try to tell him anyways.

It's him. He's the reason I'm late. I know you can't see him. I'm not crazy. What do you mean I want special treatment? Go fuck yourself. Go ahead, tell on me. No, hold on. Listen, I'm sorry, I need this job. I'm sorry. I know. It won't happen again. I'm sorry.

You always get me into trouble, don't you. You don't care about time. You don't care about money. You don't care about responsibility. Well, I have to. I have to make money. I have to pay for the house, the car, the food, the cable TV. I'm not living in your world, where nothing means anything. You're living in mine.

Walking into the maze of white and grey cubicles, I see that you've gotten into my square before me. You're wearing my headset, spinning in my chair, splitting my pencils, making so much noise my head hurts. You've eaten my mouse, stapled my files together, swallowed my newspaper, written on the memo I was writing. I can't work with you here. I can't do anything. I never can. Never. Never. Never. Never.

Hee hee hee heeeeeee, you giggle. Hee hee hee heeeeeee. Hee hee hee heeeeeee. Hee hee hee heeeeeee.

You need to go. I need to have meaning again. I need to know a time without you. I need to be alone.

There was, of course, a time before you came into my life. Well, at least I think you weren't there. Maybe if I remember, maybe if I imagine, you will leave again.

A time before you.

In a little brown boy, alone, waiting on the curb for his father to come and pick him up.

Friday. It was always on Friday when dad would come get me. The good days were when he was on time. The bad days were others, in the moments of waiting, always waiting. Waiting for rituals. Waiting for stories. Waiting for laughter. Waiting for him.

I was lost in the waiting.

Home was painful hoping, invisible nothingness, wondering if dad would come. Sitting at the end of my driveway, under that tree with my bike, waiting for the glimpse of a bumper, made it all easier. I kept busy. I watched that woodpecker. I played with stones. I sang to myself.

Other times I practiced what I would do when dad arrived. It was theatrical. Imagining that he was here, I looked away from the driveway, playing. At the last second, I pretended I saw him, turned, grabbed my bike, and raced down the pavement, trying to beat his car to the house. I practised in front of an absent audience. I got it down so perfectly I memorized every bump, every pothole. Eventually, when he did arrive, I always beat him to the front door.

But, mostly, I just waited. Waited for dad to come. Waited for the bumper to turn the corner. Waited for the soft candies that always sat beside him. Waited for the laughing to begin.

When he arrived, I knew he would be as happy as I was, joking, laughing. Then he would tell me funny stories—mostly ones that I knew were untrue, but I didn't care. They would be about how he created the world, gave the buffalo a hump, made the beaver have a flat tail. He told me hilarious stories about hunting, fishing, camping, and about the time he caught blindfolded ducks. Other times, he told me he had chased the sun, swam and played with the fish, and fooled his grandmother by pretending to be a rock.

I would laugh and laugh. You're lying, I would say. You're a postal worker, not a hunter. You don't even have a tent. You live in a house. No one can talk to animals.

Laughing, dad would hug me, tell me he loved me, and then tell me about his new life, his new home, my new sister, and how my grandfather was doing.

Together, on the expressway, we would joke and laugh, ride and laugh, laugh, laugh, laugh. I never wanted it to stop. I loved those times.

One day, at the end of a story, he told me to tell him one.

I don't know any, I said. The truth was, I didn't know any that he would laugh at.

Tell me about your school, he said, or the books you are reading.

I have a good teacher, I said.

Oh yeah, he asked, is your teacher still teaching you that Columbus discovered America?

No, I said. I told her what you told me to say. Columbus didn't discover anything. She told me that I was right. It was Jacques Cartier who discovered Canada. He's the one who founded this land.

Well, what about Indians, he asked. What about our ancestors?

My teacher told me that Indians didn't know about countries and land. We knew about animals and trading, but Cartier brought Thanksgiving, laws, and government. She told me it's important that I know the truth about Canada's history. So, I memorized it all. I can tell you who the first leader was in Canada, dad. Do you know? Sir John A. Macdonald. He was followed by Alexander Mackenzie and then John Abbott.

He said nothing, sitting quiet for a long time. It's like he was mad or something. See, I said to myself, my stories aren't funny. He said nothing until we got to his house.

It was then that I decided to never tell him true stories ever again. Made up ones were way funnier.

But I didn't know any good stories. I never hunted, talked to animals, lived in the bush. I never even pretended I was a rock to fool anyone. I needed help.

So I went to my teacher and she gave me a book.

Read this, she said, it will help you.

I looked at the cover. *Myths of the Indian.*

But there were scary pictures. Stories with big words I didn't understand. And lots of maps. Maybe Dad was right.

I recognized some of the stories as similar to the ones my dad told me, like the one about the blindfolded ducks. Others I didn't.

On one page I found a picture that said it was a story. It looked like this:

It said that the story was about a boy and his father. Just like us, I thought. I would show him this story. I didn't know what I would say about it, but I'm sure my dad would find something funny to say about it—he always did. I would show him that I knew how to tell a good story, show him that I could make him laugh too.

Carrying the book in my backpack, I waited all week. That Friday I waited and watched the clock all afternoon, hoping it would move faster so I could see him.

Racing home, I didn't even go inside. I just sat there, under the tree, and waited at the end of the driveway.

It got dark. I practiced until my legs hurt. I sat under the street lamp, just so dad could see me. I made as many piles of stones as I could. I watched that woodpecker for hours. I sang. I played until it was dark and I was alone.

In the dim light I opened up the book with the picture and the story. I strained to read. It was very dark. Giving up, I tried to remember what the story was, what the words on the page had said. I tried telling the story out loud. Frustrated, I found I couldn't remember all of the parts. I tried just making up stuff I couldn't recall, but nothing felt quite right. Exhausted, I just waited. I had the time. There was nowhere else to go.

I remember that night, so dark, so black, with only bright stars overhead. I remember the blinking street light. I remember being lonely. I remember waiting, thinking I got the day wrong. I remember being furious when I knew I hadn't.

I remember waiting and that dad didn't come. I remember wanting to forgive my dad as soon as he told me his first story. I remember hoping that dad liked mine, even if I cheated. I remember being angry, looking at my story. I remember ripping out all of the pages from that book and throwing them on the ground. I remember mom calling to me, telling me that it was time for bed.

What does a story matter, anyways, I thought. It's not mine. I'll just think of one myself. It doesn't matter.

Reaching for my bike, I left that empty book on the ground with the ripped out pages. Turning around, I grabbed my bike and headed on home.

Then, I heard you.

Hee hee hee heeeeeee, you giggled. Hee hee hee heeeeeee. Hee hee hee heeeeeee. Hee hee hee heeeeeee.

Where did you come from? Were you listening? Were you watching? Were you here the whole time? Were you waiting for me? Were you telling this story?

For the first time, I smelled you deeply, gagged, and choked. You appeared all of a sudden, your hair all over your body, your hunched shoulders, thick legs, shifting eyes, and that huge gaping mouth with no teeth. You were small then, not the fat slob you would become. Nevertheless, you started eating right away. It didn't take you long to swallow half the tree.

Are you real? I asked.

You, of course, ignored me, leaves falling from your mouth. When I grabbed a few off the ground, then you stared at me.

I remember being scared. You were frightening to look at, especially the first time. I hopped on my bike and pedalled to get away, crying. You followed, and I thought you were going to kill me. You suddenly appeared in front of me and I swerved and fell, scraping my knees and breaking my glasses. It was then that I realized, for the first time, that you had powers. I left my bike and ran into my house, hoping I could escape.

All night, you were everywhere, causing trouble. In the kitchen. In the bathroom. In my room. In my bed. Everywhere was you, your smell, your ugly face. I tried to get away. I tried to hide. I tried to run. You have been there since.

I didn't see dad again, until years later, in the big room with the old man in the black robes. I couldn't concentrate because you were there, eating the desk, playing with his wig, playing with yourself on his desk. I could barely hear that old man when he was talking to me.

What do you want? he asked me.

I don't want him in my life, I said, pointing at you.

Sole custody mother, supervised visitation rights father, the old man said.

No, I meant him. Not you, dad. Not you. Not you.

My dad gave me a hug, told me he loved me, and I scarcely ever saw him again. When I did, he was tense, nervous, and sad, and even when I asked him to tell me stories, he wouldn't. Then, he started just to phone me. Years later, he stopped coming.

Please come back, dad. I don't mind waiting. I don't care. Please, just come back.

It was weeks later when I realized your trick. You did it, I realized. You kept my father from coming that Friday. You tricked him, and then you tricked me. You're the one who did all of this. You wanted me all to yourself. You're an asshole.

And now, you play tricks on me all the time. When I draw, when I write, all I can create is you. You are all that comes out on the page. The disgusting pictures that I create are of you. You. You. You. Always you. I hate drawing, writing, living, like I hate you.

There is no reason to look back at that time. There are no answers there. There is only now, where you are today. I have to deal with you now. Now. Now. Now.

I don't know what trick you are going to play next.

No one knows you are here. Even in this office, when I tell people to look, they say they can't see you. You are everywhere, I tell them. Right there, beside you.

They say I make no sense. I should go to a doctor, they say. I have been, I respond. I have seen doctors, psychiatrists, herbalists, yoga instructors, professors, bartenders. Once a guy in a New Age bookstore told me that seeing must be a gift. I said that he was wrong and then told him your hand was on his crotch.

One time, I went to a real medicine man. He didn't tell me where he was from. He was an Indian, though. He told me that he could do a purification for me and it would wash you away. He sang and beat a drum. He told me to dance. Then, when it was over, he asked me for fifty dollars and there you were, laughing behind him, waving your ass.

I gave him a hundred. Keep the change, I told him.

I turn on my computer and you are all over my keyboard. The letters are covered in slivers of your hair and drops of your saliva. When I finally wipe them clean, I open my files and they are filled with descriptions of you. I read yesterday's reports, and they are covered with images of you laughing. My e-mails are all from you. My desktop is a photo of your huge, black mouth. You. You. You. You. Nothing else. What mean games you play on me.

I go to the bathroom to hide in the stall. I hold the door shut, but you eventually grunt and struggle as you open it and squeeze in there with me. You poop with me, beside me, through me, all over me. Oh the stink. Not again.

At lunch you eat my food. You munch off of my plate, burping, farting, swallowing whole everything. As always, you grow fatter with everything you consume. I am hungry but can't eat because being around you makes me want to get sick, so I push my tray towards you, and you swallow the orange plastic completely.

I try to work when I get called to boss's office to copy down every word he says.

Copy this down, he says. Memo. For Press Release. I, Cappuccino Meaning, President and CEO of www.redman.com do hereby announce that, following the traditions of our—ahem—more cultural brethren, from now on we will have all of our encyclopaedic entries on Indian cultures free for everyone. There will be no rules, no owners, no standards. All of our existing webpages, newspapers, picture books, and e-mails will be editable, and members of the public are now encouraged to come and add their two cents. And don't worry, everyone will be right. We're also going to stop publishing anything new on paper, and—as of next year—open up our new 24-hour information centre built in the style of a real-life tepee where real-life old Indians will share oral stories and laughter. We will be completely authentic and real, and all of us can do whatever we want with whatever we hear. This will be the last word I will ever speak on paper. Thank you. Oh, I mean, ho ho ho ho.

My boss is fat, pompous, and rude, but, hoping that he will promote me, I tell him he's lost some weight. You laugh at his jokes about his wife and roll on the floor at the stupidity that is yourself. You help yourself to his cigars, swallow them, and lick the covers of his books. I see your hairs on top of his Indian Entrepreneur of the Year Award, so I know you must have done something with that. Of course, you rub the photo of his wife on your crotch. I hand him the memo, and he laughs at the pictures of you I have drawn and tells me to come back tomorrow. Then, he tears it up and throws the pieces in the air.

Go and tell someone what I told you, my boss announces.

No wonder I am in this dead-end job. It's the same thing every day. I am unable to advance, to evolve, to grow, to do anything that would impress anyone. I will never get promoted.

Getting back to my cubicle I collapse into my chair. I feel the cold plastic grooves sticking into my ass because you've eaten the cushion.

I am paralyzed. It's always the same crap. It's killing me. You're killing me.

Hee hee hee heeeeeee, you whisper. Hee hee hee heeeeeee. Hee hee hee heeeeeee. Hee hee hee heeeeeee.

I finish work and run away. I take the stairs, and I hear you heaving behind me.

You never run, do you. Your fat belly can't keep up to me. I run and you are far behind. I race to the exit and feel my eyes screaming at the pain of the afternoon light, my legs throbbing at the newness of motion. I squint as I sprint through the parking lot.

I get to my car and rip open the door. I lock it. I lock all of them. Even if I get a few seconds until you get here, I am safe. I am alone. I close my eyes.

Of course, I am only playing a trick on myself.

I drive away. You're there. I can smell you. I can hear you struggling to breathe, and I feel the vehicle weighted down with your fat ass.

Then, the smell of a cigarette floods my nose. How nice. Now you're really going to kill me. How the hell did you get that?

White tobacco fills the air, fixing the distance between you and I. I bet you knew I am allergic, you jerk. I cough and gag and swerve all over the road. For a moment, I think about driving right into the railing. Then one of us will die.

No. I can play your game and get rid of you. Maybe that will work. I am going to hurt you, make fun of you, make your life a living hell. I am going to win.

I rip open the back door but you are gone. Did you get out? Did you know what I was going to do? Maybe that was it. Maybe I am free. Maybe I see you, standing by the ditch, puking up the cigarette you smoked. Dammit.

I chase after you, like you have done to me so many times. I run and run and run and run. But you're always one step ahead, one turn, one pace, one laugh. I can't catch you. I don't know why I thought I could this time. It never worked before.

I drive and you smoke again. You never learn. You cough. You eat the butts. You puke in the back seat. Oh, the smell. Again, always again.

When I pull in the driveway, it hits me. I am home. She will help. She will know what to do. She will believe me. She will make it all better. She always does.

You follow, panting and groaning.

Opening the door, I feel a difference. There is no light on in the living room, no voice to announce me, no soft call of my name. There is only silence. I feel the coldness of the house—a hollow, empty absence. There is no one, no her, no centre, only spaces where there once was a something.

No. Not today. Not now.

I hear the microwave bell ring. You're in the kitchen, making yourself something to eat. How insulting is that.

I run upstairs, disbelieving the truth. I hear you behind me.

Her clothes, her bags, her presence, gone, wiped away. Her plants, the only things we owned together, are gone too. I live with nothing but leased furniture, photographs of memories, and my old bachelor dishes. Well, unless I count you, giggling in the corner as you gnaw on your own crotch.

I find her note, in pieces on the bedroom floor, drenched in pools of your spit. You ripped it up, you asshole. How did you get it? Where did you find it? There are some missing. Did you swallow them? How do I make sense of these shards?

Hey.

You're weren't alone. Who was that someone else? You hurt me. This will eat me if Tell me. It's not right. Last night proved it. I suppose you are. I keep telling myself Be honest with me. Don't blame father. No more lies. That makes deeper. tears. honesty. faced . my ego. am not your undivided attention. independent. exist. normal. perhaps alone. kharma. I think she is right. I'm leaving. I care about you so much. i alone shield and deal. But I also respect you. to cope. Whatever works. survival mechanism crazy stupid say you don't care Tell me this is over. mother's cut me off. tell me love someone else. Easy? so I too want to know love where to go I want to go stop hurting. I want to stop caring but you will leave again. And I can't forgive you now. Yes. I care about you I wish it didn't hurt you re not alone

Me.

I sit on the bed and put my head in my hands. I'm defeated. You enter the bedroom, sit on the opposite side and roll in the covers. The smell of shit fills the room.

How could I not see this coming. How could I be with her this morning. How can she be gone. How can I be alone.

Hee hee hee heeeeeee, you shit. Hee hee hee heeeeeee. Hee hee hee heeeeeee. Hee hee hee heeeeeee.

You did it, didn't you? You watched her, wanted her, took her, and now you have me all to yourself. You knew that she was the only thing that kept you from destroying me. She made me happy and it drove you crazy. So you tricked her, just like my dad.

I stand up and turn to you. I'm going to make you give her back to me. This time, it's going to be different.

Where did you go? I want to see you. I want you to feel the pain that you have created. And this time, I'm not going to stop. This time I'm going to win.

There you are, under that pile of shit. I can see you moving. You can't get away from me now. I want her back, and you will give her to me.

I bet you think I won't crawl through this pool of poop to get to you. I will. I will get you, you bastard. You think you are safe in that stink but I know it is just full of you. I know what you eat. I can handle it. I can beat you. I can dig through this shit. It's only my world anyway.

I will find a way to get her back once I get my hands on you.

I take a deep breath, dive in, and wade through your powerful smell. It is thick, dark, and all over me, between my fingers and toes, grabbing me, slowing me, gripping me. Soon, I am treading in a wall of stench so much more than I thought it was. I am surrounded by it; it is everywhere. The more I flail, the more I get filled in it. I've run out of air. I open my mouth and try to scream but it fills so quickly I can't even moan. I swing my arms and legs trying to get to the surface, but I feel myself falling. Oh no. Down. Down. Down. Down. I try harder and harder, but I am too heavy, too slow, too old. The shit is too thick, too strong, too brown, too much. I am sinking, sinking, into the trap you set, filling me until all I can breathe is you.

Oh my god. I'm going to die. And you're going to live. I've lost. Fuck.

And, then, I see her. I remember her. I miss her. I love her.

In this moment, my worst, she comes back. Not in the shit, in my head—although the lines are hardly so separate anymore.

It's her story. My story. Our story. An important story. Oh, don't worry, you're there too, you asshole. It's the story where I first realize who you are, actually. You should probably hear it while I can still tell it.

It's about a time with you, but it's really about us.

The first day, in a class at that university. A professor walking in, telling everyone to pull out a book called *The Trickster: A Study in American Indian Mythology*. You sit, right behind me. For years, I try to shut you out the best I could.

But today it's impossible. There, on the front page, is you, laughing and pointing right at me. The trickster, that's what the professor, the students, and the authors call you. And, from the first words out of the professors' mouth, I can tell they're yours. They are,

> Few myths have so wide a distribution as the one, known by the name of *The Trickster*, which we are presenting here. For few can we so confidently assert that they belong to the oldest expressions of mankind. Few other myths have persisted with their fundamental content unchanged. The Trickster myth is found in clearly recognizable form among the simplest aboriginal tribes and among the complex. We encounter it among the ancient Greeks, the Chinese, the Japanese and in the Semitic world. Many of the Trickster's traits were perpetuated in the figure of the mediaeval jester, and have survived right up to the present day in the Punch-and-Judy plays and in the clown. Although repeatedly combined with other myths and frequently drastically reorganized and reinterpreted, its basic plot seems to always to have succeeded in reasserting itself. (xxiii)

I hear you snickering beside me, rolling in the aisle, holding your fat belly. You did write this, you asshole. The professor continues,

> Trickster himself, is, not infrequently, identified with specific animals, such as raven, coyote, hare, spider, but these animals are only secondarily to be equated with concrete animals. Basically he possesses no well-defined and fixed form. As he is represented in the versions of the Trickster myth we are publishing here, he is primarily an inchoate being of undetermined proportions, a figure foreshadowing the shape of man. In this version, he possesses intestines wrapped around his body, and an equally long penis, likewise wrapped around his body with his scrotum on top of it. Yet regarding his specific features we are, significantly enough, told nothing. (xxiii–xxiv)

Yeah right. You wish you had a dick that long. These words are meant to confuse those who can really see you, mislead those who could help me. I know what you look like. You are this fat slob sitting behind me. The one that follows me around, like a bad nightmare that never ends. It's like you wrote this to make sure that the truth is that no one can figure you out.

But I know you.

Other textbooks say basically the same, minor variations on a larger theme of nothingness. You've written all of them, I realize. You are everywhere. You write in different voices in different fonts in different times in different books. Still, it is your voice, playing tricks. I know that this can't be a good thing. You are taking over.

I first tell a study group that these are tricks played by you. I know what you really look like, I tell them. I even draw a picture of you, but they tell me that it's just a blank page. You obviously erased the picture, I exclaim. It would be just like you to do that.

Soon, everyone refuses to work with me.

I had to do more. One day I raise my hand and tell the professor the same thing. That I know you. That you are there, writing on the blackboard. That the truth is that you are tricking all of us.

Personal experiences shut discussions down, the professor says, in front of the class. Now I know you are Indian, and your perspective is important, but what you need to practice is more open-mindedness, more awareness of other positions, more realization that there is no truth. I would suggest you read Gerald…

I miss the rest of what the professor says, especially after you pull out your scrotum and put it on the overhead.

But I do hear the laughter. At me. The whispers. The fingers pointing. The strokes of pens as each word of my shame is copied.

Embarrassed, I retreat into silence. The class ends and I am alone with my realizations. The world thinks you are something else, and I can't do anything to stop it. Shit.

Hee hee hee heeeeeee, you dance. Hee hee hee heeeeeee. Hee hee hee heeeeeee. Hee hee hee heeeeeee.

You repeat and repeat and repeat, growing louder with each round. Your hissing and footsteps grow so loud that soon they sound like permanent whispers, deep in my ear, like dancesteps on my brain.

Until I hear her voice. For the first time since you came into my life you go silent.

How do you know tricksters? she asks, clearly.

Lost by your muteness, I confusingly say, I see one every day.

Tricksters aren't real. They're stories, she states.

I wish that were true, I reply.

I'm Aboriginal, and I don't see the tricksters you're talking about.

You're lucky.

We sit together for a long time. I enjoy the stillness and calm of her voice. You sit off on that bench, quiet for the first time in years, watching us. We talk for hours. She tells me to study you, write books about you, speak up to you, confront you. She encourages me to think different things than whimsical stories and theories of untruths.

Most of all, she trusts me. She tells me that what I experience is true. What I know was true. What I conclude is true.

But that's not the end, she states, your trickster might be beautiful too. He might even be fun, smart, and powerful.

How do you know this? I ask.

I've heard stories from my relatives.

So you've seen him?

Not yours. But one.

I don't believe it, I say. I tell her how you came into my life, how you are nothing but an asshole who makes my life hell, how you are nothing that I want to be, nothing that I want to become, nothing that reflects me or my life.

Tell me more, she asks.

We spend more and more time together, days, afternoons, evenings. She asks for details about you, about what you do, about what you say (which is nothing, I know). Then she talks about herself, her life, her interests, her dreams, and asks me about mine. It is the first time I speak about a time without you. It was easy, especially since I could concentrate. You were still there but you were calmly watching us, in the faded background of our community.

One Friday, in my apartment, she kisses me. I pull away, scared.

Okay, okay, she whispers. Don't worry. Be with me. Shhhhh. Focus on us, on me. The rest will come. Are you upset? Oh god, I didn't know. It's okay. I'll be gentle.

Kissing my neck, she takes off my shirt. I tremble, a warm chill hitting my skin.

Hearing you lick your lips, I feel your hairy hands help pull it over my head.

We move in together soon after that. One night, she tells me she loves me. We marry. I get a job. We buy a house. You come, but you subversively make your presence known, making messes only I can find. I clean up after you, take responsibility for your actions. Sometimes I even pretend you aren't there. I don't want anything to happen to us.

Once in a while, she asks if you are around, if I see you, hear you. No, no, no, no, I lie, not anymore. He's gone. It's good. The trickster is just a fucking asshole. Just a jerk. Just there to make my life shit. Everything is better now. I'm happy.

I decide to try what she said. I put up with you. I try to see the beauty in you. I try to listen to you. It's hard. You are angry that I've been ignoring you. Pissed off that I have pretended to move on. You start doing different things. You drink, party, gamble, and do some horrible things. Sometimes I find the alcohol, drugs, and money you hide in my bags. Sometimes I find your used condoms. Sometimes I find blood.

But I'm happy, I tell myself. I can't let you ruin us. I can't let you break up my first happiness. I can't let you get to her. Why are you changing? Why can't you be like you were before? Why can't you go away?

You continue to mess things up, especially when she's not around. You pant in my ear, reek of booze and marijuana, and masturbate while you watch her sleep. I start leaving in the afternoon, just to keep you away from her. I go. I stay away and let you party, hoping you will pass out. I come home long after she is sleeping and stay on the couch. I keep you busy with beers to drink, floors to piss on, places to shit. I stay away as long as I can.

In this way, I protect her. I live on an island of our love, surrounded by you.

Until last night. When I couldn't stop you. I don't remember much, except for you and your drinking and your drugs and your dark fuzzy nights together when we can't stay away any longer and we come home not alone and you convince me to fumble with the locked door and come into the living room with sweaty hands making back circles and shapes kissing lying on top singing singing singing singing calling out to god pulling pushing it out in harder harder harder harder until her face not her but her becomes you suddenly it is you I have been fucking all this time, my hands holding your coarse hair as you come into with through on me and I see her standing away looking at me crying, shaking, screaming, oh honey I'm sorry it won't happen again I'm so sorry please come back please oh please I'm sorry, you saw him didn't you you saw him didn't you you saw him didn't you you saw him.

I wait until she is sleeping and slip into bed. You, of course, are already there.

I just realized, I touched you for the first time last night. I think I'm going to throw up.

I think I'm going to die.

There's no imagining the shit I have covered all over my hands, my body, my mind. It's very real, and you created it. I can't get to you. I will never get to you. The shit is too thick. I am too weak.

I cry, little sobs at first, and then try to scream out her name, even though my mouth is so full of shit I can't close it. I can make no sound. I am pathetic. I am lost. I am alone. And I should be dead by now, but I'm not. I can hear you giggling.

I feel a long rubber staff, like a rope, near my hands. It's bendable, firm, soft to the touch, kind of like a piece of wood covered in slippery moist plastic. I grab it and wrap it around my wrist as it pulls me free from the ooze. I breathe my first breath in what feels like days. Then, as soon as I free myself, the rope slithers back into the shit pile and disappears.

Coughing and wheezing on the floor, I've got nothing more to say to you. I've got nothing more to take. I slowly walk and sob and cry, travelling down the stairs calling her name.

Walking through the house, I stink. I don't care. I look for anything she has left behind, anything that is her, anything that is normal. Every breath, I call out her name.

I hear you coming down the stairs. Go ahead. I don't care what you destroy anymore.

I'm sorry, I cry out. I'm so so so so sorry, Sky. You deserve better. I'm sorry. If only my dad kept me from waiting. If only you hadn't tricked me. If only I listened better to her. If only.

Suddenly, you come in the living room and start to eat. It's small at first. The pictures on the wall of my mother, my father, my degree, her, they all go down your throat. My jacket, my laptop, my shoes, my wallet. You eat the clock her mother gave us for Christmas.

What are you doing, I scream, what are you doing you asshole.

Then, I promptly throw up shit. When I am done, my throat is so burnt, I can only croak.

I watch, silently, as you smash the television set on the floor, and then munch on the pieces. You tip the cabinet over and it disappears into your stomach. You swallow the books whole, pages from my copies of *Bearheart, Kiss of the Fur Queen, Love Medicine,* and *Ravensong* spilling out of your mouth. You throw the bookcase across the room and it smashes into shards. You gulp those down too. You get bigger, bigger, bigger, bigger, too large for the rooms. There is no room for me anymore here.

I scramble to the kitchen. You eat all there is left in the fridge, the meat, the apples, the old milk curdles that drip down your chin. You swallow the sugar bags whole, the brown and white granules sprinkled all over your hairy palms. You help yourself to everything, turning over tables, breaking lamps, tipping over the fridge. Forget it. I'm not cleaning up your mess.

You get bigger, until your fat rolls fill up the entire floor on the first floor. All I can see when I look down is you.

I have to go. You've never gotten this big before. Something's different.

All the while you are smiling right at me. Now that she is gone you are tormenting me. Making fun of my loss. I'd scream but my voice is raw and burnt, infected with too much shit, too many words, too many yous. I can't speak.

I don't get it. I don't understand what the joke is. I don't know what is so funny, why you laugh, joke, play games. Yes, you play tricks. But they are always on others. Fucking mean tricks, too. I hate you.

At least no one can deny that you exist now. You're so huge. You take up all of the first floor, and you're oozing up the stairs. I can't even see the front door.

You're eating everything, the plaster, the stairs, the banister, the hardwood. Very soon there will be nothing left.

Oh my god. That's it. You're going to eat everything. You're going to eat it all.

The trick is that today you are going to eat me.

I run upstairs and you continue to grow.

I can't stop you, can't escape. You just destroy, destroy, destroy, destroy and eat, eat, eat, eat, and grow bigger, bigger, bigger, bigger. You start to fill up the second floor, inches at a time.

I go to open the windows in the hallway and the bedroom but they're locked, and you've eaten my wallet. You have trapped me, and I have trapped myself, you bastard. I need something to break through this glass.

You grunt and moan around me, pick up furniture, throw it against the wall, eat the pieces. I jump away from the glass, onto the bed of shit, now the only island in the room of you. Your slimy hair covers the windows and it grows dark and dusky.

I slowly start to sink. What's the point of this, I try to say, but nothing comes out.

Your hands emerge from the bubbles of your hairy fat, pick up handfuls of brown slime, and throw it at me.

But I am already sinking in this, can't you tell? You can't do anything more. Cover me completely, then. Here, I'll take off my clothes so you can cover me with your waste. Have them. There, I am naked. I'll cover myself with you. Are you happy now? Is this what you want? No history, no life, no possessions, no nothing? It is only you and me and shit now.

You stop and stare at my discarded clothes. This is what you wanted, isn't it. You want to replace me. You put them on and they explode with your fatness, your jiggling chest oozing out of my shirt and my pants bulging at your crotch. You smile. Damn you.

You start to eat the corner of the bed, yourself oozing from your mouth. When you're finished with the mattress you chew on the corner of the dresser. I grab one of your rolls and pull my naked self out of the waist-high slime, step on your jiggling back, and leap into the bathroom. Quickly slamming the door, I realize that I have nowhere else to go.

No, you can't destroy everything. No, you bastard. I won't let you do it.

I destroy everything I see, so you can't. I rip the glass shower doors off, tear the photographs of us onto the floor, smash the mirror on the wall. I kick the floor and punch the walls until tiny slivers of plaster and tile are jammed in my nails and my hands and feet bleed all over. I eat the shards of glass on the floor, the photographs, and whatever pieces of plaster, chunks of wood, that I can grab. The shards cut my throat, and my cuts spread open with each step and piece I slide in my mouth. I cry and feel my body shaking, cutting, bleeding, crying out in pain. Still, I punch, kick, and eat until I lie in the bathtub and there is nothing left. I am in so much pain. I am dying. I am really dying. I am dying. I am dying.

I smile. I have kept those little pieces from you, though. You'll see.

You eat the door and I see your stretched face cover completely the entryway. You are still wearing my clothes, but they are like shreds on your inflated self. I stand and feel all of my body scream in agony. Even if I cannot speak, my presence is ensured by this horrible struggle. I am so weak, but yet I am strong.

You see what I have done, and I can see you are angry.

I try to vomit up the shards, the wood, the pieces, the photographs, the memories, just to spite you, but nothing comes out. Nothing but blood oozing from my lips, nothing but parts of me slipping out onto the floor.

Your fatness, growing from your chin, stretches across the floor and surrounds my bathtub island. I sit down and see your bushy hands reaching out from your blubber and onto the sides of my enamel lifeboat. I see your mouth swallow down the pieces of broken toilet.

I find a piece of the mirror in the tub and look at myself. I am bloodied, hideous, mangled—just like you. Take a look, see for yourself, you asshole.

I hold up the mirror shard. You stop destroying, look at your reflection and smile. You love looking at yourself, don't you. You, dressed in my clothes, looking just like me, your overwhelming fatness covering the floor, the walls, the space.

I make you happy when I destroy, don't I? I make you happy when I wreck my life. I make you happy when I hurt myself. You didn't even know that I could do that. You thought you were doing it for me.

I laugh at the absurdity of us both, even though it hurts so much. I laugh but no sound comes from my mouth. You laugh, mimicking me, but you're so overinflated no sound comes either. For the first time you look surprised, like you didn't expect that to happen.

Suddenly, it comes to me, although I knew it the entire time. I give you life.

I laugh again. So do you. Silently.

I know what I have to do.

I'm going to wash. I reach over to the faucet and turn it on, full blast. I stand in the hot and cold water, and feel it soaking my broken feet and ankles. It is tinged red from my blood. You just stand there, smiling, staring at yourself in the mirror. I will wash us both. Our destruction will be permanent, and we will be cleansed. I sit down in the rising water and watch you silently look at yourself. You have not moved.

Water fills the bathtub and runs over the sides, covering your floor of skin.

We are going to drown. We are going to be washed away. We are going to be together. We are going to be born. This is a flood, a beginning. No one will save us. We will be cleansed in this water, filled with chemical, plaster, and glass. There will be no earth, no soil, no mud, no sand. We will have to be remade from these new things, if we are remade at all.

I watch as the water fills the room, to our waists. You reach down and nibble on the shit floating around you. You are still eating, trying to consume the world, all the way to the end. All you're doing is eating yourself.

That's it, I understand. I have finally played a trick on you.

Hee hee hee heeeeeee, I laugh, mimicking you.

Then, just then, you look. Right at me. With your eyes. Your beautiful eyes. I see my reflection in them. They are filled, filled with me. I am in you.

The water fills to our necks, and my body grows light. I'm no longer carrying it.

Hee hee hee heeeeeee, I laugh.

You're eyes tell it all. You are shaking. You are scared. After all of this time, you didn't know how this would end, did you? Amongst all of the shit, piss, vomit, saliva, grunts, and moans, you did not know the ending of this story.

Hee hee hee heeeeeee, I laugh.

You reach out with your fat hands, like tiny sticks protruding from your blob. I take them. I am scared, too. I didn't know how this would end, either. I only know how we got here.

Hee hee hee heeeeeee, we sing together, our space filling the air for the first and last time.

And with our laughter we become one, one picture, floating in water that covers our heads. We dance, weightless, merging, one. Underwater our selves return, and we sing songs with spirits of presence as we enter the next world gripped in a gaze of each other's love and hate. We are different but we are similar, each disgusting, each beautiful, each here, each there. With so many stories, so many confusions, so many thoughts, so many words, ours and others,' so many spirits, so many goods, so many bads, so many others telling our story. And we have let them. To grow, we need to tell our story now. The story of our lives together, each necessary, each important, each needing the other to tell, to listen, to write, to learn. This is how we heal. This is how we die. This is how we live. Telling our stories.

Our world fills with the blood of the earth and is cleansed of our destruction. We are remade for the world that will be created tomorrow, when we will tell this story again. It will be new and it will be different, and it will be part of a story too. It will, though, be ours. We hope.

Regardless, if we are here or we are there, you will be with me. Maybe my Dad will be with us too, laughing and telling stories with soft candies beside him. Maybe we will wait for him to arrive, but, if he doesn't come, we can't wait anymore. We have made mistakes too, and we are sorry. I pray that he knows that. But we are ready to continue.

Maybe Sky will come with us too, if she wants to come back. We have made so many mistakes. We don't blame her if she doesn't want to come back. She has her story to make too. Without her our story would have ended a long time ago, so she is acknowledged and thanked.

We don't know about tomorrow, about any of these things, because, in the end, that's all we have: each other. There will be a world that we will be born into, here or there, that we know. This place is where our story will be. We have to learn to do better, and tell it like we have been living it, like we have been doing all along. Even though we may not know that were telling it, writing it, drawing it, all along, we were.

Our trickster story.

I have a trickster story. It is my own. It is also now yours.

You are there. So am I. I am here. And so are you. We're both here and there, listening to this story as we speak it, write it, read it. We are together.

That's the trick.

It's always, for our entire lives.

Everywhere.

Boozhoo.

There is something more than survival and saving ourselves: it is continuance. (32)
—Simon J. Ortiz, *Woven Stone*

Works Cited

Johnston, Basil. "Is That All There Is? Tribal Literature." In *An Anthology of Canadian Native Literature in English*. 3rd ed. Ed. Daniel David Moses and Terry Goldie. Toronto: Oxford UP, 2005. 98–105.

Ortiz, Simon J. *Woven Stone*. Tucson: U of Arizona P, 1992.

Radin, Paul. *The Trickster: A Study in American Indian Mythology*. 1956. Rpt. New York: Schocken, 1972.

Velie, Alan. "The Trickster Novel." In *Narrative Chance: Postmodern Discourse on Native American Indian Literatures*. Ed. Gerald Vizenor. Norman: U of Oklahoma P, 1993. 121–40.

Vizenor, Gerald. *The Trickster of Liberty: Tribal Heirs to a Wild Baronage*. Minneapolis: U of Minnesota P, 1988.

Womack, Craig S. *Red on Red: Native American Literary Separatism*. Minneapolis: U of Minnesota P, 1999.

TELLING STORIES ACROSS LINES

JILL CARTER

Processual Encounters of the Transformative Kind

Spiderwoman Theatre, Trickster, and the First Act of "Survivance"

As the house begins to fill with stylish, groomed bodies, there is a delightful buzz of rustling clothing, bodies settling into seats, and hushed murmurs bearing shared secrets, which is punctuated by the occasional burst of laughter or joyous cry of recognition. In 1976, the members of this largely female audience possess the political and economic clout to decide how they will spend a Saturday night, to purchase their own tickets to the event of their choosing, and to make their way to the venue alone, in pairs, or with a select group of like-minded women. Although the feminist movement is still young, these women can afford the price of admission, and they possess the cultural capital to appreciate and assess the aesthetic and cultural values of the theatrical event they have come to witness. We could be in New York City or Baltimore or Nancy, France, or in Amsterdam. No matter. Tonight, this theatre is hosting a feminist audience, which has come to see Women in Violence created and performed by the newly mobilized feminist collective, Spiderwoman Theater. After the show, perhaps, these spectators will gather with their neighbours to enjoy a late supper or nightcap and discuss what they have seen. Others will retire to "rooms of their own" to write about the experience—not in private diaries, necessarily, but also for local newspapers, academic journals—or to prepare an upcoming lecture for the classes they teach or for the women's groups they facilitate. It is "ladies' night," 1976, and it is perfect ...

It would be perfect, except that amidst the comfortable and congenial groups of the politically astute, politically active, and like-minded, there is one who doesn't belong. No, it isn't a man. It's worse! It's a bag lady.¹ Obviously, that one doesn't belong. How could she? Certainly, that one could not afford the price of admission! Nor (judging from her tattered clothing and unkempt appearance) could that foolish one have amassed sufficient cultural capital to understand or appreciate the play they have come to see.

But what's to be done? The front-of-house staff makes no move to eject her, so she must be tolerated.

"Now, you will behave—won't you?" It's a necessary question after all, tinged with the merest cautionary edge. That one obviously does not know how to dress herself appropriately; how can she be expected to behave appropriately? In accordance with her neighbours' worst fears, the Bag Lady begins to misbehave; she's banging on some old tray she's brought with her! She's disturbing the peace! "Shhhh! Shoo! Stop it! Behave!" The audience members are outraged. So intent are they in shutting her up and shutting her down that they are scarcely aware of the guttural growling on stage, which answers the Bag Lady's performance and builds in rhythm and intensity as she persists in her outrageous behavior. This is not what they paid for— is it? Then again, maybe it is …

As it slowly dawns on them that this "infiltrator" is part of the show, the spectators begin to relax and perhaps enjoy the fact that they have been fooled. And, as the evening unfolds, more revelations will occur; this group of accomplished, educated, and politically savvy elites will be unceremoniously ushered into a hostile universe peopled with "dirty mashers," big bad wolves, abusive husbands, violent siblings, betrayers, suicides, and mass murderers by a rag-tag bunch of "clowns," each of whom embodies the "poor bare fork'd animal" beneath the quotidian mask, which conceals and protects every human actor as s/he goes about the business of living. These include a glittering Chameleon in constant pursuit of herself; a Nun whose mission it is to clean the world and the other women in it; the unruly Bag Lady; a magnificent leonine Trickster who wears a second face on her tail and who both uses and blames this marvellous appendage for all tricks and offending actions against others; and finally, a Perfect Woman—a chocolate-box blonde—whose final act in the piece is to strip off wig, gloves, and makeup and publicly "come out" as someone other than she first appears.

These clowns created by Spiderwoman Theater to carry its artists and their audiences through the stories are archetypes of contemporary feminine humanity; these archetypes are, at the end of the day, vehicles of discovery and revelation. Through their ministrations and interventions, performer and spectator alike are unceremoniously forced into confrontation with themselves and publicly called into account; the chaotic combat zones in which violence is enacted upon women and in which women play out their own violence upon themselves and each other are transformed into healing spaces wherein basic human accountability, responsibility, possibility, value, and dignity may be realized, reclaimed, and celebrated. Like Nanabozho, Weesageechak, Raven or Coyote, Br'er Rabbit, Homer Simpson,[2] the Zany of the Italian Commedia-cum-"medicine show" in the public square or the low-born European booby who gets the girl, the gold, and the Kingdom, these vehicles of primordial human impulse tease, shock, rage, bumble, and stumble—audaciously confronting us with outra-geous and uncomfortable truths about who we have become as they learn for them-selves and teach us through example what we were born to be.

Trickster in the First Person

Weesageechak is the entity inside me that I never knew.
It took an elder to show him to me,
and now I know he's alive and well.
        —Kennetch Charlette, quoted in *Canadian Theatre Review* 52

As an urban woman of mixed descent (Anishinaabe/Ashkenazi), I have come to view the contemporary stage as a potential site for ceremonial encounters. For Native artists, it is a site through which we might continue the oral tradition and remember our histories, but also chronicle recent events, struggles, preoccupations, and victories. Each theatrical event engineered by Native artists in urban settings affords the opportunity to unite a scattered body politic and to engage in relationship-building as histories, languages, lifeways, and philo-sophical principles are embodied and shared. The theatrical event, regardless of the culture from whence it springs, carries the promise of transformation for performer and spectator alike: the urban stage, then, becomes the site upon which Native artists also come together with their communities to negotiate the liminal interstices between those who we were (pre-colonization), those who we have been told we are (colonization), and those who we will become (decol-onization). Such healing and transformative ritual "acts," engendered to aid in the formation of the new, decolonized human being, require, as they always have, the intervention and ministrations of our nations' models-and-agents of transformation—our trickster-figures. Over the past generation in Canada, Weesageechak has begun his/her riotous re-emergence onto the Native stage, largely through the forceful intervention of the Committee to Re-establish the Trickster. This intervention, which began as a seed in the imaginations of our writers (Tomson Highway, Daniel David Moses, and Lenore Keeshig-Tobias), began to exercise its full efficacy within the performing body as Indigenous artists such as Gary Farmer, Rene Highway, Maaka Kleist, Doris Linklater, Billy Merasty, Muriel Miguel, and Monique Mojica (to name only a few) set about their own explorations. In 1984, Kleist, Linklater, and Mojica first formed a work-shop with Richard Pochinko and Ian Wallace dedicated to developing a tech-nique by which to access and embody traditional trickster figures belonging to

Indigenous people on this continent (Preston 139). By 1985, trickster-incarnation and/or discourse had become a central feature of most Native Earth Performance Arts productions (Preston 141). Playwrights and performers—ideas and instruments of their execution—had entered the chaos[3] in tandem and so precipitated a conscious re-engagement with an age-old process of creating a new order.

The importance of this project and the potency of its reverberations have correctly received much critical attention, and will continue to be the subject of much study and discussion for years to come. But interestingly, the discussion in academic and critical circles still revolves around the idea of the text as "the thing itself," that is, the socio-political intentions and artistic facility of a singular authority—the playwright—who has constructed the "metaphor;" and the authenticity, aesthetic value, and potency of that metaphor become the subjects for reflection, as do the personal power (presence), mimetic ability, energy, and plasticity of the performer who embodies it. Never do these discussions measure the power that these "metaphors" exercise upon the mind, spirit, emotional lives, and persons of those who think, write, and *do* them into being. Yet Native artists repeatedly voice the understanding that to access the trickster within ourselves is to discover who we are, to experience transformation, to exercise transformation, to know why we exist, and to exist fully as human creatures. Our storytellers repeatedly testify to the power of that dormant entity that, once accessed, becomes the catalyst that truly heals by converting mere survival into life fully realized (see *Canadian Theatre Review* 51–3). The trick is to access that energy, to find our way through the chaos, and so to meet the teacher who is ourself and to map the route that our compatriots and future generations may follow.

I am particularly interested in the "maps" left to us by Spiderwoman Theater, which began in 1976, and which has gone on to become the longest-running Native theatre company in North America and the longest-running feminist troupe in the world. The story of Lisa Mayo, Gloria Miguel, and Muriel Miguel (the three Kuna/Rappahannock sisters who founded the company) is in itself an epic saga of becoming. Their story, which unfolds within the production history of the company and the troupe's performances, is one that has been powered by the generations who precede its protagonists and that provides a power source for the generations that follow them. Although it is not my intention here to map that larger story of its protagonists' search for self, an exploration of the troupe's initial processual encounters with "inner clowns" and trickster discourse, which have continued to reverberate throughout the Spiderwoman canon, will go far to help us better read and organically comprehend the Spiderwoman process of Storyweaving. This process imagines the human into being, through which the creatrices and those for whom they create **become** who they were meant to be before a rapacious invader stumbled upon our garden and trampled it underfoot.

Spiderwoman's maps—the troupe's published and unpublished play texts—hold particular interest, because these texts document stories that have been written upon and from within the body. As such, they constitute the blocking notes for the human "written" in action and inter-relationship; they record the movement and represent the substance of the human doing. And, as such, they mark the continuance of the oral tradition in this postmodern industrial world and constitute a significant addition to the stores of IK (Indigenous knowledge), as they document Native survival and resistance and celebrate artful existence amidst the inhospitable concrete topography and the treacherous social architecture of urban America in the late twentieth century.

In contrast to the trickster figures, as singular entities that work their transformative magic upon and within human communities and that dance artfully through many contemporary Native plays, Spiderwoman's tricksters are literally, metaphorically, and very explicitly *born of the women who carry them*. That is to say, each trickster (or clown-persona) emerges from the body of each female storyteller in whose personal story she plays a vital role. This collective embodiment demystifies and democratizes our conception of her. Trickster-energies do not emerge from a single, isolate body; rather, all human "actors" are invested with these energies and all storytellers in a Spiderwoman production move so fluidly between the mortal realm and the metaphysical realm that the distinction between the two states of being eventually becomes imperceptible. Adding to the facilitation of this liminal dissolution is Spiderwoman's absolutely unselfconscious approach in this regard: the troupe never explicitly identifies its trickster figures or sets these "Foolish Ones" apart from the human actors. Indeed, as I have come to realize, the Miguel sisters' investment in the creative process of investigation is so intense that, at times, they themselves do not recognize trickster, even after she has insinuated herself into the work and they have begun to wrestle with her.

Spiderwoman Dives in ... Feet-First: "Plop, Plop, Plop"

It was during the AIM [American Indian Movement] and I realized how angry I was and I tried to identify it. It was very hard trying to understand my anger that would snap out of nowhere. There was this kind of frustration in walking down the street and being angry at men. I really had to examine it or get killed before it killed me.

    —Muriel Miguel, quoted in Beaucage 6, emphasis added)

In 1975, fueled by her determination to reach the age of forty (unlike so many American Indian women of her acquaintance) and to work with her sisters on the professional stage, Muriel Miguel channeled a grant she had received into the mobilization of a new, multiracial, feminist collective. Spiderwoman Theater was born in the midst of grief, pain, love, and irrepressible life. Its formation was an act of "survivance,"[4] and its first full production, *Women in Violence,* was the vehicle through which the Miguel sisters and their colleague(s)[5] wrote their resistance to the violence that affected them and that they had, in their turn, effected. In 1975–76, as Miguel assembled the new troupe and began planning its inaugural production, she was mourning the death of her best friend and was adjusting to her life as a newly single woman. The questions and concerns foremost in her mind during this time revolved around "violence in Indian homes" (Muriel Miguel, U of T lecture, 2006). On the eve of a "family reunion" that would bind the Miguel sisters together within an intense, creative partnership that would span three decades, Muriel Miguel was already mapping a processual strategy towards healing. She hoped that she and her sisters would be able to effect personal healing and to repair the sibling relationships, which had been compromised by the domestic explosions that had rocked their childhood home and her own marital home, and that continued to reverberate throughout the consciousness of each.

But the show that would launch Spiderwoman Theater onto the world stage was not to be a diatribe that simply positioned women as victims/survivors of violence. This show was not about women *and* violence. Some questions that preoccupied the women of Spiderwoman Theater dealt with personal (or witnessed) experiences that ranged from the petty, quotidian humiliations of verbal catcalls to which most women have been subjected on public thoroughfares right up to domestic violence, muggings, rapes, and murders; others brought to the table by the Miguel sisters dealt with the physical and mental violence we, as women, perpetrate upon ourselves and the violence we perpetrate upon each other. It was to be an exploration of women *in* violence—an utterly honest examination of human brokenness that held up a mirror to the oppressed and reflected back the face of an oppressor (cf. Canning 167).

Such biting honesty, albeit sweetened by a generous "spoonful" of humour, proved a difficult pill to swallow for many. Although *Women in Violence* did receive some much well-deserved praise and critical acclaim, the initial recognition of the troupe's importance came from Luis Valdez of Teatro Campesino, who had seen *Women in Violence* at the Baltimore Theater. At his urging, Spiderwoman Theater was invited to the One World Festival of Theatre in Nancy, France, and became the first feminist company to perform at an international theatre festival (Canning 96). Although its "communitist"[6] possibilities eventually manifested themselves across feminist communities throughout France and later at home, the reception of the piece in America brought in its initial wake no small degree of controversy: *Women in Violence* marks the historical moment when Gloria Miguel and Lisa Mayo (mobilized by their younger sister) began to use their voices not simply to animate other people's stories but to create and perform their own stories to save lives—their own and others.' Within the context of a multiracial, feminist troupe, the Miguel sisters publicly and performatively asserted their identity as artists, as women—as **Native** women—and as feminists, working through problematic questions that spoke to their position as women in the American Indian struggle and as Native women in a struggle that largely privileged the concerns of White, middle-class women. Ironically, this identity and their allegiances would be (often vociferously) challenged by spectators for whom the troupe did not comfortably fit into imagined paradigms of authenticity and by those discomfited by the public revelation of communal flaws.

Male audience members at New York City's American Indian Community House (where *Women in Violence* played on weekends in January 1976) demonstrated their displeasure with the troupe's work by stomping out of performances or loudly and succinctly vocalizing their critique for performers and audience alike (Canning 122). Many women were offended by the troupe's deliberate full-frontal assault on the racist and classist underpinnings of the early feminist movement. Although Spiderwoman Theater definitively allied itself with the feminist struggle, three of its founding members, as women of colour, were committed to deepening contemporary feminist analyses around violence by introducing the hitherto ignored layer of race. It is indisputable that the patriarchal attitudes imported by the settler nations and imposed upon Indigenous communities have been responsible for much of the societal chaos and individual brokenness that we experience today; but this patriarchy had also often been actively supported by and had certainly afforded privileges to members of the very community that Spiderwoman Theater now challenged. European women taught (and often abused) our children in residential/Indian boarding schools; many of the most financially successful "shamanesses" who pen bestsellers that misrepresent Native spiritual beliefs and praxis, who facilitate workshops, and who even sell weekend sweats are Euro-American women. Previous "gains" made by the suffragette grand-mothers of the movement have entitled women to buy, sell, and own lands that had been stolen from our peoples, and to vote for national leaders who continue unjust policies against "their" Native peoples and refuse even to abide by the treaties signed by their ancestors and ours (see Grande 150–1). Nor could members of the feminist community distance themselves from their own complicit behaviors—whether these took the form of an "inno-cent" ethnic joke; a pointed verbal assault on another woman (be she mother, sister, acquaintance, or stranger); a violent physical attack on a mother, daugh-ter, sister, cousin, acquaintance, or stranger; or cavalier attitudes towards and dehumanizing treatment of their economically impoverished "sisters."

As Muriel Miguel observes of the Bag Lady intervention that opened *Women in Violence*, "[i]t showed exactly what these women were—upper mid-dle class. They had no regard for homeless—homeless women. They had no regard for people of color, certainly not women of color" (Interview 2007). But who actually profited from this teaching? On whom had this momen-tary intervention wrought the most profound and enduring transformation? Although the core teaching underpinning this introductory instance of trick-ster discourse had manifested itself transparently to all, it seems that the artists onstage learned much more about the mechanics of the communi-ties, which they watched watching them, than the watchers for whom it might appear that the lesson had been intended. Women were supposed to present a morally righteous, united front against a common enemy; but, in true trick-ster fashion, Spiderwoman Theater had plunged headlong into the layers of an impossibly intricate socio-political web to reveal a vital flaw in its design. The exposure of this flaw, embodied by the enemy/oppressor within, car-ried with it the potential to undermine political unity by upsetting the col-lective assurance in the moral rectitude of the feminist cause and its fighters: "[W]e just put our big feet in the middle of feminism and went plop, plop, plop. So either you loved us or you absolutely hated us" (Muriel Miguel, quoted in Canning 123).

But the revelation of flaws within the "design" was not simply a political aesthetic employed by the troupe for *Women in Violence*, it has continued to be the governing artistic mandate of the company throughout the decades. This aesthetic is characterized by story-fragments with connections that are often initially imperceptible. Widely variegated playing styles and the delib-erate integration of flaws into the production design and performative exe-cution is an aesthetic that binds the lifeblood of the company—in the persons of the Miguel sisters—to the body of Traditional Knowledge they have inherited from their Kuna father and uncles. Furthermore, the artists' fearless excavation of and descent into the layers of human experience in search of truthful revelation naturally invites (and perhaps requires) the ministrations and interventions of that transformative agent. To understand just how she negotiates those layers, and reveals within the chaos the design that manifests the connections between spirit and material, potentiality and actuality, ancestor and descendant, and creation and destruction in *Women in Violence* and other Spiderwoman productions, we must first begin to chart those layers and come to know the decorative and performative "metaphors" that inhabit Spiderwoman's stages—not as metaphors but as patently literal manifestations of Indigenous worldview and tradition.

Dramaturging the Mola: Mola Aesthetics

Since 1976, every Spiderwoman production has included the troupe's signature backdrop—a multi-layered quilt (or mola), which has continued to expand in breadth, depth, and intricacy over the past thirty years as many of those who have worked with or been touched by Spiderwoman Theater have contributed their own material artifacts to the company's mola. It is important to recognize that this signature backdrop is not only a signifier of the Miguel sisters' connection to their Kuna ancestry, but also a material representation of the dramaturgical and performative processes, which may be seen to have evolved from the Kuna mola-makers' aesthetic.

The mola, an intricately designed fabric panel, is a key element of traditional dress for the Kuna woman; the art of mola-making lies strictly within her purview. Evolving from earlier forms of adornment, which included tattoos, piercings, and intricate designs painted on the body, the mola has become the signifier of female identity (it contains the stories she wants to tell about herself) and artistic skill. The process of mola construction involves layering fabrics of variegated colors, one on top of the other, cutting away the upper layers to reveal the colour(s) beneath out of which a complex design will emerge, and finally stitching each layer to the base layer with minute deftness so as to render the connections between the layers invisible. This layering process extends far beyond the design and fabrication of the material artifact; it is the governing principle behind Kuna philosophical, cosmological, and aesthetic principles that have governed the nation's healing practices, musical composition, and oratory from the beginning of the beginning of the beginning.[7]

Trickster Enters the Mola: Cutting the Pattern of Survivance

We begin our work [in Women in Violence *] by finding our own personal clowns. Together we sit on the floor and talk about a theme—"The Clown in Us"—and discuss all different aspects of it, good and bad, sad and happy, etc. Then we isolate a particular aspect, which we want to make fun of and keep that as a basis for a clown persona.*

— "Method of Working," Spiderwoman Theater Papers, Native American Women Playwrights Archive (NAWPA)

Each Spiderwoman show is a collective exercise in the design and construction of a performative mola. Each member of the troupe contributes one or more stories, each of which will constitute one layer in the grand design. The stories are then rearticulated by and sifted through the corpus of each company member until the inconsequential details have been cut away and the shape and colour of truthful experience (the "kernel") for each story reveals itself. But, if the stories constitute the layers, what binds these layers together and so preserves the integrity of the design? With each new project, the im/material essence of the connective tissues, which repair and reorder the chaos, varies. Indeed, these dramaturgical thread-lines, their fabric, "colour," and essence, are, in the final analysis, the ultimate and crucial object of the troupe's investigations, regardless of the questions that necessitated them. After all, without these connecting threads, the troupe's investigations have yielded only random, isolate parts, which in and of themselves on stage (as in every area of existence) carry neither meaningful utility nor medicinal value.

For *Women in Violence,* as the women of Spiderwoman Theater began to strategize their entrance into the inchoate layers of the disruption and violence that had marked their lives and interpersonal relationships, they instinctively sought to access that innate, personal essence, which is, in quotidian life, controlled, suppressed, or masked. These "personal clowns" would not only carry the women and their audiences safely through these experiential fragments, they would ultimately discover and carry the thread-lines that would bind the layers together and maintain the integrity of the larger design. Ultimately, it is just for this—the search for self, relationship, and place within an ordered cosmos—that Trickster traditionally pops up to take us through the process.

The story of Muriel Miguel—mortal woman, artist, and guiding genius behind Spiderwoman Theater—bears a striking parallel to the traditional trickster tales in the Anishinaabe oral tradition, which, as David Treuer has observed, do not concern themselves with "the issue of motivation" (54). Nanabozho wanders the world aimlessly for eternity. Her destination (if any) is of considerably less import than what she **does** and how she **interacts** with other beings while on route:

> So, you know it was like this ... groping in the dark! And I'd say, "Oh, that feels good! I think I'll try this." And then I'd go some place else and go, "Oh, that's interesting; maybe I'll try that." And that's how I faced the world [...] So, I think everything I have done was process, including Spiderwoman. (Muriel Miguel 2007)

Muriel Miguel's process to "find" her clown-anima for *Women in Violence* began with a headlong dive into an inchoate space of remembered abuse and impotent confusion. In rehearsals, she gave herself over to a story of one person calling another person an animal. As she **did** this story, Miguel took corporeal possession of all of its characters shifting moment-to-moment from abuser to abused to witnesses and back again. Eventually, as the story settled into her body and she began to settle on its shape, the story began with the words, "Animal! Animal! Nothing but an animal" (Muriel Miguel 2007); simultaneously, her abused and abased "animal" crawled rapidly across the floor, growling a rhythmic score to her physical movements. From this story, Miguel's "inner clown" began her outward manifestation. The abused and abased was transformed into a personal allegory of contemporary "Revenge." Like the Koshares (Sacred Clowns) in the Pueblo Corn Dances who often hurl abuse (and/or refuse) at Caucasian spectators, this one delighted in settling old scores and "getting people back" (Muriel Miguel 2007). She sprouted a tail bearing its own face with which she would whack fellow cast members upside the head or tickle peoples' private places. Since the offending appendage had a face of its own, Miguel's trickster could also ascribe to it a will of its own, and hence assign to it all blame and declare with picaresque sincerity, "I wouldn't do a thing like that."

Miguel now identifies this inner clown-persona as a "Contrary" (Muriel Miguel 2007)—that is, one of those Sacred Clowns who teach us who we were meant to be by forcing us to confront who we were not. That one does everything backwards and so teaches us the right course of action by demonstrating the wrong course of action. Alternatively, we may discover through the intervention of the Contrary that what we have come to regard as an odd or wrong course of action may in fact be the only possible correct course of action in the face of injustice, cruelty, and wrong action executed to effect physical or psychological harm:

> All of us would laugh at what people did to us. And out of that came my per-
> sona, especially in *Women and* [*sic*] *Violence* and other shows. I remember my
> dance teachers and my drama teachers saying, "Muriel always giggles, she's
> the first one to laugh." Well, fuck, if I didn't laugh first, they were going to
> laugh at me. (Muriel Miguel, quoted in France and Corso 183)

But, along with the anger that threatened to overwhelm the youngest Miguel
sister when she encountered or remembered deliberately violent, wrong
actions directed towards herself or those she loved, there also danced an irrepressible spirit of investigation that sought to dig into the roots of those
wrong actions and into those dark spaces where anger lived to discover and
test out possibilities of reconfiguration and repair. So, while it is apparent
that Muriel Miguel's Contrary-persona was originally conceived as a creative
antidote to the destructive spirit of Miguel's rage, what has driven her throughout her artistic career is the self-same gratuitous curiosity that fuels our
nations' tricksters' transformative moments of glorious creation or senseless
destruction: "What would happen if …?" (Muriel Miguel 2007). This curiosity is as inextricably bound up in Miguel's own ceaseless fascination with and
engagement in the process of doing art and doing life as it is in her irrepressible spirit of resistance.

During this time, Gloria Miguel was also "aimlessly" beginning a new
chapter in her life—a *processual chapter*, which would be dedicated to the
search for self:

> Was I a mother? Was I a faculty wife? Was I a wife? Was I a nursery school
> teacher? I didn't really know where I was heading, because here I'd given
> my life to my husband, my kids, and I didn't do what I wanted to do. What
> do I want to do now? And so it came out—I don't know. I have to look for
> myself. I have to look. (Gloria Miguel 2007)

It is interesting to note that it was Gloria who contributed the first actual mola,
which she had acquired in 1971 during her first trip to Kuna Yala, to what
would become Spiderwoman's signature backdrop and visual metaphor of
the troupe's process. Although it is generally her younger sister Muriel who,
as the troupe's director, facilitates what she terms "organic continuity" by identifying and facilitating the development of the connecting thread-lines for
each production (Muriel Miguel 2007), Gloria was very instrumental in bringing these to birth for *Women in Violence*. Fresh from an intensive six-month
session in clown work with Bill Irwin at Oberlin, Gloria Miguel suggested the
invocation and investigation of the "inner clowns" to facilitate the artists' negotiation of the layers of violence in their lives and to afford some comic relief
during the communication of their findings (Gloria Miguel 2007).

Her own clown-persona was a fabulous creation who protected herself with a hard hat; mirrors, which covered her entire costume to reflect back to all onlookers the things they most enjoyed viewing (reflections of themselves) or to deflect negative judgment back to its issuers; and a flashlight with which she negotiated her way through darkness and uncertainty. As Gloria's clown searched the mirrored layers of her costume to "find herself," its creatrix sifted through the layers of *herstory* to find her "*self*" and discover the connections between personhood and personation: "When they call me beautiful, I say, 'Oh yes, I'm beautiful.' When they call me exotic, I say, 'Oh yes, I'm exotic.' When they call me powerful, 'Oh yes, I'm *powerful*.' So, I'm all those things but I don't know who I am. I am whatever I reflect and I have to find my *self*" (Gloria Miguel, quoted in France and Corso 180–1).

But it would be a mistake to assume that the investigation stops here; that the answer lies in the question; that the "problem" lies quite simply in one of those universal stages of liminality that occur after illness, separation, death, or divorce—those "natural shocks"—during which the affected individual begins to question who she has been and who she wants to be. Miguel's dazzling shape-shifter had, rather, *dis-covered the "unnatural shock" that had severed those natural connections between personhood and personation.* So subtle at times, it can barely be gauged and borne upon the presumption of "genteel" racism, this form of violence assaults the dignity of all Others, calling into question their very existence as human beings:

> And because we're Indian, certain things happened to us. And we all have an experience with these certain things: Like, I'd be coming up in a Museum in NYC and a woman would come up to me and say, "Oh, look at that beautiful brooch you have on." And TOUCH me! And I said to her, "Don't touch me!" And she said, "Whoa! She doesn't want me to touch her!" And the idea she had in mind is that I was a museum piece to be touched—not a human being. (Gloria Miguel 2007)

On the one hand, Gloria Miguel's bedazzling Chameleon revealed herself to be an insubstantial wisp—an illusive shape-shifter—reflecting back to curiosity-seekers the prefabricated images emblazoned on their retinas—beautiful, spiritual, exotic, erotic, powerful, earthy, or wise. On the other hand, she confronted those who gazed upon her with vital revelations explicating not only the flaws in her own design but also revealing the skewed perceptions generating skewed behavioural responses towards the Other and a dangerous propensity towards self-deception harboured by her audience. Gloria Miguel's trickster carried a vital lesson within her mirrored layers: those who gaze out complacently from beneath the gloss of "civility" and "enlightenment" may be surprised by the brutish, mawkish reflections staring complacently back at them through their own eyes. Indeed, at every turn, trickster teaches us that things are never what they seem.

Certainly, it might appear that the discovery of Lisa Mayo, an American Indian woman, beneath her disguise as the Caucasian blonde bombshell was the show's most literal explication of this lesson. But again ... things are never what they first appear to be. Muriel Miguel has stated that the unmasking of her eldest sister's clown was the "most healing" element of *Women in Violence* (Muriel Miguel 2007). In "coming out" as an Indian to herself and to the world, Mayo publicly acknowledged her relations (onstage and off) and showed solidarity to her community. She characterizes her own experience in this inaugural production as initially "frightening" (Mayo, 2007) but ultimately liberating (see France and Corso 182). In these formative stages of a new and intense professional-sibling relationship, Mayo was being forced to recognize and confront the violence with which she had grown up, and she was being forced to confront and resolve the anger that this unearthed in her:

> I remember in the beginning when I was looking for stories in *Women in Violence*, I had put stories of those experiences so far down, I said to my sister who directed the play, "Muriel, I don't have any stories like this, any stories of pain, stories of denial," and she said, "Elizabeth—" which is my real family name, I'm called Lisa Mayo which is also phony, but I'm stuck with it because I'm in all the unions with it. [Laughter.] I began to remember, it came out slowly but when it began to come out, it came out in torrents. Things I had tried not to remember ... (Mayo, quoted in France and Corso 182)

Guided by unassailable (if unfathomable) trickster logic, Mayo resolved to "take the easy way out" and to be absolutely honest as she did so (Mayo 2007). Working through exercises[8] that Muriel Miguel had brought from her own work in Open Theater, Mayo struggled to find her clown by turning herself "inside out." But, as she has been careful to clarify for me, her "Perfect Lady" was not simply a painstakingly constructed mask to obfuscate imperfect truth until Mayo's final "reveal." Mayo's whiteface *reflected the truth of her inner life*: as she puts it, she put her "thoughts and wishes on the outside" (Mayo 2007), inscribing them all upon the mask she showed the world. Inside, she hid her dark skin and her feelings around being a "dark person in America as an actress in New York City" (Mayo 2007). One might be tempted to read her mask quite simply as the material articulation of a complex and debilitating lie, engendered by the self-loathing that comes from internal colonization. But deceptively sweet-faced and soft-spoken, Mayo's mask wordlessly articulated her accusation and indictment of the dominant society and all of its constraints and injustices: "'What's the point? You have to be White in this world.' That's what I was saying" (Mayo 2007).

On the one hand, Mayo transformed herself into the mirror that confronted her audience with the reflection of its perverse and corrupted ideal: "I look the way you look and I am seeing what you see" (Mayo 2007). But, in the same moment, she turned that mirror with its flat, accusatory stare upon herself as the one who had bought into the "ideal" and embodied its soulless reflection: "What people saw is not what I saw" (Mayo 2007). In a potent exercise of poignant, self-reflexive sovereignty, Mayo performed herself performing whiteness. The outrageous humour of Mayo's onstage performance erupted from its blatant, irrepressible honesty and self-reflexive irony. In and of itself, it was an act of "ironic compromise." Homi Bhabha identifies this particular phenomenon in the calculated, self-imposed adjustments of the colonized body that mould it into conformity with the standards and models legislated by the colonizing authority to facilitate its survival in a hostile world governed by an invader (122–3); Mayo's ironic compromise, however, emanated from the studied imitation and deliberate send-up of *herself* in the throes of such mimesis. The power and poignancy of her clowning were bound up in the desperate sincerity of the original "performance" she was imitating. Mayo's offstage, original mimetic exercise had been executed with flawless precision to repair a flawed existence. Like the Winnebago trickster who disguises himself as a woman that he might marry a good provider and so live in peace and plenty (see Radin 21–3), or the Pueblo Coyote who is tempted by a gathering of Two Hearts to disguise herself as a rabbit in order to more easily capture her prey and so feed her children (see Ballinger 102–3), or the Tlingit Raven who disguises himself as an anthropological expert to *literally re-member himself* (Dauenhauer 130), Lisa Mayo had played the offstage role of a lifetime to save her own life.

Against all expectations of the "reformed, recognizable Other," who has long been imagined as an "almost-but-not-quite" copy of the colonizing original (Bhabha 122), Mayo's offstage disguise was impenetrable (Mayo, quoted in Burns and Hurlbutt 168). She "passed." But as our nations' stories teach us, the costs (to individuals and their communities) associated with denying the authentic self often outweigh the rewards of a new identity: the Winnebago trickster deserts his wife and children, leaving them to starve, and violently reconfigures his own biological "design" to bear children for another. In a horrifying twist, the Hopi trickster, a female who has adopted the shape of rabbit that she might more efficiently hunt, is devoured by her own children who do not recognize her when she is unable to reassume her own shape. There is a price to be paid for denying self: sometimes the mask sticks; sometimes the soul dies. Sometimes, to save our own lives, we must strip off the masks before they choke off the human hosts they were meant to preserve and sustain.

Mainstream scholarship largely concentrates on counter-mimetic trickster discourse as a reactionary (and/or revisionist) strategy whereby Native artists "incorporate, play back, and parody the melodramatic lexicon of [colonial] misrepresentations" (Däwes 324) to counter the colonial gaze and shatter its stereotypes. Certainly, this is an important function of trickster discourse on the contemporary stage. But the proliferation of theoretical discussions that privilege this function and thereby position the contemporary, Native trickster as solely a political respondent to the colonial narrative remould her in accordance with their authors' imagination: examined through such a lens, contemporary counter-mimetic acts become a series of predictably unpredictable responses to a need created by the forces of colonization. Trickster discourse then functions mainly as a teaching tool for non-Native audiences. Cast in this light, trickster can only play the role of the antagonist and never the protagonist. One function has become the sole function; one face has been imagined as *the* face; and trickster dances for (or in response to) a foreign invader. She is always the reactor and never the actor—always the respondent and never the initiator of discussion.

Certainly, since the publication of Rebecca Schneider's seminal and oft-quoted *The Explicit Body in Performance*, it has become common to read incidents of trickster intervention in Spiderwoman's work as reflections of reflections "showing the show, spoofing the gaze of the white" (163). But traditionally, "showing the show" is not always about "spoofing the gaze of the white"—or indeed any gaze. From a ceremonial perspective, "showing the show"—that is, revealing the mundane behind the magic—communicates a crucial teaching around patent and spiritual realities. From a traditional perspective (which is shared by Indigenous nations across Turtle Island), the material world is merely a shadowy representation of spiritual reality. The revelation of any sleight-of-hand mechanics, which might underpin representations of metaphysical phenomena, is intended not to shake belief and foster cynicism but rather to remind the People to perceive the metaphysical essence of patent reality and to value *that* over material representation. Although on the surface our contemporary tricksters may appear to be in rapt conversation with the dominant Other, these contemporary manifestations of age-old Indigenous tradition conceal their healing essence and their exercise of sovereign, proactive self-reflection and self-discovery beneath their outrageous representations of counter-discursive response.

Onstage in *Women in Violence*, in a sovereign bid to save her own offstage life, Lisa Mayo utilized counter-mimicry as a proactive intervention to reconfigure the flawed creation of her own design. She utilized her "inner clown" to deconstruct her offstage performance; in so doing, Mayo countered the violent psychic fallout of racism and the violence she had perpetrated upon herself by ultimately stripping off her whiteface and coming out to the world and to herself as an American Indian woman. She did not simply dissolve a mask to reveal the authentic. Indeed, this was not merely a "confessional" moment. Rather, Mayo had discovered a process through which to heal herself. Having utilized the Inside/Outside exercises under Muriel Miguel's guidance to access her inner clown, Mayo was, through its ministrations, able to align her own outer and inner lives. She was finally able to align patent realities with essential/spiritual realities.

As she allowed her brown skin to surface, she wiped away a formerly skewed dream of "White perfection" that had been poisoning her spirit. Offstage, as she has testified, her patent exterior had been painted with subtle hues and carefully arranged to present a manifestation of Whiteness. At times, she had tried to align her inner essence with the outward manifestation: she had joined a folk dance group and notated traditional European folk dances in her body. She had trained operatically and learned to sing in French, Italian, and German. She had married a Jewish man and converted to Judaism; later, she married a Methodist man, adopted his son, and lived in accordance with their ways. When she was first invited to a Sun Dance, she opted instead to visit Taos, New Mexico, as a tourist with her family and to observe (as an outsider) the annual Taos Corn Dance rather than participate in a traditional event, which her husband and son could not attend (Mayo 2007). She has said of this incident:

> But I was there behind the rope with the tourists; you know, out of denial. When the Pueblos began to sing, I went out of my mind. I had fantasies and everything, standing right beside my husband. He had no idea I was going through this. I was acting almost normal. But I knew that I couldn't do this again. I had to get out there and make another arrangement. I couldn't deny anything anymore. I knew where I was and why I was there. I had to rescue myself spiritually. (Mayo, quoted in Burns and Hurlbutt 182)

Onstage, Mayo was able to turn the sharp edge of counter-mimicry on herself. Donning a uniform of exaggerated whiteness, she was able to send up her own "gaze [on] the white" and the dangerous, internal "lexicon" she had authored that had necessitated her crippling self-denial in the first place.

Layering as a Performative Tool

Each of the clowns who danced through *Women in Violence* found her basis in the personal, idiosyncratic flaws of her creatrix. This riotous, performative self-confession realized an aesthetic model that is specifically tribal and specifically Kuna at two crucial levels. First, the integration of flaws into the fabric of Spiderwoman's performative mola is a key element of the company's mandate with regards to its processual aesthetics: "We take our name from Spiderwoman, the Hopi goddess of creation who was the first to create designs and teach her people to weave. In her designs a flaw was always woven in to allow her spirit to find its way out and be free" ("Method of Working—Spiderwoman Theater," NAWPA Archives). It is only when we can "find" and learn to "love" our brokenness that it becomes possible to transcend that brokenness and finally to free our spirits (Spiderwoman, quoted in Canning 94). Incidentally, it may be worth noting that, in accordance with Kuna aesthetic criteria, while patterns and motifs are generally repeated within a mola, subtle asymmetry in the finished creation is a prime requisite of excellence (Salvador 178). The flaws that some assiduously avoid for fear of compromising artistic excellence are painstakingly sought and wrought by Others *to effect artistic excellence* by weaving into their creations the potential for transcendence and transformation.

Second, the layering of a clown-persona afforded the troupe an opportunity to inhabit the mola corporeally—peeling away the layers piece by piece until the woman beneath and her connection to the stories were explicitly and powerfully revealed. To wit, when Lisa Mayo finally pares away her mask of blonde perfection, the fabric of violence is revealed, as is the hitherto unacknowledged "race layer." Diane Cartwright has written of this experience thus:

> Matching each performer with her clown I realized that some of the stories told by American Indian women had involved violence encountered in personal relationships with men. The incidents of male-inflicted violence acted out by the other women had occurred on the street or subway, in their dreams and fantasies. (5)

For Lisa Mayo, this final "reveal" allowed her to "come out [...] to the world as an Indian," just as the process of creating *Women in Violence* had allowed her to **come in** to herself by forcing her into an honest acknowledgement of and reckoning with the "tremendous" violence that she had "completely put out of [her] mind" (Mayo, quoted in Burns and Hurlbutt 169). The "perfect woman" who had denied *herstory*, denied her family, and denied her Indian-ness to breach the gates of middle-class Elysium, completed her transforma-tion by shoving a pie into her own face, as the other women on stage pelted each other with pies. Throughout her life, Lisa Mayo would never discard the "mask" of glamour—of privileged perfection. Indeed, to this very day, she carries herself with the insouciant grace of an eternally ageless diva. But the glamorous façade is cut with a healthy dose of irony, a "little wink" as it were, as if to remind us not to be too overwhelmed by the "mask," which is as "phony" as the name with which she has always identified herself to her pub-lic (see France and Corso 182).

But the slapstick humour of *Women in Violence* was not merely a "sweet-ener" to cut the bite of the troupe's anger to please and entertain even as it educated and enlightened. Nor was it simply a "weapon" with which to sur-reptitiously attack the audience; rather, as they sought the threads with which to connect the layers of a dense and intricate performative mola, Trickster—herself a single layer in the tapestry—laconically showed them the way. It started slowly with Muriel Miguel's outrageous angry "animal." But soon all the women began to weave into their stories the racist and sexist jokes they had overheard or been told or had told about them on the streets, in places of business, or at social gatherings. As the show progressed and the layers peeled away to reveal uglier and uglier truths, so the jokes intensified in bru-tality and ugliness, sharpening the edges of the design and tightening the weave. Audiences were pulled into the fabric as they performed their own com-plicity (through their laughter) and were finally locked into a face-to-face encounter with their own brokenness, with the flaws that marred their design:

> It started with "Why do Puerto Ricans wear pointy shoes? To kill cockroaches in corners." "How can you tell an Arab at the airport? He's feeding bread to the plane." Finally, as the audience was still laughing … "What's the differ-ence between a Jew and a pizza? The pizza doesn't scream when you put it in the oven." We kept smiling, it got worse, we slaughtered them. (Miguel, quoted in Canning 168)

Societal complicity and hypocrisy were further underscored by the lewd and juicy "raspberries" with which the performers answered audiences' shocked reactions to the more "unacceptable" jokes they had delivered. Articulating the Zany's thoughtful and considered evaluation of the credibility of the spectators' collective disavowal of participation in the creation, dissemina-tion, or encouragement of these verbal atrocities, Spiderwoman "slaughtered them" by adding layers of direct accusation and pointed (albeit scatalogical) demands for personal accountability, because, as Muriel Miguel put it, "people who behave this way pull back and tell you that they are kidding" (Muriel Miguel, U of T lecture, 2006). Threading the connections between these incidents of absurd, antisocial *gest* (the "raspberry"), and the more "civilized" (social) gest of Muriel Miguel's Trickster, which manifested itself in her repeated protestation, "it wasn't me, it was my tail," the troupe challenged the identity of its spectators by shattering the illusions upon which collective, complacent assertions of the "civilized" self had so comfortably rested. Tellingly, some audience members could not or would not recognize or acknowledge their position—*our* position—in the deadly design that emerged from beneath *Women in Violence*'s layers of "humour," racism, and violence. Illustrative of this sad truth is the response of a prominent female theatre practitioner who, after seeing the show, suggested to Muriel Miguel that she substitute the climactic Jew/pizza joke with a Polish joke (Canning 168).

The personal tricksters accessed by the Miguel sisters to navigate them through their initial investigations around violence and women have followed them throughout Spiderwoman's tenure on the world stage, shape-shifting and altering tactics with the shifting tenor of each investigation. During the performance of these investigations undertaken by the Miguel sisters and their collaborators throughout the decades, there have been as many Tricksters dancing on Spiderwoman's stages as there have been women to articulate their stories. What excites me so about these transformative agents who pop up throughout Spiderwoman's works is that these are neither amorphous shadows nor mythic archetypes inhabiting the margins in splendid singularity to affect the patent business of life. Rather, these comprise a feminine-plural spirit, accessible to and embodied within the first person. These are not picturesque or picaresque metaphors. They do not evoke or pretend particular authority over "traditionalism." Rather, each one of Spiderwoman's "inner clowns" presents herself as an unapologetic, living embodiment of the loud, lewd contemporary female who is wandering "aimlessly," looking for something and savouring the process. As is true of the more recognizable (or "accessible," since s/he has been so oft-documented and discussed) tribal trickster, she is both buffoon and culture hero. But she does not stand apart from her human host(ess), self-consciously marking herself as a singular and distinct entity. Indeed, her interventions in *Women in Violence* (and throughout Spiderwoman's subsequent productions) orchestrate the dissolution of the liminal point between the mortal woman and this metaphysical Other.

At the end of *Women in Violence*, as the women assertively communicate their hard-won self-acceptance and newfound understanding of self in relationship with community, the trappings of the "inner clown" are not entirely stripped away from the public woman, as if to signify a distinction between mundane reality and heightened mythos, between victim and victor, or between comic buffoonery and human dignity. Throughout the final scenes— "Revolution" and the reinvocation of Wallace Black Elk's Plea for Peace and Unity—the outer signifiers of the inner clown remain more or less intact and part of the human actor, albeit a little the worse for wear and for pie filling. She and "She" have found each other; the layers have been connected; and it is impossible to denote where self ends and Other begins: "Even at the end, it didn't matter what we were wearing at that point in *Women in Violence*. In the revolution, woman is equal" (Muriel Miguel 2007).

As she works with and through the artists of Spiderwoman Theater, she teaches us who we are not, and she shows us how to *do* life, so that we may become who we were meant to be. In these contemporary spaces, disordered by silent siege, she brings us the "pipe" and leads us through the ceremonies she has remembered or discovered or concocted in the course of her investigations. These rites, undertaken on contemporary stages across the globe, carry the power to write artist and spectator into humans who are fully being and doing, to heal our brokenness, and, in so doing, to right our lives and our interrelationships. "Aimless" she may be—immoderate, outrageous, inappropriate, irrepressible, and tactless—yet she is no mere reactor, set into motion by the colonizer's narrative, dancing to his tune and saving all of her best quips for him. No—she is that one who weaves her people firmly into the aesthetic and philosophical traditions that inform the construction of Mythos from within our families, our clans, our communities, and our nations. She is that one who has storied us into our humanity from the beginning of the beginning of the beginning.

Notes

1   Lois Weaver's clown-character for *Women in Violence* emerged as a Bag Lady who was placed in the audience from the top of the show. While this description of a performance night in 1976 is largely constructed from my imaginings, the characterization of the audience and its reactions to Weaver's character remain true to the account shared with me by Muriel Miguel on 27 August 2007 in New York City during a personal interview.

2   I do not mean to suggest, fabricate, or explore an outright parallelism here between the transformative agents (tricksters/culture-heroes) of tribal tradition

and the clownish culture-heroes of European tradition or western pop culture. However, it is worth noting that even those figures foreign to tribal tradition—particularly those disseminated through popular media—fulfill a pedagogical function for their viewers, which, as one-dimensional as it may be, bears some similarity of effect and objective to the functioning of the trickster-figures in Native discourse. In their immoderate appetites and behaviours and gratuitous acts of creative generosity or self-destruction, denizens of the societies to which they are contemporary see themselves reflected in all their beauty and ugliness and learn something of what it is to be a "human doing" in their world—the world they have created, the world they are creating. It is important to remember that we (as colonized peoples), along with our children, often gaze into these "mirrors" that mainstream society holds up to itself and are often subtly and profoundly affected by the "reflections" that gaze back at us. It is particularly important to consider this when we consider the lessons they carry. This mainstream culture-hero may be bumbling, stupid, greedy, and destructive, but he is never more so than the community that surrounds him: generally, he is a stupid, ugly being surrounded by a community of even stupider and uglier beings. Laughter at his antics is always a signifier of audience approbation—as if to say, "Yes, that is exactly what I have done/would do." Such laughter is born of a different spirit than the laughter that denotes teasing (albeit unmistakable) disapproval with which Native observers greet inappropriate behavior in either culture-heroes, children who have not yet learned better, or contrary adults. This points to the significant differences between cultures that glorify the individual and the assertion of individual identity apart from the masses of the "great unwashed" and cultures in which individual identity is unrealizable apart from the community of which the individual is an integral part.

Part of the work that belongs to the sovereign reclamation of the Indigenous self is bound up in our engagement with these reflections, particularly with those that seem at first glance to be the most removed from us (or from which we feel ourselves to be at the greatest remove). But this discussion, perhaps, would be best left to another time and place.

3   Anishinaabe writer Lenore Keeshig-Tobias, who with Tomson Highway and Daniel David Moses co-founded the Committee to Re-establish the Trickster, has articulated her own approach to the craft of story-making as a headlong dive into the chaos [wrought by colonization] to "try to find a new order in it" (Keeshig-Tobias, quoted in Moses 47).

4   Gerald Vizenor, who has coined this term, explains that survivance denotes "an active sense of presence, the continuance of native stories, not a mere reaction, or a survivable name. [As such,] Native survivance stories are renunciations of dominance, tragedy, and victimry" (vii).

5   *Women and Violence* began as a collective project by four artists: the Miguel sisters with Lois Weaver. Later, Pam Verge and Nadja Beye joined the troupe, created their clowns, and wove these with their stories into the show.

6   I borrow this term from Jace Weaver. He has created this term as a crucible in which "community" and "activism" are fused into one ideological phenomenon. All works that promote or effect active and ongoing service to the Native commu-

nity and the larger community beyond that are "communitist" in his estimation: "[To] promote communitist values means to participate in the healing of the grief and the sense of exile felt by Native communities and the pained individuals in them" (Weaver 43). Although the Miguel sisters own their responsibility to their artistry and artistic methodology, with Spiderwoman Theater they have created a communitist project, thereby extending their responsibility to communities beyond the purview of the biological family, artistic family, studio, or stage.

Women in Violence was autobiography transformed through process into a story that spoke to women across the globe. So it is no great marvel that after a performance at the One World Festival of Theatre, an audience member was inspired to tell the Miguel sisters her own story. She had been brutally beaten in the streets by an inebriated thug. And although her attacker had been apprehended by the police and identified by her, he had been released with no penalty (Canning 96). Outraged by her plight, the Miguel sisters told her story night after night during festival performances, solicited their audiences for ideas, and organized a mass demonstration at which they performed and at which, because of their intervention, feminist groups across the French provinces were able to network and mobilize (Canning 96).

Since this time, the Miguel sisters have continued their communitist projects, facilitating talking circles and workshops, developing the political and artistic voices of children with the American Indian AIDS Task Force, and offering up the Storyweaving Process (through workshops) as a tool for Native peoples to generate art, honest dialogue, and healing.

7   Domitila DeLeón de Fernandez and Oswaldo DeLeón Kantule, "*Mola makke*— Making *Molas*," workshop at the Textile Museum of Canada, Toronto, 16 June 2007.

8   Three decades after the fact, the artists of Spiderwoman are not always able to enumerate all of the exercises that went into the creation of their characters. But it is likely that, along with CR (consciousness raising) sessions at the table and regular drills in "Transformations," which is a foundational exercise in the Storyweaving Workshops of Muriel Miguel and Monique Mojica, a combination of Joseph Chaikin's "Odets' Kitchen" with his "Perfect People" exercise would have lent themselves specifically to the creation of Lisa Mayo's clown persona. Lisa Mayo has stated that, guided by Muriel, she accessed her clown through the Odets' Kitchen—or "inside/outside"—exercise (Mayo 2007). This calls upon actors to first manifest exterior behaviour and then find a way to exteriorize the inner life beneath that. The "Perfect People" exercise, by contrast, deals solely with surface behaviour, and calls upon actors to choose icons of perfection (from media representations) and to improvise the events of their ongoing perfect lives after the movie, commercial, or magazine spread has ended. For further information, Robert Pasolli's *A Book on the Open Theatre* provides a detailed account of each of these exercises, and of Chaikin's exercises in transformation through sound and movement.

Works Cited

Ballinger, Franchot. *Living Sideways: Tricksters in American Indian Oral Traditions.* Norman: U of Oklahoma P, 2004.

Beaucage, Marjorie. "Strong and Soft: Excerpts from a Conversation with Muriel Miguel." *Canadian Theatre Review* 68 (Fall 1991): 5–8.

Bhabha, Homi K. *The Location of Culture.* 1994. Rpt. New York: Routledge, 2005.

Burns, Judy, and Jerri Hurlbutt. "Secrets: A Conversation with Lisa Mayo of Spiderwoman Theater." In *Women and Performance: A Journal of Feminist Theory* 5:2 (1992): 166–83.

Canadian Theatre Review 68 (Fall 1991). Special Issue. Ed. Monique Mojica. 51–3.

Canning, Charlotte. *Feminist Theaters in the U.S.A.: Staging Women's Experience.* London: Routledge, 1996.

Cartwright, Diane. "Spiderwoman Theatre Workshop: Women in Violence." *Alternative Theater* 1:3 (January 1976): 5.

Dauenhauer, Nora Marks. *Life Woven with Song.* Tucson: U of Arizona P, 2000.

Däwes, Birgit. *Native North American Theater in a Global Age: Sites of Identity Construction and Transdifference.* Heidelberg: Unversitätsverlag Winter, 2007.

France, Anna Kay, and P.J. Corso, eds. *International Women Playwrights: Voices of Identity and Transformation—Proceedings of the First International Women Playwrights Conference, October 18–23, 1988.* Metuchen, NJ: Scarecrow, 1993.

Grande, Sandy. *Red Pedagogy: Native American Social and Political Thought.* New York: Rowman & Littlefield, 2004.

Mayo, Lisa. Personal interview. New York City. 28 August 2007.

Miguel, Gloria. Personal interview. New York City. 26 August 2007.

Miguel, Muriel. Distinguished Lecture Series, University of Toronto. 13 November 2006.

———. Personal interview. New York City. 27 August 2007.

Moses, Daniel David. *Pursued by a Bear: Talks, Monologues and Tales.* Toronto: Exile Editions, 2005.

Native American Women Playwrights' Archives (NAWPA). King Library, Miami University, Oxford, Ohio. Accessed February 2007.

Pasolli, Robert. *A Book on the Open Theatre.* New York: Bobbs-Merrill, 1970.

Preston, Jennifer. "Weesageechak Begins to Dance: Native Earth Performing Arts Inc." *The Drama Review: A Journal of Performance Studies* 36:1 (Spring 1992): 135–59.

Radin, Paul. *The Trickster: A Study in American Indian Mythology.* 1956. Rpt. New York: Schocken, 1972.

Salvador, Mari Lyn. "Looking Back: Contemporary Kuna Women's Arts." In *The Art of Being Kuna: Layers of Meaning Among the Kuna of Panama.* Ed. Mari Lyn Salvador. Los Angeles: UCLA Fowler Museum of Cultural History, 1997. 151–211.

Schneider, Rebecca. *The Explicit Body in Performance.* New York: Routledge, 1997.

Treuer, David. *Native American Fiction: A User's Manual.* Saint Paul, MN: Graywolf, 2006.

Vizenor, Gerald. *Manifest Manners: Narratives on Postindian Survivance.* Lincoln: U of Nebraska P, 1994.

Weaver, Jace. *That the People Might Live: Native American Literatures and Native American Community.* New York: Oxford UP, 1997.

CHRISTINE KIM

Diasporic Violences, Uneasy Friendships, and The Kappa Child

In a landmark essay, "Against the Lures of Diaspora," Rey Chow demands self-reflexivity from critics working on Chinese cultural material and asks that diasporic critics make clear their self-interested positioning vis-à-vis China. The essay concludes with a warning that:

> Any attempt to deal with "women" or the "oppressed classes" in the "third world" that does not at the same time come to terms with the historical conditions of its own articulation is bound to repeat the exploitativeness that used to and still characterizes most "exchanges" between "West" and "East." Such attempts will also be expediently assimilated within the plenitude of the hegemonic establishment, with all the rewards that that entails. No one can do without some such rewards. What one can do without is the illusion that, through privileged speech, one is helping to save the wretched of the earth. (119)

The diasporic critic may be tempted to conflate her position with those in China and speak from a minoritized position, but this tendency overlooks the very significant symbolic and material differences between those located overseas and those in China. Chow urges diasporic critics to be conscious of the relative privilege they possess and the hegemonic positions they occupy, and underlines the need for this cultural capital to be used responsibly: "not merely to speak as exotic minors, but to fight the crippling effects of Western imperialism and Chinese paternalism at once" (114).

Chow's castigating comments about diasporic critics may seem like an odd place to begin an essay about trickster figures, but her urging of intellectuals to take seriously their ethical responsibilities is one that I want to try to heed in this paper. At the same time, Chow's reminder that those of us linked to the Asian diaspora must be conscious of "the historical conditions" of our articulations is also a useful way to enter into a conversation about the relations between diasporic and First Nations communities in Canada. After hearing Hiromi Goto give a reading from *The Kappa Child* in my first-year English course, Deanna Reder approached me with the idea of writing a paper for this collection of essays on the trickster, and it was one that, I admit, simultaneously intrigued and alarmed me. The question of how to write a contribution about the kappa, a creature from Japanese folklore, for a collection largely about Indigenous tricksters forced me to begin seriously considering the ethical and political responsibilities of Asian diasporic communities in Canada, and, more specifically, those responsibilities towards First Nations communities. In the end, I agreed, in part because Deanna's enthusiasm for this project was contagious, but also because the editors' goal of revisiting previous trickster representations that "conceal the colonial violence that has been enacted upon First Nations cultures, even in claiming to draw attention to these cultures" (their "call for papers") is clearly an important one. And because I believe that Goto's novel—in its writing about the encounters between the unnamed narrator, a Nisei or second-generation Japanese Canadian, with a kappa—draws attention to issues about history, the occupation of land, and the nature of knowledge, all of which are pertinent to this consideration of imperial damage and tricksters.

Forced Occupations, Unwilling Migrations

For fairly self-evident reasons, diasporic studies often demonstrate a preoccupation with issues of movement, migration, and (dis)location. Goto's novel returns us to this familiar ground but asks that it be tread with a somewhat different set of destinations in mind. Early on in the novel, the narrator makes the trek back to her parents' home, somewhere vaguely southeast of Lethbridge, Alberta, for Easter. The return to her childhood, enacted literally through the drive back from Calgary, is replayed symbolically during the disastrous holiday dinner. When the narrator's father erupts in a fit of rage over a minor mishap, the responses of the four sisters and their mother make it clear that the father is not the only one trapped in a "pattern so ingrained he can't stop" (27). The narrator's three sisters respond by fleeing the scene and bursting into angry tears, the mother by passively enduring the spectacle and the narrator by cleaning up the remnants of the dinner her mother toiled to prepare while thinking to herself that, although the girls have now grown into adulthood, their return to their parents' house com-pels them to "slip into our childhood roles. No one is exempt. Until death do us part" (28).

The text returns repeatedly to this pessimistic view of being unable to escape the violent patterns that characterize the past, on the levels of family interactions, painful friendships, and national history, perhaps in hopes of disproving the narrator's claim. The narrator's sense of being assailed by the forces of history is unsurprising given the way the domestic dramas of the family replay the injustices inflicted upon the Japanese-Canadian community during the Second World War. The family's move from British Columbia to the interior of Alberta, while not made as part of the Japanese-Canadian internment, mirrors that historical moment of the forced migration of thousands of individuals. The oppressive terms of these relocations are conveyed through the experiences of the sisters. Finding themselves stuck on an unwelcoming plot of land in the unrelentingly stifling heat, the girls are unable even to complain about the situation. Instead, they choke back their unhappiness and force themselves to eat pieces of fried chicken that their father has brought back from town. The allegorical implications of the narrator's concerted efforts to swallow the distasteful drumsticks, the "two disgusting legs, the gristly white threads growing like tapeworms in [her] stomach," without crying openly before her family members are clear for the many Japanese Canadians who quietly endured the internment (36).[1]

The historical internment is explicitly invoked as a key intertext during a conversation between the father and the local motel owner shortly after the family has arrived in their new hometown. The tense exchange between these men underlines the complicated politics of arrival that mark the family's location within rural Alberta, as well as Asian communities more broadly situated within the dominant narrative of national identity. The motel owner, in an attempt to be hospitable, expresses his disagreement with the government's internment policies but is rebuffed by the father's loud anger:

> "I always thought it was terrible what was done to you people."
> Which ones? I thought. Which ones does he think we are?
> "What you say?" Dad took a quick step toward the gulping man.
> Okasan raised one hand but it dropped heavily beside her body.
> "No offense intended," Motel Man stammered. "I figured you folks to be Japanese."
> "We are CANADIAN!" Dad roared.
> "No need," Okasan nervously plucked Dad's sleeve. "No need to shout," she murmured.
> Swinging arc of arm. Smack. A hand-shaped stain on my mother's cheek, the color of pain and humiliation. (70)

The father's violent response, spurred on by the motel owner's liberal sympathies but received by the mother, is clearly a rejection of a narrative of Canadian identity that excludes racialized bodies. It is, after all, precisely this sentiment that enabled the government to carry out and profit from its devastating internment policies. But in this dismissal of the motel owner's comment for interpellating the family as Japanese rather than Canadian, the father also utterly refuses to be read through the historical lens of Japanese-Canadian struggles. By prohibiting this conversation, the father effectively shuts down discussions about the legacies of institutionalized practices of discrimination aimed at Japanese Canadians and other racialized bodies, and refuses to acknowledge the troubling terrain the contemporary moment is perched upon. In this way, the father's lashing out at the mother as a response to his dissatisfaction with liberal sentiments warns us of the dangers of ignoring history.

The father's attempts to cultivate the family's plot of land in Alberta as rice fields further underscores the perils of neglecting history.[2] The narrator and her sisters are forced to steal water from their neighbours to feed their father's "rice-growing obsession," a task that takes a toll on their bodies and psyches (197). By refusing to acknowledge the arid reality of the Albertan landscape, the father constructs it as both inhospitable and a space to be conquered. While tilling the land much like an indentured labourer, the narrator recognizes that long ago, "the prairie was just an ancient ocean" (181). She is, however, alone in her epiphany as her father reasserts his efforts to colonize the land through the migrant labour of his family and to realize his vision of the present moment. The seemingly arbitrary nature of this aspiration, when coupled with the merciless implementation of the plan, translates into despair for the children:

> No one knew what compelled our father to try and grow Japanese rice in Alberta. No one knew what we were doing in boxcars disguised as a motel. No one knew how long we had to stay there. No one knew.
> What we did know was that no one would save us. (114)

And it is this unremitting despair that threatens to be the most overwhelming of all forces.

One of the narrator's few saving graces during her childhood is her friendship with a neighbour, Gerald Nakamura Coming Singer, who lives with his Japanese-Canadian mother, Janice. Despite the pleasure she feels while in Gerald's company, the narrator finds herself hurling cruel words at her friend after a particularly grueling episode of digging to steal the Snyders' water. Gerald appears on the scene just as the narrator is feeling despondent over her lack of escape routes. She realizes that "[g]oing to white out-siders wasn't an option for an Asian immigrant family like us. If you ditched the family, there was absolutely nothing left. When you are ten, something is better than nothing, even if something has a hand faster than the words forming in your head, let alone in your mouth" (199). In a scene that strongly resembles the earlier episode between the father and the motel owner, Ger-ald's offering of compassion and comfort is rejected as the narrator feels a "hateful coil of ugliness twisting in my gut, the words stinging something inside me, but unable to stop" (200). Upon ending this friendship, the nar-rator is met with words of praise from her father: "'Good for you,' my father nodded approvingly. 'Shouldn't be friends with weaklings'" (201). Respond-ing to her frustration with many things, including a recognition of how her father's impossible dreams have both distorted his humanity and caused similar effects in herself, the narrator turns her face up to "[t]he fat sun ris-ing keen and relentless, [and howls] until [her] mouth was parched and cracked" (201). Her despair, which cannot be articulated through conven-tional speech or through familiar narratives, understandably leaves her father feeling quite confused.

This painful episode with Gerald, however, is not the only occasion in which the narrator finds herself emulating her father. The narrator describes her complicated relationship with her father and states in a moment of hon-est vulnerability that "[i]t isn't like *I* feel an overwhelming surge of affection whenever I think of our father, but, I don't know, an emotion I can't name stays small and silent in the depths of my heart. I can't cut off my feelings from him, my monster, my hero" (245). And, earlier in the novel, when she is exhausted after long shifts at work, the narrator thinks that she may need a new vehicle "[l]ike my dad['s]!" (184). This transmission of violence and despair between generations makes the task of reconciling with historical injustices incredibly difficult. As an adult, the narrator returns to the child-hood home and demands reparation from her father for the pain he has caused her sisters, her mother, and herself. After literally choking an apol-ogy out of her father, the narrator is shocked by her own actions and forced to admit that what she longs for, "[s]omething that will erase the past, right all wrongs, so we can be whole creatures again," does not exist (260). Indeed, any resolution that seeks to place the entire burden upon the father with-out implicating the narrator is perhaps as impossible a fantasy as Albertan rice fields.

The book begins by implicating the narrator within a neo-colonial land-scape littered with the signs of commodity culture. Indeed, she introduces her-self to the reader in the first line of the text by stating that "I am a collector of abandoned shopping carts" (9). By profession, the narrator is one who collects debris from the urban landscape and reclaims that which has been discarded and forgotten. And yet, despite her function as one who reinte-grates neglected elements of capitalist culture, recycling past products into the present, the narrator tells us that, once she has realized it is Easter and therefore time for the family reunion, she would "rather go on collecting the lost carts than make the pilgrimage home" (10). The marked preference for inhabiting her current role as an extension of commodity culture in the contemporary moment instead of returning to the difficult landscape of parental homes and histories depicts the ongoing work of colonial conquest. The connection between past and present activities and the troubling posi-tions of father and daughter are made explicit in an early description of the holiday: "This weekend is a long one, and the business shuffle turned into a mass exodus for the markets. Instead of bidding for pipes, steel cables, real estate, and crude oil, human suits are clamoring in long lineups for carcasses of meat, fowl, and the limbs of large mammals" (9). This passage then ren-ders visible the doubled meaning of the word "occupation," as both profes-sion and colonization of land, and the interconnections that run through this novel. Any return to the past implicitly requires a consideration of the spatial dimensions of that existence and the problems of occupation, position-ing, and territory—and, in this way, ultimately asks for a consideration of the contiguous and often overlapping existences of Asian diasporic and First Nations communities in Canada.

Contiguous Tricksters

Towards the end of the narrative, the narrator finds herself off duty and driv-ing through the downtown area of Calgary. It is a moment of desolation, both in terms of the cityscape and the narrator's emotional state. She looks at the empty urban core and thinks,

> Abandoned, I can imagine a post-apocalyptic world of crumbling concrete, the struggle for clean water. Or maybe, when humans are gone, our myths will come alive, wander over the remnants of our uncivilization. Kappa, water dragons, yama-uba, oni. Selkie, golem, lorelei, xuan wu. The creatures we carry will be born from our demise and the world will dream a new existence. (223)

Hers is a vision that disrupts conventional understandings of the present as civilized. She dreams instead of a future born from the bowels of the contem-porary moment in which global mythologies are able to coexist. This simultaneously utopic and dystopic vision suggests that cultural stories may be able to teach us how to construct more hospitable futures. At the same time, this post-apocalyptic vision also asks us to consider how such stories and those who tell these tales are located within landscapes.

As a child, the narrator remembers one year when her father was actually successful in his rice-growing endeavour. For once, the prairies received an abundance of rain and the rice flourished, a spectacle their neighbour Janice called an "unnatural sight" (227). It is also the same summer that the narrator spotted kappa footprints in the muddy rice fields. The footprints suggest "a gleeful creature had ran jubilantly over every inch of the amazing wetness, jumping, leaping, dancing, stepping exquisite toes, perfectly webbed," and this sense of joy spreads to both the narrator's father and mother when they behold the marks (228). Upon seeing the traces of the kappa, the father becomes visibly softer and more human, but also wonders to himself: "But how?" he murmured, "in this country, this climate? Where would it have come from? Emigrated like us?" (229). The question of how a Japanese kappa comes to exist in Blackfoot territory, southeast of Lethbridge, somewhere between the Oldman River and the Milk River, is never resolved for the father, and the possibility that it, like the family, might have emigrated is never one that he entertains seriously. The aridity of the prairies suggests that the Albertan landscape would be hostile for the kappa, given its distinctive dependency on water. The narrator describes the difficulty of obtaining water for the rice fields in other years because the two nearby rivers are both distant and inadequate sources with "Old Man River flowing sluggish brown north of us and the Milk River, chocolate, winding too far south" (126). And yet, the kappa clearly is able to exist and bestow good fortune upon others in this Canadian landscape.

Perhaps, then, the more pressing question raised by the kappa is not, as the father asks, how did it arrive here, but instead, how does it manage to flourish while others like the narrator's family struggle to exist? The answer to this problem seems to lie in the relationship that each has to the local space. When the narrator comments on the coincidence of the successful rice crop and the sighting of the kappa that year, she contemplates the possibility that

> Okasan's and Dad's good-luck kappa must have left some green goodness behind, despite all my pooh-poohing and cynical comments. We had an incredible crop, handpicked in the old-fashioned way, and each grain so sweet it flooded our mouths with juicy longing.
> Dad's one and only ever rice crop. Something he wouldn't get over for the rest of his life.

> But we were thankful, that year, that summer, and at Christmas, I received a diving watch that could withstand water pressure up to fifty meters. Me inwardly snorting, when the hell had I ever gone diving? Where would I go that was fifty meters deep? Milk Chocolate River perhaps? The Old Man? But I was touched, all the same, and wore the gift constantly. Sending thanks to a questionable creature from a different clime. A creature much greener than Santa. (231)

Throughout the text, the narrator constantly meanders through Blackfoot territory, but fails to recognize it as such. For instance, she refers repeatedly to Naapi, the Old Man, without ever realizing that the river's name comes from Blackfoot legends about this land. The difference between the kappa and Santa/Naapi is described in terms of degrees of greenness rather than as absolute difference, but the narrator never seems to realize fully the implications of her insight.[3] And, while Gerald's narrative echoes and overlaps with the narrator's in multiple interesting ways, especially given his own displacement once his parents part ways, these intersections completely elude the narrator's attention. When Gerald's father decides to return to the Blood reserve, Gerald is left in limbo. His mother Janice notes that "Gerald didn't want to go with him and he didn't want to stay with me. So now's all he got is attitude" (163). Given the timeline of the novel, it is likely that Gerald would be without Native status and therefore unable, even if he had wanted, to accompany his father to the reserve.[4] Gerald's eventual relocation to Vancouver to live with his aunt reverses the migration pattern of the narrator while remaining shaped by the paternalistic authority of the Canadian government.

Fixated on surviving her own childhood, the narrator's unhappiness prevents her from seeing the rich history of the Albertan space around her and from making connections with others. By explicitly linking the family's move to the prairies with the Japanese-Canadian internment, the novel implicitly draws upon the dominant perception of the interior as empty land, filled only with abandoned mining and other ghost towns. The language of national security mobilized by the government during the Second World War becomes a way of allowing the government to appropriate property and strip people of their citizenship rights while also forcing Japanese Canadians to participate in a colonial myth of unoccupied territory. The relocation is perceived as emptying the west coast of Japanese Canadians to protect the nation, all without inconveniencing anyone else. Thus, when the narrator as a ten-year-old child takes her shovel to the land in order to try to produce the rice paddies her father demands, she engages in a violent relationship with the land, but this repetition is more complicated than previous settlement narratives that deliberately neglected Indigenous presences. Although the narrator's participation within this framework is clearly coerced, this factor does not make her speech or actions any less damaging in either the past or present tense. The transplantation of the rice, with the exception of that one year when it flourishes, represents an impossible set of cultural relations that operate through imposition and ahistoricism, and that radically differ from those embodied by the kappa. The migration of the Japanese kappa then gives us a way of imagining harmonious coexistences that do not resort to strategies of colonial violence. The kappa's ability to live alongside Blackfoot tricksters without claiming the social imagination in absolute terms opens up ways of reading the intersecting narratives of Japanese-Canadian internment, the family's relocation to the prairies, and the ongoing displacement of the indigenous inhabitants.

Cultural Baggage

Intersecting with these traumatic childhood memories and descriptions of collecting shopping carts are the narrator's intimate encounters with a mysterious Stranger. She describes the Stranger she meets at a wedding banquet in Chinatown as "beautiful beyond belief" at first and then later, upon closer scrutiny, as having "an oddly shaped head, strands of thin hair hanging long and limp.... In the strange glow of the streetlight, the Stranger's complexion looked almost olive" (85). These shifting appearances are initially easily explained as the result of distance and lighting, but take on increasing significance when the Stranger's appearance shifts again. The narrator and the Stranger head to the tarmac of the Calgary airport to watch the lunar eclipse, but find themselves wrestling Japanese-style. When disrobing, a necessary prerequisite according to the Stranger, the narrator realizes that "the Stranger looked almost greenish, skin hairless and moist" (122). As the Stranger turns to face the narrator, she says she "could only gaze with wonder. No nipples. Nor a bellybutton" (122). This sumo tori, intensely physical contact, has significant consequences for the narrator. When she manages to wrestle the Stranger to the ground and accidentally knocks off her hat to reveal "a strangely shaped head," the narrator describes how "something cool-wet spilled, covered me in a liquid sweetness. I thought she came. Came in waves of pleasure" (124). This extensive and intimate physical contact has significant consequences, but not ones that the narrator could have imagined or is able to understand. Although she believes that this act has impregnated her, despite realizing how such a condition would contradict the fundamentals of human biology, the reader is encouraged to interpret this encounter and the idea of pregnancy slightly differently. The description of the Stranger as green, with a bowl-shaped head filled with water, and as able to shift forms, makes it clear that the narrator's wrestling partner is a kappa. Although the narrator's sense of being literally pregnant is never completely confirmed or refuted, the text also introduces a metaphorical reading of her condition. The splash of liquid that the narrator interprets as an orgasm is also the source of life for the kappa. Without it, the consequences are unbearable:

> *And when kappa despair, when their green skin grows dry and brittle, when kappa eyes succumb to pain, when kappa parents turn aside their kappa children, when kappa deny water, they rip the tender skin from between their fingers and toes. They rip their water bowl from atop their noble heads. They tear off their turtle shells and expose their flesh to the sun. They turn their eyes away from all things kappa.*
>
> *They become humans.* (176, emphasis in original)

The kappa's willingness to have her water bowl spilled allows for a moment of intense vulnerability and intimacy. The life that the narrator then feels growing inside her can also be read as the planting of hope. The encounters with the kappa serve to educate the narrator about the connections between pleasure, intimacy, and regeneration.

But the kappa's lessons are neither simple nor easy to learn, and this difficulty is illustrated by an exchange between the kappa and the narrator that occurs towards the end of the novel. After stumbling upon two of her sisters having lunch together, the narrator sits down with them and is surprised by who her sisters have become. She realizes that each of her sisters, Slither, PG, and Mice, have grown out of their childhood selves and are no longer people with whom she is familiar. Her ongoing worries about PG's safety, the narrator thinks to herself, have been "nothing but the reflections of my own sorry circumstances and I really need a kick in the butt" (245). This epiphany highlights how much more self-aware the narrator has become. Slither's gift of a beautician's business card leaves the narrator feeling "[e]xasperated, annoyed, and also touched for her way of expressing concern," a response that is markedly different from her earlier angry reactions (246). This increasing willingness to accept her sister's affections are encouraged by the kappa, who suddenly reappears in the restaurant's washroom after a prolonged absence in the narrator's life. Instead of beginning by discussing the narrator's pregnancy, for which the kappa is somehow partially responsible, the kappa encourages the narrator to visit the hairstylist, stating, "We don't come from a Samsonite culture" (247). The narrator responds by retorting, "[t]hat's a suitcase company!" (247). Without providing any significant insight into the narrator's possibly pregnant condition, but extolling the pleasures of visiting a barbershop, the kappa then vanishes.

I find this exchange between the narrator and the kappa provocative for the misreading that the narrator commits, but also for the misreading that she does not commit. The narrator finds the kappa's comment ludicrous because her immediate referent for the term "Samsonite" is the Japanese luggage maker. In this way, she implies that the company's description of its corporate vision to "transform itself into a leading global lifestyle travel company," and presumably to become synonymous with travel, has achieved a level of success that surely surpasses even the corporation's initial hopes. The kappa's intention seems to have been to invoke the Christian story of Samson's betrayal by his lover Delilah and the subsequent loss of his strength when his hair was shorn. Although there are potentially interesting ways of interpreting that missed reference, I am more intrigued by a third layer of meaning that is overlooked. Despite the multiple lawsuits filed in Alberta by various Cree bands (including the Samson Cree, whose claims were worth billions of dollars) during the late 1980s and early 1990s, a period of much legal action that intersects with the timeline of this novel, the narrator does not make the connection between the kappa's words and the land claims.[5] The narrator's instinctive association of "Samsonite" with the corporation suggests that her narrative, a *Bildungsroman* of sorts, is nestled between at least two other epistemological frameworks. That she does not catch the Biblical allusion might imply a certain shift away from the settler ideology that she had embraced earlier (a connection made explicit through her childhood obsession with Laura Ingalls and *Little House on the Prairie*), but the narrator's inability to connect the term "Samsonite" to the ongoing land claims, even then later to reject the link as a misreading, suggests that it is not easy to unlearn colonial ideologies. This (mis)understanding occurs towards the end of the text rather than the beginning, which underscores the impossibility of reading Goto's novel as a successful novel of kappa education. The narrator's understanding of the Samsonite reference then becomes a moment that gestures the reader's attention to the difficulties of working through one's cultural baggage in all the senses of that term.

The kappa's response to the narrator's dismissive comment, "We don't come from a Samsonite culture," is to state, "You're not listening" (247). The narrator's sense of being overwhelmed by her own pain and complicated family history leaves her wondering, "When do memories lose their power? There must be an expiry date. Maybe PG's choice of physical distance isn't such a bad idea. Maybe PG's family baggage is still in heaps in the

downstairs bedroom, cluttering the floor until Okasan finally boxes it up"
(171). Instead of connecting to others who also feel hurt by their realities,
the narrator's experiences serve to isolate her from the larger social world.
This Samsonite exchange, then, has significant implications, given that the
narrator's inability to listen, a condition diagnosed by the kappa, occurs precisely at the moment when the narrator is the most receptive she has ever been
throughout the entire text. If, after all of this work that has been undertaken
by the kappa, the narrator, and her sisters, she still cannot hear, then what
possibilities exist for undoing colonial violence?

The novel reminds us that there are differences between the narrator
and her father, and that it is possible to work towards the closing of past
injuries once the extent of those wounds has been understood. Historical
pain, in this novel, is experienced by all parties; the father is certainly not
exempt. His nostalgic efforts to grow rice—"All he knew was that we needed
water to make the flooded soft mud of his childhood thought-place, years
disremembered and half a world away"—speak to a sense of urban dislocation as an adult in Japan as well as to displacement in rural Alberta (126–7).
It is, however, his desire to create a past long gone without being conscious
of the price extorted by it from those in the present moment that translates
into material and symbolic violence. Consequently, the narrator is left burdened by historical pain, but is also being given an opportunity to address
these fractured narratives. Her friendship with Gerald introduces her to
ongoing attempts at dialogue and companionship between Asian Canadian
and First Nations communities, and, as the narrator's description of her first
visit to Gerald's home makes clear, opens up the possibility of entering into
this conversation for her:

> Gerald Nakamura Coming Singer was incomprehensible. In Laura Ingalls'
> book-world, Indians meant teepees on the prairies and that was that. Indians
> didn't equal someone who was both Blood and Japanese-Canadian. Indians
> certainly never meant someone who lived next door on a chicken farm.
>
> "Call me Janice," she croaked and thumped me on my arm, when I called
> Gerald's mom, Mrs. Nakamura Coming Singer.
>
> I eye-glanced at Gerald's face for signs. Flipping from his face to his
> mother's, searching for where the ancestry bled into more Japanese and less
> Indian, but I couldn't tell, and only stared with my pea-sized eyes until Jan-
> ice noticed.
>
> "Whatchya staring at, kiddo? You never seen a First Nations person
> before?"
>
> "First Nations?"

"Yeah, kiddo. Don't cut me any of the 'Indian' crap, how they keep teaching that shit in school, I'll never understand!" (188–9)

The narrator reflects upon this exchange and tells us that when she had first moved east, "I didn't really think about Indians, First Nations or otherwise. I didn't really think" (189). Although the blossoming friendship with Gerald becomes an opportunity to rectify this gap in her thinking, it is one that causes her to feel guilty and apprehensive. When Gerald and the narrator speak on the telephone as adults, he tells her that he has long since forgiven her for those terrible comments she made as a child. And yet, when he invites her to visit him on his mother's farm, she waffles, afraid to take him up on his offer even though her heart yells, "Go see him!" (240). This hesitation is, however, a sign of the important distinction between the narrator and her father, since it comes out of her desire to handle this relationship with care.

Water

The novel ends with the narrator in the company of her friends and a new romantic interest. Having driven outside of the city limits to watch a planetary conjunction, the characters look up and, although they are unable to see the planets, they are greeted by an unexpected rain shower. Surprised by the precipitation, the narrator and her companions embrace this new turn of events by leaping into the rain:

> We hold out palms to catch the wet in the cups of our hands, tip our heads, drink from the skies.... Soaring, we leap skyward, leave perfect footprints in the rich mud. New green shoots of life twine at our feet, rising leafy in the warm night air. And in the collage of green, the movements of our bodies, I can see kappa rising from the soil, like creatures waking from enforced hibernation, they stretch their long, green limbs with gleeful abandon. Skin moist, wet, slick and salamander-soft, kappa and humans dance together, our lives unfurling before us.
>
> And the water breaks free with the rain. (275)

This depiction of the women reveling in the rain appears to be a clear moment of hope and a sign of the kappa's effectiveness. This link between the kappa, the narrator's present, and joy are further underscored when the narrator picks up her new girlfriend, Bernie, and feels "a flow of sweet liquid fil[l] [her] ... veins" (272). Although this representation is unarguably an optimistic one, it occurs on the penultimate page of the text. The final pages of the novel are instead filled by an invitation that reads, "*I am a creature of the water. / I am a kappa child. // Come, embrace me*" (276). And after that, the text provides the reader with a glossary of kappa-related terms and pertinent history, and then finally the author's acknowledgements.

Reading this ending that unfurls for a few pages, eventually meandering towards a conclusion, is quite suggestive given the kinds of discussions this novel makes possible. Although I realize that the positioning of the author's acknowledgements at the end of the text may simply be the result of the publisher's preferences, I nonetheless think they suggest a way of moving outside of the text in a way that foregrounds acknowledging support and friendship, but also heeding the effects of neglect and violence. The rolling ending of this text then moves between the ideas of pleasure and transformation invoked by the image of the women in the rain, to the world outside of this narrative, all the while encouraging the reader to heed the kappa's call for sustained pleasure and intimacy. The glossary suggests ways in which the kappa exists outside of the pages of the novel in the space of cultural mythology as well as in the everyday world, having been sighted "on mainland Asia" (277). The glossary reminds us again that the kappa "lives in the borders between natural and human environments ... [and] can be beaten only by spilling the water from its bowlshaped head," reiterating the interdependent nature of survival, risk, and intimacy (277).

Goto's novel as a whole, but especially its conclusion, assumes a new and particularly urgent set of meanings for me now as a reader newly located on the west coast of Canada. The glossary reiterates ways to defeat the kappa in what is really the final page of the novel proper and therefore the novel's, if not the text's, final words. These instructions about emptying the kappa's water bowl resonate in particularly discomforting ways, given the ongoing efforts to privatize water in British Columbia. Given the ways that this novel stresses the symbolic significance of water for a Japanese-Canadian community more specifically, but also for Asian diasporic communities more broadly, larger questions about the responsibilities of diasporic communities to public resources are raised. The dereliction of these duties results in both enormous ethical and cultural dilemmas given the vision the kappa puts forward. Moreover, this current debate over water as a potentially private resource asks us to consider how we, just like Goto's narrator, occupy particular positions within this same public.

It is, of course, a plight that echoes the narrator's crime of stealing water from her neighbours. Although hers is a fictionalized account, the consequences are still worth considering for their relevance to this current and very real-life situation. While taking a break from stealing water for her father's impossible rice paddy, the narrator looks for the first time at the landscape:

> The stars were loud. They buzzed with light and the summer breeze cooled the sweat along my hairline. Only then did I notice the sweet sound of the crickets. Breathed in the fresh scent of corn ripening into peaches and cream, summer grass turning into hay.
>
> How beautiful it could be, I thought, and trembled I don't know why. I plunked down in the sea turned desert, lay in brittle grass. Huge, shiny crickets crawled across my body, paused and played their songs before passing. I stared at the incredible sky, rich, dense, almost dizzying. The stars quivered. (199)

This moment produces a recognition of the double bind in which she is caught. The narrator perceives fully the futility of her father's efforts to recreate Japan in Alberta and feels immense shame at being forced to undertake this theft of resources. At the same time, she is also bound to her despotic father by love, kinship, and a recognition of their shared similarities. Her ensuing callous treatment of Gerald occurs at this point in the novel, after she realizes her very limited options. The decision to survive by lashing out with cruelty comes at the cost of her humanity, as she is consequently unable to appreciate falling stars or feel desire. The attempt to resume this friendship is never fully actualized and indeed cannot be until the narrator can be sure that she is capable of true friendship. Although the narrator never reaches that point and never fully relinquishes the past narratives that have shaped her, she strives towards a more hopeful future. Her sister Satomi tells her that "[i]f you don't let the hatred go, he continues to oppress your life, just like if you were still living in his house" (266). Although the narrator accepts this advice, she is deeply entangled within various complicated narratives that refuse easy solutions.

The father's theft of water is motivated by nostalgia, a desire to remake the land into home, and a fear of surviving outside of this narrative. *The Kappa Child* gives us a complicated representation of this paternal figure, complete with insight into how he came to personify such violence and how it damaged his children and wife. Before moving to Canada, he was a husband that Okasan's friends admired because he was a teetotaler. It is only after the family migrates that the father is transformed into a monstrous figure and addicted to nasal spray. The narrator speculates that somehow the aridity of the interior "filled my father's head so mucus-full he couldn't breathe without it. Nasal spray. His cavities filled with memories lost, or maybe the unattainable future" (126). Even if this explanation of

304 TELLING STORIES ACROSS LINES

her father's frustrations does not justify his actions, it does suggest a diasporic relationship to both a public and its communal resources that requires
both self-criticality and compassion.

Reading this novel in the contemporary moment invites pressing questions about how to reconcile the failed dreams of diaspora with the violences
they have helped enact, and about the possibilities for forging new narratives not laden with guilt but still mindful of the past. The goal of thinking
through these kinds of questions is not to stuff our Samsonite luggage with
more liberal guilt or reach easy milktoast answers, but to think about our
contiguous existences that often overlap in challenging ways. These various
trickster figures, whether they be Indigenous or diasporic ones, operate as
provocations to thinking, acting, and being. As ethical and political guides
that intersect in many ways, one visible instance being that of water, these
tricksters give us a means of thinking through potential conversations around
specific common issues and suggest ways of moving in new directions.
Through its use of the trickster figure, *The Kappa Child* reminds us of the
importance of curiosity and the need to make space for it in the world. It is,
after all, the kappa's curiosity that gets it into difficulties, but these dilemmas
more often than not become situations of learning. The kappa's willingness
to explore opens up new possibilities for readers, but also lets us remain conscious of the shaping forces of culture, history, and geography. For Asian
diasporas, one of the lessons the kappa tries to teach is the need to participate in new conversations that are not necessarily spaces of safety, but contain risk and ask us to reckon constantly with the unknown.

Notes

1 Not all Japanese Canadians and Japanese Americans co-operated with their governments' attempts to relocate them. As Roy Miki documents in his important work
on the Japanese-Canadian redress movement, many protested the injustice of
the government's actions. He cites the Nisei Mass Evacuation Group, mostly Nisei
men, "who protested the federal government's policy of breaking up the family
unit," as an example of resistance by Japanese Canadians (58).

2 In sharp contrast with the father's ahistorical method of growing rice, Blackfoot
ways of growing tobacco involve rituals that incorporate historical and mythical
elements: "While they're away, they must camp in four different places of increasing distances from the garden while mythical 'little people' tend to the crop.
'Some say the seeds are the dwarf people,' wrote Wissler. 'No one must ever try
to see the little people for if you do you will die.' At the fourth campsite, the
women make tiny moccasins about five centimetres long and bags of food about
seven centimetres long and put them out for the little people. The group then
spends the rest of the summer hunting and gathering" (Chandler 35–6). These

tobacco rituals and farming practices provide a way of seeing the geography of Alberta in deeply historical terms and as requiring balance amongst multiple kinds of forces: "As well as the mythical bringing of the original tobacco seed, the beaver and its aquatic habits played a leading role in ensuring the success of the crop by imparting information crucial for timing and locating tobacco" (Chandler 36).

3   This linking of Santa and Naapi draws on Eldon Yellowhorn's reading of Santa as an appropriation of Naapi. Please see his essay earlier in this collection.

4   I thank Deanna Reder for making this astute observation. Given the multiple ways that the Indian Act excluded many from holding status and that Bill C-31, the Act that amended the former one and restored status to people such as those whose parents were not married, it is entirely possible that Gerald would have had no legal right to live on his father's reserve.

5   Judging by the narrator's viewing of the "last total eclipse of the twentieth century," which took place in September 1996, the novel seems to span a period that runs roughly from the mid-1960s to mid-1970s, and on until November 1996 (119).

Works Cited

Bastien, Betty. *Blackfoot Ways of Knowing.* Calgary: U of Calgary P, 2004.

Chandler, Graham. "Growing Their Own." *The Beaver* (February/March 2005): 33–6.

Chow, Rey. "Against the Lures of Diaspora." In *Writing Diaspora.* Bloomington: Indiana UP, 1993. 99–119.

Goto, Hiromi. *The Kappa Child.* Calgary: Red Deer, 2001.

Laird, Gordon. "This Land Is Whose Land?" *This Magazine* (March–April 2000). <http://www.thismagazine.ca/issues/2000/03/whoseland.php>. Accessed 19 May 2008.

Miki, Roy. *Redress.* Vancouver: Raincoast, 2005.

Samsonite Corporation. "Vision and Heritage." <http://corporate.samsonite.com/samsonite/about/vision_heritage/>. Accessed 26 February 2008.

THOMAS KING

"How I Spent My Summer Vacation"
History, Story, and the Cant of Authenticity

According to the 1991 Neiman Marcus Christmas catalogue, you can buy a custom carved totem pole or a painting by Rosie the Elephant. These two advertisements did not sit on opposing pages, although they should, for they form a wonderful cultural diptych; the poles are carved by an authentic Native carver, and the paintings are rendered by an authentic elephant.

This has little to do with my essay, which is not available in the catalogue, but it did suggest certain things to me about the power of advertising, the value of authenticity, and the need for essential Truths. And it reminded me of my summer vacation.

Last summer, I was at the Sun Dance on the Blood reserve in southern Alberta. Old friends had invited me up. I had never been to a Sun Dance before. When I told several of my neighbours in St. Paul where I was going, their eyes slowly glazed over and I imagined them conjuring up images of Catlin's romantically rendered Indians hanging about by their pectorals from poles.

In all honesty, I was not sure what to expect myself, but I was reasonably sure that I would have better luck seeing this kind of white-male eroticism at the theatre than I would on the Alberta prairies.

As it turned out, I was right. If my neighbours had gone with me that July, they probably would have been disappointed, for the major activities at the Sun Dance involved an incessant coming and going: go to the store to get bread; take the kids in for a doctor's appointment; grab another load of wood; run to town for more ice; drive the bags of garbage to the dumpster in Standoff; duck home and take a shower.

And constant preparation. Each lodge had coffee. Food was everywhere. Not a conspicuous show of food, just its constant presence—a pot of stew, soup, a picnic ham, bread, apples and bananas. And all around, elders, adults, and children were on the move, circling the camp, visiting. You can sit in one lodge all day, and, in between the preparations, and the dances, you will be able to meet and greet many of the people in the camp, for the Sun Dance is a consummate social ceremony as well as a religious one, and that is the way it should be. It is also an occasion for storytelling.

I was sitting in my friend's lodge enjoying yet another cup of coffee, minding my own business, when the flap of the teepee was pulled to one side and two elderly women and a younger man entered. We greeted each other; the women settled themselves on their side of the lodge and the man and I settled ourselves on our side. For a while, no one said a word.

Finally, one of the women, a woman named Bella, leaned forward, looked at me, looked at the ground, and looked back at me.

"I hear you're a historian," she said.

I quickly told her it wasn't true, that I was a writer, a novelist, a story-teller. But she waved me off.

"Same thing," she said, and she began to tell this story.

There was a young man who came to the reserve to talk to elders. He was from a university (Bella didn't say where), but when she said the word university, she slowed down and stretched out each syllable as if she were pulling on an elastic and the man sitting next to me started to laugh as if he had just heard an excellent joke. Bella waited until he stopped and then she continued.

The man, Bella explained, wanted to hear old stories, stories from back in the olden days, stories about how Indians used to live. So she told him about how death came into the world, how Old Man and Old Woman had argued over whether human beings should live forever or whether they should die. Old Man thought they should live. Old Woman thought they should die.

So they made a wager, a bet. Old Man got a buffalo chip and they agreed that if they threw the chip in the river and it sank, then human beings would live forever. If it floated, the human beings must die.

There are no surprises here. The chip floated, and, as Bella explained to the man, that was how death came into the world.

At this point in her story, Bella told me that the young man, all eager and full of sound, jumped in and said that whites had the same sort of story. And before anyone could stop him, he began a recitation of Genesis, how everything was perfect in the garden, how there was no death, how Eve found the apple, how she ate the apple, how she seduced Adam, how Adam and Eve acquired knowledge, and how, from then on, things got gloomy. He concluded by noting what a coincidence it was that women, in both cases, were responsible for these disasters.

After he finished, the elders thanked him for his remarks and the man from the university thanked the elders and everyone went their own way.

When Bella finished telling this story, she settled back in her chair and drank some coffee. Then she looked right at me, and she said, "And that's why he never heard the rest of the story."

The first thing that flashed through my mind was Paul Harvey. The second was to keep my mouth shut, for I understood that attached to the story Bella had just told was a caution to mind my manners and not to interrupt as the other man had done.

So I shut up, and I waited. Bella finished her coffee and had another cup. There was some soup in the pot and that was passed around with bread and more coffee.

Then Bella said, "So you see, Old Woman was right. If there had been no death, there would have been so many people, the world would have sunk into the ocean. Just look at it now! Old Woman understood the need for balance."

I think I started to smile, but Bella cut me off quickly. "And that Eve woman was right, too," she said. "No point in being stupid all your life."

We sat in the lodge for a long time and talked about family and children, the price of gas, the weather, Martin's new fan, Dixie's cellular telephone, and Thelma's new boyfriend from Calgary.

Finally, the three of them got up to leave and move to the next lodge.

"You work at a university just like that young man?" Bella asked me.

I told her that I did.

"It's real frustrating, you know, to have to keep telling that story. Maybe you can find that young man and tell him he should get it right.

"Tell him," she continued, "to remember that Eve woman of his and to use the brains she gave him."

I followed Bella outside. The rains had been heavier than usual that July and the prairie grass was tall. Here and there in the distance, sections of canola were in full bloom, bright gold against the deeper greens and blues, and from the camp on the Belly Buttes, you could see the sky in all directions and watch the land roll into the mountains.

"You write stories?" Bella asked me.

"Yes, I do."

"About us Indians?"

"Most of the time."

She smiled and shook her head. "You're kinda young to be a historian."

I had to leave that day to go down into eastern Oregon for a writers' conference and, all the way down, I chewed on what Bella had suggested about story and history. I was, of course, able to dismiss her contention that story and history were the same, knowing that she had never studied history, knowing that she was not aware of the fine distinctions that separated the two. Of course, history *was* a story, and, as with all stories, it carried with it certain biases that proceeded from culture, language, race, religion, class, gender. It was burdened with the demands of nationalism, subject to the vagaries of scholarship, and wrapped up in the myth of literacy. Nonetheless, as one of my professors told me, history dealt with a series of facts rather than fictions, and, while the interpretations of those facts will vary, these small truths would remain.

I was comforted by that. I am not sure why, but I was.

When I finished the conference at Lake Wallowa, I headed back to the Sun Dance. I wanted to get there in time to see the men dance. But the first thing I did was look up Bella. I found her sitting in a folding chair outside one of the lodges enjoying the panorama of the prairies and the Rockies.

"You again!" she said.

She motioned me to sit down beside her and I did. I did not know what to say or how to start. I wanted to tell her about history and story, but instead, we sat there and watched Chief Mountain turn blue and then purple as the light deepened.

"You know," Bella said, "there was this guy about your age came out to visit us. He was from Ottawa. Reporter. Wanted to know what we thought about Meech Lake, so Florence told him about how Coyote won a bet with Old Woman and how death came into the world. You know the story?"

I said I thought she had told me a story like that several days ago.

But did I remember it, she wanted to know. Could I tell it again?

I made the mistake of saying that I thought I could. Bella settled into the chair, waved at the mosquitoes, put her hands in her lap, and closed her eyes.

I thought she was going to sleep. But she wasn't.

"You waiting for winter?"

So I began to tell the story, and I thought I did a pretty good job. When I finished, I settled in the grass, put my hands in my lap, and closed my eyes. As I sat there, I could hear Bella shifting her weight in the chair.

"Okay," said Bella. "There was this Mormon guy from Cardston came to visit us. Wilma brought him by. He was an old guy, had a bad leg, you know. He said he was collecting oral history for the church. So Francis told him about how Duck and Buffalo had a bet and how Duck won the bet and how death came into the world."

And Bella proceeded to tell the story once again. It was the same basic tale, but, each time she told it, some of the facts changed. First it was Old Man and Old Woman who had made the bet. Then it was Old Woman and Coyote. Duck and Buffalo got into the act in a third telling. Sometimes it was a rock that was supposed to float. Once the bet involved a feather. The man from a university/Ottawa/Cardston changed, too. First, he was young, then middle-aged, and finally, old. The only thing that remained truly constant was that death came to the world.

"That's history," Bella told me when she had finished the fourth telling of the story. "You got any questions?"

I was dying to tell Bella that this wasn't history at all, that this was ... well ... myth. But I didn't get a chance.

"Some of those white people call this story myth because they figure it never happened. Is that what you're thinking?"

I was in full retreat by now and was willing to do or say anything to get out of the way.

"Maybe it's a little of both," I said.

"You think that, do you?"

"Well, for instance," I said, "Stanley Fish suggests that there are interpretative communities composed of groups of people who share commonalities, who agreed on how things such as history and myth are interpreted, how the universe is ordered."

"That so?" said Bella.

"And Adrienne Rich talks about the politics of location and how your subject position, your gender, race, class all determine what you see and how you interpret what you see."

"Okay," Bella said with a sigh. "There were these two guys from France came to visit us. They wanted to hear old stories, so Latisha told them about Old Man and Old Woman and how death came to the world."

It was almost dark when I left Bella.

I do not know exactly what Bella was trying to tell me about history and story. Indeed, I do not know if she was trying to tell me anything at all. Perhaps, as she said, she just wanted to make sure I got the story straight.

But I do not believe this. The elements of her story were too well placed. The conflict too cleverly organized. The resolution too pointed and axiomatic. I even suspect that the frame of the story—the man coming to hear a story— is apocryphal. But curiously, while the supporting facts changed in each telling of the story, the essential relationships—the relationship of humans to death and the relationship of balance to chaos—remained intact. Bella had begun here and crafted a set of facts to support these relationships, to create a story, to create a history.

Then, too, the language itself shifted as ceremony gave way to instruction. Metaphor, imagery, the rhythmic and repetitive syntaxes, the rhetorical interrogatories gave way to more didactic structures that marched lockstep from beginning to end, from premise to conclusion. These shape changes were not a product of frustration, the having to tell a story again and again, making it progressively simpler and simpler, but rather the concern with purpose, allowing Bella, who told one version all full of colour and motion, to declare that this was story, and, as she told another version all full of instance and example, to insist that this was history.

Of course, we know we cannot trust authorial intent, and you should be rightly appalled that I bring it up at all.

Yet in considering what Bella told me and what I know, I am struck by how thin the line between history and story is, resting as it appears to do on a single question, a single concern—did it happen/is it authentic/can it be verified/is it real—and on the assumption of the pre-eminence of the literary within non-Native culture. Patricia Limerick, in her fine critical study of the West, *The Legacy of Conquest*, questions this very assumption. Speaking specifically about history and anthropology and the West, Limerick says that "human differences that hinged on literary assumed an undeserved significance." This significance that Limerick speaks of is, I believe (and I think Limerick would agree), not merely a function of the ability to read but rather the blind belief in the efficacy of the written word.

As an example, let's take my own trip to Alberta. When I am famous, some bright graduate student in search of a thesis or an assistant professor in search of tenure might consider a history of my life as a writer. Chapter five might start out with several paragraphs that recount my journey in July of 1991 to the Sun Dance in southern Alberta where I met with a Blood woman named Bella; how over a period of days, with a short break during which I went to eastern Oregon to attend a writers' conference, Bella and I discussed the relationship of history to story and how that discussion inspired a most interesting paper that I later gave at the American Studies Coffee Hour in November of 1991.

Ah, history. Ah, story. What if I never went to the Sun Dance? What if I made all this up? What if I went to the Sun Dance, but Bella is a fiction? What if I went to the Sun Dance and talked to a woman named Bella, but I completely made up our conversation on history and story? What if I went to the Sun Dance, met a woman named Bella, had a conversation such as I described, and could produce trustworthy witnesses to swear that my account of that conversation is accurate?

Perhaps what really happened was that someone, say a historian, said something in passing about history that set me thinking and that, during my stay at the Sun Dance and talking with some of the people and listening to the stories they told, I decided to use that particular setting as a backdrop to give my personal thoughts and remarks an authentic context.

We like our history to be authentic. We like our facts to be truthful. We are suspicious of ambiguity, uneasy with metaphor. We are not concerned with essential relationships. We want cultural guarantees, solid currencies that we can take to the bank.

I tried to explain this to Bella with one example that I knew would carry the day. As we were sitting there on the Alberta prairies, I turned to the east and said in my best matter-of-fact voice, "It's the facts that separate history from story. For instance," I droned on, "the sun rises every day in the east."

Bella half-turned, smiled, and nodded her head. "Has so far," she said.

So that is it. Bella, if she exists, believes that history and story are the same. She sees no boundaries, no borders, between what she knows and what she can imagine. Everything is story, and all the stories are true. Whereas I am forced to try to separate them. To put fancy in one pile, facts in another, so the two will not get mixed up. By training (and I am speaking here of culture and society rather than just the university), I go forth into the world, not to question the presence of God in the universe, nor to confront the mysteries of birth and death, nor to consider the complexities of being, but simply to ascertain what is authentic and what is not.

Harry Truman and Paul Revere, for instance.

Harry Truman, when he was President, ordered the military to drop two atomic bombs on Japan, one on Hiroshima and one on Nagasaki. We can read about it. We can go to Hiroshima and see the monument. We can see the aftermath of its destruction.

Paul Revere, when he was a young silversmith in Boston, rode through the city streets to alert the citizenry to the impending British invasion. We can read about it. We can go to Boston and see the Old North Church. We can walk the path he took that fateful night, and follow the drama in Longfellow's poem.

Well, so much for literacy.

Thank God, then, for Neiman Marcus and the Christmas catalogue and the certificates of authenticity they provide. While questions of history and story may continue to plague me, I can tell you I sleep easier knowing that I own a painting by a real elephant, and that the totem pole in my back yard was not chainsawed into existence by an out-of-work lumberjack. Bella prob-ably wouldn't care, but then she wouldn't care that Paul Revere never made his ride, either.

All levity aside, I want to assure you that this essay is, in the best sense of the word, authentic. In a world that believes that wisdom is, in the main, a mat-ter of keeping facts and fictions straight, it's the least I can do.

APPENDICES

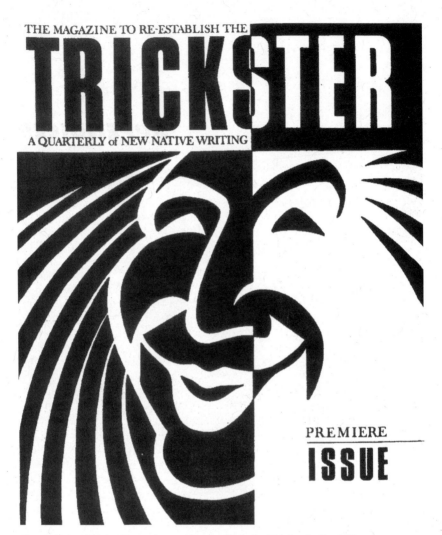

Cover design for the Committee to Re-establish the Tricker by David Beyer.

LET'S BE OUR OWN TRICKSTERS, EH

FOR ANYONE involved in the making of culture in Canada there is a very real concern that Native peoples are not seen as active participants. The need and desire for more Native images and more stories by and about Native peoples is world wide.

But who determines whether a piece of writing or a story is "too Indian" or "not Indian enough"? Who knows best how to present the Native perspective? How many times have you heard "We've already done Indians this week"? Well, today it seems, there's a host of professionals dealing with the printed word (editors, publishers, producers, directors, writers, storytellers, journalists), all non-Native, who have taken over the work of the missionaries and the Indian agent. They now know best how to present the Native perspective, never dreaming, of course, it is basically their own perspective coloured with a few canoes, beads, beaver ponds, and a buffalo or two - romantic cliches of how they see Native peoples or how they want to see Native peoples.

(Artifacts and history do not make Native culture, or any culture, for that matter. The collection of mental constructs, ideas do. These describe how a people think and how they determine things.)

The loss of Native sensibility through the benevolent and fine professional efforts of these people, is of little concern. When Native people advocate WE CAN TELL OUR OWN STORIES - IN OUR OWN WAY, there is always great lamentation from those who see it as their god-given right, as Canadians, as editors, publishers, producers, directors, writers, storytellers, and journalists, to tell the Native Canadian stories. (The country is theirs now, why not our stories too, eh?) Our most basic right - to speak for ourselves, to tell our own stories - threatens them! No matter the goodness in their hearts and intentions, they cannot or they refuse to see that to continue telling our stories, writing our stories, is to continue speaking for us and paraphrasing us.

As Native Canadians, we don't have hundreds of years of a written literary legacy supporting us! But, we do have hundreds and hundreds of years of a vibrant and vital "oral literature" to support us.

Native cultures in Canada are basically oral cultures, and a major component in any oral culture is the body of ceremonial stories and songs, games, incantations, prose cycles (Trickster tales), the popular stories, and songs/poems (lullabies, work songs, jokes, anecdotes). These in a traditional or contemporary setting reflect the deepest perceptions, relationships and attitudes of Native cultures.

Symbols, figurative and metaphoric bendings, themes, organization and structure that characterize tribal rural and urban life, from traditional times to now, contribute to a variety of cultural meanings. Only the most perceptive and careful translator (Native writer/storyteller) should confront these. They know best what goes on in the hearts and minds of Native peoples.

The Native and non-Native have basic differences about the universe and basic reality ... space for one is spherical and time is cyclical; for the other, space is linear and time sequential. The universe moves and breathes for one, but not the other. It is this particular detail that is reflected in work by Native writers, and it is this particular detail that will give this body of work its universal appeal.

And sure, some of our stories do not look good on Canadian society and Canadian people. Heck some of them don't even look good on us, but these stories deal with the experiences of humanity, and as such they are not always pretty or pleasant. Let's cut out the anthro-apologizing and anthologizing. Let's be our own tricksters, eh.

The formation of the Committee to Re-Establish the Trickster (CRET) in 1986 arose out of awareness by a group of Native writers to consolidate and gain recognition

for Native contributions to Canadian writing - to reclaim the Native voice in literature.

To facilitate the creation and the promotion of literature by Native writers, CRET offers a series of workshops and seminars dealing with relevant themes, readings by CRET members, critiquing and consultation services, and publications. CRET encourages literacy on all levels and in all languages used by Native people. The production and appreciation of a literature of artistic excellence is its goal.

The Trickster is a figure found in oral cultures the world over, but he is special and central in the cultures of North America. Among his names here, in Canada, are Glooskap, Nanabojoh, Weesakejak, Napi, Raven, Hare, Coyote. Half hero, half fool, this figure is at once like each one of us and like none of us. Trickster tales are at once admonitions, instruction and entertainment. Storytellers say he disappeared with the arrival of the white man. We believe he is still here, having assumed other names. And, in certain instances, it now seems that the Trickster [is] re-emerging as female also.

Become a friend of the Trickster by supporting CRET ... and may the Trickster be with you.

Lenore Keeshig-Tobias

THESE stories deal with the experiences of humanity, and as such they are not always pretty or pleasant.

The Committee to Re-establish the Trickster was conceived in 1986 and founded in 1987 by Daniel David Moses, Lenore Keeshig-Tobias, and Tomson Highway in order to draw attention both to their own work and to that of other Indigenous artists. As part of this project, they developed *The Magazine to Re-establish the Trickster* (two issues were published), from which this essay, by Keeshig-Tobias, is reprinted in facsimile form. It appears with the permission of Lenore Keeshig-Tobias.

Copyright Acknowledgements

The general editors and the publisher are grateful to those copyright holders who granted permission to reproduce works under copyright.

Sonny Assu, for the essay "Personal Totems" and the three images that appear with it.

Lenore Keeshig-Tobias, for the article "Let's Be Our Own Tricksters, Eh" and the cover art for *The Magazine to Re-establish the Trickster: A Quarterly of New Native Writing*, premiere issue.

Thomas H. King, for the poems "Coyote Sees the Prime Minister" and "Coyote Goes to Toronto," both of which were published initially in *Canadian Literature* (Spring 1990), and for the essay "'How I Spent My Summer Vacation': History, Story and the Cant of Authenticity," which was published initially in *Landmarks* (1998).

Steve Sanderson, for the artwork reproduced in the chapter "Sacred Stories in Comic Book Form: A Cree Reading of *Darkness Calls*" and on the front cover of this volume.

University of British Columbia Press, for the excerpt from *Indigenous Storywork: Educating the Heart, Mind, Body, and Spirit*, by Jo-ann Archibald. Copyright © 2007 University of British Columbia Press. All rights reserved by the publisher. The excerpt is taken from pages ix–x and 153.

Richard Van Camp, for the story "Why Ravens Smile to Little Old Ladies as They Walk By ..."

Contributors

Jo-ann Archibald (Stó:lō) is the Associate Dean for Indigenous Education at the University of British Columbia (UBC) and the Acting Director of the Native Indian Teacher Education Program. She has recently released *Indigenous Storywork: Educating the Heart, Mind, Body and Spirit* through UBC Press.

Sonny Assu (Laich-kwil-tach) received his BFA from the Emily Carr Institute of Art and Design in 2002 and his certificate in Multimedia Studies from UBC in 2004. He has held solo exhibits at Equinox and the Belkin Satellite Gallery, and group exhibits at several galleries.

Warren Cariou (Métis) is the Canada Research Chair in Narrative, Community and Indigenous Cultures at the University of Manitoba, where he also directs the Centre for Creative Writing and Oral Culture. He has published fiction, non-fiction, and criticism dealing mainly with Métis culture.

Jill Carter (Anishinaabekwe) is completing her dissertation, *Repairing the Web: Spiderwoman's Grandchildren Staging the New Human Being*, at the Graduate Centre for Study of Drama (University of Toronto). She has published in *Canadian Woman Studies/Les Cahiers de la Femme: Indigenous Women in Canada* (26:3,4) and *Stanislavsky and Directing: Theory, Practice and Influence* (Legas, 2008).

Kristina Fagan (Labrador Métis), an Associate Professor of English at the University of Saskatchewan, specializes in Aboriginal writing and storytelling in Canada. She has published articles on methodology in the study of Aboriginal literature and on the depiction of Aboriginal people in settler-Canadian literature. Her current research is on autobiography and storytelling among her people, the Labrador Métis. She is also increasingly interested in oral traditions and the ways in which the study of such traditions challenge our usual methods of literary analysis.

MARGERY FEE is a Professor of English at the University of British Columbia. She has been specializing in post-colonial studies, particularly in the comparison of indigenous literatures in Australia, New Zealand-Aotearoa, and Canada, since the early 1990s. Recently she has been writing about racializing narratives associated with the "'aboriginal' thrifty gene." She is the editor of *Canadian Literature.*

DANIEL MORLEY JOHNSON is a PhD candidate in Comparative Literature at the University of Alberta, where he has taught courses in the Faculty of Native Studies. He has also taught at Maskwachees Cultural College in Hobbema, Alberta. His dissertation is a Cree literary history. Johnson is a graduate of the Aboriginal Studies program at the University of Toronto.

LENORE KEESHIG-TOBIAS (Anishinabe), a member of the Chippewas of Nawash First Nation, is a fiction and children's literature writer, storyteller, essayist, and playwright. Her publications include *Emma and the Trees* (1995) and *Bird Talk* (1991). She was a founding member of the Committee to Re-establish the Trickster (CRET).

JENNIFER KELLY teaches in the International Indigenous Studies Program at the University of Calgary. Her interests include Indigenous Literatures and Interpretive/Pedagogical Practices, Indigenous Film, and Research Ethics. She is a co-ordinator (with Delia Cross Child, Ramona Big Head, and Georgette Fox) of "'You May Laugh': Surviving, Remembering, and Transforming Residential School Experience," with members of the Kainai Nation, Southern Alberta.

CHRIS KIENTZ (Cherokee) traces his Native ancestry back to the Eastern Cherokee nation of Tennessee and the Dawes Rolls. He has worked as an independent producer and animator, developing multimedia projects for commercial clients in both Canada and the United States for over ten years. He has scripted, produced, and directed award-winning video, animation, interactive media, and website projects for numerous clients. Growing up among the Navajo, Zuni, and Hopi people of New Mexico gave Chris a great respect for North American Aboriginal art and culture. *Raven Tales* (both a company and an animated series) represents the culmination of this interest.

CHRISTINE KIM is an Assistant Professor in the Department of English at Simon Fraser University. Her teaching and research focus on Asian North American literature and theory, contemporary Canadian literature, and diasporic writing. She has recently published articles in the journals *Open Letter* and *Studies in Canadian Literature*, as well as the collection *Asian Canadian Writing Beyond Autoethnography* (Wilfrid Laurier University Press, 2008). She is currently working on a book-length project entitled *From Multiculturalism to Globalization: The Cultural Politics of Asian Canadian Writing*, and is co-editing a collection of essays entitled *Cultural Grammars of Nation, Diaspora and Indigeneity in Canada*.

THOMAS KING (Cherokee) is a professor of Native Literature and Creative Writing at the University of Guelph. He is renowned for writing such novels as *Medicine River* and *Green Grass, Running Water*.

JUDITH LEGGATT is an Associate Professor in the Department of English at Lakehead University. She teaches post-colonial, First Nations, Canadian, and women's literatures, and has published articles on Lee Maracle, Salman Rushdie, and post-colonial pedagogy. Her present research interests include the representations of dirt and disease in First Nations literature, and the intersections of science fiction and post-colonialism.

LINDA MORRA, an Associate Professor in the Department of English at Bishop's University, specializes in Canadian Studies/Literature, with a particular focus on twentieth-century Canadian writers. She has published articles and given papers about Tomson Highway, Jack Hodgins, Pauline Johnson, Sheila Watson, and Mordecai Richler. In 2009 she worked collaboratively with professors from other departments at Bishop's University to establish the Indigenous Studies Minor program.

DEANNA REDER (Cree-Métis) holds a joint appointment as assistant professor in Simon Fraser University's First Nations Studies Program and Department of English. Her main fields of study are Indigenous literary theories and autobiography theory, with a particular focus on Cree and Métis lifewriting. She has recently published on Edward Ahenakew in *Studies in Canadian Literature*, and is about to begin a term as series editor for the Aboriginal Studies series at Wilfrid Laurier University Press.

STEVE SANDERSON (Cree), a member of James Smith Cree Nation, is currently a resident of Vancouver, BC, where he works as a professional cartoonist. Sanderson provided the cover art of this book from his work on *Darkness Calls*, a comic book about suicide prevention distributed by The Healthy Aboriginal Network. Besides authoring his own scripts, Sanderson has also provided the interior art in Daniel Heath Justice's *The Way of Thorn and Thunder* trilogy put out by Kegedonce Press.

NIIGONWEDOM JAMES SINCLAIR (Anishinabe) is a graduate of the Native American Literatures program at the University of Oklahoma, and is currently a PhD candidate in the Department of English at the University of British Columbia. His dissertation is an Anishinaabeg literary history. Niigon is originally from St. Peter's (Little Peguis) Indian Reserve in Manitoba and is the proud father of a little girl, Nimiizhiian-Nibiens, or Sarah. His creative work has appeared in *Prairie Fire* and *Tales from Moccasin Avenue: An Anthology of Native Stories*, while his critical work will appear in two anthologies in 2009 and 2010, the former with Broadview Press and the latter with Michigan State University Press. He also writes a monthly column entitled "Birchbark Bitings" in *Urban NDN*, Manitoba's monthly alternative Native newspaper. Niigon dedicates both contributions in this book to his father.

RICHARD VAN CAMP (Tlicho) is a proud member of the Dogrib (Tlicho) Nation from Fort Smith, Northwest Territories, Canada. A graduate of the En'owkin International School of Writing, the University of Victoria's Creative Writing BFA Program, and the Master's Degree in Creative Writing at the University of British Columbia, Richard currently teaches Creative Writing with an Aboriginal Focus at the University of British Columbia in Vancouver, BC. His novel *The Lesser Blessed* will soon be a movie with First Generation Films. Director Kelvin Redvers has now completed the film adaptation of Richard's short story "firebear called them faith healers," with Cross Current Productions, and will be screening the film at various film festivals internationally. Richard's new collection of short stories, *The Moon of Letting Go*, will be published by Enfield and Wizenty later in 2009. His new novel, *Blessing Wendy*, will be released in 2010 by Orca Book Publishers. This novel is about a young Dogrib man who begins to train as a ninja in his quest towards revenge after learning that his cousin is molested by the high school principal in the fictional town of Fort Simmer, NWT.

ELDON YELLOWHORN (Piikani) is an Associate Professor in Archaeology and Director in First Nations Studies at Simon Fraser University. Presently he is working towards defining the tenets and objectives of internalist archaeology and examining its contributions to archaeological theory. He is the co-author of the oft-used textbook, *First Peoples in Canada*.

Index

Water Beetle, 121
Watson, Sheila, xi, 14, 77, 80–83, 86, 89n2
Waub-Ameek, 25
Waynaboozhoo stories, 24–25
Weaver, Jace, 41, 203, 204, 205, 215, 232
Weegit, 79
Weesageechak, 265
Weesakeechak, 13
Weesquachak, 221
Wendigo, 179
werewolf folk tales, 159–60
werewolves, 157, 159, 160, 164
Wesakecak, vii, 179, 180, 183, 184, 186–90, 190n1
"'What About You?': Approaching the Study of 'Native Literature,'" 47
Wheeler, Winona, 180
When the World Was New, 101, 113
"white man's burden," 229, 231, 232
White Paper (1969), 36, 61, 234
whitestream, 204, 213, 215n3, 216n9
"Why Raven Is Black," 114
"Why Ravens Smile to Little Old Ladies as They Walk By ...," 95–97, 99–119

Wiebe, Rudy, 69
Wihtiko, 179, 184, 185, 186–89, 190n1
Wiintigo, 188
Willmott, Glenn, 83
Winnebago tribe, 33, 34
Winnebago trickster, 277
wîsahkêcâhk, 185, 188, 215n1
Womack, Craig, 3, 10, 11, 38, 44, 202, 205, 207, 215, 232, 239
Women in Violence, 263, 268–83, 284n6
World War II, 32, 291
Woven Stone, 255
Writers Guild of Canada, 64, 68
The Writers' Union of Canada (TWUC), 62, 63, 73n8
"Writing Thru Race" conference, 4, 62
Wyile, Herb, 7

"Yamoria Lives with the Beavers," 122n19
Yamoria the Lawmaker: Stories of the Dene, 112

Zemans, Joyce, 69
zhaanganaashiikwe, 222

Books in the Indigenous Studies Series

Published by Wilfrid Laurier University Press

Blockades and Resistance: Studies in Actions of Peace and the Temagami Blockades of 1988–89 / Bruce W. Hodgins, Ute Lischke, and David T. McNab, editors / 2003 / xi + 276 pp. / map, illustrations / ISBN 0-88920-381-4

Indian Country: Essays on Contemporary Native Culture / Gail Guthrie Valaskakis / 2005 / x + 293 pp. / photos / ISBN 0-88920-479-9

Walking a Tightrope: Aboriginal People and Their Representations / Ute Lischke and David T. McNab, editors / 2005 / xix + 377 pp. / photos / ISBN 978-0-88920-484-3

The Long Journey of a Forgotten People: Métis Identities and Family Histories / Ute Lischke and David T. McNab, editors / 2007 / viii + 386 pp. / maps, photos / ISBN 978-0-88920-523-9

Words of the Huron / John L. Steckley / 2007 / xvii + 259 pp. / ISBN 978-0-88920-516-1

Essential Song: Three Decades of Northern Cree Music / Lynn Whidden / 2007 / xvi + 176 pp. / photos, musical examples, audio CD / ISBN 978-0-88920-459-1

From the Iron House: Imprisonment in First Nations Writing / Deena Rymhs / 2008 / ix + 147 pp. / ISBN 978-1-55458-021-7

Lines Drawn upon the Water: First Nations and the Great Lakes Borders and Borderlands / Karl S. Hele, editor / 2008 / xxiii + 351 pp. / illustrations, maps / ISBN 978-1-55458-004-0

Troubling Tricksters: Revisioning Critical Conversations / Deanna Reder and Linda M. Morra, editors / 2010 / xii + 336 pp. / illustrations / ISBN 978-1-55458-181-8